Values and Ethics
in Organization and
Human Systems Development

WILLIAM GELLERMANN
MARK S. FRANKEL
ROBERT F. LADENSON

Values and Ethics
in Organization and
Human Systems Development

Responding
to Dilemmas
in Professional Life

Jossey-Bass Publishers

San Francisco   •   Oxford   •   1990

VALUES AND ETHICS IN ORGANIZATION AND HUMAN SYSTEMS DEVELOPMENT
Responding to Dilemmas in Professional Life
by William Gellermann, Mark S. Frankel, and Robert F. Ladenson

Copyright © 1990 by: Jossey-Bass Inc., Publishers
         350 Sansome Street
         San Francisco, California 94104

         Jossey-Bass Limited
         Headington Hill Hall
         Oxford OX3 0BW

         American Association for the
         Advancement of Science
         1333 H Street, N.W.
         Washington, D.C. 20005

Library of Congress Cataloging-in-Publication Data

Gellermann, William.
  Values and ethics in organization and human systems development :
responding to dilemmas in professional life / William Gellermann,
Mark S. Frankel, Robert F. Ladenson. — 1st ed.
    p. cm. — (Jossey-Bass management series) (Jossey-Bass
social and behavioral science series)
  Includes bibliographical references (p.   ) and index.
  ISBN 1-55542-296-9 (alk. paper)
  1. Organizational change—Moral and ethical aspects. 2. Personnel
management—Moral and ethical aspects. I. Frankel, Mark S.
II. Ladenson, Robert F. III. Title. IV. Series.
V. Series: Jossey-Bass social and behavioral science series.
HD58.8.G45 1990
658.4—dc20   90-4946
                                        CIP

Manufactured in the United States of America

The material in this book is based upon work supported by the National
Science Foundation under Grant Nos. RII-8409933 and RII-8696147. Any
opinions, findings, and conclusions or recommendations expressed in this
material are those of the authors and commentators and do not necessarily
reflect the views of the National Science Foundation.

JACKET DESIGN BY WILLI BAUM

FIRST EDITION

Code 9099

A joint publication in
The Jossey-Bass Management Series
and
The Jossey-Bass Social and
Behavioral Science Series

Contents

IIIIIIIIIIIIIIIIIII

ix

We dedicate this book to Herb Shepard,
a founder of the Human Systems Development profession,
whose vision for its development was global and
who saw "life loving" as its primary value.

Preface

The evolution of any profession is characterized, in large part, by efforts to increase the influence of ethics in professional life for its members. This process includes efforts to define the principles of ethical conduct for professional activity and to deepen the commitment of members of the profession to those principles. It also includes striving to help members realize the ideals that infuse professional life with meaning. This certainly holds true with respect to the Organization and Human Systems Development (OD-HSD) profession, which since 1981 has been involved in a worldwide effort to identify core values and ethical guidelines applicable to research and practice in the field. One outcome of this effort is "A Statement of Values and Ethics by Professionals in Organization and Human Systems Development" (presented in an annotated version in Chapters Four and Five and without annotation in Appendix B and hereinafter referred to as the Statement), which seeks to support ethical judgments by OD-HSD professionals by ensuring that they are informed by shared values and experience.

Values and Ethics in Organization and Human Systems Development seeks to help OD-HSD professionals become more aware of and more insightful about ethical issues in their work. We hope it will make a practical difference, proceeding as it does from the premise that thinking about ethical issues before action is required increases the likelihood of ethical conduct. This volume is intended to (1) heighten the sensitivity of OD-HSD professionals to the profession's core values and ethics as expressed in the Statement, (2) engage them in the process of affirming or refining the Statement, and (3) improve their ability to perform their work according to high ethical standards by encouraging them to be alert to ethical problems, to pursue the solution of those problems in a rational manner, and to use the Statement as a frame of reference for anticipating and responding to ethical concerns. The book also seeks to contribute to a collective professional development by helping to foster a sense of membership in a professional community bound by a shared commitment to the highest standards of ethical practice.

This volume draws on the experience of many OD-HSD professionals who have thought seriously about the profession's ethical standards and underlying core values. This is especially important for those who are new to the field. A systematic approach to ethical decision making is presented to help individuals think through the proper course of action in particular situations. The book also includes material that challenges members of the profession to ponder carefully what are referred to as "context, content, and frontier issues" for the OD-HSD field, all of which have important implications for the profession's maturation as an ethical enterprise.

In addition to OD-HSD professionals, their clients may find this book useful in helping them understand the profession's values and how its ethical guidelines promote or constrain work in OD-HSD. (For those readers, it is important to recognize that the profession's values and ethics are still a work in progress and that much of this book was written as a contribution to the dialogue among OD-HSD professionals about what they want to stand for as a profession. At the same time, in accordance with the value the profession places on openness, we expect that OD-HSD professionals generally are willing to let those who use their services listen in on the profession's internal dialogue and, if they wish, contribute to it.) Many other professions also seek useful ways to think about their professional responsibilities. In presenting the unfolding story of how one profession is responding to the ethical concerns facing its members, the book offers ideas, information, and insights that we hope will be useful in other professional contexts.

By including certain analytical material in this work, we aim to contribute to the further development of scholarship in applied and professional ethics. The book's reflective, analytical essays serve in some instances to bridge the gap between analysis centered on OD-HSD and the larger body of scholarly literature from other professional fields; the case analyses illustrate alternative ways to assess the ethical issues highlighted in the scenarios. It provides an additional potential link to scholarship in other fields relating to professional ethics by offering a detail-rich "case study" of how one profession has viewed the role of ethical guidelines in its development and the process by which the guidelines have evolved.

Overview of the Chapters

The book is organized into twelve chapters. Chapter One provides a broad context within which to consider the values and ethics of OD-HSD; it reflects on the centrality of values and ethics for professions generally, then introduces OD-HSD as a field and as a profession and offers an overview of some key ethical issues faced by OD-HSD practitioners and researchers. Chapter Two describes two distinct ways of thinking about ethics—"ethics as morality" and "ethics as the quest for a good life"—and examines some of the ethical issues in OD-HSD from both perspectives. Chapter Three presents a five-step model for ethical decision making and includes a discussion between two of the authors regarding its appropriateness and utility for anticipating and responding to ethical dilemmas in OD-HSD. Chapters Four and Five present the most recent annotated version of the Statement. The process of developing the Statement has been coordinated by William Gellermann, one of the authors and an experienced OD-HSD external consultant. This process is a dynamic one that continues today, with an increasing number of people participating in the Statement's further refinement. In Chapters Six through Eleven, we offer six cases with accompanying analyses prepared by the book's authors, as well as a selection of commentaries from other contributors. We anticipate that this mix of perspectives will contribute to the discussion about ethical issues in OD-HSD by making it better informed and more genuinely engaged. Chapter Twelve concludes the volume with an examination of "frontier" issues — issues that are currently unresolved but that will continue to confront the profession as it matures both technically and ethically.

Readers are also encouraged to consult the appendixes, which include a variety of materials intended to inform, educate, and serve as resources: an essay describing the background of the Statement; the most recent version of the Statement (without annotation); the April 1985 version, which was used by the commentators in preparing their case responses; six additional case scenarios prepared for the project, with commentaries; a listing of ethics resources; and a description of how the statement was developed.

Background

This volume traces its origins to a project that began in September 1984 and concluded in late 1987. Although OD-HSD had experienced rapid growth as a professional field prior to this project, very few resources had been committed to the systematic examination of OD-HSD values and ethics and their implications for professional practice and research. The project, funded by a grant from the National Science Foundation, was intended to remedy that situation through a collaborative effort between scholars at the Center for the Study of Ethics in the Professions at the Illinois Institute of Technology (IIT) and OD-HSD professionals associated with the Human Systems Development Consortium, which represents several leading OD-HSD professional groups, primarily in the United States and Canada. Two of the authors — Mark S. Frankel and Gellermann — were co-directors of the project; when the former left IIT to join the

American Association for the Advancement of Science (AAAS), the association become the host institution for the project. However, project ties with IIT were maintained through the third author, Robert F. Ladenson, a philosopher and faculty associate with the Center for the Study of Ethics in the Professions.

The project sought to bring experience and informed opinion to bear on the values and ethics that underlie and guide the professionalization of the OD-HSD field. It was a catalyst for energizing the participation of OD-HSD professionals, their clients, behavioral scientists from related fields, and moral philosophers in a concerted effort to document, analyze, and assess the values and ethics of the profession.

The project employed a number of strategies. Twelve original case scenarios were prepared, taken in part from responses to an open solicitation of critical incidents. Each scenario illustrated a set of critical value conflicts and ethical issues in OD-HSD. Ten of these scenarios were presented at a series of six professional meetings (OD Information Exchange, May 1985; Organizational Behavior Teaching Conference, June 1985; OD World Congress, June 1985; Association for Creative Change, June 1985; American Psychological Association, August 1985; OD Network Conference, October 1985), where two to five commentators offered their analyses of the issues before a larger audience. The other two cases were reviewed by eight scholars and practitioners invited to prepare written commentaries. In total, thirty-four persons prepared forty-nine commentaries, many of which are included in this book.

Another strategy was to encourage presentation of the cases at national and local OD-HSD meetings and in university courses. Some examples of where this was done include meetings of the Chicago and Los Angeles chapters of the OD Network, in October 1985 and March 1986, respectively; a graduate seminar on Organization Development and Change at the University of Illinois, Chicago (Winter 1986); and a course in the University of San Francisco's Master's Degree Program in Human Resources and Organization Development (Spring 1987). Additionally, several presentations about the project were made at various professional meetings by project staff. These

included the 1986 and 1987 annual conferences of the U.S. OD
Network and the 1987 International OD Association's annual
conference in Poland.

The project also contributed directly to the development
of the Statement and produced an annotated bibliography: *Values
and Ethics in Organization and Human Systems Development* (Washington, D.C.: American Association for the Advancement of
Science, 1987). However, this book is the capstone of the project.

Acknowledgments

Many people and organizations have contributed to the
preparation of this volume. We acknowledge the institutional
support given the project and the writing of this book by the
American Association for the Advancement of Science and the
Illinois Institute of Technology. We are grateful for the early
encouragement and support of members of the Human Systems
Development Consortium. We were aided throughout the original project by a distinguished advisory board, which included
Richard H. Blackwell, Local Union No. 165 of the International
Brotherhood of Electrical Workers, Chicago; Norman E. Bowie,
Curtis L. Carlson School of Management, University of Min-
nesota, Minneapolis; Jeanne Cherbeneau, Cherbeneau and Associates, Berkeley, California; Mary Ann Von Glinow, Department of Management and Organization, University of Southern
California, Los Angeles; Stanley R. Hinckley, Jr., Hinckley
and Associates, Cincinnati, Ohio; Linda M. Lampkin, American Federation of State, County, and Municipal Employees,
Washington, D.C.; and Philip H. Mirvis, psychologist in independent research and consultation, Sandy Spring, Maryland.
Two additional members of the advisory board—Frederick Elliston, a philosopher, and Herbert Shepard, a founder of the
OD-HSD profession—died during the course of the project. Both
made important contributions to developing the original concept for the study and to its execution. We acknowledge their
roles in our work and honor their memories.

The project might never have been were it not for a grant
from the National Science Foundation and the support of Rachelle

Hollander, program officer at the foundation. The thirty-four case commentators whose analyses appear in the volume deserve special recognition, as do the professional groups that agreed to host panels at their meetings at which some of the cases were discussed. We also appreciated the constructive comments by several anonymous reviewers on earlier drafts of this manuscript.

William Gellermann would like to express his personal appreciation to Robert Tannenbaum and Herbert Shepard, both among the founders of the OD-HSD profession, who gave him support and encouragement early in the process and helped him make the necessary personal and organizational contacts to move the Statement development process forward; to Jeanne Cherbeneau and Frank Friedlander, whose support on the U.S. OD Network board gave him the feeling of legitimacy he needed in order to view his role as serving "the profession" and not just doing what he thought the profession needed; to Jean Pollara Muni and Karen Davis, whose love, critical comments, and guidance have been invaluable; and to the 700 or so OD-HSD professionals from all over the world who have endorsed the Statement development process and/or affirmed their acceptance of it in one of its forms or made constructive suggestions for improving it.

Both Gellermann and Frankel gratefully acknowledge the efforts of Donald Cole, founder and current director of the OD Institute, whose initial attempt at drafting on "OD Code of Ethics" sparked Frankel's interest in the work of the OD-HSD profession and whose support for Gellermann ignited the Statement drafting process. Frankel expresses his personal appreciation to Cheryl Jackson at AAAS; her work in deciphering successive drafts of this manuscript based on the writings of three authors was absolutely critical to producing the final product.

Postscript

We make no claim to having addressed in this single volume all the important issues related to the values and ethics of OD-HSD. We believe, however, that it is the most comprehensive, detailed, and interdisciplinary treatment of such matters presently available and that it thereby pushes the issues forward to a new level of understanding and deliberation. We invite readers to build on this foundation.

September 1990   William Gellermann
                                          New York, New York

                                          Mark S. Frankel
                                          Washington, D.C.

                                          Robert F. Ladenson
                                          Chicago, Illinois

The Authors

William Gellermann is an independent consultant in Management and Human Systems Development with his own firm, Dialogue Associates, based in New York. He received both his B.A. degree (1950) in economics and his M.B.A. degree (1953) in accounting from the University of Washington and his Ph.D. degree (1964) from the University of California, Los Angeles, in business administration.

      Gellermann has been an external Organization Development consultant with Westvaco, a Fortune 500 corporation, over a fifteen-year period; a facilitator for the American Management Association's Executive Effectiveness Course for ten years; and coordinator of a process for clarifying the values and ethics of the Organization and Human Systems Development profession since 1981. He has had consulting and facilitation experience with a wide variety of organizations — large and small, in both the public and private sectors, profit and not-for-profit, including governmental (federal, state, and local) organizations, labor unions, and religious and civil rights groups. In 1972 he was included in American Men and Women of Science, Social and Behavioral Sciences, and in 1984 he was given the

Outstanding Organization Development Consultant of the Year award by the International Registry of Organization Development Professionals. Gellermann's publications include "Values and Ethical Issues for Human Systems Development Practitioners" in *Human Systems Development* (R. Tannenbaum, N. Margulies, F. Massarik, and Associates, 1985) and "Integrating the *Business* and *Human* Dimensions of Management and Organization Development" (with N. Frizell) in *The Practice of Management Development* (S. Mailick, S. Hoberman, and S. Wall, 1980).

Gellermann was co-director, with Mark S. Frankel, of a Study of Values and Ethics in the Organization Development Profession, a project funded by the National Science Foundation (1984 to 1987); chair of the Ethics Task Force of the Human Systems Development Consortium; and United States Liaison for the International OD Association.

Mark S. Frankel is head of Scientific Freedom and Responsibility Programs at the American Association for the Advancement of Science and staff director of the association's Professional Ethics Program. He received his B.A. degree (1968) from Emory University in political science and his Ph.D. degree (1976) from George Washington University in political science.

Frankel's research has focused on the ethical and policy implications of advances in biomedical research and technology, the development and enforcement of professional codes of ethics, and, more broadly, professional self-regulation. His work has been supported by grants from the National Science Foundation, the National Endowment for the Humanities, and the Exxon Education Foundation. He has conducted workshops on professional ethics issues for professional societies, corporations, and federal laboratories. In 1969–70, he was awarded a Rotary International Fellowship for study at the University of Bonn, West Germany. His publications include *Professional Ethics Activities in the Scientific and Engineering Societies* (1980, with others), *Values and Ethics in Organization and Human Systems Development: An Annotated Bibliography* (1987), and *Science, Engineering and Ethics: State-of-the-Art and Future Directions* (1988).

Frankel was assistant professor of political science at Wayne State University from 1975 through 1979 and director of the Center for the Study of Ethics in the Professions at the Illinois Institute of Technology from 1980 to 1986.

Robert F. Ladenson is professor of philosophy at the Illinois Institute of Technology, Chicago. He received his B.A. degree (1965) from the University of Wisconsin, Madison, in philosophy, his Ph.D. degree (1970) from Johns Hopkins University in philosophy, and his J.D. degree (1980) from DePaul College of Law. He is also a labor arbitrator and mediator. Since 1975 he has been a faculty associate of the Center for the Study of Ethics in the Professions at the Illinois Institute of Technology.

Ladenson's main areas of scholarly interest are ethics, political philosophy, and the philosophy of law. He has written numerous articles on these subjects and is the author of *A Philosophy of Free Expression* (1983). Ladenson's current work focuses on ethical issues in the workplace and on free speech issues related to scientific and technical information bearing on national security.

The Commentators

Kenneth D. Alpern, assistant professor of philosophy, DePaul University, Chicago

Ian Barber, director general, Q2, S.A., Madrid

Fred R. Berger, professor of philosophy, University of California, Davis

Lee G. Bolman, lecturer on education, Graduate School of Education, Harvard University, Cambridge, Massachusetts

Beverly P. Brown-Hinckley, manager of organization effectiveness, soap division, The Procter & Gamble Company, Cincinnati

John C. Bryan, president, Bryan*Weir-Bryan Consultants Ltd., Toronto

Barbara Bunker, associate professor of psychology, University of Buffalo-SUNY

Jeanne Cherbeneau, president, Cherbeneau and Associates, Berkeley, California

Allan R. Cohen, Walter H. Carpenter Professor of Management, Babson College, Wellesley, Massachusetts

Donald W. Cole, executive director, Organization Development Institute, Chesterland, Ohio

Michael Davis, senior research associate, Center for the Study of Ethics in the Professions, Illinois Institute of Technology, Chicago

Jerilyn Fosdick, president, Fosdick & Company, Minneapolis

Ophie A. Franklin, executive director, The Door — A Center of Alternatives, New York

Herman Gadon, director of executive programs, USCD Extension, University of California, San Diego

Robert T. Golembiewski, research professor, University of Georgia, Athens

Leonard D. Goodstein, consulting psychologist, Washington, D.C.

Stanley R. Hinckley, Jr., president, Hinckley and Associates, Cincinnati

Bailey W. Jackson, associate professor of education, University of Massachusetts, Amherst

Daniel L. Kegan,, president, Elan Associates, Chicago

Pessy Krausz, executive director, Shalshelet (Israel)

Martin J. Lonergan, associate professor of professional studies, University of San Francisco

Rodney L. Lowman, director, Career Development Laboratory, Houston, Texas

Newton Margulies, professor of management, Graduate School of Management, University of California, Irvine

Bernard Mohr, president, The Synapse Group, Inc., Portland, Maine

Matjaz Mulej, professor of dialectical systems theory, School of Business Economics, University of Maribor (Yugoslavia)

John Nirenberg, Management Insight, Stamford, Connecticut

Hugo Prein, associate professor of social and organization psychology, University of Utrecht (The Netherlands)

Zofia Rummel-Syska, faculty of management, Warsaw University (Poland)

Joan E. Sieber, professor of psychology, California State University, Hayward

Robert Tannenbaum, professor emeritus of the development of human systems, Anderson Graduate School of Management, University of California, Los Angeles

Robert W. Terry, director, Reflective Leadership Center, Hubert H. Humphrey Institute of Public Affairs, University of Minnesota, Minneapolis

Dorothy M. Tucker, consulting organization psychologist, Los Angeles, California

Peter B. Vaill, professor of human systems, School of Government and Business, George Washington University, Washington, D.C.

Patricia H. Werhane, Wirtenberger Professor of Business Ethics, Department of Philosophy, Loyola University of Chicago

Values and Ethics
in Organization and
Human Systems Development

Confronting Professional Values and Ethical Issues

In Part One, we stand back from the practice of Organization and Human Systems Development in order to provide a broad perspective for the rest of the book. Chapter One examines the centrality of values and ethics to professional life generally, focuses more specifically on the field of OD-HSD practice, and then explores the possibility of defining OD-HSD as a profession. It introduces a model of some of the primary elements involved in the emergence of OD-HSD as a mature profession and assesses the degree to which practice within the field has developed in terms of each of those elements. And, finally, it discusses the importance for professionals of being clear about their ethics (the standards they use to guide thought and action about good-bad and right-wrong behavior) and briefly surveys some of the most important ethical issues currently facing OD-HSD professionals.

Chapter Two provides a philosophical perspective for thinking about ethics generally, including two fundamentally different, though compatible, views about the nature of ethics: "ethics as morality" and "ethics as the quest for a good life." It then shows how applying such a philosophical perspective can

1

help OD-HSD practitioners respond more effectively to some of the dilemmas they are likely to face.

Chapter Three reviews a range of possible moral (or ethical) orientations based on where people look for the source of their ethics. The range includes orientations to external authority, to the groups or the society to which one belongs, to one's own reasoning, and to an "inner light" (called conscience by some). From this perspective, a five-step model for ethical thought and action is described and applied to a specific situation. The first part of the chapter, in which the model is described and applied, was written by one of the authors of this book (William Gellermann). In a separate section, a second coauthor (Robert Ladenson) gives a critique of the model. In a final section, the author of the model responds to that critique.

CHAPTER ONE

Organization and Human Systems Development: The Field, the Profession, and the Ethical Issues

To provide a larger context for thinking about values and ethics in the Organization and Human Systems Development* (OD-HSD) profession, we will begin by considering the centrality of values and ethics to professions and professionals generally. From that perspective, we will then examine the field of knowledge covered by OD-HSD, explore OD-HSD as a profession, and investigate the primary ethical issues presently faced by OD-HSD professionals. But first it will help to reflect on a specific situation.

An Ethical Dilemma?

Imagine that you are an internal OD consultant. You have been asked to work on a cost-cutting project that is likely to

*"Organization and Human Systems Development (OD-HSD) is a professional network or community of professionals whose practice is based on the applied behavioral sciences, a human systems perspective, and both human and organizational values. [OD-HSD professionals . . . seek to promote and facilitate the process by which human beings and human systems live and work together for their mutual success and well-being" (see the Preamble of "A Statement of Values and Ethics by Professionals in Organization and Human Systems Development" in Chapter Four).]

result in the laying off of approximately 3,000 people at a plant that currently employs 9,000. The plant is the primary employer in its community. Gathering the data that would make recommendations possible is expected to involve interviewing a large number of people, many of whom are likely to be among those laid off. How do you feel about what you have been asked to do? How do your values affect your reaction, if at all? Does this assignment involve you in an ethical dilemma — namely, a situation in which you are not sure about the right thing to do? Do you consider yourself a professional? If so, has your profession given you any preparation for approaching a situation such as this? What are you going to do? How will you make a decision?

We will return to this case in Chapter Three after establishing a frame of reference for considering this and similar concrete situations.

The Centrality of Values and Ethics to Professional Life

As knowledge becomes more specialized and as the decisions of experts become increasingly essential to the operation of society, the professions acquire new power and prestige. Not only do they affect the interests of growing numbers of individuals, but, within their areas of interest, they may also exert near monopolistic control over the implementation of social policies that, at least in theory, are aimed at the common good. As societies become more dependent on professional services, it is vital that professions and professionals be held accountable for their conduct and for their commitment to public service. This holds true for OD-HSD as much as for other professions.

In Western societies, we have constructed a number of legal mechanisms — for example, licensing and civil and criminal suits — to protect us from professional malfeasance. But these alone are not sufficient. We must also rely on the moral commitments of the professions and the ethical integrity of individual practitioners. This is so because the law typically delineates what cannot be done; it rarely prescribes what should be done. Surely we seek more from professionals than behavior that merely avoids injury to others. We expect them to aspire to behavior that promotes the welfare of those they serve and the common good. Toward that end, the force of law is a cumbersome, if not counterproductive, strategy. By appealing to the moral conscience of professionals, society may evoke from them a higher level of integrity than that which it can command through law. And when that evocation is supported by professional norms, the likelihood of moral behavior is substantially increased since individual professionals are simultaneously serving their consciences, their professions, and their societies.

Building a Foundation Through Professional Values. "To be a professional is to be dedicated to a distinctive set of ideals and standards of conduct" (Jennings, Callahan, and Wolf, 1987, p. 5). Members of a profession are bound together by common aspirations, values, and training, and to varying degrees the professions "develop social and moral ties among their members who enter into a community of [common] purpose" (Merton, 1982, p. 203). These community members "are distinguished as individuals and as a group by widely shared goals [and by] beliefs about the value of those goals, . . . about the appropriate means for achieving them, and about the kinds of relations which in general should prevail among themselves, and in many cases between themselves and others" (Camenisch, 1983, p. 48). The professions, then, are a major normative reference group whose values and articulation of appropriate conduct serve as guidelines by which individual practitioners organize and perform their work and by which outsiders can understand and evaluate practitioners' performance (Frankel, 1989).

With respect to their own members, the professions seek to cultivate values and moral commitments considered significant to the profession and, in the process, to help define the kinds of relations that professionals establish with those outside the field. It is, after all, the profession's core values that infuse professional life with meaning and, ideally, provide a foundation for its articulated ethics of conduct. Such ethics would be meaningless unless they were connected to the profession's aspirations,

which give foundation and purpose to expectations of character and to specific ethical duties.

The mediating influence of the profession between the expectations and needs of clients and the provision of services by
individual professionals also highlights the critical role of the
profession's core values. "The collectivization of appropriate
norms and their transmission to individual practitioners are the
cornerstones" (Wolfson, Trebilcock, and Tuohy, 1980, p. 192)
of the trust relationship clients expect between themselves and
individual practitioners. This is so because "we place our trust
not only in individual professionals, but also in the professional
group. We rely on the group to guarantee that its members fulfill
their agency obligations" (Tuohy and Wolfson, 1977, p. 67).
Hence, what is essential to protecting the interests of clients
reaches beyond the independent professional-client relationship;
it has as its lifeline the core values of the profession itself as a
stable and enduring entity.

The commitment of professionals to the values central to
their professions is what leads society to grant them — individually and collectively — the authority and resources to pursue
those values in the service of others. Professionals are, writes
Alan Goldman (n.d., p. 48), "viewed as morally committed to
pursuing the dominant value that defines the goal of their professional practice . . . . They are expected to pursue such goals on
a social as well as individual level . . . and they are expected
to do so *even when self-interest may have to be sacrificed in that pursuit*"
(emphasis added). That commitment can be identified as enlightened self-interest, in contrast to narrow self-interest, which
tends to focus only on one's short-term individual interest. If
a sizable number of the members of a profession are unwilling
to subordinate their narrow self-interest to the interest of the
profession-as-a-whole, the practices of the deviant members can
reflect back on the whole and thereby jeopardize the profession's
autonomy and status. Hence, narrow self-interest may not in
fact serve one's own interest in the long run if enough other so-
called professionals follow the same practices and the continued
functioning of the profession and its members is threatened. Enlightened self-interest acknowledges that the benefits society ac-

cords to a recognized profession and to members of that profession are important enough so that individual professionals need to be willing to forgo the short-term advantages of letting themselves be guided by their narrow self-interest.

The commitment to sacrifice narrow self-interest, continues Goldman, "is reflected in every code of professional ethics, although each profession differs essentially in the dominant value to be pursued . . . . Society expects this sort of commitment as a return for the professional's training, status, and power" (p. 49). For Goldman, this reflects a model "of a moral division of labor, in which crucial values are to be protected and advanced by special segments of the population whose special concerns they are" (p. 49). However, while each profession draws on its own distinctive traditions and experience in pursuing its dominant values, any major departure from the fundamental values of the larger society will inevitably fuel public anxiety and may endanger the profession's stature and autonomy.

The values and ethics of a profession are central to ensuring a good fit between that profession and the larger society of which it is a member, on the one hand, and between the profession and its members, on the other. This is especially true for the OD-HSD profession because its practice is potentially so important to the functioning of society and to the various human systems of which it is composed.

Translating Values into Professional Conduct. The evolution of any profession is, in large part, characterized by its efforts to define the expected character of its members and the behavior that is considered ethically proper. Indeed, the normative feature of professions in our society has traditionally been defined as the articulation of ethical standards, and it is the profession's core values that both anchor and trigger the virtues and duties expected of its members.

The institutionalization of a process whereby a profession's values and moral commitments are regularly discussed and assessed, in terms of changing conditions both inside and outside the profession, offers a period of critical self-examination both by individual members and by the profession as a whole.

It is a time for testing one's personal and professional ethics against one another and against those of one's colleagues and for testing the profession's ethics against the experience of its members and against the values and norms of society. Members' participation in such an effort helps reinvigorate and bring into sharp focus not only their own individual underlying values and moral commitments but also those of their profession. This process of self-criticism, codification, and consciousness raising helps reinforce or redefine and realign the profession's collective responsibility, and it is an important learning and maturing experience for both individual professionals and the profession.

For its members, the profession's ethical standards are central to understanding what constitutes proper conduct as well as expectations of the virtues professionals should possess. We do not expect professionals simply to act in a particular way; we also expect them to *be* a particular kind of person—that is, to embody a certain type of character. After all, acting ethically and being ethical can be quite different. One can do the right thing, but for the wrong reasons. The profession's ethical standards, writes Karen Lebacqz (1985, p. 75), "are more meaningful when interpreted as an ethics of character or virtue than simply as an ethics of action. They tell the professional not only what to do but whom to be." The very essence, then, of being a professional, and not just acting as one, is understanding and committing to the spirit as well as to the letter of the profession's values and ethical prescriptions. At the same time, the essence of being a *profession,* and not just a collection of individuals who call themselves a profession, is that such understanding and commitment be widely shared among the members of the group.

The Field of Organization and Human Systems Development

The field of OD-HSD practice is still in the process of definition. According to Tannenbaum, Margulies, and Massarik (1985, p. 1), it "has to do with some kind of explicit approach to the study of people and how they work together toward specified ends. . . . [Its] origins are . . . lost in ancient years . . . however, . . . the past five or six decades have witnessed an increasing outpouring of research, formulation of theory, and modes of professional practice (managing, consulting, and teaching) that have shared a common thrust: to enable us *to better understand and/or effectively influence human behavior in organizational settings.*"

When the practice deals with organizations, it is generally recognized as Organization Development (OD). However, in recent years, there has been increasing recognition that "the field" includes more than organizations. Although individual practitioners may limit their focus to part of the field, the whole encompasses the entire range of human systems, including the following levels (with examples of professionals working at each level included in parentheses):

- *Individuals* (career counselors, individual therapists, and management consultants)
- *Small groups* (couples counselors, family therapists, and team-building facilitators)
- *Organizational subsystems* (managers of divisions, regions, plants, and other major organizational units and their consultants)
- *Organizations* (CEOs, other senior managers, and their consultants)
- *Larger systems* (social scientists, politicians, and consultants whose work aims toward improving the functioning of communities and entire societies)
- *Systems composed of societies* (those who work with the European Economic Community or those seeking to develop cooperation throughout the Americas or the Pacific Rim)
- *The global human system as a whole* (delegates to, the staff of, and consultants to the United Nations)

This broader view of the field is known as Human Systems Development (HSD). However, in order to acknowledge that the field includes Organization Development, it seems best to call it OD-HSD as a means of giving explicit recognition to the roots of its practice. With this broader concept we can then extend the definition given above by saying that the purpose of OD-HSD is to enable us *to better understand and/or effectively influence the behavior of people in human systems.*

But what do we mean by human systems? By *human* we mean, in the words of one widely accepted definition, life conscious of itself. By *system* we mean wholes composed of parts or subsystems that are interdependent with one another, with the whole, and with the macrosystem(s) of which the whole is a part. The force that tends to hold human systems together and keep their parts functioning in coordination with one another is common purpose. Therefore, drawing on the definition of human as life conscious of itself, we can say that a system is human to the extent that its members are conscious of their common purpose, their identity as a whole system, their relationships as parts within the whole, and their relationships with the environment of the whole system, especially the larger systems of which they are parts.

And what do we mean by development? To answer this question, it helps to consider the fundamental tendency for human beings to grow and develop. The philosopher John Dewey (1958, pp. 13–14) described the conditions that evoke this tendency: "Life consists of phases in which the organism falls out of step with the march of surrounding things and then recovers unison with it — either through effort or by some happy chance. And in a growing life, the recovery is never mere return to a prior state, for it is enriched by the state of disparity and resistance through which it has successfully passed. If the gap between the organism and the environment is too wide, the creature dies. If its activity is not enhanced by temporary alienation, it merely subsists. Life grows when a temporary falling out is a transition to a more extensive balance of the energies of the organism with those of the conditions under which it lives."

To this concept of the organism adjusting to its external conditions we need to add the concept of an inner tendency to grow in a particular way or direction — that is, a tendency to realize the potential that lies latent within individuals and the human systems they form. For individuals, this is sometimes referred to as "self-realization." For organizations, we can speak of something similar, something that is a unique combination of the potentials of all the people who make up the organization. The metaphor of the acorn, which has latent within it the oak that it will become, can be helpful in understanding this idea of inner tendency. However, we need to think beyond this metaphor because its focus is limited primarily to innate tendencies. We must acknowledge that human beings, in addition to their rich endowment from nature, generally have an abundance of potential based on their life experiences. Therefore, without trying to resolve the argument about which is more important, we can say that nature and nurture combine to create the uniqueness of the potential that exists within human beings and human systems.

From the perspective provided by the preceding discussion, we can differentiate two concepts that are basic to the point of view described here.

- By *human systems development (hsd)* we refer to the continuing living process by which people express their tendency to search for a better way to be as they cope with their life conditions and seek to realize their full potential.
- By *Human Systems Development (HSD)* we refer to the field of professional practice devoted to supporting or facilitating the full realization of the hsd tendency.

Having differentiated HSD from the more fundamental living process (hsd) on which it is based, we can now look more closely at HSD as a profession. This distinction does not require us to continue talking about "hsd," but only to keep its existence in mind as we focus on HSD (or OD-HSD).

Defining the OD-HSD Profession

Can OD-HSD be considered a profession? Most practitioners implicitly consider themselves professionals, but there is substantial difference of opinion about whether they constitute a profession or should aspire to become one. For example, some hold that OD-HSD will not be a profession until it (1) has a set of standards that both define professional practice and provide a base for regulating harmful practice and (2) consciously relates theory and practice. Others oppose OD-HSD's becoming a profession because they are concerned that (1) by becoming "professionals," practitioners will put themselves above their clients or (2) by becoming "a profession" they will become a regulatory clique that controls entry and practice, as has happened with medicine and law (Gellermann, 1984b).

The number of people who are actively working to create an OD-HSD profession based on conscious choices about the kind of profession they want to become is still relatively small. Without such active commitment to conscious evolution, however, the profession's evolution is likely to follow the typical developmental pattern described by Shepard (1983). Its phases include:

- Learning and market differentiation (phases through which the profession has already passed)
- Legitimization (the phase it is in now)
- Monopolization and exploitation (phases toward which it may be moving)
- Defensiveness (a phase in which clients begin to rebel)

This book, as an element in a process of consciously creating the OD-HSD profession, is intended to contribute to the prevention of monopolization and exploitation by creating in their place a mature profession that truly serves humanity.

Since organizations are the primary clients of most OD-HSD practitioners, it is understandable that Organization Development would be the most widely used name for the profession. However, a substantial minority prefer Human Systems Development, and others prefer alternative names (Gellermann, 1984b). Although organizational clients may comprise the bulk of the profession's practice, an emerging acceptance of Human Systems Development as the name for the field seems likely since that will enable all people who work with human systems to be included within it and thereby increase their potential for cooperative effort.

No other concept allows OD-HSD professionals to view their efforts, both individually and collectively, in such a useful way; nor does any other such concept provide so essential a perspective for the work they do, even when their attention is focused exclusively on a single organizational client. As noted earlier, the field of OD-HSD encompasses such professionals as individual therapists and counselors, family therapists, group facilitators, mediators, trainers, management consultants, OD consultants, and consultants who work with multinational systems. This concept enables individual practitioners who focus on parts of the field to see themselves as members of a larger whole, and it enables them collectively to conceive of their potential in ways that no single person and no single specialization (such as OD) could conceive of alone.

In fact, OD-HSD can be defined, in part, by its emphasis on the systems approach. It is a logical evolution from its initial focus on the development of organizations as systems to encompass other human systems as well. So the systems concept is central to OD-HSD professionals' concepts of who they are and what they do. For the same reason, but from another point of view, it differentiates OD-HSD from fields such as Human Resource Development (HRD) and Personnel Administration, which tend not to emphasize a systems perspective, although there is substantial overlap with and interdependence among them.

In the context of the earlier definition of human systems, it is important to note that OD-HSD practitioners are themselves an emerging human system — or, more precisely, a professional community — to the extent that they share a common purpose and are conscious of themselves as a profession. That consciousness is being enhanced by the process of developing a consensus throughout the profession on a statement of its values and ethics. An annotated version of that statement ("A Statement of Values and Ethics by Professionals in Organization and Human Systems Development," hereafter referred to as the Statement) is presented in Chapters Four and Five; the Statement appears without annotation in Appendix B. The Statement begins by stating that the purpose of OD-HSD professionals is *"to promote a widely shared learning and discovery process dedicated to the vision of people living meaningful, productive, good lives in ways that simultaneously serve them, their organizations, their societies, and the world"* (emphasis added). Other descriptions of the profession's purpose exist, but this one is sufficient to orient our discussion.

Another issue related to defining the scope of the OD-HSD profession involves its relation to transformation. Some people differentiate transformation from development by defining *transformation* as "change in composition and structure" and "the act of becoming a different thing." In contrast, they define *development* as "gradual unfolding," "expansion by a process of growth," and "growth and differentiation along lines natural to one's kind." The latter broad definition is particularly important for our purposes. When development is narrowly defined as gradual unfolding, transformation is significantly different. But if development is defined as growth, without limiting it to gradual unfolding, then transformational growth can also be a form of development. In order to make it explicit that OD-HSD encompasses transformation, the Statement defines development broadly as "referring to all forms of growth toward full realization of potential, including transformational growth." That definition does not deny the importance of the distinction between transformation (in the sense of change in form) and the narrower definition of development (in the sense of gradual change). Just as physicians who use medicine and those who use surgery benefit by conceiving of themselves as members of the medical profession, OD-HSD practitioners who use transformational methods and those who use developmental methods (narrowly defined) can benefit by conceiving of themselves as members of the same profession.

OD-HSD is best described as an emerging profession, since it has clearly not yet fully established itself. Generally, what can be said about HSD is also true of OD; yet OD's emergence is clearer than that of the more inclusive HSD, and so most of the profession's concrete experience has been with OD. Therefore, much of the following discussion deals with examples from OD.

A Model of the OD-HSD Profession

At a 1986 conference on the theme "Growing: My Profession/Myself," sponsored by Certified Consultants International (CCI), a model of the elements in the OD profession's emergence as a full-fledged profession was described. With slight modification, it can also describe the OD-HSD profession (see Figure 1).

In reviewing the model, George Harding, a leading external OD consultant, asked conference participants to rate (using a scale of 0 to 10) the degree to which OD was characterized by each of the elements in the circle (values, ethics, educating the public, educating practitioners, body of knowledge, standards of acceptable practice, and monitoring the practice and its practitioners). By that test, he observed that, in his opinion and that of most of the participants, OD professionals have a long way to go in establishing themselves as a full-fledged profession — no ratings were higher than four. If that is true for OD, it is even more true for OD-HSD.

The model directs attention to some of the principal elements in the emergence of the OD-HSD profession — namely: its core values and ethics; its practitioners; its body of knowledge, educating its practitioners, and monitoring its practice and practitioners; its standards of practice; and educating the public about its practice. We will look at each of these more closely in the following subsections. Our purpose in doing so, however, is not to deal with each element extensively but to put a bit of flesh on the bones of the model so the profession will be more recognizable, in terms of both its current reality and its potential.

Values and Ethics: The Core of the OD-HSD Model. In terms of the definition that the practitioners of a profession "profess" or "stand for something," OD-HSD is beginning to qualify as a profession.

Figure 1. The OD-HSD Profession (A Process Model).

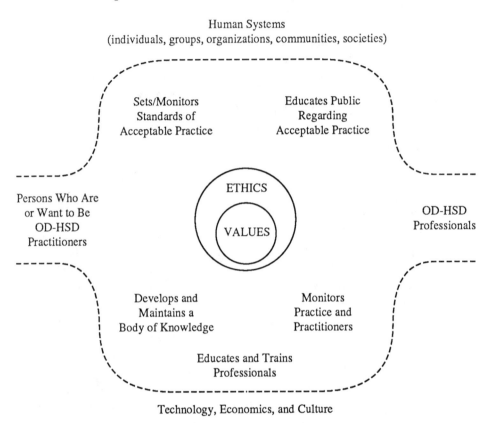

Human Systems
(individuals, groups, organizations, communities, societies)

Sets/Monitors
Standards of
Acceptable Practice

Educates Public
Regarding
Acceptable Practice

Persons Who Are
or Want to Be
OD-HSD
Practitioners

ETHICS

VALUES

OD-HSD
Professionals

Develops and
Maintains a
Body of Knowledge

Monitors
Practice and
Practitioners

Educates and Trains
Professionals

Technology, Economics, and Culture

Note: This should be understood as a dynamic process involving a high degree of interaction among the elements within the profession's boundaries and between the profession and its environment.
Source: Peters, Gellermann, and Herald-Marlowe, 1986, p. 1.

Values have been explicitly recognized as important within the field for a long time (for example, see Tannenbaum and Davis, 1969). In 1981 a conscious process of developing an explicit statement of an ethical-value position for the profession began. That process is outlined in Appendix A. A goal in drafting the Statement has been to establish a consensus among practitioners. We should recognize that the goal is not the statement itself but rather consensus in the minds, hearts, and souls of those who consider themselves OD-HSD professionals. In addition, we should acknowledge that the emergence of a consensus, both in breadth and depth, is still very much in process. Generally speaking, however, there does seem to be an emerging consensus around a position that encompasses the profession's purpose, as quoted from the Statement earlier, and certain core values and ethical standards. Among the *values* (standards of importance) about which consensus is emerging are: life and the quest for happiness; freedom, responsibility, and self-control; justice; human potential and empowerment; respect, dignity, integrity, worth, and fundamental rights of individuals and other human systems; authenticity, congruence, honesty and openness; understanding and acceptance; flexibility, change, and proaction; learning, development, growth and transformation; whole-win attitudes, cooperation-collaboration, trust, community, and diversity; and widespread, meaningful participation in system affairs, democracy, and appropriate decision making.

Among the *ethical guidelines* (standards of behavior) emerging as part of that consensus are:

1. Responsibility to ourselves:
   - Acting with integrity and authenticity
   - Striving for self-knowledge and personal growth
   - Asserting individual interests in ways that are fair and equitable
2. Responsibility for professional development and competence:
   - Accepting responsibility for the consequences of our acts
   - Developing and maintaining individual competence and establishing cooperative relations with other professionals
   - Recognizing our own needs and desires and dealing with them responsibly in the performance of our professional roles
3. Responsibility to clients and significant others:
   - Serving the long-term well-being of our client systems and their stakeholders

- Conducting ourselves honestly, responsibly, and with appropriate openness
- Establishing mutual agreement on a fair contract

4. Responsibility to the OD-HSD profession:
   - Contributing to the continuing professional development of other practitioners and the profession-as-a-whole
   - Promoting the sharing of professional knowledge and skill
   - Working with other OD-HSD professionals in ways that exemplify what the OD-HSD profession stands for

5. Social responsibility:
   - Acting with sensitivity to the consequences of our recommendations for our client systems and the larger systems within which they are subsystems
   - Acting with awareness of our cultural filters and with sensitivity to multinational and multicultural differences and their implications
   - Promoting justice and serving the well-being of all life on earth

Among the most fundamental influences on the profession's practice is the idea that OD-HSD professionals approach their client systems with a holistic, systemic perspective that values "the whole person in the whole organization in the whole society" (Tannenbaum, Margulies, and Massarik, 1985, p. 16). The vision that guides their practice encompasses:

- Facilitating the development of human systems as healthy settings within which individuals can grow in ways that enable those systems to survive and thrive so they can continue to be healthy settings
- Serving both systems and the individuals who are their members by supporting the simultaneous empowerment of
  - Individuals in the context of the human systems within which they live their lives, thus supporting the empowerment of those systems
  - Human systems composed of individuals, thus supporting the empowerment of their individual members (*Note:*

This supports the people involved in being the best they can be, individually and collectively.)

- Approaching the empowerment of all levels of human systems in optimal (whole-win) ways that ultimately serve the whole global system

One of the most important benefits of developing a widely shared position about the values and ethics of the profession is that it will help focus energy in the OD-HSD professional community by providing a common frame of reference. Even with such a reference, most practitioners will probably continue to act in substantially the same ways they have been, but they will do so with greater consciousness that their actions affect the functioning of a larger whole (comprised of their own global professional community and, ultimately, the entire global community). It is worth noting, however, that although the individual behavior changes are likely to be small, their collective effect may be very great because of their high leverage potential.

OD-HSD Professionals. Across the range of human systems levels, from individuals to the whole global system, those who practice at the OD level are easiest to identify because, among other reasons, they have a clearer sense of their own identity as members of a common profession. Among those in the field, OD is a term they recognize and with which they can identify. They can be found as internal and external consultants, managers, teachers, and researchers. They are in increasing demand by universities and major corporations. Many of the Fortune 500 companies maintain entire staffs devoted to OD. The professional organizations represented in the Human Systems Development Consortium (HSDC), composed of most of the leading OD-oriented organizations/associations/networks based in the United States and Canada, have experienced substantial growth in membership since the early 1960s. That growth has included scholars and practitioners with established credentials in basic and applied research in the behavioral sciences. And similar growth is going on all around the world, as indicated by the fact that during the U.S. OD Network's 1986 national conference, leaders of organized professional groups from countries in many different parts of the world participated (including Canada, France, Germany, Great Britain, Hong Kong, Ireland, Mexico, Singapore, South Africa, and Yugoslavia).

Consciousness of the need to expand the boundaries of the profession's practice to encompass all human systems emerged with the formation of the HSDC by a group of professional leaders, originally convened by Herb Shepard, who is generally recognized as one of the founders of OD. That group was designed as a consortium of OD-oriented professional groups, but it soon became clear that people who belonged to several of the member groups could not identify their practice with OD. After calling itself the Inter-Organization Group for a while, the leaders finally settled on Human Systems Development as the term most descriptive of the field they represented.

In acknowledging that HSD professionals work across the range of human system levels, we should note that work at one level of system complexity does not necessarily prepare one for working at other levels. For example, an HSD practitioner whose experience is in work with small groups is not necessarily prepared to work as a consultant on large-scale, complex system change and vice versa. In such cases, the importance of membership in a profession is clear: a common profession can facilitate cooperation among professionals who are working with different expertise in different parts and at different levels of single systems. When the client is a large, complex system, no single professional can adequately serve its needs for system development alone.

As noted earlier, OD-HSD practitioners may limit their focus to part of the field, including work with individuals, small groups, organizational subsystems, whole organizations, communities, societies, and more inclusive systems that are international, multinational, and transnational in scope. This diversity of possible orientations raises the questions, How inclusive is the OD-HSD professional community? and Who are the members of that community? There are no simple, clear-cut answers to those questions, but we can identify some of the primary characteristics of the community. It is an open system composed of people who (1) regard themselves as professionals (they provide service as a means of earning income and not just for the fun of it), (2) share a holistic, systemic perspective in their work (they recognize systems, subsystems, macrosystems and their interdependencies), (3) possess a professional level of competence (including ethical competence), (4) share the entire system of interrelated beliefs, values, and ethics generally accepted as primary by OD-HSD professionals (which are gradually being made explicit in the Statement), and (5) choose to consider themselves OD-HSD professionals by freely aligning themselves with the common purpose and vision that are the core of their professional community's identity.

To illustrate how people who would not consider themselves OD practitioners because their work does not focus on organizations might nevertheless consider themselves members of the OD-HSD profession, we can refer to those professionals whose primary focus is on individuals, such as psychotherapists and management consultants. They might consider themselves OD-HSD professionals if they include the membership of their clients in organizations and other human systems as factors that contribute to the way they approach their work. In contrast, practitioners whose focus is on community development might also consider themselves OD-HSD professionals if they approach their client communities as human systems composed of individuals.

Given the OD-HSD context, we can say that all professionals who work with or in relation to human systems — including organization behavior and organization development theorists, researchers, and academics; management development specialists; human resource developers and planners; industrial/organizational psychologists; and managers — are HSD professionals if they meet the criteria just specified. Of particular importance among those criteria is that they use "a holistic, systemic perspective in their work." Among other things, such an outlook implies that their work is guided by the following ideas:

- Human systems are open systems — that is, they influence and are influenced by their environments, including the larger, more inclusive macrosystems of which they are part.

- Systems are wholes composed of subsystems, and they are simultaneously subsystems of more inclusive macrosystems.
- Regardless of which systems are their clients, OD-HSD professionals pay attention to the interdependencies among their client systems, their subsystems, and the macrosystems to which they belong.
- The interests of clients served by OD-HSD professionals are best served in the long run within the context of serving the good of the whole, including the client, its subsystems, and the macrosystems of which it is a part; this view of service can be called the "whole-win approach."

Finally, if those who consider themselves OD professionals because they focus primarily on organizations also consider themselves HSD professionals, then they are more likely to seek ways of cooperating with management consultants-therapists on the one hand and community development professionals on the other. By virtue of such cooperation, all those involved can expect to be better able to serve their clients. In other words, Human Systems Development provides a context within which cooperation among OD professionals and all other specialists within HSD can become particularly meaningful and effective.

Body of Knowledge, Educating Practitioners, and Monitoring Practice and Practitioners. As suggested by the model in Figure 1, there is a close relationship among the profession's body of knowledge, the education of its practitioners, and the monitoring of both practice and practitioners: therefore, it is useful to discuss them together.

Writing in 1973, French and Bell observed that "Organizational Development represents one of today's leading edges of applied behavioral science as organization theorists and practitioners endeavor to find ways to improve organization effectiveness and achieve organizational excellence (p. 192). It is probable that organization development will be around for a long time and will increasingly be a methodology chosen for effecting organizational change and improvement" (p. xv).

Nearly two decades later, their observation is still pertinent and, for reasons mentioned earlier, it is also applicable to HSD. OD remains a highly visible application of behavioral science theory and methodology to effect change in complex organizations. Though there is no single, well-defined body of knowledge, many American colleges and universities — including Case Western Reserve, Harvard, Massachusetts Institute of Technology, Stanford, the University of California (Los Angeles and Berkeley), the University of Chicago, the University of Southern California, and Yale — have courses or entire programs in OD or Organizational Behavior (OB) at the master's or doctoral level. Major studies of OD have been funded by the federal government (see, for example, Cummings and Molloy, 1977, financed by the National Science Foundation, and Fullan, Miles, and Taylor, 1980, supported by the National Institute of Education).

Although there is no single generally accepted scientific paradigm in the field, it is evident that research about and the practice of OD have matured considerably over the past twenty years and its effects are being felt by a growing number of organizations and persons. During that time, there has been an explosion of literature describing and evaluating the effectiveness of OD interventions. Such interventions draw on behavioral science theories and methods in such areas as problem solving, planning, interpersonal relationships, role definition and role relationships, values clarification, communication, leadership, group and intergroup dynamics, conflict management, organizational behavior, the systems approach, and systems dynamics. Its maturation as a science is best illustrated by the number and improved quality of empirical studies produced over that twenty-year span. Much of that research is assessed in five major reviews published between 1974 and 1986 (Cummings and Molloy, 1977; Friedlander and Brown, 1974; Porras and Berg, 1978; Nicholas, 1982; and Beer and Walton, 1987). The review by Nicholas (1982) included approximately sixty-five studies and 168 outcome variables, and concluded that certain OD interventions are clearly effective in producing organizational change. It is no less important to note that OD research and application have made important contributions to behavioral science

theory and methods by helping to identify and differentiate types
of change and by developing criteria for measuring them (Golembiewski, Billingsley, and Yeager, 1976; Terborg, Howard,
and Maxwell, 1980).

Within the profession's body of knowledge and closely
related to the education of practitioners is the ongoing work to
clarify competencies needed by OD-HSD professionals. Among
other efforts in this direction, a continuing Delphi Conference
has been in process since 1986 (Eisen, Steele, and Cherbeneau,
1988), which includes as its three stages (1) Environmental Scan:
Trends and Implications, (2) Core and Emerging OD Competencies, and (3) Experiences for Learning and Professional
Development. Clearly, the latter two stages focus on competencies and educating practitioners. Another related study was
reported by the American Society for Training and Development in 1983, which identified thirty-one critical competencies
needed by people in training and development, many of which
are important for OD-HSD professionals (McLagan, 1983,
1989). In addition, the Statement includes as one of its major
sections Responsibility for Professional Development and Competence (Guideline II, Chapter Five), which lists a number of
the more important competencies that can be expected of practitioners. As studies like these continue, we can expect substantial
improvement in the clarity with which we understand the knowledge and skills required for competence in the profession.

In this connection, however, we should also note that truly
being an OD-HSD professional involves more than mere "competence." In view of the attention still given to "the methods and
techniques of OD," the profession seems to have difficulty understanding what Tannenbaum, a founder of the profession,
has pointed out for a long time — that the ultimate professional
competence, paradoxically, does not involve professional competence. Rather, it involves the ability of the person who is functioning as a professional to apply him- or herself with authenticity and integrity.

As for monitoring practitioners, nothing has been done
on any comprehensive, systematic basis. Holders of advanced
degrees from certain university programs — including some in

business, education, human services, industrial and labor relations, management, nursing, psychology, public administration,
and social work — presumably have been monitored as to their
ability to practice, although such monitoring is probably more
related to knowledge than to the ability to practice. Certified
Consultants International and the Association for Creative
Change (ACC) both developed peer review processes which enable those professionals who choose to do so to monitor their
own practice with the help of colleagues who have participated
in a similar review. However, the fact that CCI disbanded in
the late 1980s suggests that support for an organization whose
primary purpose was to serve the purpose of "certification" was
not strong enough to make it financially viable, although it is
worth noting that at the time of its dissolution, more than 120
leaders in the profession had qualified for membership by means
of its peer review process.

Other professional associations/networks/institutes have
a variety of qualifications for membership, ranging from minimal
to extensive, and some grant members with certain qualifications the right to use professional designations that might become meaningful if their use were more widely recognized. For
example, the OD Institute requires commitment to the Statement, which the institute calls the "OD Code of Ethics," as one
of the conditions for recognition as a "Registered OD Professional." It seems clear that, in spite of the understandable resistance by a number of people, the process of monitoring practitioners offers substantial opportunity for the profession to
develop itself as a human system which takes collective responsibility for its functioning.

Setting and Monitoring Standards of Acceptable Practice.
There are few, if any, generally accepted, explicit standards of
practice. Implicit standards do exist, however, and the Statement development process is the profession's primary means for
making those standards explicit. Most practitioners seem to value
developing the Statement. Their reasons include: (1) The Statement is individually clarifying. (2) It clarifies a widely shared
view. (3) The Statement development process is evolutionary

and not static. (4) The Statement can provide guidance for professional education. (5) It can be used to educate clients and the public generally about what to expect from OD-HSD professionals (Gellermann, 1984b). Differences of opinion are not so much about whether to develop a statement but about what the Statement should encompass.

The Statement the profession seeks to develop can have different purposes, including aspirational, educational, and regulatory. An *aspirational* statement generally describes ideals toward which professionals strive. In contrast, an *educational* statement is more precise; it seeks to describe and explain professional norms in enough detail that it can be used in preparing practitioners to resolve ethical dilemmas they experience in their practice. And, finally, a *regulatory* code is even more precise, since it is buttressed by rules that are specific enough to govern behavior.

Although some practitioners feel differently, a regulatory code does not seem feasible for the profession now. Existing organizations may develop their own regulatory codes if they so choose, but for the profession generally, it seems more appropriate to proceed one step at a time, achieving consensus first on an aspirational statement and then on an educational one. Ideally, regulation will emphasize individual self-regulation and, therefore, until a clear educational code and materials to support it exist, it seems premature to talk about a regulatory code with sanctions imposed by the profession on those who violate its ethics. Most professionals and the leaders of their associations strongly prefer not to have a regulatory code at this time, based, at least in part, on the value the profession places on self-control, with motivation based on understanding and commitment rather than compliance enforced by professional sanctions and supports.

The Statement is explicit in saying that it is aspirational and educational. It is intentionally silent about whether it is regulatory. Further work, including work with the cases and case discussions in this book, can be expected to lead to an enhanced version of the Statement that is truly an educational Statement. The Annotated Statement in Chapters Four and Five represents substantial progress in that direction. As for its usefulness as a regulatory code, it is worded so that any network/ association/institute that wants to experiment with using it for regulatory purposes with its members can do so, and the profession can learn from their experience. However, as has already been said, it seems premature to think about a statement for regulatory use on a widespread basis.

The current Statement specifies its three purposes as (1) to increase professional and ethical consciousness and responsibility among OD-HSD professionals, (2) to guide OD-HSD professionals in making more informed ethical choices, and (3) to help the OD-HSD profession itself function at the fullness of its potential. People's responses indicate that there are different ways of valuing those purposes. In particular, several people have focused on the second one and emphasized completion of the Statement with its set of guidelines. Such responses have reflected an impatience to "get it done." But the "it" encompassed by the totality of the above purposes consists of much more than the completion of the written Statement. And, as OD-HSD professionals know, establishing ownership of the ideas behind the Statement is essential to fulfilling those purposes. Therefore, as long as significant suggestions for improvement continue to be received, keeping the Statement open to revision seems advisable.

The number and magnitude of revisions have decreased over the last few years, but more important suggestions continue to come in. For example, among other substantial changes, the latest have included:

1. Sharpening the purpose statement of the first paragraph
2. Making an explicit shift from being an aspirational statement to being educational as well
3. Reorganizing the Statement so that it can be summarized in a more concise form
4. Sharpening the list of values, including explicit recognition and definition of "life" and "the quest for happiness" as primary values
5. Explicitly including "justice" as one of the profession's primary values

6. Adding sections on moral rules and ideals and on justifying violations of morals and ethics
7. Establishing "responsibility to ourselves" as a major category of a professional's ethical responsibility
8. Clarifying the shift from a United States perspective to a global perspective for the profession
9. Making responsibility for dealing with cultural differences more explicit, especially when one is practicing in a culture that is not one's own
10. Explicitly recognizing that prospective clients may have purposes one considers morally wrong and providing guidelines for such situations
11. Making more explicit the responsibility of OD-HSD professionals for knowing about labor union issues and their responsibility to labor unions
12. Defining development broadly to include explicitly transformational change so that practitioners who deal with transformation will be included (and will include themselves) as members of the OD-HSD profession

For the next few years, periodic revision of the Statement may be needed to deal with suggestions for improvement, but thereafter the number and importance of suggested changes seems likely to decrease enough to allow less frequent revision. When that happens, we can say that the goal of "substantial consensus" has been achieved; however, attempting to move more quickly would be to put form ahead of substance.

An issue that has surfaced repeatedly during the evolution of the Statement has been its length. Some people feel that it is too long; others feel that the length is necessary to do what needs to be done. This difference is inevitable as long as people differ in their ideas of what purposes the Statement is intended to serve. For now, though, an educational statement such as the Annotated Statement in Chapters Four and Five, supported by educational materials such as this book, seems most reasonable. However, the people who object to the Annotated Statement's length also have an important point. A statement intended only to convey a sense of our aspirations need not be so long. Therefore, a more concise version has also been prepared (see

Appendix B). As can be seen, that Statement is abstracted from the Annotated Statement and is substantially shorter.

Educating the Public Regarding Acceptable OD-HSD Practice. Because of the diversity of its practitioners, it is not possible to give one concise description of OD-HSD practice, although in time, the Statement may serve such a purpose. For now, during its developmental period, it has been written primarily for the purpose of orienting discussion within the profession.

In addition, because of the recency of its emergence as a conscious field of practice, there have been few attempts to educate the public about OD-HSD. Although OD practitioners have been at work in the field for about four decades, the profession itself has made few, if any, conscious, systematic attempts to educate the public about its practice; a number of individual attempts can be identified, however, particularly in recent years.

For a general idea about the nature of OD-HSD practice, it will be helpful to look briefly at some primary kinds of practice. Throughout the literature on OD, a set of frequently used and quite specific techniques for introducing change and for measuring and evaluating its impact can be identified. Rush (1973) has identified three general forms of interventions: technical, administrative, and social.

- *Technical* interventions are intended to improve the effectiveness of technical resources or structural arrangements affecting the organization's operation. They may include experimenting with new organizational structures and assessing their effectiveness or designing new ways of applying available technology to the problems of the organization.
- *Administrative* interventions seek to improve the organization's policies and procedures by, for example, revising personnel practices or procedures for performance planning, performance appraisal, and compensation.
- *Social* interventions are concerned with such things as leadership and management, interpersonal relationships, group, intergroup, cultural, and systemic aspects of the organization.

In all three types of intervention, there is strong emphasis on systematically collecting data, assessing it along with the members of the organization who are affected, and then involving those members in planning whatever needs to be done as a means of improving the plan's quality and ensuring their full commitment to it.

Underlying these interventions is a fourth form of intervention that is not mentioned by Rush but that is at least as important, if not more so:

- *Personal* interventions focus on each individual's unique characteristics and dynamics, including beliefs and values, goals and roles, needs and aspirations, thoughts and feelings, hopes and fears, knowledge and abilities. They include such activities as personal counseling, life and career planning, and learning from the T-Group experience. For many people, the T-Group experience has had profound, positive effects on their self-esteem, self-confidence, and their commitment to the full realization of their potential.

To put "the personal" into perspective, some practitioners, including Tannenbaum, Margulies, and Massarik (1985, p. 6), "are personally committed to research and practice that help individuals reach as nearly as possible their basic potential." They add that they consider it important "that organizations be entities in the service of people rather than the other way around." And from a slightly different perspective, Stan Hinckley (1986), former CCI chairperson, contends that the clearest part of the profession's mission is "empowering human beings in the context of the human systems within which they live and work."

We can conceive of the practice of OD-HSD as aiming broadly to further the general process of development or growth with respect to individuals, organizations, and other human systems. More specifically, we can say that OD-HSD seeks to further such development in three primary ways. First, it seeks to help systems and their constituents establish or clarify their purpose and vision. Second, it provides systems with a variety of means for improving the goodness of fit between themselves and their external environments; between themselves and their internal constituents, especially their individual members; and between all of their constituents themselves. Third, it seeks to help systems and their constituents clarify more precisely what development means for them, given their purposes, their visions, their environments, and their constituent elements.

This last point comes into focus more sharply when we contrast the development of nonhuman organisms with that of human beings. For a nonhuman creature, development occurs when its struggle to reestablish equilibrium with its surroundings results in increased ability to satisfy basic instinctual needs. This development-defining purpose is, so to speak, programmed into the organism. By contrast, development for human beings and organizations consists of more than just increased ability to satisfy fixed, or programmed needs, such as hunger or safety. It also involves broadly based development in terms of intellect, imagination, and emotion that help people reflect on the purposes and goals to which they *choose* to aspire. And, as will be seen in the discussion of the profession's values and ethics as it develops throughout this book, freedom of choice is a primary value, and many, if not all, of the profession's ethics are rooted in that value in one way or another.

Conclusions. With the perspective provided by the above discussion, we can now consider the prospects for OD-HSD as a profession. As noted earlier, some practitioners are concerned that if it were to become a "profession," following the same evolutionary pattern as seems to have been followed by the professions of law and medicine, it would become exclusionary, monopolistic, and exploitive. Most seem to consider themselves professionals in the sense of the dictionary's definition of "participating for gain in an activity often engaged in by amateurs," and many would also apply the definition of "a calling requiring specialized knowledge and often long academic preparation" to their practice. Moreover, many would acknowledge that the practitioners of OD — but not necessarily practitioners of HSD — constitute a "whole body of persons engaged in a calling," although there would be differences of opinion about who is "in" and "out" and how the boundaries are defined.

In conclusion, we can say that although most OD-HSD professionals acknowledge that their profession is not highly developed, most seem to accept that:

1. OD-HSD is an evolving, emerging profession.
2. OD-HSD does not have to follow the developmental pattern of such professions as medicine and law; it can avoid their exclusionary, monopolistic, and exploitive tendencies (in fact, the profession may be able to learn from the experience of those other professions and avoid or at least minimize their mistakes).
3. OD-HSD needs some boundary clarification to protect itself and its clients, but how much and how to do so are still open questions (with some practitioners holding that by its nature the profession *must* be inclusionary).
4. OD-HSD is capable of becoming a profession in ways that make the world better for everyone and not just for the profession and its members, including ways that enable others to do what OD-HSD professionals do and that do not put the "professionals" above their clients.
5. OD-HSD practitioners can be both professionals and persons without getting so caught up in their roles that their sense of their own identity as persons gets lost in their identity as professionals (Gellermann, 1984b).

Later chapters will examine the values and ethics of the OD-HSD profession more closely, as well as explore ways of applying them in thinking about how to act in specific situations. To provide context for doing that, the closing section of this chapter will briefly identify some of the key ethical issues currently faced by the OD-HSD profession.

Ethical Issues in OD-HSD Practice and Research

Because ethics can serve as guides to thought and action when people are uncertain about the good and right thing to do, they can be particularly helpful when people are under powerful influences to act in ways they feel are not good and right. That raises the question of how we know what is "good and right," but we will defer that discussion until later. For now it is enough to say that, generally speaking, most people have a sense of right and wrong. For example, imagine the situation of an engineer who knows that one of her company's products is seriously unsafe — so unsafe that it is likely to cause the deaths of many people if appropriate action is not taken. At the same time, imagine her experiencing pressure from her boss to say nothing about it or at least to not continue asserting her view because higher-level management has decided that the risks are "acceptable." Without some guidelines for how to act in that situation, she could easily succumb to the pressure in spite of an uneasy feeling that she is doing something wrong.

An important way of preparing for ethical action is to identify in advance the qualities of virtue expected of professionals and the kinds of situations they are likely to face in which good-bad and right-wrong may be considerations, and then establish guidelines and rules for reference when such situations actually arise. For a professional community, in contrast to individual professionals, it is important, and some would even say essential, that its members collectively follow a similar procedure as part of establishing the ethical component of what they stand for as a profession. And having a profession's ethics as support for his or her conscience can strengthen an individual's ability to do what he or she* feels is right. This book, particularly the case discussions and the Statement, are intended as contributions to the establishment of ethics for the OD-HSD profession.

One of the first steps toward establishing ethical guidelines is to identify the ethical issues OD-HSD practitioners currently face. As part of the project on values and ethics in OD supported by the National Science Foundation, we asked practitioners to tell us about the issues they considered most important to the profession. We made this request publicly in most

---

*Rather than use the awkward "he or she" and "him or her" throughout the book, we will in some instances vary the gender of the pronoun, thus giving approximately equal attention to female and male.

of the leading OD-oriented publications in the United States. In addition, the process of developing the Statement, as described in Appendix A, has helped us identify additional issues.

Ethical issues in OD-HSD can be grouped using the same categories as those in the Statement. According to those categories, the primary issues identified include:

Responsibilities to Self

1. *Responsibility to Themselves.* In committing themselves to the service of others, it is easy for OD-HSD professionals to ignore the effects of that commitment on the quality of their own lives. To what extent, if any, are they also responsible to themselves and their families?

Responsibilities for Professional Development and Competence

2. *Responsibility for Professional Competence.* Do individual professionals have an obligation to ensure that they are competent to deliver the kinds of service they offer and, if so, how? Does the OD-HSD profession have an obligation to ensure the competence of all practitioners who claim to be members of that profession? If so, how should that obligation be discharged? Under what conditions, if any, is it acceptable for a professional to work at the edge of his or her competence?

3. *Multinational and Multicultural Competence.* When OD-HSD professionals practice or conduct research in countries with cultures that are significantly different from their own, do they have any special responsibilities? For example, would a consultant from a Western, Judeo-Christian culture invited to practice in a Middle Eastern, Moslem culture be obliged to practice in any special ways? And, if so, how? Does work with an organization within their own culture whose members come from different cultures or subcultures than their own give OD-HSD professionals any special responsibilities? For example, under a contract that would affect most members of a client organization, would a white

American OD-HSD professional be under any different obligations if the membership in the organization were a mix of white, black, and Hispanic than if that membership were predominantly white?

Responsibilities to Client and Significant Others

4. *Who Is the Client? Responsibility to Whom and for What?* What are OD-HSD professionals' responsibilities for the effects of what they do or do not do? Do those responsibilities extend to people other than the person(s) who contract with them to pay for their services? Do they extend to people who may be harmed by the change? If so, in what ways? When OD-HSD professionals contract with managers to achieve results based on the organization's values, particularly economic values, may they also seek to serve human values, such as "life," "the quest for happiness," "dignity," "empowerment," and "self-realization"? When the achievement of organizational results is in conflict with the good of the human beings who work for the organization, what, if any, are the responsibilities of OD-HSD professionals? When OD-HSD professionals help people increase their productivity, to what extent, if any, are they obliged to see that the people who create the increase receive a share of that increase?

5. *Participation in Change Decisions.* Because the actions of OD-HSD professionals are intended to change the conditions of life in their client organizations/systems, they raise serious ethical issues relative to the rights, abilities, and opportunities of people affected by such changes to participate freely in informed and voluntary ways (Walton, 1978; Walton and Warwick, 1973). Even without direct pressures, subordinates may perceive refusal to participate as putting them in jeopardy (Elliston, 1985). What are the responsibilities of professionals for seeing that people who currently have little power or influence in the system are allowed to participate in making decisions for change that may have major impact on their lives, as in down-sizing, plant closings,

and changed working conditions? What obligation do consultants have for seeing that the people who are affected by decisions about organizational change are fully informed? If a change exposes certain people to risks, should they be told? Should they be informed even when they are likely not to understand what the information means? Under what conditions, if any, is it ethical for OD-HSD professionals to advocate or support directive leadership, authoritarian decisions, and the use of power to impose change?

6. *Deception.* Under what conditions, if any, would withholding or misrepresenting relevant information be acceptable? For example, would deception be permissible as a means of generating research knowledge? If so, under what conditions?

7. *Confidentiality.* OD-HSD's data-gathering techniques (for example, interviews, surveys, and participant observation) may uncover sensitive information about persons or organizational units (Warwick, 1982). Information about dissent or incompetence may place some people at risk if it is reported. Yet professionals are under pressure from managers to diagnose and report the causes of difficulties. How can the ethic of confidentiality be reconciled with the organization's need for timely, accurate information that could improve its functioning? What is the professional's responsibility when information reveals improper actions by the organization? Does that responsibility differ according to whether the organization is public or private?

8. *Contracting and Contract Termination.* What are professionals' responsibilities for ensuring clear, full, and mutual understanding of the objectives of their engagements and the means to be used in accomplishing them? Must the contract be in writing? How does that contract affect the responsibilities of professionals during and after its fulfillment? If, during the course of an engagement, an OD-HSD professional concludes that responding to his client's demands or expectations may do more harm than good, does he have a responsibility for terminating the contract?

What other conditions might make termination necessary? And, in the event of termination, what responsibilities do professionals have in the termination process? Or, in contrast, if the contract creates unforeseen needs for service, what are the professional's obligations with regard to serving those needs? In other words, when is it fair to conclude that the professional's responsibilities have been fulfilled?

9. *Responsibilities to Third Parties.* Do OD-HSD professionals have obligations to third parties outside their client organizations? For example, do OD-HSD professionals have any responsibility to the communities within which their clients exist? To the organizations' suppliers? To their labor unions? More specifically, do OD-HSD professionals have responsibilities to labor unions as well as management when, while working under contracts with management, conflicts arise between management and the unions? For example, would it be ethical for a professional to consult with an organization's managers on how to decertify a union or to keep one from organizing and seeking certification as a representative of the organization's workers? Or, in contrast, if the leadership group of a union asked for help in team building, what should the consultant do?

10. *Conflicts of Interest Between the Professional and the Client.* When a professional finds herself in a conflict of interest with a client, what is she obliged to do? For example, what should a consultant do if she has an opportunity to establish a major contract with a prospective new client and she discovers that the prospect is in direct competition with one of her existing clients? If an external consultant develops new technology during the course of her work for a client, what are their respective rights to that technology? Who owns it?

11. *Divergent Client and Consultant Expectations.* When a prospective client brings in an OD-HSD consultant to serve a specific need as perceived by the prospect, the professional may soon perceive the client's needs differently. And, in fact, their expectations may conflict, at least as understood

by the consultant. Does the consultant have an obligation to make their differences fully known at the beginning of their relationship? If not, how is that reconciled with the value the profession places on openness and honesty? If a prospective client seeks help in achieving short-term objectives that the professional believes will do long-term harm to the organization, what is the professional's responsibility? Would it make any difference if the prospect seems unaware of the potential for such harm? What if appropriate long-term approaches would almost certainly be unacceptable to the prospect and the alternative is doing nothing?

12. *Researcher-Practitioner Role Conflict.* OD-HSD's use of action research combines commitments to both action and research, but the tension between helping and studying precipitates ethical dilemmas (Benne, 1959; Bennis, 1963). Because researchers try to augment the body of knowledge, they may undervalue the client's need for timely information. Who "owns" the data? What arrangements for access to it and its release are appropriate for researchers to negotiate into their contracts?

(*Note:* Within the area of "Responsibility to the Client," we should also acknowledge the extensive analysis by White and Wooten [1986], who identified thirty-one potential ethical dilemmas that could arise at the various stages of Organization Development, ranging from "misrepresentation of the consultant's skill base and background" to "failure to monitor change.")

Responsibility to the Profession

13. *Relationships Between OD-HSD Professionals.* What obligations exist between internal and external consultants? In case of conflicts, what are their obligations to one another, the client system, and the profession? What about relationships between different professionals who are serving the same client? To what extent, if any, are practitioners

responsible for sharing the knowledge, technology, and abilities they develop with one another? By what values — professional, economic, and personal — should such sharing be guided? When professionals use technology developed by other professionals, what are their responsibilities to one another? When one professional develops new technology that builds on the work of others in the profession, what are her ownership rights and responsibilities?

14. *Responsibility to the OD-HSD Profession.* Are ethics of OD-HSD professionals matters only of individual choice or do they also encompass obligations to the profession? If so, what are they? For example, one professional may be willing to risk his reputation on practices whose consequences, if they fail, will affect the profession as well as himself. What are his responsibilities to the profession in such a situation? In contrast, the opportunities open to OD-HSD professionals come, in part, because others in the OD-HSD profession have behaved responsibly and credibly. As a consequence, do professionals have an obligation to their profession? How can individual freedom and responsibility to the profession be reconciled?

Social Responsibility

15. *Morality of the Client's Purpose.* Are OD-HSD professionals responsible for making a moral judgment about their clients' purposes and, more specifically, about the degree to which their professional activities seem likely to serve those purposes? If so, in the case of activities that might serve immoral purposes, are OD-HSD professionals obliged to withhold service? Are there any conditions under which such service might be permissible?

16. *Social and Economic Justice.* To what extent, if any, are OD-HSD professionals responsible for social and economic justice? For example, do those who work with organizations which have historically practiced discrimination in their hiring, compensation, development, and promotion practices have any obligation to act affirmatively in order

to influence those organizations to change? If so, in what ways? Would that hold true even if affirmative action is in no way a part of their consulting contract? Under what conditions, if any, are OD-HSD professionals obliged to offer their services free (as in the case of pro bono work by lawyers) or at a discount in order to serve justice?

We intend this listing only as a broad survey of the current state of the primary issues faced by the OD-HSD profession. Additional issues will become clear as this book proceeds. With this chapter's discussion as background, we are now ready to look more closely at values and ethics in the OD-HSD profession. The next chapter presents a philosophical overview to provide a general perspective for the more specific practical focus of later chapters.

CHAPTER TWO

▮▯▮▯▮▯▮▯▮▯▮▯▮▯▮▯▮▯▮▯▮▯▮▯▮▯▮

A Perspective
for Thinking
About Ethics

▮▯▮▯▮▯▮▯▮▯▮▯▮▯▮▯▮▯▮▯▮▯▮▯▮

Professional activity in Organization and Human Systems Development raises important ethical issues. Exploring these issues in a systematic way, however, is difficult, since no single framework for analyzing them does full justice to their diversity and multifaceted character. Nonetheless, it seems useful to provide a context for thinking about such issues, at least from a preliminary standpoint, by focusing attention on the concept of ethics itself.

There is, to be sure, no universally agreed-upon way to analyze that concept. There are, however, two distinct views of ethics that have played important roles in Western philosophy and that correspond to important aspects of the way in which most people think about ethics. The first of these conceptions, which one might term "ethics as morality," treats ethics as being fundamentally concerned with rules of interpersonal conduct. Under this conception, ethics consists, at its core, of a set of rules that apply to human beings over the totality of their interrelationships with one another and that take precedence over all other rules. In contrast, the second conception, which one might call "ethics as the quest for a good life," is fundamentally concerned with values that are ultimately personal rather than interpersonal. Under this conception, ethics is concerned with determining the ends, or values, to be sought in a genuinely good human life and with the means for their realization.

One need not make a judgment about which of the two conceptions is superior. Each provides special illumination with respect to different areas of human ethical experience. Ethics as morality and ethics as the quest for a good life thus may be viewed as complementary rather than opposed to one another.[1] The following discussion will briefly examine both conceptions of ethics and identify some major ethical issues in OD-HSD from their different perspectives.

Ethics as Morality

The concept of ethics, as understood in one significant way, involves a system of interrelated ideas within which the notion of a code of moral conduct plays a critical role. Such a code has particular characteristics.[2] First, the code is paramount. Its dictates take precedence over any other considerations a person might take into account when making decisions. While paramount, however, the code is not all-encompassing. It does not even come close to providing complete guidance on how to live one's life. In most personal decisions, it is not usually even a factor. But when its dictates bear upon a decision, they outweigh all other considerations.

Second, the moral code of conduct is general. One important way to think of an act as immoral involves regarding it as forbidden by a code of paramount significance not only for oneself but for other people as well. Philosophers disagree as to just how generally the code applies, whether universally to all rational people or in ways conditioned by factors such as time and place. Nonetheless, the idea of a moral code, in one of its major forms, involves the conception of dictates that extend in scope of application far beyond the individual.

Third, the code of moral conduct is rationally grounded. The paramount status and general scope of the code are viewed as resting upon an objective, rational foundation. The precise nature of this foundation, however, is elusive. Different philosophical theories, all highly plausible, explain it in different and, in some cases, radically incompatible ways, reflecting deep disagreements over how to understand the idea of reason itself, as it applies to human conduct.

According to one major philosophical theory of morality, Utilitarianism, the value of pleasure ultimately grounds the basic moral rules. Utilitarians, at least of the classic form exemplified by John Stuart Mill, conceive of pleasure as the one thing that is desirable for its own sake (see Sher, 1979). Everything else properly thought of as desirable, including the basic moral rules, derives its status as such from its means-to-an-end relationship with pleasure. According to Utilitarianism, this relationship, in the case of the basic moral rules, consists in the net increase in pleasure, over an entire society, presumably obtained when a large number of individuals adhere to those rules.

By contrast, another major philosophical theory of morality, the Kantian or, as it is sometimes called, the Deontological approach, emphatically rejects the Utilitarian account of the grounding of the basic moral rules. Under the Kantian theory, the paramount status of the basic moral rules cannot be accounted for by their relationship to pleasure or, indeed, to any other value the idea of which is identifiable independently of the basic moral rules. In the words of Immanuel Kant, "the purposes which we may have in our actions, as well as their effects regarded as ends and incentives of the will, cannot give to actions any unconditioned and moral worth" (Ellington, 1981, p. 13). In contrast, "unconditioned and moral worth" of actions, according to Kant, stems from their conformity with a principle, derived from reason itself, independent of the desires and inclinations of human beings, that Kant calls the *categorical imperative*. According to this principle, a person should "[a]ct only on that maxim whereby you can at the same time will that it should become a universal law" (Ellington, 1981, p. 14).

The idea of a code of moral conduct has a fourth important characteristic that relates to its content and structure. The code contains at its core a set of rules that forbids various kinds of behavior that cause severe harm to others or substantially increase the likelihood that others will suffer grave harms.[3] The rules, however, are not absolute. The code also specifies circumstances in which a person may justifiably violate the rules. If a person violates the rules unjustifiably, however, then this makes him or her liable to punishment according to the code.

The idea of a moral code described above thus contains the ideas of two kinds of norms that enter into moral thinking at different points: (1) moral rules such as "Do not kill," "Do not cheat," "Keep your promises," and so on, and (2) norms that indicate the morally relevant considerations with respect to the justified violation of basic moral rules. The importance of moral rules is largely conceptual rather than practical. They provide relatively little guidance in dealing with concrete moral issues — that is, questions of morality about which rational people may disagree. They define for us, however, the very concept of a moral issue. No matter how strongly one objects to certain conduct, if it involves no violation of a moral rule, then the conduct raises no moral issues.

Thus, whenever a moral issue exists, the actual or possible violation of a moral rule is involved. If one decides that such a violation has or may have occurred, the question becomes the moral justifiability of the actual or possible violation at issue. This question, in turn, concerns identification and weighing of the various factors deemed relevant under the code of moral conduct for reaching a decision about this matter. In this connection, Bernard Gert has identified the following eight factors (Gert, 1989, pp. 141–146, 285).

1. The moral rules violated
2. The evils (a) avoided, (b) prevented, (c) caused by the violation
3. The relevant desires of the people affected by the violation
4. The relevant rational beliefs of the people affected by the violation
5. The authority to violate certain moral rules with respect to a person given one's relationship to that person
6. The good promoted by the violation
7. Whether the violation prevents an unjustified violation of the basic moral rules

8.   Whether the violation results in the punishment of a person for unjustifiably violating the basic moral rules

   The above list, though not necessarily comprehensive, indicates the diversity and breadth of scope of the morally relevant factors for justifying the violation of basic moral rules. According to the list, one needs to consider probable consequences of a violation. One also, however, must take into account "nonconsequentialist" factors, such as the desires and beliefs of people affected by the violation and the nature of one's relationship to an individual (for example, judges have authority to violate rules that other people do not have). There is no universally agreed-upon formula for weighing such diverse factors to reach a moral decision. The idea of a moral code underlying the concept of ethics as morality thus leaves open a large gray area wherein rational people may disagree about moral issues. This disagreement, however, occurs within a broader framework identifying the agreed-upon basic moral rules and the morally relevant factors concerning their violation.

   As stated at the outset, the conception of ethics as morality involves a system of interrelated ideas having at its core the notion of a moral code with the four characteristics described above — specifically, that the code is paramount, universal (but not absolute), grounded in reason, and concerned principally with forbidding behaviors that tend to cause severe harm. It was noted that the notion of such a code defines the very idea of a moral issue. That is to say, a moral issue arises only if someone has violated a basic moral rule in a given set of circumstances. If so, then one may proceed to consider whether the violation was justifiable. The claim that an act is immoral can be understood as the assertion that it involves the unjustified violation of a basic moral rule. Likewise, one may interpret the statement that one has a moral obligation to do something as expressing the idea that in the circumstances, a basic moral rule requires doing it. One may define *guilt* as an uncomfortable feeling caused by the belief that one has unjustifiably violated a basic moral rule. A morally bad person is best thought of as someone who does not regard the basic moral rules as paramount, while one best conceives of a morally good person as someone

who follows the basic moral rules out of a belief in their paramount status. In less direct but no less integral ways, the notion of basic moral rules also enters into the ideas of moral virtue and moral vice, and moral judgment as it relates to social
institutions and practices, rather than to the conduct of individual
human beings (Gert, 1989, chaps. 8, 9, and 12).

Some of the ethical issues in OD-HSD enumerated at the
end of the previous chapter primarily involve questions of moral
justification — that is, of whether in a specific situation the acts
of a consultant unjustifiably violate basic moral rules. The deception of research subjects, for example, raises questions of
moral justification, questions that in particular circumstances
inevitably relate to factors one, four, and six on Gert's list. The
conception of ethics as morality also relates to the kinds of ethical issues cited at the end of Chapter One in two other ways.
The first of these concerns the issue of moral responsibilities of
OD-HSD consultants. The second has to do with an issue best
characterized as "how to avoid morally hazardous situations."
The following two sections respectively discuss these two issues.

Moral Responsibilities of OD-HSD Consultants. OD-HSD
consultants frequently engage in activities that may significantly
affect the interests of many individuals. The question of the
responsibilities of consultants with respect to such individuals
thus often becomes an important issue in particular situations.
The preceding discussion indicated that, according to ethics as
morality, the basic moral rules have to do with avoiding behavior that either causes harm to others or significantly increases
its likelihood. Furthermore, such rules may not be violated unless one has a valid moral justification for doing so. Accordingly, ethics as morality has a clear implication at the outset
with respect to the moral responsibilities of OD-HSD consultants. They must not unjustifiably cause harm or act in ways
that increase the likelihood of anyone suffering harm.

The foregoing statement seems straightforward at a general level. Complexity sets in quickly, however, when one becomes more specific. As noted above, although the system of
concepts that comprises ethics as morality identifies the rele-

vant considerations for determining when an act unjustifiably causes harm, it does not include a formula upon which all rational people agree for weighing those considerations. A further element of complexity surrounds the concept of *cause* that figures in judgments about whether or not someone's act caused harm. In the most clear-cut cases in which an individual causes harm, he specifically intends to produce harmful consequences for another person. In circumstances, however, in which no such specific intent obtains, the issue of whether a person's act caused harm tends to become much less clear.

Consider, for example, the case of an internal OD-HSD consultant who assists in developing a plan to improve the competitive position of her firm, which, if implemented, will result in large personnel reductions. Or consider the situation of an external consultant, hired to facilitate development of a job restructuring plan by a joint labor-management committee, who becomes firmly convinced that the emerging plan is unfair to the employees in significant respects. Does the internal consultant in the first case have a responsibility to fight for specific measures that would reduce the adverse impact of the plan on affected employees? Does the external consultant in the second case have a responsibility to depart from his neutral role as facilitator and intercede actively on the employees' behalf? Suppose that neither consultant takes the above steps, or any other like them, to minimize the potentially adverse consequences for affected employees of organizational decisions resulting, in part, from the activities of each consultant? Under this circumstance, should one hold that the consultants, through their respective activities, caused harm to the employees? Or, rather, should one conclude simply that they chose not to try to prevent that harm?

The above distinction, between causing a harm and not preventing it, is critical from the standpoint of ethics as morality. The basic moral rules require everyone to avoid causing harms such as death, pain, disability, loss of freedom, and loss of pleasure. They do not, however, require people to prevent these harms. By contrast, the statement that everyone should seek to prevent harm expresses a moral ideal, as opposed to a basic moral rule (Gert, 1989, chap. 8). That is, from the standpoint of ethics as morality, the objective of preventing harm should be universally encouraged, though not universally required. Moreover, as noted in the previous section, ethics as morality treats the preventing of harm as a morally relevant consideration for determining whether a moral rule was justifiably violated in particular circumstances. For example, one may justifiably violate a basic moral rule, such as "Do not cause pain," in circumstances in which the amount of harm preventable by violating the rule significantly outweighs the amount of harm caused by violating it, as in the administration of a rabies shot. Under ethics as morality, however, no basic moral rule, by itself, *requires* everyone to prevent harm, although moral ideals *encourage* its prevention.

Questions about the responsibilities of OD-HSD consultants, such as those raised above, thus involve an issue of classification, or description — namely, whether to characterize certain patterns of consultant activity or inactivity in certain circumstances as the cause of harm, or, alternatively, as the choice not to prevent harm. Reaching agreement about this matter of description is difficult in many cases for the following reason: There is a basic moral rule to the effect that one should meet one's responsibilities (Gert, 1989, pp. 154–157).[4] In the context of this rule, the term "responsibilities" does not refer broadly to the requirements of the moral rules. So understood, the rule "Meet your responsibilities" would be logically equivalent to the circular statement that one is morally required to do what one is morally required to do. Instead, the term *responsibilities,* as it functions in this basic moral rule, refers to the behavior required of a person by virtue of an occupied position or role, such as parent or teacher; a voluntarily incurred obligation, such as a promise; or, in some instances, simply being in a certain situation, as with proximity to a small child drowning in a pool. There are circumstances in which failure to prevent harm involves unjustified violation of the basic moral rule to meet one's responsibilities. Such a failure from the standpoint of ethics as morality is equivalent to the unjustified causing of harm.

How then do OD-HSD consultants identify their professional responsibilities to determine when not preventing a given harm, in the context of professional practice, amounts, morally speaking, to causing it? This question has no single, clear-cut answer but instead involves unavoidably ambiguous issues concerning interpretation of the professional role of an OD-HSD consultant. One might conceive of the consulting role in Organization Development primarily from the standpoint of economic and legal relationships. According to this conception, the role emerges through an exchange process wherein the consultant authorized to act on behalf of an organization offers an economically valuable service to another party in exchange for some reciprocal economic benefit. The consultant's primary responsibilities under this conception are delineated by the specific terms of the contractual agreement with the organization. To the extent that the services rendered under the agreement affect other individuals, those individuals' rights and the consultant's correlative responsibilities are determined entirely by the legal system — that is, by statutes, common law, and so forth. The foregoing economic and law-based account of the OD-HSD consultant's role thus implies that consultants cause harm to others through their activities only insofar as they contravene the contractual agreement that created the consulting relationship or violate the legally enforceable rights of others.

In contrast, one may view Organization Development not merely as a set of techniques to enhance the economic productivity of organizations but also — and principally — as a profession committed to making organizational life of all kinds more fully expressive of human values, such as autonomy, self-realization, fairness, cooperation, and concern for human well-being. Viewing the practice of OD-HSD in this way strongly suggests that consultants have a responsibility to promote the realization of these values as an inherent part of their professional role. Accordingly, under this conception, OD-HSD consultants cause harm to others adversely affected by their professional activity not only by breaching the terms of their consulting contracts, or by violating the legal rights of others, but also by failing to act in specific circumstances so as to further the human values at the heart of OD-HSD.

In all likelihood, few OD-HSD consultants would accept either the economic or human interpretation of their professional role in a categorical way that absolutely excludes the other. Nonetheless, the two views are not easily reconciled, and it seems that in most cases one or the other of them tends to predominate in the outlook of particular consultants. Which of them does so predominate determines how an OD-HSD consultant identifies the circumstances in professional practice in which not preventing harm is morally equivalent to causing it.

As noted above, OD-HSD consultants disagree in real and substantial respects on this matter. Such disagreement, however, does not preclude the possibility of meaningful dialogue among them on a continuing basis about significant professional values. To the contrary, one may think of practitioners in the field of OD-HSD as constituting what the philosopher Ronald Dworkin (1986, pp. 46–48) has termed an *interpretive community*. This means not only that they participate in a common social practice, namely OD-HSD consulting, but also that they regard the nature of the practice as an appropriate subject for interpretation. Such an outlook toward OD-HSD, or any social practice, according to Dworkin (1986, p. 47), has the following two components: "The first is the assumption that the practice . . . does not simply exist but has value, that it serves some interest or purpose or enforces some principle—in short, that it has some point—that can be stated independently of just describing the rules that make up the practice. The second is the further assumption that the requirements of [the practice]—the behavior it calls for or judgments it warrants—are not necessarily or exclusively what they have always been taken to be but are instead sensitive to its point, so that the strict rules must be understood or applied or extended or modified or qualified or limited by that point." Dworkin (1986, p. 47) notes that by regarding a social practice in the above manner, people thereby seek to impose meaning upon it, "to see it in (what they consider) its best light—and then to restructure it in the light of that meaning."

Questions about the moral responsibilities of OD-HSD consultants thus connect inextricably with broad interpretive issues about their professional role, issues that no single discussion may realistically seek to close. Instead, under any reasonable view, the discussion of these interpretive issues must be conceived of as ongoing, multifaceted, and broadly based. The drafting process, described in Appendix A, that has produced the Statement represents one aspect of a continuing discussion about interpretation of the professional role in OD-HSD. So also do the analyses of critical incidents presented in Chapters Six through Eleven and Appendix D. More generally, perhaps the best way to think about the purpose of this book would be to view its use as an exemplification, in the context of OD-HSD, of Dworkin's description above of the nature of discourse among the members of an interpretive community.

Avoiding Morally Hazardous Situations. The work of OD-HSD consultants often places them in ambiguous, complex, or delicate situations that present ample possibilities for errors in judgment. Such errors, in turn, can contribute to the creation of even more difficult situations in which (1) the consultant feels compelled to choose among alternatives that all seem to involve serious moral problems or (2) for other reasons, circumstances increase the likelihood of morally unjustified behavior on the part of the consultant. OD-HSD consultants thus face the following major moral issue: How can a consultant function effectively in a complex, difficult human environment, and yet avoid errors of judgment that may lead to nearly intractable problems of moral choice, or to circumstances that increase the likelihood of morally unjustifiable behavior on the part of the consultant? More concisely, how can an OD-HSD consultant avoid morally hazardous situations?

Two kinds of morally hazardous situations were alluded to in the immediately preceding paragraph. The first involves risk of error on the consultant's part that may lead to a situation in which every alternative poses serious problems from a moral point of view. Many OD-HSD professionals consider the initial contracting process critical to avoiding these kinds of situations. They believe that establishing a clear understanding with the client about basic aspects of the consulting relationship at the outset substantially enhances the avoidance of morally agonizing situations at later stages. In this regard, consider the problems that OD-HSD consultants face concerning disclosure of confidential information. Consultants may obtain information in confidence from individuals and then find that circumstances later develop under which they feel impelled to disclose the information to others. This kind of problem may be unavoidable at times. However, such problematic situations may stem in part from a failure on the part of the consultant to clarify adequately the nature of his or her commitment to confidentiality at the beginning of the consulting relationship. This suggests that problems concerning disclosures of confidential information in an OD-HSD consulting relationship might be approached constructively by concentrating on the general guidelines consultants should adopt in this regard and on the most effective means of communicating them at the outset to everyone concerned.

In the second kind of morally hazardous situation there are circumstances that increase the likelihood of serious, morally unjustified behavior by the OD-HSD professional. Conflict of interest between a consultant and client represents a classic instance of this kind of situation. As another example, consider a T-Group program that does not have adequate provisions to ensure genuinely voluntary participation. In such a program, participants may be uninformed or not fully informed about the nature of the T-Group experience. They may feel subtly pressured to join the T-Group or, having joined, to avoid withdrawing from it. Under these circumstances, the T-Group leaders risk becoming involved in morally unjustifiable forms of coercion. A crucial question thus arises of how to structure T-Group programs to secure the uncoerced participation of members within client organizations.

Another example concerns a far more general phenomenon. A variety of motives, such as financial reward, career advancement, or, for academics, the desire to test various research hypotheses, may impel consultants to accept work in areas in which they have little experience and thus are not fully competent. This can set in motion a train of events involving major expenditures of money, time, or even emotional energy on the part of a client with no remotely commensurate benefits. At times, an OD-HSD consultant may decide to become involved in such a situation fully aware of the gaps in his or her experience and knowledge that may cause subsequent problems. In all likelihood, however, this occurs most often because the consultant's decision involves a large element of self-deception, a state of mind that in some ways resembles, but in other ways differs from, willful disregard of one's deficiencies in the areas of experience and knowledge. Avoiding self-deception plays an important part in the ideal of professionalism for most vocations, and it has a special relevance for OD-HSD (Davis, 1982). The problem of how to avoid the above described morally hazardous situation thus merges with the problem of devising effective means to foster high standards among OD-HSD practitioners with regard to a critical, though elusive, aspect of the ideal of professionalism.

Ethics as the Quest for a Good Life

The conception of ethics as the quest for a good life has a fundamentally different emphasis from that of ethics as morality. Ethics as the quest for a good life does not allot a critical role to the idea of a code of moral conduct that defines the basic obligations of human beings. Instead, it focuses on the very different idea of flourishing, or fulfillment, for the human individual; that is, it focuses on the ends, or values, to be sought in a genuinely good human life and on the means for realizing them.

Aristotle's *Nichomachean Ethics* (Aristotle, 1941) is the clearest, and historically most important, example of the conception of ethics as the quest for a good life. The *Nichomachean Ethics,* like other works by Aristotle, presupposes that every object has a natural end, or *telos,* toward which it strives that determines the course of its natural development. For Aristotle, the *telos* of a human being is to attain a good life through full development of his or her natural capacities within the context of membership in a society supporting that development.

Aristotle views the virtues as natural human capacities in their proper working order — that is, in balance between excess and deficiency. Thus, for example, Aristotle defines courage as a mean between rashness and cowardice, and he views generosity as a mean between prodigality and stinginess. The mean between deficiency and excess, which constitutes virtue, according to Aristotle, cannot be determined with precision. Much is necessarily left to the judgment of the person of practical reason with wide experience.

Aristotle maintains that the good life, or happiness, consists in the full development of the human virtues, among which the highest are those associated with theoretical contemplation, the most satisfying and worthwhile human activity. Furthermore, Aristotle views human beings as naturally social. For this reason, he believes that the development of virtue can occur only within the context of social existence. More specifically, Aristotle holds that such development requires conditions of social cooperation that provide security and material prosperity. The primary purpose of society, for Aristotle, is thus the fostering of virtue.

The basic thrust of Aristotle's *Nichomachean Ethics* significantly diverges from the conception of ethics as morality. Aristotle's ethical theory emphasizes the idea of human excellence, the full realization of human capacities. It deemphasizes the idea of moral obligation, rules that specify the basic requirements of social living. In the words of the late noted legal philosopher Lon L. Fuller (1964, p. 5), Aristotle "recognized, of course, that a man might fail to realize his fullest capabilities. As a citizen or as an official, he might be found wanting. But in such a case he was condemned for failure, not for being recreant to duty; for shortcoming, not for wrongdoing. Generally with the Greeks instead of ideas of right and wrong, or moral claim and moral duty, we have rather the conception of proper and fitting conduct, conduct such as beseems a human functioning at his best."

Aristotle's specific conclusions about the quest for a good life, at least as he formulated them in the *Nichomachean Ethics,* no longer exert a strong active influence on philosophical thought. The general structure of his ethical theory, however, with its emphasis on aspiration toward development of important human capacities to their full extent, continues to play an important role in modern philosophical and psychological writing about ethics. One finds the aspirational element of Aristotelian ethical thought exemplified over a broad spectrum of works by major intellectual figures ranging from Friedrich Nietzsche (see Kaufman, 1966) to Abraham Maslow (1943). As will become apparent in Chapters Four and Five, it significantly underlies one important and continually evolving contribution to ethical thought about OD-HSD—namely the Statement.

Some further implications of the contrast between ethics as the quest for a good life and ethics as morality are important to note. The ends, or values, to be sought in a genuinely fulfilled human life range far more widely than the basic moral rules central to the idea of ethics as morality. As noted previously, ethics as morality essentially involves the idea of a code of moral conduct that is paramount and general, but not all-encompassing. To state the matter another way, one may associate the basic moral rules at the core of ethics as morality with a corresponding set of moral values which constitute a subset within the totality of human values. For example, to the extent that a person is motivated to follow the basic moral rules, he or she identifies with the rule "Do not deceive," and accordingly values honesty. Likewise, such a person identifies with the rule "Keep your promises," and thus values trustworthiness, and so forth. Such moral values are conceived of as paramount under ethics as morality in the sense that one presupposes the existence of rational, objective grounds in support of the view that a society should have effective means to bring about their general inculcation. The specifically moral values, however, do not, and cannot, by themselves completely guide a person in living his or her life. A meaningful life involves identification with many other kinds of values as well, which are not derivable directly from the basic moral rules.

There is, however, no code of the values to be sought in a genuinely good human life analogous to the basic moral code that underlies the conception of ethics as morality. According to that latter conception, objective, rational considerations dictate that everyone should be brought up to identify with the values directly derivable from the basic moral rules. Society should influence each person in such a way that he or she positively values honesty, trustworthiness, dependability, and so on, and negatively values cruelty, callousness, deceitfulness, and the like. As a corollary, if a person who does not have these values expresses his or her lack of identification with them in overt immoral behavior, then, based on the code, the person should be thought of as liable to punishment.

The conception of ethics as the quest for a good life, however, does not correspondingly imply a set of values — beyond those derivable directly from the basic moral rules — which from an objective, rational standpoint everyone must likewise regard in the above mentioned ways. Different human lives may derive meaning from identification with very different values, or from very different orderings of them. This point holds even for extremely important values such as knowledge, friendship, love, wealth, and pleasure, which, though extremely important, do not have the direct relationship described above with basic moral rules.

As noted earlier, the conception of ethics as the quest for a good life significantly underlies the Statement. This is understandable because many values issues for OD-HSD consultants largely involve clarification of the values that infuse lives with meaning, both their own lives and the lives affected by their professional work. Such clarification requires consultants to identify their values and then develop a conception of how they relate to one another — that is, the extent to which they complement or conflict, and if the latter, their relative rankings. The process of values clarification in this sense involves continuous interplay between experience and critical reflection, each influencing the other.

This process plays a key role in a number of areas in which ethical issues of a personal nature arise for OD-HSD professionals. For example, questions related to fundamental career choices about the kinds of work in OD-HSD a person wants to do involve a balancing of diverse values. The balancing of values figures likewise in problems stemming from divergent client and consultant perceptions of issues the consultant should address. As noted in the first chapter, a consultant hired to serve a need specifically identified by the client may soon perceive the client's needs differently. Furthermore, in that regard, the consultant may recognize underlying problems of a sensitive nature that, in his judgment, the client requires further preparation to face. Should the consultant make his or her perceptions of the client's needs known at the very beginning of the consulting relationship, and possibly imperil its success? If not, how may such a course best be reconciled with the value of openness in professional relationships? The above issues call for striking a balance between competing values based on reflection, personal experience, and insights derived from the relevant experiences of other professionals.

The conceptions of ethics as the quest for a good life and of ethics as morality do not inherently conflict. A significant theoretical issue exists, however, about the relationship between the two conceptions. More specifically, one may inquire about the exact relationship between the good life for human individuals and adherence to the basic moral rules at the core of ethics as morality, namely those that forbid killing, causing pain, deceiving, cheating, breaking promises, and so forth.

Regrettably, one must reject at the outset in this regard the straightforward idea of inevitable rewards for moral virtue — that is, the idea that those who respect the basic rules of morality can, with confidence, count on living deeply satisfying lives. Should one hold alternatively, then, that by respecting the basic moral rules one thereby avoids the most deeply unsatisfying kind of life? Plato characterizes the unjust man as enslaved by his appetites, as utterly lacking in the kind of internal controls requisite for psychological well-being. There may well be a connection between total, or near total, disregard of basic moral rules and the desperate psychological condition Plato attributes to the tyrant in the *Republic* (Plato, 1974; see *Republic* XIII 562a–IX 588a). More systematically limited forms of immoral behavior appear to avoid this problem. Thus, someone who happened to acquire a kind of myopia that made it possible for him to confine serious breaches of the basic moral rules to certain contexts and not to others (for example, only in business dealings) might well have his cake and eat it too. Such a person might derive whatever benefit accrues from selective immorality while avoiding the disintegration of self that very possibly attends complete abandonment of basic moral rules.

One can state the difficulty in a more striking way. Plato's account of the unjust life concentrates exclusively upon the disastrous consequences that flow from *too much* unjust behavior. Such an account would thus appear by implication to counsel not the complete avoidance of injustice but only greater moderation with regard to indulging in it. Under such a view, justice would not involve respecting a general prohibition of killing, inflicting pain, deceiving, cheating, and so on; rather, it would involve not doing these things in excess.

Respecting the basic moral rules absolutely guarantees neither a deeply satisfying life nor the avoidance of a deeply unsatisfying life. One might, however, conceive of a proper regard for basic moral rules in a third way, namely, as making possible, rather than as absolutely guaranteeing, the most deeply satisfying kinds of life. Under this idea, there is a range of deeply satisfying lives that fit different characters and circumstances. Respecting the basic moral rules, according to this view, is an essential element in all of them. The above idea has an enormous emotional appeal, but one needs to find careful answers to a number of difficult questions before accepting it as fully credible. What are the most deeply satisfying forms of life, or at least what are some of them? How does proper regard for the basic moral rules fit into these ways of life, and why must it fit so inevitably? Are the most deeply satisfying ways of life reasonable objects of personal aspiration? Or do many of these ways of life presuppose conditions whose attainment lies beyond the reach of most individuals?

Although the above kinds of philosophical issues seldom need to be addressed by OD-HSD professionals, there is one important instance in which the practical and the philosophical viewpoints would appear closely intertwined. An OD-HSD consultant working in a cultural environment significantly different from her own — for example, in a Third World country — may encounter practices that, at least on first impression, appear to the professional as unjustified violations of basic moral rules.

Such an impression, however, may lead the consultant to raise further questions, such as: How reliable are a consultant's moral judgments when applied to cultural environments significantly different from her own? When so applied, do the judgments tend to reflect inadequate understanding of the different culture? Do basic aspects of the consultant's conception of morality even apply to that culture? Alternatively, by declining to make a moral judgment, would a consultant be guilty of bad faith — in this case by failing to evaluate the practice from the standpoint of moral standards she genuinely regards as paramount and general? Such questions can be extremely difficult to resolve. It would seem that any reasonable effort at their resolution would require serious thought of a philosophical nature about the very idea of ethics itself.

Aristotle's ethical theory, it may be recalled, implies that the process of values clarification must necessarily leave substantial discretion to people of practical reason with wide experience. One cannot, however, reject out of hand the idea that advantages may accrue from seeking to introduce an element of systematization into the process of clarifying values. In this regard, Chapter Three contains a systematic five-step approach to guide the interplay between experience and critical reflection in defining the values and ethics of OD-HSD. This approach was developed by William Gellermann, a coauthor of this book. The chapter also contains a brief section by another coauthor, Robert Ladenson, that raises some basic questions about the five-step approach.

As noted at the beginning of this chapter, there are no universally agreed-upon ways of thinking about the concept of ethics. The foregoing conceptions of ethics as morality and of ethics as the quest for a good life nonetheless correspond to widely shared patterns that play a significant role in the ethical thinking of most individuals. Whether or not the conceptions provide a comprehensive framework within which to locate the diverse ethical issues in OD-HSD, it is hoped that they supply at least a measure of initial guidance. The material presented in the remaining chapters is intended to raise many more issues, to examine these issues from a variety of viewpoints, and, most importantly, to stimulate thought.

Notes

1. Some recent philosophical writings have challenged the complementarity of ethics as morality and ethics as the quest for a good life. See MacIntyre (1981) and Williams (1985). The above cited works, although very interesting, express a distinctly minority point of view among contemporary philosophers that, in effect, rejects as incoherent the very idea of ethics as morality.

2. The following discussion of the characteristics of a moral code of conduct draws heavily on the work of Gert in his book *Morality: A New Justification of the Moral Rules* (1989). This volume is an extensively revised and enlarged version of the moral theory that Gert first presented in *The Moral Rules* (1970).

3. The discussion that immediately follows draws upon chaps. 5, 6, and 7 of Gert's *The Moral Rules* (1970).

4. H.L.A. Hart also makes this point in *The Concept of Law* (1961, pp. 189-195).

▐▌▐▌▐▌▐▌▐▌▐▌▐▌▐▌▐▌▐▌▐▌▐▌▐▌▐▌▐▌▐▌▐▌▐

CHAPTER THREE

Making Ethical Decisions in Organization and Human Systems Development

▐▌▐

In most of day-to-day waking life, we live within an ongoing stream of consciousness in which we make decisions about how to live our lives without paying conscious attention to ethics. Generally, either what we need or want to do does not seem to require consideration of ethics or the ethical thing to do seems clear enough that consciously attending to our ethical standards is unnecessary. But when our stream of consciousness leaves us in doubt about the right thing to do, it can help to have a systematic approach to thinking carefully about what our ethical problems and options are and then deciding on action.

This chapter will examine one such approach, called the *five-step model*. It will examine the model's primary elements, outline its specific steps, and apply them to a sample situation as a way of giving concrete meaning to the steps. However, be-

Note: In writing this chapter, I want to acknowledge several sources: reflection on more than twenty-five years of my own experience as an OD-HSD consultant; communication with my coauthors; communication with participants in sessions on ethics at professional meetings in Canada, Europe, Mexico, and the United States; and correspondence with OD-HSD professionals from all over the world. — *William Gellermann*

fore looking at the model, it will help to consider the moral orientation that provides the context within which ethical decision making takes place.

Kinds of Moral Orientation

The ideas in this section[1] are based on the ideas of John Dewey, Jean Piaget, Lawrence Kohlberg, and Gordon Shea (Shea, 1988) about what have been called "levels" and "stages" of "moral development." It is important to acknowledge those ideas, but, in view of differences of opinion about the validity of those concepts, it is also important to recognize that the differences do not matter for our purpose. Our purpose here is to use these ideas in differentiating the *orientations* people have toward morality without necessarily arguing that they reflect levels or stages of development.

Identifying people's moral orientation helps us understand the source of their ethics. Adapting the analyses of Kohlberg and Dewey, different moral orientations can be identified as follows:

I.   Preconventional morality (external authority or narrowly defined self-interest seen as moral source)
   1.   Obeying orders — seeking to avoid punishment
   2.   Marketplace morality — maximizing pleasure, minimizing pain
II. Conventional morality (the groups or society to which one belongs seen as moral source)
   3.   Conforming to group norms — seeking to belong and be accepted
   4.   Focusing on law and order — desiring to preserve the structure of society even if force is needed to do it
III. Postconventional morality (one's own reasoning seen as moral source)
   5.   Principled morality — guiding one's self freely and responsibly based on individual soul searching and the evolution of ethical principles derived from open discussion
   6.   Universal morality — transcending national and cultural boundaries based on the fundamental belief that

every individual is of equal importance as a human being and possesses the same fundamental rights as every other human being

IV. Transcendent morality (an "inner light" within one's self, called conscience by some, seen as moral source)

7. Moral integrity—integrating thinking and feeling (in ways that are creative, caring, sensitive, and aligned with one's inner or higher nature)

Shea (1988, p. 86) describes transcendent morality and moral integrity as an orientation in which "the spirit soars." In that connection, he notes that Lande and Slade (1979) have pointed out that universal morality (orientation 6) is similar to the guiding philosophy of the Quakers, which is dependent on the triumph of principles conforming not to the world but to "an inner light" (or conscience). It is also worth noting that the inner light could be a manifestation of either universal or transcendent morality, depending on whether one conceives its source as "self" or "higher self" (also called "spirit" or "soul"). (It is relevant to note that one of the frontier issues in the development of the ethics of the OD-HSD profession is, To what extent, if any, do we recognize "spirit" as a dimension in OD-HSD practice? That issue is discussed in Chapter Twelve.)

Given the different kinds of orientation to the morals/ethics on which one draws in thinking about moral/ethical problems, we are now ready to look more closely at ethical thinking. In this connection, it is helpful to note that when Swiss psychologist Jean Piaget studied moral reasoning, he concluded that "moral development results not from parents imprinting moral virtues on their children but, rather, from a modification in *the way they think*. Imprinting produces certain automatic, subconscious, and essentially unthinking responses to events, which are sometimes perceived as moral. But useful as such behaviors might be, they do not involve moral decisions any more than tying one's shoes or slamming on the brakes to avoid an accident do" (emphasis added) (Shea, 1988, p. 26).

The potential usefulness of the model described below is based on the assumption that, in accordance with the importance given it by Piaget, conscious attention directed at helping people examine the way they think can enable them to improve their ability to make ethical decisions. Although the model may be helpful for people with any of the moral orientations, it is expected to be particularly helpful for those with postconventional and transcendental orientations because they accept responsibility for the morals/ethics by which they guide their lives.

Ethical Thought and Action: A Basic Model

If we are clear about our values and morals/ethics, then we can often readily decide what to do. But how do we decide when we are not sure about the right thing to do? In such a situation, we have an "ethical problem." Even with an extensive code of professional ethics, we can be in doubt about how to proceed ethically because of complicated situations, lack of clarity about which of our values and ethics are relevant, conflict between our values and ethics, and uncertainty about how to apply those ethics to our specific situation. When faced with such doubt, having a systematic way of thinking can be helpful. In this section, I will examine a model (Figure 2) that can provide such help.

My purpose in describing the model (see Figure 2) is to encourage ethical sensitivity, thought, and action in real situations. Though easily expressed, this idea needs fuller explanation.

First, the model is intended as a tool for use in:

- Increasing *sensitivity* to situations that require ethical thought and action
- Developing *ability to think* about possibilities for ethical action
- Developing *ability to act* in ways consistent with thinking (namely actions that yield consequences consistent with one's values and ethics)

Second, ability to think about ethical problems can be thought of as a matter of "fluency" analogous to fluency in use of language, since it literally involves conversation with one's self. The smoothness with which that dialogue flows is fundamental to making decisions based on understanding and commitment rather than on mere compliance.

Figure 2. A Five-Step Model for Ethical Thought and Action.

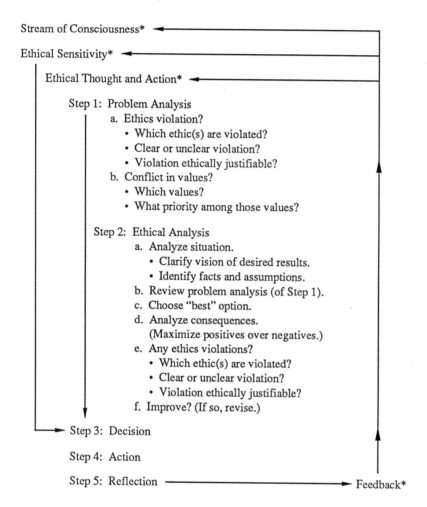

Stream of Consciousness*

Ethical Sensitivity*

Ethical Thought and Action*

Step 1: Problem Analysis
a. Ethics violation?
• Which ethic(s) are violated?
• Clear or unclear violation?
• Violation ethically justifiable?
b. Conflict in values?
• Which values?
• What priority among those values?

Step 2: Ethical Analysis
a. Analyze situation.
• Clarify vision of desired results.
• Identify facts and assumptions.
b. Review problem analysis (of Step 1).
c. Choose "best" option.
d. Analyze consequences.
(Maximize positives over negatives.)
e. Any ethics violations?
• Which ethic(s) are violated?
• Clear or unclear violation?
• Violation ethically justifiable?
f. Improve? (If so, revise.)

Step 3: Decision

Step 4: Action

Step 5: Reflection ——————————————→ Feedback*

*Note: Drawing on our store of knowledge and experience, our "stream of consciousness" calls attention to our need for "ethical sensitivity." The ethical thing to do may be clear immediately, in which case we can make a decision without further thought. Or we may need to consider our situation more carefully, in which case our thinking, with reference to our ethics and values, can help clarify whether we have an ethical problem (Step 1). This may enable us to make a decision without further thought, but, if necessary, we can analyze our situation even more closely (Step 2). This thought process involves a combination of reason and intuition. Our ethical competence depends in large part on the extent to which we have (1) informed our intuition with clear vision, accurate beliefs,

Third, the model is best understood in the context of "ethics as the quest for a good life," as described in Chapter Two. Though the model focuses on sensitivity, thought, and action as they relate to a specific situation, it is best understood as describing a cycle within a continuing process in which reflection on experience continually informs consciousness and intuition, thus yielding continued improvement in one's ability to live a *truly good life.*

Fourth, the model is consistent with "ethics as morality," as described in Chapter Two, in that its steps include reference to morals (as the core of all ethical systems), identifying potential violations, and considering the possibility of moral justification for violations.

Basic Terms Underlying the Model. Terms basic to understanding the model include: *values, moral values, ethics, moral rules* and *moral ideals, ethical principles, ethical guidelines,* and *professional values and ethics.* Although other meanings for these terms exist, the following definitions should be used for the purpose of understanding the model.[2]

Values is the most fundamental term. Values are the standards of importance (desirability, worth, goodness, and rightness) human beings use in making judgments. They represent the ideals implicit in the visions people have of the world (including themselves and their lives within the world) as they would like the world to be. They are the ideals that guide people in their "quest for a good life." For example, pleasure, freedom, honesty, justice, integrity, productivity, efficiency, and profitability are all values.

Among values, *moral values* are the standards of good and evil (bad, harm, or wrong) accepted by people generally. For example, life, freedom, honesty, pleasure, and justice are generally

clearly understood values and ethics, and an understanding of our potential ethical problems, (2) reflected on our experience and given feedback to our store of knowledge, and (3) practiced the use of our values and ethics in ways similar to those outlined in the model, so that they are available to our minds when we need them.

considered moral values in contrast to productivity and profitability, which, though valued, are not generally considered matters of morality. In contrast, death, pain, disability, dishonesty, loss of freedom, loss of pleasure, and injustice are among the standards by which evil is generally measured. Moral values refer to the subset of values within the totality of human values that are reflected in the moral rules of ethics as morality and that are generally regarded as applicable to everyone.

This raises the question, "How are moral good and evil determined?" In the context of personal decision making, we each decide for ourselves. Culture and the institutions that reflect it (schools, churches, societies, and their subcultures, such as businesses and professions) exert powerful influence on individual decisions, but in the final analysis we each decide. That decision may be to accept the judgments of others with a minimum of our own thought, as in the case of people with conventional and preconventional orientations toward morality. Consensual validation provides a more sound basis for refining and improving our individual judgments. This means that individuals can influence and be influenced by the emerging consensus about what is good and evil. We cannot know for certain whether absolute, objective standards exist, but since consensus is based on logic and reason, it seems likely that consensus based on a diversity of points of view can come close to specifying such standards. It is important to remember that consensus does *not* involve compliance with a vote; rather, it is a process of pooling individual judgments into a collective judgment that individuals can freely accept.

This brings us to *ethics,* the third basic term required for understanding the model. Ethics are standards of behavior grounded in values, which, in contrast to ethics, relate to importance. There are four kinds of behavior standards: moral rules, moral ideals, ethical principles, and ethical guidelines.[3]

Moral rules and *moral ideals* are universally applicable, generally accepted standards for morally good and bad behavior that are grounded in moral values and whose aim is to minimize harm or evil. Moral rules focus on not causing evil ourselves; for example: "Do not kill" (grounded in valuing life), "Do not cause pain" (grounded in valuing pleasure), "Do not deceive" (grounded in valuing honesty), and "Keep promises" (grounded in valuing trustworthiness). In contrast, moral ideals focus on preventing or lessening evils, such as death, pain, deception, and promise breaking as just specified in relation to moral rules. Moral ideals can be summarized as "Prevent evil" or "Do those things that lessen the amount of evil suffered by anyone." More specific examples include: "Prevent killing," "Prevent the causing of pain," "Prevent disabling," and "Prevent the deprivation of freedom" (Gert, 1989).

Ethical principles are behavior standards that provide general guidance in contrast to the specific prescriptions of moral rules and moral ideals. The most fundamental principle, in fact a meta-principle, is, "Act so that you would be willing to universalize the principles underlying your acts" (grounded in those values considered fundamental to "good life" for all). Examples of such universal principles are: "Do unto others as you would have them do unto you" (grounded in the values of respect and empathic understanding of others' values, not naive projection of one's own values onto others) and "Always treat people as ends, never only as means" (grounded in such values as respect, dignity, integrity, worth, happiness, and love of life).[4]

Ethical guidelines are behavior standards that are less universal in their application than moral rules, moral ideals, or ethical principles. Guidelines are oriented toward the unique conditions of "the quest for a good life" by a person, profession, organization, or other human system; for example, "Define and protect confidentiality in client relationships" (grounded in the value of trustworthiness) and "Promote the sharing of professional knowledge or skill based more on professional than commercial values" (grounded in the specific values of a profession). In some cases, guidelines reflect a principle's more universal meaning in words focused on the conditions of a person, profession, or other human system. For example, for OD-HSD professionals, "Respect other people's integrity; do not seek to manipulate or coerce them into doing what we want them to do only for our reasons without regard for what they want for themselves" is a more focused version of the principle about always treating people as ends, never only as means.

Professional values are those values about which substantial consensus exists among the members of a profession. For example, the values of the OD-HSD profession include justice, freedom, respect, authenticity, honesty, growth, whole-win attitude, widespread participation in system affairs, and effectiveness.

Professional ethics are those standards of behavior about which substantial consensus exists among the members of a profession (and which are constrained by broader social values, including those reflected in public opinion, legislation, and court decisions).[5] Among those standards are the generally accepted moral rules and moral ideals and those ethical principles and ethical guidelines most applicable to the profession's practice. In the practice of OD-HSD, for example, "Always treat people as ends; never only as means" is a principle of particular relevance to the profession's work with people in organizations and other human systems because, without consciousness of that principle, the profession's emphasis on *system* development could lead to violations. And, as an example of an ethical guideline, we can refer to the following from the Statement: "Fully inform people about activities in which they will be asked to engage so they can freely choose their participation," which reflects the value the profession places on independence and freedom.

Given these definitions of professional values and ethics, we need to acknowledge that professional values and ethics may be considered "bad" based on other standards. For example, if the values and ethics of a profession orient its members toward serving the interests of their profession at the expense of society, those could be considered bad standards. In order to avoid such self-serving standards, it is generally advisable to engage users of a profession's services and other interested stakeholders in the process of defining the profession's standards.

The Flow Process Implicit in the Model. At its best, the process described by the model is a smoothly flowing dialogue one has with oneself. It is more a condition of "letting it happen" than of "making it happen," though one needs to prepare one's mind with the knowledge and ability necessary for "it" to happen. The process is not a rote following of predetermined steps, although steps are involved and they tend to follow a logical sequence. It is more a process of iteration and reiteration that uses both reason and intuition. The intuition referred to is the kind Isenberg (1984, p. 85) found being used by senior managers when he noted that "early on, managerial action needs to be thought through carefully. Once the manager is 'fluent' at performance, however, and the behavior is programmed, executives can execute programs without conscious effort."

As noted earlier, the model encompasses both views of ethics described in Chapter Two—namely "ethics as morality" and "ethics as the quest for a good life." The steps in the model in Figure 2, adapted from Frankel's (1984) ideas, start with a series of thought-provoking questions, followed by decision, action, and reflection. The steps are easy to remember, but in actual use the thought process can become quite complex. Without such an approach, however, the complexity is likely to become overwhelming. And without preparatory thinking based on such an approach, the pressures of your immediate situation are likely to make conscious, ethical decision making difficult.

In summary, the process emerges from within your moment-to-moment *stream of consciousness* and is triggered by *ethical sensitivity* that alerts you to the possibility that you may face an ethical problem. The process begins with *problem analysis* (Step 1), during which you analyze whether the problem involves ethics violation, conflict in your values, both, or neither. In and of itself, that analysis may clarify your problem sufficiently that you can act without further analysis, in which case you can skip *ethical analysis* (Step 2) and move directly to *decision* (Step 3), *action* (Step 4), and *reflection* (Step 5)—which feeds back into your *stream of consciousness* and *ethical sensitivity,* thus improving your ability to make ethical decisions in the future.

In contrast, if after Step 1 you have not been able to solve the problem, then Step 2 guides you through a series of substeps in clarifying the ethical thing to do (or not do). These substeps involve a combination of intuition and reason aimed at maximizing realization of your values as reflected in the consequences that flow from your actions in ways consistent with your ethics. Advance thinking about potential ethical problems increases the probability that you will in fact maximize the realization of your values in ways consistent with your ethics. Without such preparation, your narrowly defined self-interest is likely to be overvalued.

Although the thought process may look complicated, as noted earlier, much of it actually goes on unconsciously and intuitively, since your mind is capable of moving much faster than you can consciously control it. In fact, many people would say that attempting to base our ethical decisions solely on conscious, logical reasoning, when our intuition is telling us something is "wrong," is likely to be ineffective because intuition is capable of tapping into the vast reservoir of our knowledge and experience with much greater rapidity than we can consciously control. You can develop your intuitive ability by slowing the process down at times and consciously thinking about situations you have faced in the past or are likely to face in the future, thus adding to the reservoir of knowledge and experience from which your intuition can draw. And, for the same reason, by consciously choosing your values and ethical standards and reflecting on their use, you can increase your fluency in making ethical decisions.

(Note: Chapters Six through Eleven describe several cases along with commentaries. Before reading the commentaries, you may find it useful to identify some of the decision points in each case and think about how you would decide. For example, at the end of the "Clash of Cultures" case, the consultant is faced with a decision about whether to continue. The commentary on that case shows how that decision might be approached using the model described in this chapter. Before reading the commentary, I suggest that you think about what you would do and why, perhaps trying out the model as a guide.)

Key Process Terms in the Model. Key terms required for understanding the process described by the model — in contrast to the basic terms, such as *values* and *ethics,* which underlie the model — include *stream of consciousness (consciousness), ethical sensitivity, ethical problems, problem analysis, ethical violations, ethical justification, conflict in values, ethical analysis, ethical decision, ethical action,* and *reflection.*

Stream of consciousness is the ground of being, out of which and within which the entire process of ethical thought, action, and reflection takes place. Although its focus is consciousness, it can draw on unconscious knowledge and ability by means of intuition, and so it should not be conceived only in terms of consciousness. For example, the so-called "voice of conscience" can be conceived as a channel between consciousness and unconsciousness during the process of contemplating ethical problems.

Ethical sensitivity refers to alertness to situations in which one faces ethical problems, based on one's understanding of ethics both as "morality" and as "the quest for a good life" and, more specifically, on the clarity of one's values and ethics, both personal and professional, and one's ability to apply them in concrete situations. It triggers the process of ethical thought and action in much the same way that the settings of a rocket's navigation and control instruments guide its flight. *Ethical sensitivity is at the heart of the process described by the model.* Without it, the process would not emerge from within the stream of consciousness. In fact, the process outlined is aimed both at making decisions in immediate situations and at heightening ethical sensitivity in the future. (See Feedback in Figure 2.)

Ethical problems (or dilemmas) are situations in which we are uncertain about how to behave because we may violate our ethics or experience conflict in our values. For example, in working with a quality of working life (QWL) group, the question of whether to provide day care for employees with young children has arisen. The problem is that ethics related to keeping the ratio of costs to output low are in conflict with ethics related to enhancing the quality of people's lives; the value we give to efficiency is in conflict with the value we place on life.

Ethical violations are the result of behavior that violates ethical standards (morals, principles, or guidelines). For example, closing a plant without regard for the effect on people's lives would violate the ethical principle, "Always treat people as ends; never only as means."

Ethical justification refers to reasoning based on conditions in a specific situation by which one can reasonably conclude that ethical violation in that situation is ethically acceptable. As noted in Chapter Two, Gert (1989) has identified the classes of factors involved. Those factors, modified to apply to all ethical violations and not just moral violations, are:

1. The ethical standard(s) violated
2. The bad-evil avoided, prevented, and caused by the violation
3. The relevant desires of the people affected by the violation
4. The relevant rational beliefs of the people affected by the violations
5. The authority to violate certain moral rules with respect to a person given one's relation to that person (such as judges to convicted felons)
6. The good promoted by the violation
7. Whether the violation prevents an unjustifiable ethical violation
8. Whether the violation results in the punishment of a person for unjustifiably violating the basic moral rules

It is important to note that in thinking about such justification, one needs to consider the probable consequences of violation. There is no universally agreed-upon formula for the relevant factors or their relative weights. Thus, as noted in Chapter Two, the idea of a moral code that underlies "ethics as morality" leaves open a large gray area wherein rational people may disagree about the solution of ethical problems. However, it is also important to note, as was done in Chapter Two, that this disagreement occurs within a broad framework of agreement about basic moral rules and the factors relevant to justifying their violation.

Conflict in values refers to a situation in which one's standards of judgment give contradictory guidance. As noted in Chapter Two, "ethics as the quest for the good life" concerns the values sought in a genuinely good human life and the means for their realization. Ethical problems arise during the quest when a person feels conflict between the differently valued consequences that would result from opposed courses of action. For example, imagine being an OD-HSD consultant directed to participate in laying off 3,000 people in order to keep a plant economically viable within a community in which it is the primary employer. You face a conflict in values if, on the one hand, you value plant efficiency and, on the other hand, you value the well-being of the 3,000 people who would be laid off and the community to which the plant belongs.

Ethical analysis is a process that aims at making ethical decisions based on logical reasoning, including answers to such questions as: Who will benefit or suffer? By what values will benefit and suffering be measured? By what rules/principles/guidelines do we choose to guide our decisions/actions, and what are the values underlying them? What decision/action will best balance the positively and negatively valued consequences of our action? Though the aim of this analysis is a decision based on logical reasoning, as noted earlier, in actual practice it is likely to involve a combination of reason and intuition.

Ethical decisions are decisions about how (or how not) to behave that are consistent with our values and ethics. Values are included here because, although they are not ethics, ethics are implicit in them. For example, valuing honesty has implicit within it the ethic "Do not lie."

Ethical action is behavior consistent with our values and ethics.

Reflection, though identified as the last step in the model, might actually be considered the first step, since it refers to looking back on experience and learning/discovering/creating generalizations about ethical thought and action that, through *feedback* to *consciousness,* inform intuition and heighten *ethical sensitivity.*

The above definitions are fundamental to the step-by-step approach to ethical decision making described in this section, and it is important to understand the following description in terms of those definitions.

A Five-Step Model of Ethical Thought and Action

The steps in the model[6] (Figure 2) can now be described with emphasis on their logical sequence, although, as noted earlier, in actual practice, intuition may not limit itself to rigidly following that sequence.

Ethical Sensitivity

As noted earlier, the process is triggered by ethical sensitivity, which enables you to recognize situations in which you may have an ethical problem. After first thought, your ethical sensitivity may make it clear what to do — you are reasonably certain either about the good-right thing to do or that ethics are not an important consideration and, therefore, you have no apparent ethical problem. If so, you proceed to decision, action, and reflection. That reflection may later enable you to recognize that you did have an ethical problem and thus enable you to heighten your ethical sensitivity in the future. On the other hand, first thought may leave you unsure about what to do, in which case the thought process described by the model begins. At this first point in the process, it is important to recognize that clarity about your values, ethics, and potential ethical problems is a primary determinant of your sensitivity and its ability to alert you to the need for further thought.

> *Is further analysis needed?*
> *If No, move directly to Step 3 (decision).*
> *If Yes, move to Step 1 (Problem Analysis).*

> COST-CUTTING EXAMPLE: *Imagine you are an OD-HSD consultant. Your manager has asked you to work on a cost-cutting project that is likely to result in laying off approximately 3,000 people at a plant that currently employs 9,000. The plant is the primary employer in its community. Gathering the data that would make recommendations possible is expected to involve interviewing many people, including many likely to be among those laid off. Are you willing to accept the assignment? (For the purpose of this example, let's say that you are not sure, which alerts you to the need for further thought, and thus takes you to Step 1 in the model.)*

Step 1: Problem Analysis

Step 1a: Ethics Violation? Does the situation involve a problem of ethics violation?
> *If No, move to Step 1b.*
> *If Yes, do a preliminary analysis of the violation, as outlined below.* (This will be reviewed and examined more deeply in Step 2b.)

- *Which ethic(s) are violated?* (Moral rules or ideals? Ethical principles or guidelines?)
    - (a) *Moral rules?*
      Examples: Do not kill, cause pain, deceive, or break promises.
    - (b) *Moral ideals?*
      Examples: Prevent killing, pain, deception, breaking of promises.
    - (c) *Ethical principles?*
      Examples of principles (less prescriptive than morals, more general than guidelines):
        - Act so I would be willing to
            - universalize the principles underlying my action
            - live with the costs of my action if I had to live with those costs.
        - Always treat people as ends; never only as means.
    - (d) *Ethical guidelines?*
      Examples of guidelines (less general than principles and more focused on your own ethical commitments, particularly those you make as a member of a profession or other human system):
        - Define and protect confidentiality in client relationships.
        - Promote sharing of professional knowledge and skill based more on professional than commercial values.
- *Clear or unclear violation?* Is the violation black-and-white or gray? If clear, ethical justification is essential. If unclear, you may have more discretion, although ethical justification would still be necessary. In any case, this is a matter of judgment, which can be improved by reference to the experience of others and with practice in thinking about possible violations.
- *Violation ethically justifiable?* Is the violation ethically justifiable? (See the discussion of "Ethical Justifica-

tion" earlier in this chapter.) If the violation is clear and ethically justifiable, then you may be able to move through the ethical analysis of Step 2 with little difficulty, although Step 2 may still enable you to avoid the violation. On the other hand, if the violation or ethical justification is in the gray area, then the ethical analysis of Step 2 needs to be followed with greater care.

After the violation is analyzed, skip to Step 2a (for analysis in greater depth) or, if you think the problem may also involve conflict in values, move to Step 1b.

COST-CUTTING EXAMPLE: (To demonstrate the meaning of the various steps and substeps, I will refer to the cost-cutting example introduced earlier. Since I am doing this only to demonstrate the meaning of key ideas mentioned at each step, I will not be giving as much detail as might be appropriate to the full analysis of a real situation.)

If you do not *have clear ethics relevant to the cost-cutting situation, your answer at Step 1a would be No (the problem seems not to involve violating your ethics), so you would move on to Step 1b.* (Note: *This demonstrates the critical importance of ethical sensitivity, first in alerting you to ethical problems and then in keeping you alert to ethical considerations as you think about your options. Without such sensitivity, you are likely either to ignore ethical problems or to rationalize violations rather than thinking honestly about* ethical *justification.)*

If you do *have relevant ethics, then the possible violation needs to be clarified and the possibility of ethical justification considered before moving on to Step 2. For example, two ethics may be violated, namely, the principle "Always treat people as ends; never only as means," and the OD-HSD guideline "Explore the possible implications of any OD-HSD intervention for all stakeholders likely to be significantly affected; help all stakeholders while developing and implementing OD-HSD approaches, programs, and the like, if they wish help and we are able to give it" (Guideline III–A–4). Such violations might be ethically justified, based in part on (1) the bad avoided by enabling the plant to survive and thus to continue serving the good of the community and (2) the good promoted for the people who would remain employed, the larger society, and all the communities, stockholders, and other stakeholders the plant serves.* (Note: *This is not a complete analysis, but it alerts us to think more carefully during Step 2 about such things as whether the principle and guideline referred to are violated and, if so, how clear the violations are and whether they can be justified ethically.*)

Step 1b: Conflict in Values? Are your values in conflict? In other words, as you think about the value you give to the different consequences of the actions you might take in your "quest for a good life," do your values conflict? This step is intended to help you clarify whether your problem involves conflict in values and, if so, to help you to look at it more closely before moving on to Step 2.

If No,

- either *skip to Step 3,* if you have resolved your ethical problem (having considered both the possibilities of ethical violation and value conflict)
- *or move to Step 2a,* if at Step 1a you identified an ethical violation that needs more extensive ethical analysis.

If Yes, make a preliminary analysis of the value conflict.

- *Which value(s)?* Are they related to the action you are contemplating or to the consequences of that action?
- *What priority among these values?* Which are most important, and how important are they relative to one another?

After the value conflict is analyzed, move on to Step 2a for more extensive ethical analysis.

*COST-CUTTING EXAMPLE: You identify that, among
other things, you value organizational efficiency, which is
in apparent conflict with the value you place on the quality
of the lives of the people whose jobs may be eliminated and
the quality of life in the community where the plant is located. You are also clear that you "seek to facilitate the development of systems as healthy settings within which individuals can grow in ways that enable those systems to
survive and thrive economically so they can continue to be
healthy settings" (from annotation following the Annotated
Statement's Preamble). Conclusion: Move on to Step 2a.*

Step 2: Ethical Analysis

Step 2a: Analyze Situation.

- *Clarify vision of desired results.* In your imagination, think
  about the results you want (your vision) in this specific situation. This involves letting your imagination
  play with possibilities on a preliminary basis in order
  to clarify your vision of "a good life" (for you and
  others), the precision with which it reflects your values,
  and how you would like to see the emergent situation
  you are presently facing fit into that vision. (*Note:* [1]
  situational analysis begins with vision rather than facts
  and assumptions because it is better to start with clarity about what you want than to start with facts and
  assumptions that may unnecessarily limit your ability to think clearly about what you want, and [2] for
  OD-HSD professionals, many of the elements of their
  common vision are either explicit or implicit in the
  Statement. Clarifying their vision relative to a particular situation is to some extent guided by thinking
  about how their immediate situation might best be
  changed in ways consistent with their more inclusive
  vision.)

*COST-CUTTING EXAMPLE: Your vision will prob-
ably include the plant thriving, the individuals involved*

living lives that are good for them (though not necessarily at the plant), the community surviving and thriving, and minimal harm to all the other stakeholders affected by the prospective layoff.

- *Identify facts and assumptions.* Strive for a reasonably comprehensive and detailed specification. Recognize that the ethically relevant features of the situation have an extremely broad range, as suggested in the discussion of factors relevant to "ethical justification." Therefore, you cannot be sure, prior to more complete ethical analysis, which facts and assumptions are relevant to this decision. It is also helpful to note that when we speak of "facts" we refer to observations about the past and present and not to assumptions about the future. Assumptions about the future are facts insofar as they affect the way people think in the present; however, the contents of assumptions are not facts and your ability to discover or create ethical options may depend on freeing yourself from the limits of unnecessary or inaccurate assumptions. Assumptions are necessary to plan future action, but they need to be understood for what they are. With greater clarity about facts and assumptions, you are in a position to move to Step 2b's review of your earlier problem analysis and then to Step 2c's preliminary focus on a "best" option.

COST-CUTTING EXAMPLE: *In this discussion, we cannot illustrate all the possible relevant facts and assumptions, but we can identify some. For example, it would be important to know such facts about the plant as: (1) it has operated at a loss for the last two years, (2) in spite of those losses, it is still in reasonably sound condition, and (3) it is by far the largest employer in its community, currently employing 9,000 people in a community of 25,000. It is also important to note some assumptions: (1) the plant's survival is likely to be seriously threatened if income and expenses continue at the same rate as in the prior two years, and (2) the assignment you have been given necessarily involves laying off 3,000 people. On examination, the first assumption seems reasonable, but the second needs to be questioned, since it may be unnecessarily limiting. For the purposes of this example, let us say that you conclude that you have other options than simply accepting or rejecting the assignment, particularly the option of engaging your manager in a discussion of possibilities. It may even be possible to engage him or her in dialogue based on* ethical *reasoning. And, even if he or she is not open to ethical reasoning, economic reasoning will almost certainly be acceptable. (Note: This raises the possibility of a major addition to the accepted qualities of competence of OD-HSD professionals: namely, the ability to engage managers in* ethical *reasoning. See Chapter Twelve for further discussion of this as a frontier issue.)*

Step 2b: Review Problem Analysis (of Step 1). How do you see your ethical problem now? After your problem analysis of Step 1 and the situation analysis of Step 2a, you have probably clarified the nature of your problem. You are probably clearer about: (1) whether it involves potential ethics violations, values in conflict, or both, (2) whether any ethics violations are clear or unclear and on what grounds they may be justified ethically, and (3) which values are involved in a values conflict and their relative priority.

COST-CUTTING EXAMPLE: *On the one hand, you value organizational survival, efficiency, and profitability; and, on the other hand, you value the quality of the lives of both the people affected by your work and the community within which the plant is located. You begin to recognize the possibility that you can serve all those values, at least to some extent. Your problem at this point might be stated as: How can I help the plant with its layoff and, at the same time, help the people who are laid off find other work, preferably within the community? (Note: If this is possible, then the problem involves only a possible conflict in values, and the potential violation of ethics noted at Step 1a will have been minimized.)*

Step 2c: Choose "Best" Option. Which options occur first? Which option seems best? In doing this, you are likely to rely heavily on intuition. Your purpose is to identify an alternative you can assess in terms of its potential for maximizing good over bad consequences and doing so in ways compatible with your ethics (morals, principles, and guidelines).

> COST-CUTTING EXAMPLE: *In the example, most OD-HSD consultants are likely to feel that there is something "wrong" with just gathering the data; their intuition might suggest trying to negotiate a contract with their manager that permits being open with employees about the purpose of the interviews and that aims to balance all stakeholders' interests. That intuition is likely also to be supported by economic reasoning. For example, longer-term inefficiencies due to decreased motivation, trust, loyalty, concern for quality, and morale generally by the 6,000 people still employed are likely if the savings due to layoffs aren't carefully created. Options include a combination of attrition, retraining, transfers to other locations, and outplacement, rather than simply laying off the 3,000 people. At this point, however, being clear about your reasoning isn't necessary. A "hunch" about what is "best" is enough to give you a place to begin. For illustrative purposes, let us assume that your hunch is that your "best" option will involve going ahead with the layoff but providing the maximum feasible assistance to the people laid off.*

Step 2d: Analyze Consequences (maximize positives over negatives). How well do the positive and negative values associated with the consequences of your "best" option balance to serve "the good life"? (Note: This kind of approach is sometimes conceived as seeking "the greatest good of the greatest number." The human systems orientation of OD-HSD is oriented more toward the good of whole systems, rather than the good only of the largest number of individual system members, so our analysis is oriented more to "the greatest good of the whole," as indicated below.)

- *What likely benefits?* For whom? By what values? How likely?
- *What likely costs?* For whom? By what values? How likely?
- *How well do benefits and costs balance to serve the greatest good of the whole?* At this point, you may be back to using intuition, but it is intuition informed by reason. Your objective is to maximize the benefits over costs so as to achieve the highest net benefit for the whole system. In striving for the greatest good, you may be able to discover or create ways of improving the "best" option.

COST-CUTTING EXAMPLE: *One approach to balancing is to draw a line down the middle of a sheet of paper and record "positive" on the left side and "negative" on the right and list as many stakeholders and the kinds of positive and negative effects on them as you can think of in the appropriate columns. Thus, in the example, if the chosen action was to go ahead with the layoffs but with maximum feasible assistance to the people laid off, on the positive side would be the plant (survival), its owners (profits), the people not laid off (continued employment), people laid off (potential benefits initially unclear), and all other stakeholders (benefits also initially unclear). On the negative side would be the people laid off (who would be affected negatively by the disruption in their lives), their families, and the community, including the plant's suppliers (all of whom may be faced with severe loss of income). These negative effects suggest things to think about as possibilities for improving your "best" option. So, too, does the check for ethics violations in Step 2e. Examples of how to improve your "best" option are given below under Step 2f.*

Step 2e: Any Ethics Violations? Does your best option violate any of your ethics? (Note: The reason for this step is that action that maximizes good over bad consequences might still involve violation of your ethics and you would therefore need to make a different decision than analysis of consequences alone would suggest. For example, a person engaged in the testing of an experimental drug that had the potential for saving many lives — but also for causing the deaths of a few experimental subjects — might reason that the potential for good consequences over bad was so great that it was worth the risk. But if he had an ethic about informed consent by experimental subjects, then he would need to rethink his action. In applying your ethics at this step, you will be reviewing your Step 1a analysis.)

If No, move ahead to Step 2f.
If Yes, consider each of the following questions.

- *Which ethic(s) are violated?* Are any of your morals, principles, or guidelines violated? At this point, consciously chosen ethics are important. And for OD-HSD professionals, the Statement can be a valuable resource. It also seems likely that people who are highly conscious of their ethics will have intuitively considered them in choosing their "best" option at Step 2c, thus increasing the probability that they are already working with a high-quality option and thus there may be little or no need for revision.
- *Clear or unclear violation?* Is the violation black-and-white or gray? As noted under Step 1a, the more clear the violation, the more careful you need to be in deciding whether the violation is ethically justifiable. It is particularly important not to use ethical justification as an excuse for rationalization. It is better to look for ways of improving the "best"

option so that violation is avoided, or at least minimized, than to create "ethical justification."

- *Violation ethically justifiable?* Is there basis for ethically justifying any violation(s)? After weighing all
the ethically relevant factors in considering the possibilities for ethical justification (see discussion of
"ethical justification"), the critical question is what
would be the effect of those violations if they were
generally allowed. For example, in the OD-HSD
profession, if members of the profession generally
allowed themselves such violations, would that be
acceptable? (This is a variation on the ethical principle "Act so that you would be willing to universalize the principle underlying your action.")

*COST-CUTTING EXAMPLE: Among other consider-
ations in analyzing the problem during Step 1a, we mentioned the ethical guideline of exploring the effects of OD-
HSD activities on all stakeholders and helping them if we
can. If we disregard them, we would be in clear violation
of that ethic. To keep from doing that, we need to consider
ways we might improve our "best" option by helping the
community and working with the people who are likely to
be laid off to see if they can create even better alternatives
than those noted earlier.*

Step 2f: Improve? *(If so, revise.)* Can you improve on your
"best" option?

*If "No," move on to Step 3.
If "Yes," you may choose to repeat the analysis of Steps 2a through
2e.* Repeating your analysis may involve: reanalyzing
your situation, reviewing your problem analysis, choosing a revised "best" option, analyzing consequences, and
checking your revised "best" option against your ethical standards. As suggested in Figure 2, you can repeat
that analysis until you arrive at an alternative that is
at least acceptable and as close to "best" as you can reasonably make it.

COST-CUTTING EXAMPLE: You might help make
life better for the individuals who would be laid off, the
community, and the company by helping community leaders
and the individuals affected to identify additional possibil-
ities. For example, by working as a group, the individuals
may be able to create a new way of using their combined
knowledge and skill in one or more new enterprises that
would be located in the community. These enterprises might
serve company needs directly and serve new customers in
ways that would appropriately be included within the com-
pany (thus justifying the creation of new organizational
units), or the company could help the enterprise(s) get off
the ground as independent enterprises by guaranteeing loans
or providing capital, training, consulting, and other resources
during their start-up period. In any case, harm to the com-
munity and the people would be minimized and the net effects
might even be positive.

(Note: *Acting on the above analysis will require*
willingness by your manager to engage in dialogue with you
about alternatives. That dialogue may create further alter-
natives. If your manager or the people to whom he or she
reports are unwilling to accept or discuss such alternatives,
you may decide that you must refuse the assignment [or even
resign] after explaining your reasons [see Guidelines III–
B-6 and III–D-3 in Chapter Five].)

One Final Test Before Committing Yourself to a Decision: If you
have any serious doubts about whether you are making an ethical
decision, it is advisable to consult with a professional colleague
who can give you a different perspective on your situation. This
can probably help you sharpen your understanding of your ethical problem, create alternatives that you might not be able to
see alone, and identify pitfalls (such as rationalizing ethical violations rather than honestly and ethically justifying them).

COST-CUTTING EXAMPLE: On reviewing the above se-
quence of steps, you can probably identify improvements in

the analysis and conceive of alternatives not included which could lead to an even better decision.

Step 3: Decision

Choose the option that seems best (recognizing that your decision is likely to be based on a combination of intuition and reason).

Step 4: Action

(No action is also a possibility.)

Step 5: Reflection

Reflect on the results of your action; clarify your vision and beliefs; refine your values and ethics; and give feedback to your consciousness as a means of heightening your ethical sensitivity and developing your ability to act ethically in the future. (Note: If you do not do this, you fail to learn from your experience and are doomed to repeat your mistakes. Therefore, learning from experience is an ethical imperative for OD-HSD professionals.)

Summary

To enhance your effectiveness in using the model just outlined (or some modification that seems appropriate to you), these ideas can help:

1. Be clear about:
    *   Your *vision* (it helps clarify your concept of a good life and thus establishes the context within which you relate to situations in your life that require ethical sensitivity)
    *   Your *beliefs* (they affect your ability to understand the past and present, to imagine the future, and to plan effective action)

- Your *values* and their priority (they guide you in clarifying your vision and deciding how to act so as to bring it into being)
- Your *morals* (they provide universal prescriptions for action)
- Your *ethical principles* (they provide general guidance for action that is less prescriptive than morals)
- Your *ethical guidelines* (they provide guidance for action that is less general than principles and more focused on the unique conditions of your life and your profession)
- The *conditions for ethical justification* (they provide guidance in thinking through the possibilities for *ethically* justifying violation of your ethics in specific situations)

2. Recognize that under the pressure of immediate situations, your decisions will often be intuitive and, therefore, you need to *inform* your intuition by reflecting on:
   - All the elements listed above (under 1) that affect your ability to think and act ethically
   - Your way of thinking about ethical problems
   - The kinds of ethical problems you are likely to face *before* you need to think about them
   - The ethical problems you have faced, how you handled them, and how you might have handled them in closer accord with your values and ethics
3. Develop your ability to approach ethical problems systematically (based on the five-step model or a variation that works better for you based on your experience)

Conclusion

Of central importance in this discussion has been recognition of the need to clarify and refine our values and ethics before we need to draw on them. We can do that alone, and in the ultimate sense we must each do it alone, since, at their best, values and ethics are deeply personal. But for a person to belong to a "profession," in the sense that he or she "professes" or stands for something in common with all those who belong to the same profession, a substantial consensus about values and ethics is necessary among all the members of that profession. At the same time, for such a consensus truly to exist, rather than only the appearance of consensus, it must be based on a process that allows for each professional freely to align his or her personal values and ethics with those of the profession *and* for the professional position to be open to change in order to allow such individual alignment.

A related idea is expressed by Marvin Brown (1988–1989, p. 1) in discussing the ethics of organizations: "More often than not, discussions about ethics in organizations reflect only the 'individualistic approach' to moral responsibility. According to this approach, every person in an organization is morally responsible for his or her own behavior, and any efforts to change that behavior should focus on the *individual*.

But there is another way of understanding responsibility which is reflected in the 'communal approach.' Here individuals are viewed not in isolation, but as members of communities that are partially responsible for the behavior of their members. So, to understand and change an individual's behavior we need to understand and try to change the *communities* to which they belong.

Any adequate understanding of, and effective solutions to, ethical problems arising in organizations requires that we take BOTH approaches into account" (emphasis added).

Brown's point about the importance of both approaches for organizations applies equally well to professional communities. In other words, in thinking about professional ethics, we are faced with an apparent paradox: individual professionals are considered completely responsible for their behavior and, at the same time, the profession is considered responsible for the behavior of its individual members.

We in the OD-HSD professional community can make important progress toward fulfilling our individual and collective responsibility by achieving substantial consensus on the values and ethics of our profession and by facilitating shared learning from our collective experience. As noted earlier, that has been a primary goal of the Statement development process since it began in 1981.

Critique of the Five-Step Approach
to Ethical Decision Making
— *Robert Ladenson*

A joint intellectual project, such as the writing of this book, inevitably requires of the participants a significant amount of give and take, through which most disagreements get resolved over the course of time. Occasionally, however, different points of view emerge and remain unreconciled even as the project nears completion. In this regard, two coauthors of this book, William Gellermann and myself, have strikingly divergent opinions about the idea of a systematic method for making ethical decisions. One should not, however, regard this area of disagreement as posing a problem but rather as creating an opportunity to explore an important subject in greater depth. The following brief remarks contain my critical response to the five-step approach to ethical decision making that has been set forth in this chapter.

Insofar as the idea of a systematic approach for making ethical decisions appears to promise enhanced clarity and precision of thought, it has an obvious appeal. As Aristotle says in *Nichomachean Ethics* (Aristotle, 1941), however, in thinking about ethical matters one can achieve only "as much clearness as the subject matter allows." It seems to me that in the case of any approach that analyzes the ethical decision-making process primarily in terms of a determinate, well-defined, and ordered sequence of steps, there is a near total lack of fit between subject matter and method. Such an approach, by its very nature, cannot clarify the most critical aspects of ethical issues, at least not the kinds of ethical issues that arise in OD-HSD.

As noted in Chapter Two, if a given act clearly violates one or more of the basic moral rules, the issue arises of whether the violation was justifiable in the circumstances. As was also noted, the notion of ethics as morality involves various factors relevant for reaching a decision about issues of this kind. The factors, however, are highly diverse and wide-ranging. Among the relevant factors, one needs to consider not only the probable consequences of a violation in terms of the harms that it prevents or causes but also "nonconsequentialist" factors, such as the desires and beliefs of people affected by the violation and the nature of their relationships to the individual who violates the basic moral rule. No formula exists on which all rational people agree for weighing such factors. For this reason, an ethical decision-making procedure, such as the one proposed, that simply identifies morally relevant factors for the justified violation of basic moral rules and advises people to consider them provides distinctly limited guidance.

As a related point, difficult controversies over whether a person's act unjustifiably violates basic moral rules often involve disagreements about factual issues rather than about the ranking of relevant factors with respect to justifying morally the act in question. Though one can perhaps theoretically distinguish between moral and factual judgments, in practice they often become inextricably combined. What would be useful in such cases is a method for identifying true and morally relevant *factual* beliefs. I know of no one, however, who considers such a method possible. Accordingly, the instructions, such as those in the five-step model, simply to identify the pertinent facts and assumptions, does not take a person far in the process of moral decision making.

A systematic approach to ethical decision making provides extremely limited guidance concerning justified violation of basic moral rules, and such an approach is entirely inapplicable to the kinds of issues discussed in Chapter Two under the heading "Moral Responsibilities of OD-HSD Consultants." As noted there, the critical questions in such issues concern determination of the circumstances in which not preventing a given harm, in the context of professional practice, is morally equivalent to causing that harm. Such questions, it was pointed out, involve unavoidably ambiguous interpretations of a person's professional role.

Questions about the moral responsibilities of OD-HSD consultants thus require a kind of *interpretive* reasoning wherein one reflects on the basic purposes of Organization Development and then seeks to understand or criticize various aspects of its practice in terms of those purposes. Such interpretive reasoning

in connection with a social practice such as Organization Development has significant affinities with other kinds of interpretation — for example, in literature, religion, or law. All interpretive reasoning is constructive in the sense that it involves the
attempt to impose meaning upon the object of interpretation.
As Dworkin (1986, p. 47) says, in adopting an interpretive attitude toward an object or phenomenon, one seeks to "see it in
its best light — and then to restructure it in light of that meaning." Interpretation of the professional role in Organization Development thus no more lends itself to a systematic, sequential
analysis than does the interpretation of Shakespeare's comedies,
the biblical passages about Jacob's dream, or the first amend-
ment to the United States Constitution.

When one focuses attention on the category of issues discussed in Chapter Two under the heading "Avoiding Morally
Hazardous Situations," the five-step model again has little application. The discussion in Chapter Two pointed out that the
work of OD-HSD consultants often places them in ambiguous,
complex, or delicate situations that present ample possibilities
for errors in judgment. Such errors, in turn, can contribute to
the creation of even more difficult situations in which the consultant feels compelled to choose among alternatives that all seem
to involve serious moral problems, or in which, for other reasons, circumstances increase the likelihood of morally unjustified
behavior on the part of the consultant. An issue thus arises of
how a consultant can function effectively in a complex human
environment and yet avoid errors of judgment that may lead
to nearly intractable problems of moral choice or to circumstances that increase the likelihood of morally unjustifiable behavior by the consultant.

In light of the inherently complex and ambiguous circumstances of OD-HSD practice that give rise to issues of how to
avoid morally hazardous situations, it appears that such issues
are best addressed on a collective rather than an individual basis. Questions, for example, about appropriate standards concerning confidentiality or measures to ensure voluntary, uncoerced participation of T-Group members in an organizational
setting call for the adoption of general policies. Effective policy

making, in turn, requires a method that taps the wisdom, insight, and, most importantly, experience of many individuals. In this connection, one may note that professional codes of ethics in fields such as law and government service have many rules forbidding behavior that, though not morally wrong in itself, tends to lead a practitioner into morally hazardous situations. Rules against representing both parties in a divorce proceeding, commingling a client's funds with the attorney's own funds, and accepting gifts as a public servant under certain circumstances come to mind as examples. Accordingly, open, broadranging, and collective decision-making processes, not unlike those relied on to draft a sound code of professional conduct, represent the best means of dealing with questions about how to avoid morally hazardous situations in OD-HSD consulting. The five-step model, with its essentially individualistic orientation, seems inapplicable to questions of this kind.

Finally, the discussion in Chapter Two identified a second conception of ethics besides ethics as morality — namely, ethics as the quest for a good life. This conception focuses on the idea of flourishing, or fulfillment, for the human individual — that is, the ends, or values, to be sought in a genuinely good human life and the means for realizing them. Such ends, or values, it was noted, range far more widely than do the basic moral rules central to the idea of ethics as morality. Different human lives may derive meaning from identification with very different values or from very different orderings of them. This point holds even for extremely important values, such as knowledge, friendship, love, wealth, and pleasure, which, despite their importance, do not have the same direct relationship with basic moral rules as do values such as truth, kindness, and dependability. For this reason, the five-step model provides, at most, only a small measure of guidance with respect to the making of personal decisions in the context of ethics as the quest for a good life. The model directs a decision maker whose values conflict to identify the conflicting values, determine their priority, and then, after analyzing and reviewing the situation, to choose the "best" option. Given the enormous range of values potentially relevant for decision making in the context of ethics as the quest for a good life, these directions become so vague as to be essentially nonsubstantive.

There is another reason, however, for regarding the five-step model as inapplicable to decision making in the context of ethics as the quest for a good life. The philosopher Alasdair MacIntyre (1981) has pointed out that despite the absence of an overall formula for ranking human values, we all make choices throughout our lives about the best way of life for ourselves. Not only do we identify and choose between "better" and "worse" with respect to discrete courses of action, but our choices frequently involve the conception of our life experiences as parts of an essentially unified, unfolding narrative (pp. 199–204). Indeed, the fact of looking at our experiences in this way accounts for the aptness of the phrase "ethics as the *quest* for a good life"; that is, in making personal decisions, we often view our lives as a quest for fulfillment or meaning—in short, as a search for something with elusive characteristics we can never identify in a precise way at any given time.

The above observations lead to an important point suggested by Dewey (1958, pp. 80–81): Under ideal circumstances, decision making, in the context of ethics as the quest for a good life, has an esthetically creative aspect. It involves viewing one's life as a not-yet-completed story, written by oneself, and looking on particular decisions as choices about how to continue the story in ways that make it better. It seems to me that one cannot accommodate this vital esthetic component of personal decisions to an approach that conceives of the ethical decision-making process primarily in terms of following a determinate, well-defined, and ordered sequence of steps. For this reason, the five-step model has no more application to ethics as the quest for a good life than to ethics as morality.

Before concluding, I want to stress that the above critical remarks should not be taken as an endorsement of the view that ethical decision making has a fundamentally irrational character. Quite the contrary—I think that ethical decisions have a logic, or better yet, a rational structure. That structure, however, in its complexity and depth resists characterization in terms of models such as the five-step model proposed in this chapter.

Response to the Critique of the Five-Step Approach
— *William Gellermann*

Ladenson's critique of the five-step model raises some important questions about its utility. However, I think the points he makes can most fruitfully be viewed as cautions for those who use the model rather than as proofs that the model cannot be useful. In responding, I would first like to make some general comments and then deal with his points one at a time.

My first general comment is that, though the critique suggests limitations to or refinements needed in the use of the model, I see the model as having potential applicability in all situations in which practitioners feel they *may* have an ethical problem. Its use may facilitate a quick solution, especially if their ethics are clear and comprehensive, since the model would help them move easily through Steps 1a, 3, 4, and 5 without having to bother with any of the other steps. (The Annotated Statement in Chapters Four and Five is intended to help OD-HSD professionals develop such clarity and comprehensiveness.) Or the approach may at least alert them to the needs for modifying the model to make it applicable to their specific problem. In one way or another, I expect that it will be a useful, systematic approach for people who experience an ethical problem and that they will be able to apply it in much the same way as I applied it to the "Cost-Cutting Example" earlier in this chapter. However, I do *not* consider it a necessary or sufficient approach to making ethical/moral choices in all situations, as the critique seems to imply.

Second, the critique seems to deny or minimize the model's general usefulness when it denies or minimizes the model's applicability to particular situations considered by the critique. Even if it is not useful in those situations, that does not mean it cannot be useful in other situations. Having said that, however, I hasten to add that in my view the model has potential utility in each of the situations mentioned in the critique. To understand my reasoning, one needs to understand the model as a systematic way of thinking that can help people:

1. Enhance their ethical sensitivity so they will be alert to potential ethical problems (a precondition necessary for using the model)
2. Clarify the nature of their problems so they can think about them with greater precision than if they had no systematic way of thinking (Step 1)
3. Think about their problems and their options (Step 2)
4. Choose (Step 3)
5. Act (Step 4)
6. Reflect on their experience (Step 5) so their ethical sensitivity will increase and they will be better able to deal with future situations

With that model in mind, we can now focus on each of the separate points. I will take them one at a time, summarizing my understanding of each one and then commenting, with the comments addressed directly to readers as potential users of the model.

1. *The diversity of factors to be considered in deciding whether violation of a moral rule is morally justifiable is so great that a procedure such as the five-step model "provides distinctly limited guidance."*

I agree. But the model does provide *enough* guidance to be useful, even when potential violations of moral rules are involved. It helps you heighten your sensitivity to situations in which your ethics (including moral rules) may be violated, and it encourages you to (1) think about whether violations can be morally justified, (2) devise options that might not require violations, and, finally, (3) reflect on your actions and their results so that, in case of violation, you will be better able to deal with future situations that seem to require violation. The model does not purport to encompass the factors relevant to moral justification; its purpose relative to such factors is only to call attention to them and to provide a context for dealing with them meaningfully.

2. *Deciding whether specific action would violate moral rules is difficult because in any given situation people can disagree substantially about*

facts, factual judgments, and moral judgments. Therefore, when the model suggests that the person using it "identify facts and assumptions," it "does not take a person very far in the process of moral decision making."

I agree. But the model needs to be considered as a whole. Its suggestion that people identify facts and assumptions is only one substep (under 2a) in the set of considerations toward which it directs people's attention. No matter what one's approach, failure to differentiate facts (is and is not) and assumptions (*beliefs* about is and is not) will almost certainly lead to error. Such differentiation may be difficult and may not take one "very far," but the distance one does go can be significant. The person who does not do his or her best to differentiate assumptions and facts as elements in ethical problem solving risks serious error.

In the context of ethical reasoning, it is also important to be aware of the potential distorting effects on judgments of "self-fulfilling prophecies," particularly false beliefs about the future that, when acted upon as if they are facts, cause the future to be consistent with the beliefs. In other words, false beliefs can lead to true reality. People who seek to make moral/ethical decisions need to be aware of that possibility, for without such awareness they can make serious errors as they try to learn from their experience.

To comment on a second aspect of the above criticism, I think the model might be improved by calling attention to the difference between descriptive judgments (is and is not) and normative or prescriptive judgments (ought and ought not), which are comparable to the factual and moral judgments referred to in the critique. The model does call attention to "facts" of the "is and is not" variety that lie behind descriptive judgments (Step 2a) and to the need to make judgments of the "ought and ought not" variety when it raises the issue of ethics violations as part of both problem analysis (Step 1a) and ethical analysis (Step 2e). However, it does not explicitly separate violations of basic moral rules from violations of other ethics. A strong case could be made for doing so. I assume that, although making moral violations explicit would give the model greater precision, it

would lessen the model's usefulness by making it more complicated. In any case, I agree that it is important to use the model
with the consciousness that when questions of ethical violation
are being considered, violations of moral rules and ideals are
more important than are violations of nonmoral ethical guidelines.

3. *Answering questions about "Moral Responsibilities of OD-HSD
    Professionals" requires an interpretive approach to the field and its
    practice by trying "to see it in its best light—and then to restructure
    it in the light of that meaning," and the five-step model is "entirely
    inapplicable" to discuss such issues.*

Although the model may not be directly applicable to answering questions about the moral responsibilities of OD-HSD professionals, it still can contribute to creating the conditions under which members of the profession behave in ways consistent
with such moral responsibilities. As we strive to answer such
questions, our answers may be found in or at least suggested
by the ethical principles or guidelines in our Annotated Statement (see Chapters Four and Five). Those professionals who
use the model and who accept those principles and guidelines
will behave in accordance with them, by virtue of their experience with the model (at Steps 1a and 2e). (*Note:* The word "virtue" in this context is particularly appropriate, since moral virtue has been defined as "a rightly habituated will" [Adler, 1988,
p. 273], and one of the outcomes that can be expected from
repeated practice applying sound ethics under the model's guidance is a rightly habituated will. See the discussion under point 6.)

Furthermore, I think that, far from being "entirely inapplicable" to dealing with issues of the moral responsibilities of
OD-HSD professionals, the model can be extraordinarily helpful. For example, one of the moral principles to which I think
most OD-HSD professionals subscribe, although perhaps not
exactly in this form, is "Always treat people as ends—never only
as means"; as illustrated in the "Cost-Cutting Example," this
principle is relevant to situations in which practitioners are asked
to facilitate reductions in personnel, large-scale layoffs, and plant

closings. I also think that OD-HSD professionals generally would agree that preventing harm to the people involved in such reductions, layoffs, and closings — and, as illustrated in the example, to the communities within which those people live — is, by virtue of the principle, a moral responsibility of the profession. In addition, OD-HSD professionals have a responsibility to serve the economic values of the organizations and the people with whom they contract, even though serving those values seems (often an assumption) to conflict with serving the good of the people or at least with preventing harm to them. As demonstrated in the "Cost-Cutting Example," the model can be helpful in thinking through the complexity of such situations on the basis of both conscious reasoning and unconscious intuition. Furthermore, by virtue of reflection on the results of such decisions (Step 5), we can make refinements in both our logical and our intuitive abilities to cope with similar situations in the future. By pooling such reflective interpretation, we can collectively and individually strive to see our practice "in its best light and then restructure it in light of that meaning."

Another example: Many consultants seem to consider an absolute commitment to confidentiality a necessary condition for their effectiveness. Experience indicates that such a commitment can lead to morally hazardous situations in which the consultant's other responsibilities are in irresolvable conflict with responsibilities to the individuals to whom such a commitment has been made. For instance, most OD-HSD practitioners do not have the same legal protections with regard to confidentiality as do ministers, priests, rabbis, psychiatrists, and clinical psychologists, so they cannot reasonably give an absolute commitment to confidentiality. Therefore the Annotated Statement includes the following: "Define and protect confidentiality in our client relationships. (1) Make limits of confidentiality clear to clients and participants. (2) Reveal information accepted in confidence only to appropriate or agreed-upon recipients and authorities" (Guideline III–E). When awareness of the need for defining and making the limits of confidentiality known is part of consultants' ethical sensitivity and when it is among the ethics consultants apply in analyzing ethical problems, consultants are better prepared to avoid morally hazardous situations involving commitments to confidentiality.

In ways similar to the "Cost-Cutting Example" and the confidentiality issue just described, other issues involving the moral responsibility of OD-HSD professionals can be examined with the aid of the model; and the results can be shared throughout the profession so that, over time, we can expect to develop an increasingly comprehensive view of the moral dimensions we choose to help define the meaning of our profession's collective practice.

4.   *The ambiguity and complexity of OD-HSD practice presents opportunities for errors in judgment that can create situations in which all alternatives seem to involve serious moral problems. Avoiding such morally hazardous situations is best addressed on a collective basis because the pooled wisdom, insight, and experience of many individuals will be superior to that of single individuals, and collective decision making can be used in "forbidding behavior which, though not morally wrong in itself, tends to lead . . . into morally hazardous situations." The critique concludes; "The five-step model, with its essentially individualistic orientation, seems inapplicable to questions of this kind."*

Ethical sensitivity, the first element in the model, can be vital to avoiding morally hazardous situations, since such sensitivity alerts practitioners to potential problems. Thus alerted, practitioners can use the model to facilitate their problem analysis, with the first consideration (Step 1a) being "Do I have a potential ethical violation?" and, if so, "Which ethic(s) are applicable?" At that point, in a real situation, the model can help practitioners when their ethics sensitize them to the need for avoiding hazardous situations. It can help them clarify the nature of their problems and then analyze their situations (as described in Step 2) not only for the purpose of avoiding the hazards but also to help them identify their "best" options or at least a reasonable approximation of the "best." Repeated use of the model in such situations can also be expected, by virtue of reflection (Step 5), to help professionals refine their relevant ethics and heighten their sensitivity to future potentially hazardous situations. Both the "Cost-Cutting Example" and the discussion of confidentiality illustrate how the model can be used in this way.

This still leaves us with the question, "Where do the ethics come from that inform people's sensitivity and that are applied at Steps 1a and 2e in the model?" I agree with the critique about the superiority of collective over individual decisions about ethics; this is why a widely participatory process has been used in developing the Statement. Furthermore, as OD-HSD professionals know, widespread participation in the process of deciding on the profession's ethics substantially increases the probability that individual professionals will feel ownership in those ethics and use them to guide their actual behavior. That is, when individuals use the ethics, they will do so because the ethics are theirs and not only the profession's. Thus they will behave in accordance with the ethics based on personal commitment and not just in compliance with or obedience to the dictates of the collective. It is important, however, to note that when decisions about ethics are made collectively, the fact that they are individually applied makes the model's individualistic orientation particularly applicable to helping individuals avoid morally hazardous situations.

5. *"Given the enormous range of values potentially relevant for decision making in the context of ethics as the quest for the good life," the guidance of the model "to identify the conflicting values, determine their priority, and then, after analyzing and reviewing the situation, to choose the 'best' option [seems] essentially nonsubstantive."*

This idea about the substance of the model's guidance for thinking about values explicitly during ethical problem solving needs to be considered in the context of the whole model. Experience with the model can heighten an individual's ethical sensitivity to situations in which she may face an ethical problem. If she has clearly applicable ethics — assuming that she (and her profession) have reflected on similar situations — her decision is likely to be easier. If the alert feeling is not based on potential violation of her ethics, then the model calls her attention to her values and, perhaps, to a conflict in her values. If there is no conflict, her decision is likely to be easier than if conflict exists. If she has thought about what is *truly important* to her—namely, about her values and their relative priority—it will be easier for her to identify how her values apply to her situation and, if her values are in conflict, she will be better able to understand her problem in terms of that conflict. With greater clarity about her problem, the model then helps her analyze her situation, choose her "best" option (or a reasonable approximation), consider its ethical consequences, seek to improve upon it, decide, act, and finally reflect on her experience. As a result, she heightens her sensitivity to future situations involving value conflict and her fluency in thinking about ways of coping with such situations. Based on reflection, she may even refine her ethics so that she will be able to deal with similar future situations more readily, particularly situations in which the ethical implications of her values had not previously been made explicit.

As noted, when values are involved, use of the model depends on clarity about one's values. The participatory process of developing the section on values for the Statement and the sections dealing with values for the Frontier Issues discussion (Chapter Twelve) has been intended as a resource for helping OD-HSD professionals develop such clarity for themselves, individually and collectively. Such an approach carries with it the benefits of the superiority of collective judgment and of heightened personal commitment for those who participate.

It seems to me that the model fits easily into the thinking about ethics in the context of the quest for a good life. Given some degree of clarity about one's values and ethics, it provides a means for alerting oneself to situations in which one needs to proceed carefully in one's quest, thinking about how to proceed and reflecting on the results of one's actions in order to achieve greater clarity as the quest continues. The model does not tell people what their values should be, but it can help them think about how their values apply to their quest; and, in the course of that quest, it can help them continually refine their understanding of what is truly important.

6.   *The five-step model is inapplicable to decision making in the context of ethics as the quest for a good life because "in making personal decisions, we often view our lives as a quest for fulfillment and mean-*

ing — in short, as a search for something with elusive characteristics we can never identify in a precise way at any given time" and such decision making involves an esthetic aspect that cannot be accommodated by an approach that "conceives of the ethical decision-making process primarily in terms of a determinate, well-defined, and ordered sequence of steps."

I agree about the elusiveness of the quest and the importance of the esthetic aspect. At the same time, I believe that using the model does not necessarily prevent us from applying our esthetic/creative abilities to ethical problem solving during the quest. I also agree that the model is "a determinate, well-defined, and ordered sequence of steps," but, rather than being "inapplicable," I believe it can help people heighten their sensitivity to questions of ethics and values in the course of their elusive "quest for fulfillment and meaning." Such questions are almost literally the essence of that "quest." The model helps one answer the meta-question, "What are the questions I need to ask in my quest for a good life?"

Because the questions the model suggests are expressed in words, they may seem less evocative of esthetic creativity than they actually are in my experience. In particular, by encouraging people to contemplate their situation, their vision (Step 2a), their "best" options (Step 2c), and the consequences of those options, the model's questions can evoke within imagination the kind of esthetic/creative answers that are essential to the quest.

The questions in the model are not the only questions. And in real life, they may be asked in a different order. Nevertheless, for a person to develop the ability to quest in a way consistent with his or her values and ethics, it can help to have experience with such a systematic procedure. It is a means of helping one prepare one's mind by consciously clarifying one's values and ethics and developing ways of applying them to thinking about real situations. As was said earlier in this chapter, "at its best, the process described by the model is a smoothly flowing dialogue one has with oneself . . . [It] is not a rote following of predetermined steps, although steps are involved and they tend to follow a logical sequence. It is more a process of iteration and reiteration that uses both reason and intuition." Without some conscious preparation of this kind, the complexity of many situations and the pressures of having to respond immediately to them tend to make conscious, ethical decision making extremely difficult, if not impossible.

In conclusion, I would say that I think the model can be a highly useful tool for people in their quest for a good life. The nature of that personal quest and the more inclusive multi-personal context within which it takes place is well described, I think, by Adler (1988) in his summary of Aristotle's central ideas about ethics.

> For Aristotle, happiness (or a morally good human life as a whole) is a *common* good, the same for all men. When the individual directs his life toward happiness as the final end of all his actions, he is aiming not only at his own ultimate goal but at the ultimate goal he shares with all other individuals (p. 270).
>
> Happiness consists in a complete life well lived in accordance with moral virtue (a rightly habituated will), and accompanied by moderate possession of health and wealth along with other external goods that are, to some degree, beyond the power of the individual to obtain by his or her own efforts, and that are, therefore, the blessings of good fortune . . . Moral virtue and good fortune are both necessary . . . neither by itself is sufficient (p. 273).
>
> The four cardinal aspects of moral virtue are temperance, courage, justice, and prudence . . . The morally virtuous man in seeking his own happiness through temperate, courageous, and prudent choices . . . also seeks it through just choices. . . . What are such choices? *Negatively,* not to do anything that injures others or frustrates them from succeeding in their pursuit of happiness. *Positively,* to act for the good of the organized community, the public common good, in which all individuals participate and which contributes to their individual

happiness by providing them with real goods they
need to lead good lives, goods they cannot obtain
for themselves entirely by their own efforts. The
best state, says Aristotle, . . . is one that aims at
the happiness of all its citizens (p. 271).

For me, that view of the quest for happiness is consistent
with the purpose of the OD-HSD profession as I understand
it, and I see nothing in it that is inconsistent with the use of
the model. I also acknowledge that the model is clearly not a
sufficient guide for such a quest.

In general, I view the points in the critique as limits and
cautions to be kept in mind by those who use the model. In and
of themselves, I do not think the points prove that the model
cannot be helpful. Perhaps the best way for you to decide on
the usefulness of the model *for you* is to try working with it on
some of the key decisions involved in the cases in Chapters Six
through Eleven and Appendix D and then make your own judgment. As with any new skill, your use of the model is likely to
be slow and somewhat deliberate at first, but your ability to use
it is likely to become more intuitive with practice. You will probably need to revise, adjust, and adapt it so that it will work for
you in the kinds of situations you expect to find yourself facing.
However, at least during the period when you are consciously
working on improving your decision-making ability, I expect
you will need a systematic procedure of some kind, and I think
the model can help you create one that works for you. After
you have developed your ethical sensitivity and your awareness
of the variety of elements you need to consider in making ethical decisions, and after you have applied that sensitivity and
awareness to a number of real situations, you may well shift
into a way of choosing that cannot be described by any model.
In spite of that, however, I believe that both the model and the
critique can help you along the way.

Notes

1. Much of this section on moral orientation is based on ideas
    in a booklet by Shea (1988).

2.   The definitions of key terms given here are qualified to apply to decision making only in a context of either ethics as morality or ethics as the quest for a good life. Decisions viewed from the former standpoint deal with whether an actual or possible course of action is morally justified. Decisions viewed from the latter standpoint deal with which of the courses of action open to an individual under a given circumstance best serves his or her overall, evolving conception of a genuinely good life.

   The above qualification is essential given the broad wording of the definitions. In particular, "values" and "ethics" are respectively defined as "standards of importance (desirability, worth, goodness, and rightness) people use in making judgments" and "standards of behavior grounded in values." These two definitions jointly imply that the word *ethics* refers to *absolutely anyone's* standards of judgment or conduct, even racists, sadists, and the like. The qualification in this note aims to avoid that problem. Given the context of the basic moral code central to ethics as morality, the decisions of racists, sadists, and so forth are automatically excluded from the province of ethics. As for ethics as the quest for a good life, it was noted in the preceding chapter that the relationship between this conception and the basic moral rules raises deep philosophical problems. Such problems notwithstanding, however, the authors of this volume proceed on the assumption that racism, sadism, and other grossly immoral practices cannot be part of a genuinely good life for any human being.

3.   Some people conceive of *ethics* and *morals* as meaning substantially the same thing. As we use those terms here, although all morals are ethics (standards of behavior), not all ethics are morals (standards of behavior aimed at minimizing harm or evil). For example, the Statement includes as one of its guidelines, "Work actively for ethical practice by individuals and organizations engaged in OD-HSD activities and, in case of questionable practice, use appropriate channels for dealing with it" (Guideline IV–D). That ethic may be a matter of morality under circumstances re-

quiring the avoidance of morally bad behavior; yet, under other circumstances, the same ethic may involve behavior that is ethically desirable but not a matter of morality. Thus it would be *ethically desirable* to confront commercialism by individuals who disregard professional values in deciding how to share professional knowledge with other professionals, but it would be a *moral requirement* to avoid malpractice that risks serious harm to one's clients (thus violating a moral rule). And, in further contrast, it would be *morally desirable* (but not necessarily a moral requirement) to confront moral malpractice by other professionals.

4. "Act so that you would be willing to universalize the principles underlying your acts" is a variation of Kant's categorical imperative. "Do unto others . . . " is the "golden rule" of Christianity, a variation of which is found in most of the world's major religions. (In this connection, I should note that Gert (1989) points out that the Golden Rule has limits as a principle. For example, it is an inappropriate guide for judges and policemen. However, with such limits in mind, it can be a useful guide. [See Chapter Four for further discussion.])

5. It is important to note that individual practitioners can hold their own ideas about values and ethics and call themselves professionals. However, since this book concentrates on the values and ethics of the OD-HSD profession as a whole, we are using substantial consensus among professionals as the basis for our definitions of the values and ethics of that profession. It should be noted that the process for establishing such consensus is intended to be open to influence by all those who consider themselves OD-HSD professionals as well as by others of the profession's stakeholders and that, although there are indications of convergence on a substantial consensus, the process of achieving that consensus is far from over.

6. The five-step model is a heuristic (problem-solving) model based on dialogue between the three authors and including input from participants in sessions on ethics at several professional meetings where the model was a central ele-

ment in the presentations. I have tried to reflect on the question of how to make ethical decisions *from the point of view of an OD-HSD professional while he or she is facing an ethical problem.* I offer the model as a contribution to co-creating an approach all professionals can use and from which all professionals can learn. I expect to continue refining it in dialogue with interested colleagues.

PART TWO

▮▯▮▯▮▯▮▯▮▯▮▯▮▯▮▯▮▯▮▯▮

Developing
a Statement of
Values and Ethics

▮▯▮▯▮▯▮▯▮▯▮▯▮▯▮▯▮▯▮▯▮▯▮▯▮▯▮▯▮▯▮▯▮

The following two chapters present the most recent version of "An Annotated Statement of Values and Ethics by Professionals in Organization and Human Systems Development." It is a Statement in process, being developed with the participation of professionals in Organization and Human Systems Development (OD-HSD) throughout the world.

Chapter Four deals with the purposes, beliefs, values, and ethical principles on which our work as professionals is based, and Chapter Five outlines the ethical guidelines for practice that have evolved out of a participatory process that began in 1981 (see Appendix A for a description of some of the key events in that process). In combination with Appendix F, which presents detailed information about how the Statement was developed, Chapters Four and Five constitute an annotated version of the entire Statement. As a companion document, we have also developed a more concise Statement encompassing the primary elements in the Statement without annotation (see Appendix B).

Earlier in this statement-development process, we also prepared an Issues Discussion as a means of identifying participants' suggestions on which there seemed to be significant difference of opinion within the profession. Setting those issues apart in a separate discussion allowed us to explore them more deeply than we could in the Statement alone. The Issues Discussion is not presented here as a single document; however, several parts of this book in combination — the annotation in Chapters Four and Five; Chapter Twelve; and some of the material in Chapter One, particularly the section headed "Ethical Issues in OD-HSD Practice and Research" — constitute the most recent version of the Issues Discussion. (For an earlier version, see Gellermann, 1985, in the bibliographic references at the end of Chapter Five.*)

It is important to note that calling this a Statement "by" professionals in OD-HSD is an expression of our aspiration. Ultimately we expect to have a reasonably well-established consensus on this Statement in virtually all respects — including consensus on our view of ourselves as a global professional community and on our purpose, vision, beliefs, values, and ethics. Therefore we expect that in time this Statement will come to reflect our community's position well enough that members will freely align themselves with it and that we can truly say that it is a Statement *by* them. However, we want to keep the process open to influence, growth, and change, thus not making compliance with the Statement a necessary condition of membership. For now we want to encourage people to demonstrate their membership in our professional community by taking a position on this Statement. That can be accomplished by acknowledging one's substantial agreement with it and/or suggesting *specific* changes. Please write to William Gellermann, c/o Mark S. Frankel, Scientific Freedom and Responsibility Programs, American Association for the Advancement of Science, 1333 H Street, N.W., Washington, D.C. 2005.

*Note: To facilitate copying of this Statement, the references corresponding to the citations throughout Chapters Four and Five are presented in the bibliography at the end of Chapter Five.

CHAPTER FOUR

An Annotated Statement: Purposes, Beliefs, Values, and Ethical Principles

Preamble

Organization and Human Systems Development (OD-HSD) is a professional network or community of professionals whose practice is based on the applied behavioral sciences, a human systems perspective, and both human and organizational values. As OD-HSD professionals, we seek to promote and facilitate the process by which human beings and human systems live and work together for their mutual success and well-being. Our purpose is to promote a widely shared learning and discovery process dedicated to the vision of people living meaningful, productive, good lives in ways that simultaneously serve them, their organizations, their societies, and the world.

Note: All of Part Two (Chapters Four and Five) and Appendix F, which constitute the complete Annotated Statement, may be copied for professional use without written permission. When copying, please include reference to this book as the source: namely, W. Gellermann, M. S. Frankel, and R. F. Ladenson, *Values and Ethics in Organization and Human Systems Development: Responding to Dilemmas in Professional Life.* San Francisco: Jossey-Bass, 1990.

111

The field we call Organization and Human Systems Development is generally recognized by the name Organization Development (OD). An increasing number of OD-HSD professionals now conclude that Human Systems Development (HSD) is the most appropriate designation for our field, since our potential clients range from individuals to the whole world. With this expanded focus, the profession can, and some professionals would say *must,* be oriented toward being aware of whether what we do is good for the global system as well as for our specific clients. For most practitioners, especially those in OD and Human Resource Development (HRD), this may mean a change not in the focus of their practice but only in the context within which they view their practice. With such a perspective, the profession has the potential to become a professional community whose collective action has global significance.

These initial words about the scope of our profession raise the question "How inclusive is the HSD professional community?" The answer is neither simple nor clear-cut; some of its essential elements include the following: (1) Our community is an open system. (2) Our members are people who consider themselves professionals; share a holistic, systemic perspective in their work with their clients; possess a professional level of competence (see Guideline II-B); and choose to consider themselves members by freely aligning themselves with the purpose and vision expressed in this Statement.

Another perspective on the field of OD-HSD deals with the issue of how development and transformation are related. They can be differentiated from one another by defining the word *transform* as "to change in composition and structure" or "to change into a different thing" in contrast with *develop,* defined as "to unfold gradually" or "to expand by a process of growth." When development is narrowly defined as *gradual* unfolding, it differs significantly from transformation. But development can be more broadly defined as "all forms of growth toward full realization of potential," thus including transformational growth. It is this broader definition that we use in conceiving of development in OD-HSD. By defining development broadly, we do not deny the importance of the distinction between transformation and development; that difference needs to be recognized, along with the potential for system integration and coordination at the level of spirit, which, for many, is the essence of the "form" toward which "transformation" aspires. We define OD-HSD broadly in order that practitioners who emphasize transformation and those who focus on more narrowly defined development may cooperate more effectively as members of the same profession.

Among other things, we seek to facilitate the development of human systems as healthy settings within which individuals can grow in ways that enable those systems to survive and thrive economically so they can continue to be healthy settings. In contrast, we seek to help human systems grow away from being settings that demean people and hinder their growth. At a deeper level, our OD work has been described as "enabling organizations to find their souls."

In dialogue about past versions of this Statement, the issue was raised: *Are our ethics too culturally specific? Is our thinking oriented primarily toward practice in the United States?* In response to a questionnaire about an earlier version of the Statement, a majority of the OD-HSD professionals surveyed felt that it was *not* too culturally specific. Most recognized that it did have a cultural bias, but they thought that the words were still acceptable as an aspiration for OD-HSD professionals throughout the world. Respondents from Africa, India, Japan, Norway, the United Kingdom, and West Germany considered the words more or less acceptable, with minor modification needed. Others disagreed. For example, a respondent from Saudi Arabia said, "the typical Arab has trouble understanding how anyone cannot be 'all he can be'. To suggest something different is to suggest that God (as they see Him) has overlooked someone. People don't become; they are." Others pointed out that some cultures require behavior that would seem to be counter to the Statement, such as bribery and accepting the subordination of women. Someone else (from the United Kingdom) said, "The whole concept is alien to some cultures even in our own country. But I can't see how this can be avoided."

With regard to the criticism that the Statement has a United States bias, one respondent from Yugoslavia said, "It is not true. It is rather UNO (United Nations Organization) specific. It is only 'a smaller-part-of-the-USA-culture specific'.

It has a lot in common with the Yugoslav Constitution of 1974."

For our profession to develop an ethical stance that is acceptable across cultures, it seems essential to acknowledge cultural bias and to view the creation of such a transcultural stance as a continuing process of dialogue between, among, and within the cultures that comprise our global community.

This Statement recognizes cultural differences in several different guidelines, including:

- Practice within the limits of our competence, culture, and experience in providing services and using techniques (II-D)
- Practice in cultures different from our own only with consultation from people native to or knowledgeable about those specific cultures (II-E)

Nature and Purposes

For OD-HSD to exist as a profession, substantial consensus is necessary within the profession about its primary beliefs, values, and ethics. The process of co-creating this Statement is a means of establishing such consensus, but it is important to remember that *this Statement is not our primary objective. It is only a means to increase ethical consciousness and practice throughout our profession.*

We recognize that technically there is no such thing as "substantial" consensus, but for a group as large and diverse as the OD-HSD profession, we find the concept useful, since pure consensus is probably an unrealistic goal.

A primary duty of a profession, as we see it, is to institutionalize a process whereby the moral and ethical commitments of its members are regularly discussed and assessed. Widespread participation in such a process helps individual members clarify and align their personal and professional values and ethics by comparing them with those of their colleagues and their society; it also allows them to test their ethics in terms of their own and their colleagues' experiences. This self-assessment and consciousness raising reinforces or redefines the ethical commitments of professionals individually and collectively. We understand that these ideas about professions in general apply to our profession in particular, and we commit ourselves to supporting and participating in such a process.

This Statement is an *aspirational* guide, a statement of ideals toward which OD-HSD professionals throughout the world can strive. In addition, we intend this annotated version as an *educational* statement in which the norms of our professional community are more fully described and explained.

By providing a common reference for OD-HSD professionals throughout the world, we seek to enhance our sense of identity as a global professional community. However, two warnings are necessary about this Statement. First, its development from within the perspective of the United States may require some modification in its application to different cultural conditions. (Professionals who encounter such need for modification please write to William Gellermann, c/o Mark S. Frankel, Scientific Freedom and Responsibility Programs, American Association for the Advancement of Science, 1333 H Street, N.W., Washington, D.C. 20005 with specific suggestions for improving the Statement.) Second, the English wording may create difficulties for those whose first language is not English, since the intended meaning of some words may not be the same as the translated meaning. We have tried to minimize that difficulty by providing clarifying annotation, but there are still some inevitable gaps. Over time, we expect to minimize such gaps.

We expect the educational functions of this Statement to be developed more fully over time. The annotations in this Statement are intended as steps in that direction. In addition, an Issues Discussion and case studies, an annotated bibliography (Frankel, 1987), and other educational materials in process are all intended to add substance to the Statement and to aid in its interpretation.

The purposes of this Statement are to:

1. Increase our professional and ethical consciousness and our sense of ethical responsibility
2. Guide us in making more informed ethical choices
3. Help our profession function more effectively

In conjunction with a variety of other activities — including writing articles and holding case discussions and forums — we are using this Statement development process to stimulate:

- Discussion of beliefs, values, and ethics underlying OD-HSD
- Clarification of major differences
- Reconciliation of those differences when feasible
- Articulation of generally accepted OD-HSD values and ethics

In this Statement we seek to provide a generally accepted set of beliefs, values, and ethics. In doing this, we recognize that many OD-HSD professionals belong to professional associations or other organizations that have published formal codes of ethics. When those codes cover significant matters not covered in this Statement or when the Statement conflicts with such codes, we ask OD-HSD professionals to inform the Statement Coordinator (William Gellermann — see address on previous page).

Since our profession is itself a human system, we consider it essential that we strive toward the same level of competency we offer to help others develop. Within that competency, consciousness of values and ethics is primary. In brief, we seek to live our theory.

We intend this Statement as a resource to help us make responsible, informed choices about our behavior by helping us be clear about our:

- Vision, since it enhances our sense of common purpose
- Beliefs, since they affect our ability to see the truth
- Values, since they are the essential element underlying our choices
- Moral rules and ideals, since they are fundamental to our being responsible members of the human community
- Ethical principles, since they provide general guidance for our choices
- Ethical guidelines, since they provide more specific guidance in the kinds of situations we encounter as OD-HSD professionals

Using this Statement as a guide involves living consistently within its spirit and not just its words, particularly in ambiguous situations in which the good or right thing to do is not clear.

_____

Clarity of the kind referred to here is important as preparation for making ethical decisions. Without preparation, one is less able to avoid morally/ethically hazardous situations. In addition, insufficient preparation makes one particularly vulnerable to making mistakes of judgment or, even worse, rationalizing when faced with dilemmas under pressureful conditions.

_____

Because we view ethical practice as continuing and developmental, we encourage all OD-HSD professionals to use this Statement as a resource in (1) reflecting on their own values and ethics, ethical problems, and problem resolutions, and (2) communicating about the results of their reflection with other OD-HSD professionals and, when appropriate, with their clients.

_____

For now, we intend this current version of the Statement primarily as a stimulus for discussion within the profession. Its words are words that we generally understand in our communication among ourselves. However, for communication with clients and others outside our profession, we probably need to revise the words in order to make sure they can be readily understood by people who are not familiar with our jargon.

As our experience with and knowledge about helping human systems increases, so, too, we expect the precision of our beliefs and ethical guidelines to increase. We expect OD-HSD professionals to tell us and others about the results of their reflection so that we can accumulate the information, refine the Statement and the Issues Discussion, and develop the case studies and other materials needed to support ethics education.

Beliefs

As OD-HSD professionals, we recognize the fundamental importance of the following beliefs, which guide our practice and provide context for our ethics. We believe that:

1. *Human beings* are:
   a. Equally worthy regardless of race, creed, age, nationality, gender, ability, socioeconomic status, or any other attribute that distorts people's perceptions of their essential equality

   OD-HSD professionals recognize that humans have different characteristics and competencies that people may value differently. But as OD-HSD professionals, we view humans as being of equal inherent worth, and we support the development of just human systems based on the belief that all humans are created equal and endowed with inherent rights to liberty and opportunities to create lives fully worth living.

   b. Rightfully entitled to equal opportunity in their lives

Here we are referring to equal opportunity and not to equal results. However, when we see differences in life results, we feel that they should bear a reasonable relation to individuals' contributions. In cases of significant inequity, we are committed to affirmative action. (See annotation following Guideline V-C-1 in Chapter Five.)

c. **Interdependent economically, politically, socially, culturally, and spiritually**

Some people object to the reference to people's being interdependent spiritually. We use that term in the broadest sense of its meaning, ranging from the spirit of "esprit de corps" to the spirit of the most profound religious meaning. In so doing, we mean to acknowledge the fact that our field includes people with diverse theological and religious orientations who share a sense of community in spite of their differences. (For more, see Frontier Issues in Chapter Twelve.)

d. **Rightfully responsible for taking charge of their own lives, functioning autonomously and interdependently, and for controlling and facilitating their own growth**

We believe that people are rightfully in charge of realizing their talents and abilities and making choices about how they will live their lives. As much as possible, we proceed on the assumption that the ability to act responsibly, or at least the potential to do so, exists. We recognize that people's ability to do this may be limited, particularly in light of the economic, social, and political conditions under which they live.

We also recognize that human beings may not act responsibly or be capable of making responsible choices. For example, people who are emotionally disturbed or who have been disempowered by such conditions as poverty, discrimination, and oppression need to be approached with sensitivity to the effects of those experiences.

We generally believe that if people try to shift responsibility for their growth to others or if others act as if they can take on such responsibility, people's growth will be fundamentally hindered. But we recognize that we can help our clients by suggesting alternatives that encourage them to reexamine and accept responsibility for their choices, and we consider such help an important part of our role. We also recognize that not all people are able to control their own growth, for such reasons as those just mentioned above.

---

2. *Human systems* — including individuals, groups, organizations, communities, countries, and transnational systems — are:
   a. Interdependent economically, politically, socially, culturally, and spiritually

---

This interdependence involves whole systems that simultaneously are composed of subsystems and are themselves subsystems of more inclusive macrosystems — ultimately the world. The component subsystems are interdependent with one another, with the whole, and with the macrosystem(s) of which the whole is a part. And the whole system, because it is itself a subsystem, is similarly interdependent.

The "spirit" in "spiritual interdependence" is defined by OD-HSD practitioners in a variety of ways, ranging from team spirit to the deepest religious meaning. [See also Belief 1-c in this chapter and Frontier

Issues in Chapter Twelve for further discussion of "spirit" in OD-HSD practice.]

---

b. **Unique configurations of energy — derived from needs, desires, beliefs and values, purposes and visions, goals, talents, and resources — shaped by tensions among system, subsystem, and macrosystem dynamics**

We see these tensions as primary sources of the energy that leads to growth and greater maturity. Among them are those attributable to differences — such as beliefs, values, purposes, and goals — at different system levels and between different subsystems. Among the more mature forms of growth are those that respect differences and diversity.

We seek to encourage the development of intermediate structures and processes in societies that mediate between the individual and the state so as to minimize the alienation caused by the social systems to which people belong. Among other things, this means we tend to support the debureaucratization of organizations and societies' other subsystems and to encourage growth toward higher levels of participation and self-determination.

We recognize that there may be a significant difference between the values that people express and those by which they actually live. An important part of our role is helping our clients become conscious of those differences and then helping them make their words and their behavior congruent by changing one or the other or both.

---

c. **Open systems whose actions influence and are influenced by a variety of stakeholders**

The stakeholders of a business organization may include customers, managers, workers, suppliers, clients, patrons, investors, labor unions, committees, communities, governments, societies, and, ultimately, the world.

---

3. *Human beings and human systems* are:
   a. **Interdependent and therefore positively or negatively affect one another's lives, survival, productivity, and growth**

In earlier versions of this Statement, some people asked that this interdependence be made explicit, since, without it, our profession's emphasis on human values might be perceived as not valuing the systems. This point stresses our belief that an individual's quest for happiness is dependent on the health of the systems within which that quest takes place and, reciprocally, systems depend on the individuals who comprise them.

---

   b. **Interdependent with the earth's ecosystems**
   c. **Responsible for living in harmony with all beings so as to ensure a sustainable future**

Note: Two additional sets of ideas focus on our profession and on ourselves as professionals. They have been included in this annotated Statement because they give meaningful perspective for its educational purposes, but they have been excluded from the more concise Statement in order to help keep it brief.

---

4. *The OD-HSD profession* **aspires to help people realize their highest potential, individually and collectively, by various means, including:**

a. Helping them clarify their purposes and visions and develop their ability to serve their purposes and bring their visions into being

b. Viewing human behavior from the perspective of whole system(s) that influence and are influenced by that behavior

c. Recognizing the interests that different stakeholders have in the system's results and valuing those interests fairly and justly

---

We are not saying that we value all stakeholders' interests equally. We are explicit about valuing them "fairly and justly." At times this can seem like an impossibly complex thing to do, but we accept responsibility for doing the best we can rather than ignoring it because it seems too complex.

---

d. Enabling human systems as wholes and the subsystems within them to align themselves with one another and with their environments

---

In this Statement, the words *align* and *alignment* refer to people's energy being freely coordinated in a common direction. As we conceive it, alignment is not based on coercion of any kind; nor does it mean adaptation to external conditions, although adaptation may be necessary in the short run. And, from the point of view of individuals, we support their right to try to change the common direction, even while they are "in line."

We facilitate people's alignment by helping them clarify:

1. Essential elements in system functioning
    • Common purpose, vision, and mission
    • Philosophy (beliefs, values, norms, ethics)

- Strategies, goals, objectives, and plans
- Structures, roles, and functions
- Systems, methods, and procedures
- Relationships and interdependencies
- Personal alignments with system purpose
- Environmental and other external conditions
2. Problems, priorities, solution options, and plans

In addition, we help people understand and deal with their needs for review and revision as conditions change and as they realize ways of improving their alignment with one another, with the system as a whole, and with its environment, including external stakeholders and the larger systems of which it is a part.

We believe that alignment among a system's parts, within the system as a whole, among the system's stakeholders, and throughout the system's environment will make the system more effective and efficient because the system will avoid wasting energy and the environment will support the system. We acknowledge, however, that this does not deny the possibility of productive behavior by the system directed at changing the environment in order to achieve more enduring alignment.

------

e. **Helping individuals within our client systems (1) accept responsibility for their lives, (2) recognize the extent of their freedom and the constraints on it, their power to choose how they live their lives within the system, the impact of the system on their lives, and their potential for affecting the system, and (3) recognize the possibilities for promoting justice**

f. **Supporting the creation and maintenance of a climate within which freedom, mutual trust, respect, and love prevail**

Many people in our field explicitly or implicitly refer to love, but some would prefer to exclude it from our Statement. Part of the concern about referring to love is the fear that it may not be acceptable to our clients; so some say that, even though we may value it, we shouldn't talk about it. Several years ago, Robert Tannenbaum asked, "Does this path have a heart?" Answering that question requires us to ask ourselves what we stand for. This issue is still to be resolved. It is discussed further as a Frontier Issue in Chapter Twelve.

5. *As OD-HSD professionals,* **we:**
   a. **Recognize the importance of both process and task in our work**

This involves recognizing that the process by which systems function is as important as the tasks directly connected with producing results. For example, when a group works on decision making, *process* includes such things as how people listen, argue, fight, withdraw, and generally support, confront, or undercut one another, whereas *task* usually refers only to the communication content specific to the problem-solving or planning task. In other words, *both* process *and* task are valued, rather than *either* process *or* task. Since our contribution is primarily to improving process, some of us have had a tendency to overvalue it in the past. In contrast, our clients tend to value task primarily and therefore ignore process. One of our primary challenges is to help them add process consciousness to their task consciousness.

b. Acknowledge the influence of values and ethics on
    the effectiveness and growth potential of individ-
    uals, organizations, and more inclusive human sys-
    tems and consider them in our practice

    _____

        As noted earlier, we recognize that in the realm
    of values and ethics what people say and what they
    do can differ. Thus we seek to help others be congruent
    while striving to do so ourselves.

    _____

c. Consider conflicts involving values or ethics in-
    evitable in our practice, including recognition that:
    1. Practice according to the values and ethics
        described in this Statement may have to be mod-
        ified for us to practice under certain cultural
        conditions

        _____

        When cultural conditions affect or limit our
    ability to follow the guidelines in this Statement,
    we accept responsibility for the consequences of
    our action or inaction and seek to be clear about
    the guidelines we choose to guide our action in
    their place.

    _____

    2. Choices that may seem unethical in the short
        run may be ethical in the longer run

        _____

        As an illustration, we may work with clients
    whose purpose we consider "morally wrong" be-
    cause we believe that serving them may serve a
    greater good in the longer run.

    _____

3. Respect for peoples' right of free choice also involves responsibility for discussing with clients the consequences of their choices and how different choices might yield different consequences

---

Our ethics make us responsible for withdrawing from a consulting contract if we experience too much dissonance between what our clients choose and what we consider to be right. (See Guideline III-B-6.)

---

4. Conflict resolution based on the whole-win value generally seeks to serve the greatest good of the whole, but exceptions may be necessary to serve more fundamental principles

---

We tend to be guided more by "the greatest good of the whole" than by the more commonly known guideline of "the greatest good of the greatest number" because we recognize that the rights and interests of minorities can be ignored, undervalued, or denied by placing primary value on the interests of a majority. We also recognize that "the good of the whole" may conflict with other considerations that we value even more, such as fundamental human rights. For example, we cannot accept experimenting with people without their knowledge and informed consent, even though it might generate great benefit for the "whole," because we consider free and informed choice a fundamental right. (Also see discussion of whole-win under Value 3-b.)

---

d. See ourselves as members of:
1. A global professional community, recognizing that:
    a) Our accomplishments as individuals and as a profession are interdependent.
    b) Our responsibilities to one another are mutual.
    c) The fullest use of our potential will be realized to the extent that we coordinate our efforts in the service of our common vision.
2. The more inclusive global community of scientific professionals by virtue of our grounding in the applied behavioral sciences

As members of the scientific community, we support the efforts being made to create a "Hippocratic Oath" for that community, such as the "Buenos Aires Oath" of the April 1988 international conference on Scientists, Disarmament and People (see also Guideline V-E under Social Responsibility):

> Aware that, in the absence of ethical control, science and its products can damage society and its future, I pledge that my own scientific capabilities will never be employed merely for remuneration or prestige or on instruction of employers or political leaders only, but solely on my personal belief and social responsibility—based on my own knowledge and on consideration of the circumstances and the possible consequences of my work—that the scientific or technical research I undertake is truly in the best interests of society and peace ("In the News," 1988, p. 1).

e. Understand that our values and ethics are simultaneously personal and professional, including awareness that:
  1. In the ultimate sense our values and ethics are deeply personal
  2. We need clarity about our values and ethics prior to the time we act on them in real situations, especially those involving ethical dilemmas
  3. We are in a *service* profession in which we make ourselves and our expertise available, and we are prepared to discuss with colleagues and participants in our consulting the way we do this

Our professional practice is more than just enacting a role based on our professional expertise. It is also, and even more fundamentally, an expression of our essential humanity and our uniqueness as persons. In other words, as we see it, our professional practice is and must be aligned with our personal integrity. By referring to our "selves" we intend only to point in the general direction of what we mean. Each of us accepts responsibility for deciding what it means for us.

Values

We acknowledge the following values or *standards of importance* as the foundation of our ethics as **OD-HSD professionals.**

Values are standards of *importance* (desirability, worth, goodness, and so on). They are fundamental to the ethical concepts covered later in this Statement. Those concepts are as follows:

- *Ethics* (including moral rules and ideals and ethical principles and guidelines), in contrast to values, are standards of *behavior* based on values.

- The *fundamental principle* is an adaptation of what Kant called the "categorical imperative," a principle about principles (a meta-principle).
- *Moral rules and ideals* are generally agreed-upon injunctions that seek to minimize harm or evil: *Rules* focus on not doing harm oneself, while *ideals* focus on acting in ways that will prevent or alleviate suffering from harm or evil. Together moral rules and ideals can be identified as basic to the existence of a viable, global human community.
- *Ethical principles* give more general guidance for action than moral rules and ideals; yet, like them, principles tend to be shared with most individuals, professions, and other human systems that have reflected on their ethics.
- *Ethical guidelines* as outlined in this Statement tend to focus more specifically on the conditions of OD-HSD practice than do the other ethical standards, although many of them are general and their guidance does not become specific until the level of their subpoints is reached.
- *Moral-ethical justification* allows for the fact that following the rules/ideals/principles/guidelines is not always moral or ethical and that it is sometimes necessary to justify violations.

Our value system is based on life and the quest for happiness; freedom, responsibility, and self-control; and justice. By making these concepts primary and then building on that foundation, we give them the priority that is implicit in our vision of "people living meaningful, productive, good lives." Beyond such prioritization, it is difficult to identify the relative importance of our other values. We want to stress that (1) although this list of values is composed of separate items, several of them are value clusters and (2) together the entire list represents a system of interdependent values in which no single value can be understood without seeing its relation to all the others. We also consider other values important, but in this section we have limited ourselves to those we consider most important.

1. **Fundamental values**
    a. *Life and the quest for happiness:* **people respecting, appreciating, and loving the experience of their own**

and others' being while engaging in the search for
and the process of co-creating "good" life

One of the founders of OD-HSD, Herb Shepard,
when asked what he considered the most important
single value of OD-HSD, said "life loving." The experience of loving life embraces all the other values
since their ultimate value can be measured in terms
of their contribution to life. For example, system effectiveness can encompass the life value to the extent that
life-serving results are sought by the system; so, too,
can all the other values ultimately be valued in terms
of their contribution to the quality of life.

We refer to the "quest" for happiness, rather than
the "pursuit," in order to avoid unnecessarily biasing
this Statement with a perspective based on the United
States Declaration of Independence. It is helpful to
note, however, that the ideas behind the Declaration
of Independence were derived from the thinking of European philosophers.

When we refer to "happiness" in "the quest for
happiness," we mean whole lives well lived—namely,
lives lived in accordance with what is really good for
us, individually and collectively. We do *not* mean the
"happiness" associated with satisfying momentary desires, since that is not necessarily consistent with what
is really good for us. (See Frontier Issues in Chapter
Twelve for more on "happiness.")

We do not limit the value we place on life to
those uses of human life that serve system purposes.
For example, we value all of life and believe that for
work life to serve system purposes fully it must serve
personal purposes as well. To the extent that work life
is seen as frustrating the satisfaction of personal purposes, energy to serve system purposes tends to be in-
hibited. In other words, the higher the alignment of
system and personal purposes, the greater is the amount
of energy available to serve both purposes.

b. *Freedom, responsibility, and self-control:* people expe-
    riencing their freedom, exercising it responsibly,
    and being in charge of themselves

The freedom we value is limited by responsibility for the consequences of its use — especially for
respecting the rights of others, including *their* freedom.
Some people question whether people do in fact have
"free will" or "free choice," but most practitioners agree
that we enhance such freedom by acting as if it exists
and that we therefore value it. Furthermore, in valuing people's freedom, we support their empowerment;
and, from an HSD point of view, when people's purposes are aligned with those of the system, valuing freedom also empowers the system.

c. *Justice:* people living lives whose results are fair and
    equitable

By *justice* we mean economic, political, and social justice in general and organizational-system justice
in particular. For example, we are concerned about
people having equal employment opportunity within
the larger society of which they are a part; thus even
though it may not be part of our contract, we are alert
to opportunities to help our clients bring about equal
employment conditions.
    In thinking about justice, we find it helpful to
be conscious of the following three aspects: "(1) the
securing of all inalienable or natural human rights; (2)
the fairness involved in the equal treatment of equals
and the unequal treatment of unequals in proportion
to their inequality; and (3) the service of the public
or common good, the good of the community as a

whole" (Adler, 1987, p. 98). Although each of these ideas obviously could be developed more fully, doing so is not appropriate here. However, the second point and its reference to treating people unequally is illustrated by Guideline V–C–1–c, which states that we "encourage fairness in the distribution of the fruits of a system's productivity." On the one hand, all system members have equal rights to health and safety and, therefore, fair use of system resources requires treating people equally in that respect. On the other hand, we recognize that people make unequal contributions to productivity and, therefore, that fair distribution would allow treating people unequally. (For fuller discussion of justice, see Guideline V–C–1.)

2. Personal and interpersonal values (may also be larger ˎ system-level values)
   a. *Human potential and empowerment:* people being healthy and aware of the fullness of their potential, recognizing their power to bring that potential into being, growing into it, living it, and generally doing the best they can, both individually and collectively

Among OD-HSD professionals there is general recognition that individual human beings have unique potentials that are barely being realized. For example, Tannenbaum and Davis say, "We are struck by the tremendous untapped potential in most individuals yearning for discovery and release" (1969, p. 8). Most OD-HSD professionals share that view and place great importance on empowerment, by which they mean enabling people to fully realize their potential both individually and collectively. By *realize* we refer to both meanings of the word—namely "to become aware" and "to bring into being."

In this connection it should be noted that, since the "power" in "empowerment" exists within each human being, no one can empower anyone else; that is something we can only do for ourselves. However, we can *encourage* other people to empower themselves and so, in a sense, we can talk about empowering others. For example, one of the most empowering things one person can do for another is to ask the questions, "What would your life be like if it were exactly the way you would like it to be?" and "What can you do to make that possible for yourself?" A second empowering action is listening to the answers in a genuinely supportive, caring way. Answering those questions is likely to have an empowering effect on the person who does so. Asking the questions in a way that supports or evokes honest answering can be thought of as empowering, but only in the sense that it supports the real empowerment done by the person himself or herself. It is also worth noting that acting as if empowerment is something we can do for others actually has a disempowering effect since it encourages those we are trying to support to look outside themselves for their power.

We can also talk about the empowerment of human systems. In that regard, the idea of mutual support is important because human beings and the human systems of which they are members can support one another. From the individual's point of view, the connection with system power is identified by the answer to such questions as, "What would your job (career, organization, community, country, world) be like if it (they) were exactly the way you would like it (them) to be?" From the organization's point of view, the connection with individual power is identified by the answer to such questions as, "What would you like the relationship to be between the organization (the system) and its members?" When there is reciprocity between those answers, we can speak of mutual support.

The reciprocal effect of that mutual support can be highly reinforcing. On the one hand, as the human beings become more powerful, more power is available to the system through those human beings and, simultaneously, they are in a stronger position to support the system's empowerment. On the other hand, as the system becomes more powerful, that power can be experienced as increased support by the members of the system for their own empowerment.

b. *Respect, dignity, integrity, worth, and fundamental rights of individuals and other human systems:* people appreciating one another and their rights as human beings, including life, liberty, and the quest for happiness

In valuing these aspects of being, we apply them not only to individuals but also to organizations, communities, societies, and other human systems. They are a cluster of closely related, interdependent values:

Respect encompasses such meanings as "to feel and show honor or esteem," "to show courtesy," "to show consideration for," and "to avoid intrusion on."

Dignity is defined as "the quality or state of being worthy, honored or esteemed," "true worth," and "excellence." OD-HSD professionals value it according to those definitions—for themselves, for the people with whom they work, and for the people affected by their work (both individuals and the more inclusive human systems to which they belong).

Integrity, for some practitioners, means people being "true to themselves." This idea, of course, is based on the belief that there is a self to which each person can be true; this is not yet a generally shared belief. For almost everyone, however, integrity— in the sense of honesty, candor, and living up to commitments—is a generally shared value. At the level of organizations and more inclusive human systems, it is possible to think of integrity both in the sense of being true to self *and* in terms of honesty, candor, and living up to commitments.

Worth was referred to earlier when we said "Human beings are . . . equally worthy." This means that we believe that, although people may be valued differently by societies because of different competencies or other attributes, they are of equal inherent worth. At the level of more inclusive human systems, we can think of the worth of the systems as being grounded in the worth of the people who comprise them.

Fundamental human rights refer to "natural" rights, which have been defined as having their foundation in natural, human needs—in contrast to constitutional or civil rights, which are not founded in natural need (Adler, 1987). Adler's discussion of those rights helps clarify why they are so important in guiding our profession: "The primary right is the pursuit of happiness, having its foundation in our moral obligation to make good lives for ourselves" (p. 59). In this connection, it is important to note that the right is "pursuit of happiness" and not "happiness." Although we value happiness, it is not a right; the *right* is limited to people's opportunities/obligations to "make good lives." Note also that these views are consistent with our earlier discussions of how the quest for happiness is among the profession's primary values and of empowerment as something that people can do only for themselves.

Adler goes on to say that "the rights to life and liberty are subordinate rights because they are rights to means indispensable for the pursuit of happiness and also because [they] are dependent on external circumstances that are within the power of an organized society and its government to control" (p. 59). This second point puts into perspective the OD-HSD profession's role as facilitator of human systems development, including government, business, all the other subsystems of society, and ultimately society itself. Given that role, OD-HSD professionals have the potential to affect both people's ability to fulfill their "moral obligation to make good lives for [them]selves" and the "external circumstances" of the human systems on which people's rights to life and liberty depend. Given that potential, it is particularly important that we and our profession value fundamental human rights.

Specific fundamental rights we value include: (1) life, liberty, and security of person; (2) freedom of thought, conscience, and religion; (3) freedom of opinion and expression; and (4) freedom of choice. In general, we accept the United Nations' *Universal Declaration of Human Rights* as a guide. This position is based on responses to earlier drafts of this Statement in which a few wanted to drop the reference to "fundamental human rights" and others wanted the reference to be more specific. Among the latter, several supported the idea of incorporating the United Nations' Declaration into the profession's ethical position, including one person who said that "using it may be a step toward 'world cultural bias' rather than 'U.S. bias'." That the declaration does represent a generally acceptable world view is indicated by the fact that it was adopted by the United Nations in 1948 by a vote of forty-eight to zero, with only eight abstentions.

---

c. *Authenticity, congruence, honesty and openness, understanding and acceptance:* people being true to themselves, acting consistently with their feelings, being honest and appropriately open with one another

(including expressing feelings and constructively
confronting differences), and both understanding
and accepting others who do the same

In general, this value cluster encompasses being true to oneself in the moment and to the full realization of one's potential over time while also respecting others in their quest to do the same. From the
perspective of OD-HSD practice, it refers to supporting or creating the conditions that make this possible.
To clarify this general idea, it will help to discuss some
of the underlying values further:

Openness. It is helpful to differentiate openness from
   honesty since it is possible to conceive of people being absolutely honest about what they express without being completely open. It is the difference between speaking the truth and speaking the whole
   truth. Within the OD-HSD profession, there is a
   clear preference for openness as well as honesty.
   However, some people advocate openness without
   qualification, while others qualify openness depending on conditions, such as the usefulness and relevance of what is being expressed. For example, being open about something a person or a larger
   system cannot change may be unnecessarily harmful; being open beyond a system's ability to cope with
   the information may be destructive; and being open
   about things that are likely to harm a relationship
   may be helpfully filtered. Furthermore, all "openness" is not truly "open," as in the case of name calling and judging in ways that do not clearly acknowledge that the expression is a statement about the
   speaker and not about the object of the speaker's expression. (For further discussion, see Morton, 1966.)
      We recognize that there are conditions under
   which people cannot realistically be authentic and

open. At the extreme, for example, conditions of dependence and oppression clearly make such behavior dangerous, if not suicidal. However, even when such behavior is not realistic, we value it and seek to change conditions so that it can become realistic.

Empathy or listening with understanding. This might be called *"receptive* openness," since it refers to receiving actively the expressions of others and understanding them from their point of view. It means not distorting other people's meanings with one's own, not reacting defensively, and using questions to help people express what they want to say and not what the listener wants them to say. Empathy is essential for authentic relationship.

Appropriate and effective communication of feelings as well as thoughts. This value recognizes that feelings are facts that informed decision making must consider, although it need not be ruled by them. It also recognizes that feelings are an essential element in the formation of human relationships over and above the minimal mechanistic task relationships required to get work done. It is generally recognized that, even from the point of view of serving the organization's purposes alone, tapping into the deepest levels of human potential and motivation requires communication about feelings. And when happiness is also valued, communication about feelings is essential.

It is important to recognize that communicating about feelings is different from reacting to feelings; communicating about and acknowledging feelings are not the same as being blindly controlled by them. That is the reason for including the words *appropriate* and *effective* in our description. They emphasize communication that serves the higher values underlying individual and organizational/system purposes.

Appropriate confrontation. This value is a logical consequence of the preceding values noted under this
authenticity value cluster. It is grounded in recognizing that difficulties, differences, and conflict are
facts of organizational life and that problem solving, productivity, creativity, happiness, personal
growth, and many other organizationally desired
results require honest, constructive, whole-win confrontation. Failure to confront appropriately is generally recognized among OD-HSD practitioners as
being dysfunctional both organizationally and personally.

d. *Flexibility, change, and proaction:* **people changing
themselves on the one hand and acting assertively
on the other in a continuing process whose aim is
to maintain or achieve a good fit between themselves and the external reality within which they
live**

We recognize that change is continuous and inevitable as a characteristic both of the way of the world
in general and of the growth dynamics of human beings and human systems in particular. We view life
as a continuing process of change; thus we value flexibility in responding to such change. At the same time,
we also value proaction, in contrast to reaction, and
recognize our own and other people's responsibility for
doing what it takes to serve our purposes and realize
our visions.

3. System values (may also be values at personal and interpersonal levels)
    a. *Learning, development, growth, and transformation:*
        people growing in ways that bring into being greater

realization of their potential, individually and collectively

---

This cluster of values, although different from them, is grounded in several of the other values. For example, it is grounded in such values as human potential and empowerment, but it goes beyond them to value the collective growth and development of the system in ways that bring into being the fullest realization of individual potential in the service of the whole. Since human systems are defined as "wholes comprised of parts or subsystems that are interdependent with one another, with the whole, and with the macrosystem(s) of which the whole is a part," *system* growth and development are valued at all levels from the individual to the macrosystem.

At levels above the individual, system growth involves the ongoing creation of a system composed of human beings. At times this creation process involves a transformation — literally a change in form — that is analogous to the change from caterpillar to butterfly, as when an organization shifts from a hierarchical, bureaucratic, authoritarian form to one that is more egalitarian, democratic, and participative. During the unsettled period of transformation, the system can appear to move in opposition to the effectiveness and efficiency values; but an increasing number of practitioners value transformation because they see it as essential for creating systems capable of simultaneously being efficiently effective and achieving at the highest levels of human potential and aspiration.

---

b.   *Whole-win attitudes, cooperation-collaboration, trust, community, and diversity:* **people caring about one another and working together to achieve results that are good for everyone (individually and collectively),** experiencing the spirit of community and honoring the diversity that exists within community

_____

In their simplest terms these values refer to people respecting one another and working together for common purposes. They do not necessarily exclude competition in the service of a greater good, but they seek to minimize win-lose competition (which requires a loser in order for someone to be a winner) and seek to maximize whole-win competition, in which winning, even by one, can be valued because of what it means for the good of the whole. For example, many Olympic athletes view their competition from a whole-win perspective — namely, celebrating human excellence and achievement — and decry the overemphasis that is placed on which individuals and which countries win gold medals. In cases of competition for scarce resources, emphasis is on working together to find alternative resources that serve everyone's needs and, when that is not possible, to resolve differences based on shared higher values. (For descriptions of experiences with cooperation, see Simmons and Mares, 1983.)

Whole-win attitudes. The whole-win attitude involves valuing from the point of view of systems as wholes. For example, an organization is a system composed of interdependent subsystems; simultaneously the organization is an interdependent subsystem within a higher-level socioeconomic system. The holistic view recognizes interdependencies among all system levels and values the purposes of all levels, from individuals to macrosystems, rather than valuing only from the organization's point of view (which tends to subordinate all other interests to those of the organization, rather than coordinating all interests).

Whole-win valuing is gaining increasing acceptance among practitioners with a stakeholder orientation. Although related to the systemic view, whole-win valuing is different in that it focuses attention on equity for all those who have a stake in the system's results. In the case of a business organization, these might include stockholders, customers, workers, labor unions, suppliers, communities, nations, and transnational systems (such as the United Nations, the European Common Market, and our whole global socioeconomic system).

Cooperation-Collaboration. In earlier versions of the Statement, cooperation was referred to as "collaboration." Several of our European colleagues pointed out that the word *collaboration* has strong negative connotations because of its association with Nazi collaborators during World War II, so we stopped using the word and replaced it with *cooperation.* Subsequently, a number of colleagues outside of Europe pointed out that for them "cooperation" does not denote the same depth and richness of meaning as "collaborating." Thus both words have been used on the assumption that in translation people with different backgrounds will use the word(s) appropriate for them. In any case, the meaning we want to stress is one of people working together wholeheartedly.

We recognize the difficulty of taking a whole-win approach when others are taking a competitive, win-lose approach, especially when others define their winning in ways that require us or other people to lose. As a fall-back position in such cases, we seek no-lose outcomes, but we recognize that lose-lose results may be necessary in the short run. If possible, we try to avoid such results by informing those who take a win-lose approach of the no-lose or lose-lose consequences of their actions as a means of encouraging them to shift to a win-win (whole-

win) approach. To the extent that we can, we seek
to serve the best interests of all those affected by us
as well as our own interests.

Trust. The kind of system that is created out of
all the preceding values involves a high level of trust
among all members of the system. This is particularly true in cases of conflict and competition. At
the moment that any conflict or competition is recognized, the presence or absence of trust determines
whether people will direct their energy and attention to working *with* one another to solve the problem in whole-win ways or *against* one another in win-
lose ways.

---

c.   *Widespread, meaningful participation in system affairs,
     democracy, and appropriate decision making:* **people
     participating as fully as possible in making the de-
     cisions that affect their lives**

We value participation and democracy in the
same way that we value integrity, freedom, and justice.
The latter values are grounded in people's fundamental right to seek happiness. They are also valued extrinsically because of their demonstrable importance
for system effectiveness and efficiency. The appropriate degree of participation depends on the conditions
surrounding the need for decision making. For example, making an authoritative decision without participation may be necessary under emergency conditions
or when people do not have the necessary information
or the ability to use that information.

We define "appropriate decision making" as decision making that serves human well-being. Most OD-
HSD professionals value "democracy"; but they realize
that democratic decision making is not appropriate under all conditions because, among other things, it re-

quires *informed* participation, the ability to process and discuss information, and sufficient time.

In earlier versions of this Statement, we spoke of valuing "democratic" decision making; later we shifted to "appropriate" decision making because we recognized the possibility of conditions under which democratic decision would not be appropriate. However, because we value democracy in the sense of "rule by the people," most of us see the creation of conditions under which it *is* appropriate — rather than acceptance of conditions that may make it inappropriate — as an important part of our role. Even in situations in which authoritative rather than participative decision making is appropriate, however, ideally the authority is based in some way on the consent of the governed. When authority is not so based, we support movement toward democracy.

As we conceive it, democratic decision making means substantially more than just voting and political process. It involves enabling and empowering people to participate meaningfully in making the decisions that affect their lives. Therefore OD-HSD's role can be seen as facilitating the development of the structures, procedures, knowledge, abilities, and information needed to make full, effective participation possible.

The issue of explicitly valuing democracy is still an open one. OD-HSD professionals generally seek democratic participation whenever it is practical because of its power to motivate and contribute to organizational excellence, effectiveness, and efficiency. But there is wide variation in the extent to which practitioners see empowering people to control their own lives as a primary value in and of itself. In practice, some are willing to subordinate freedom and self-control to organizational values, while others would subordinate organizational values to individual values. Most of us are convinced that both democratic and organizational values can be achieved without subordinating either. Based on the whole-win value, we believe that coordination is possible, and we see its realization as one of the primary challenges faced by our profession.

Although it may seem to contradict the freedom value, we also value authority, power, and influence in decision making when they serve system effectiveness and do not unnecessarily limit freedom. However, there is wide difference of opinion about what this means in particular situations — especially as it relates to the conditions under which limiting independence and freedom is "necessary." Generally speaking, we prefer authority of knowledge and skill over authority of position and authority of influence over coercive power.

-----

d.   *Effectiveness, efficiency, and alignment:* **people achieving desired results with an optimum balance between results and costs, and doing so in ways that coordinate the energies of systems, subsystems, and macrosystems — particularly the energies, needs, and desires of the human beings who comprise those systems**

Effectiveness refers to achieving desired results (purposes, visions, missions, goals, objectives, and so on). In the early days of OD practice it was sometimes overlooked because of the field's emphasis on process. Effectiveness is now clearly a primary value, although issues remain about what to treat as desired results and whose desires to consider. For example, in our work with business organizations we are frequently faced with conflicts between business results and human or personal results, and there is wide difference of opinion about how to resolve those conflicts. (For example, see Frizell and Gellermann, 1988.)

Efficiency refers to achieving the maximum ratio of desired results to costs. It was also sometimes overlooked during the early days of OD practice, again because of the attention given to process. Efficiency, too, is now a widely shared value. However, issues remain as to what should be recognized as costs and desired results. Because of this we refer to "optimal balance," by which we mean achieving a reasonable balance between costs and benefits. In doing this, we recognize the difficulties of establishing a common denominator for measuring both and establishing their relative weights, thus making a simple calculation of efficiency virtually impossible.

Alignment exists to the degree that the results desired for the organization/system are coordinated with what people desire for themselves and vice versa. This state is illustrated in Figure 3.

Figure 3. Alignment.

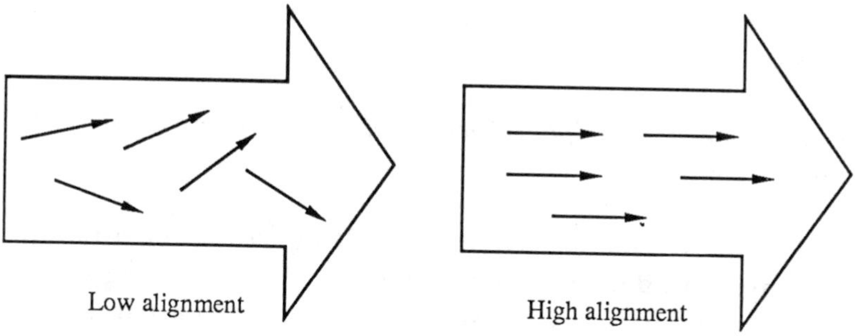

Low alignment   High alignment

Source: Adapted from Kiefer and Stroh, 1983, p. 32.

In the figure, the small arrows represent the direction of people's individual energies, while the larger arrows represent the direction of the system. Alignment is high to the extent that people's work lives simultaneously serve them and the system. For people working with an organization, this means that their work lives enable them to use their full potential *and* their work contributes meaningfully and valuably to them personally, to their organization, to their community, and to the larger society. Perfect alignment may not be possible all the time, but it can be a useful ideal toward which to strive.

Some professionals are concerned that alignment can be defined in ways that allow for its achievement through manipulation or coercion; they add "attunement" to their set of core values in order to make it explicit that the alignment truly comes from within the people involved. The above definition does not need that addition since it is grounded in the idea that people freely align themselves in their "quest for happiness."

Ethics: Principles, Moral Rules and Ideals, and Justifying Violations

We commit ourselves to the following *standards of behavior.*

Fundamental Principle (elements of a meta-principle underlying all our ethics)

Act so that we would be willing to universalize the principles underlying our action and live with the consequences of our action if everyone else were to act in accord with its underlying principles.

The first part of this principle about universalizing is an adaptation of Kant's "categorical imperative." It is a meta-principle: a principle about principles. If we had full comprehension of what this meta-principle means and the ability to apply it on a day-to-day basis, we might not need any other principles or guidelines. With the qualification we have added regarding living with the consequences of our action, the "categorical imperative" provides a good foundation for our ethics. The rest of this Statement may, in fact, be viewed as an attempt to clarify the moral rules and ideals and some of the principles and guidelines that make this fundamental principle specific to the conditions of OD-HSD practice.

Moral Rules and Ideals

Morals (rules and ideals) are ethics aimed at minimizing harm or evil. We believe they are fundamental to living responsibly as members of the global human community.

1. *Moral Rules.* Do no harm: do not kill, cause pain, disable, deprive of freedom, deprive of pleasure, deceive, cheat, break promises, disobey the law, or fail to do our duty.

Moral rules contrast with moral ideals. Both lists are adapted from *Morality: A New Justification of the Moral Rules,* by Bernard Gert (1989). The moral rules are each more specific versions of the general rule, "Do not cause harm (or evil)." They are the most basic dimension of morality and, according to Gert's reasoning, they all meet the test that "all impartial rational persons" would take the following attitude toward them: "Everyone is always to obey the rule except when an impartial rational person can advocate that violating it be publicly allowed. Anyone who violates the rule when an impartial rational person could not advocate that such a violation be publicly allowed may be punished" (p. 284). These rules, including the prescription that violators be punished, are the core of a system of morality, which Gert defines as "*a public system applying to all rational persons governing behavior which affects others and which has the minimization of evil as its end*" (p. 6).

Moral rules and ideals need to be understood in the context of possible moral justification for violation, particularly those relative to "disobeying the law" and failing to "do our duty." There would be moral justification for disobeying bad laws or failing to do one's duty when obeying or doing one's duty would be immoral (by causing harm or failing to prevent or lessen it). These two rules tend to be based on the assumption of a social context within which obeying the law and doing one's duty are consistent with minimizing harm.

2. *Moral Ideals.* **Prevent (or do those things that will lessen) harm suffered by anyone: prevent death, pain, disability, deprivation of freedom, deprivation of pleasure, deception, cheating, breaking of promises, disobeying of the law, and neglect of duties.**

In contrast to moral rules, for which compliance is *required* by our moral system, following moral ideals is encouraged but not required. It is impossible for people to follow them impartially with all people all the time, so it is unrealistic to expect it. For example, at this moment, the person reading this Statement could instead be preventing or lessening harm for someone somewhere. Also, there are so many possibilities for preventing or lessening harm that we must each decide for ourselves which ones we think are most important to act on.

It is also important to note that, as Gert (1989, p. 163) says: "Moral ideals are not revolutionary, except in those societies where immoral action by those in power is taken for granted, or when there are great numbers of deprived persons. Unfortunately in the world today there are many societies where moral ideals are revolutionary." As OD-HSD professionals, we have a professional as well as a personal responsibility to identify the degree to which the moral ideals are revolutionary in our own societies and then to decide what we are morally obliged to do. Since we are HSD professionals, it is appropriate to say "obliged," as we have a professional duty other people do not have.

Justification of Moral-Ethical Violations

We recognize that violation of ethical standards (including morals) may be justified under certain conditions because such violation is required to minimize harm or to serve most fully the ideals represented by our values and ethics as a whole.

Justifying violation of morals and other ethical standards involves such considerations as: the standards violated; the harm avoided, prevented, or caused and the good promoted; the kinds of good or harm; their seriousness, duration, and probability of occurring; the number of people who will suffer or benefit; and the distribution of the benefit and suffering. In seeking to balance all of these considerations, we seek to serve the "greatest good of the whole," which includes valuing the "good of the individual" and respecting individuals' rights.

In considering possible ethics violations, we are guided by the following:

1. Do not violate moral rules without clear *moral* justification.

Generally speaking, violation of moral rules requires *moral* justification — that is, justification based on minimizing harm. For example, harming a few people (a moral rule violation) to minimize harm to a larger number would be moral justification, whereas harming a few to serve the good of a larger number would not. More concretely, laying off a large number of people (harm) to avoid laying off an even larger number (greater harm) would be a *moral* justification, whereas laying off a large number of people (harm) to make a larger profit for stockholders (good) would not be. That is why we can say, especially in the latter case, that an organization has a *moral* obligation to consider harm-minimizing alternatives, such as attrition, retraining, and outplacement as means of staff reduction.

In specifying that the justification must be clear, we mean that it must be reasonable to rational people and not just a self-serving rationalization. A primary test of reasonableness is determining whether the reasoning supporting the justification could be accepted by impartial rational people as a basis for advocating that the violation be publicly allowed. All rational people would not necessarily agree with the reasoning, but they would accept the idea that a rational person could use such reasoning.

Violating moral rules *requires* moral justification, but violating moral ideals or other ethical standards does not. In the latter case, ethical justification may be desirable, for reasons explained in the following discussion.

2. **Do not violate moral ideals, ethical principles, or ethical guidelines without appropriate, clear, *ethical* justification.**

As explained in the annotation following Moral Ideals, it is unreasonable to expect people to comply with moral ideals for all people all the time. Therefore justification cannot be *required*. Generally, however, it would be *appropriate* to justify failure to prevent harm under conditions where we might reasonably be expected to do so. For example, if we fail to prevent harm or to serve the good under conditions where we might reasonably be expected to do so, we will hold ourselves accountable for appropriate, clear, ethical justification.

In contrast to moral rule violations, violating moral ideals, ethical principles, or ethical guidelines involves *ethical* justification. That is, rather than being based on minimizing harm, justification is based on a combination of minimizing harm and serving the good (as explicitly defined by our ethics and implicitly defined by our values). If rule violations are involved in violating an ethical guideline, our justification must be consistent with *moral* justification as well as with appropriate ethical justification. For example, an ethical guideline such as III-B-3, which directs us to "encourage and enable people to provide for themselves the services we provide, rather than foster continued reliance on us," implicitly involves both the moral rule about not disabling and the professional ideal/value about encouraging people's development and growth. Fostering continued reliance (disabling) would require moral justification. At the same time, justification for failing to encourage development would be desirable, though not required.

When violations of our ethics involve unclear situations — that is, situations that are gray rather than clear-cut black and white — we allow ourselves less clarity in our ethical justifications. However, we will be as clear as we reasonably can be. In other words, as noted earlier, we will seek to think in terms of reasons that impartial rational people could accept as a basis for advocating that such violations be publicly allowed. This does not mean that all rational people would necessarily agree with the reasoning — only that all would accept it as being based on reason. For example, in justifying failure to encourage development, we might give reasons with which all OD-HSD professionals would not agree, but all would agree that the justification is based on reason.

Although, for reasons already noted, we neither expect nor require justification of all ethical violations, we do acknowledge that we are responsible for making the judgments that lead to our failures to prevent harm or to serve the good. And, generally speaking, if we fail to prevent harm or to serve the good under conditions where we might reasonably be expected to do so, we will hold ourselves accountable for appropriate, clear, ethical justification.

To illustrate, consider the following example of how ethical justification may allow for the violation of an ethical principle: We may sometimes have to violate the principle about not acting in ways that increase the power of more powerful over less powerful stakeholders (Principle #4 below, under "Ethical Principles") because those with whom we work often are among the more powerful members of our client systems. But such violations may be ethically justifiable, particularly when they enable us to show those more powerful people how they can accomplish their goals by supporting their subordinates' empowerment, which means a simultaneous increase in both their power *and* that of their subordinates—but it is power *with* rather than power *over*. The justification for violating the principle in the short run would be that it would keep open the opportunity for us to exert our influence in the longer run, whereas not violating the principle could lose us that opportunity. As noted above, however, such justification must be reasonable to rational people and not just self-serving rationalization.

Ethical Principles

1. Serve the good of the whole.

      This encompasses the affirmative, aspirational dimension of our ethics. It is helpful to note the relationships among the moral rules (variations of "do no harm"), the moral ideals (variations of "prevent or lessen harm"), and the first ethical principle ("serve the good of the whole"). The moral rules *require* us not to cause harm, and that applies to everyone. The moral ideals *encourage* us to prevent or lessen harm regardless of who causes it, but, in contrast to the moral rules, we cannot realistically be expected to do that with regard to everyone. And, finally, the affirmative prescription to "serve the good of the whole" *encourages* us to act in ways that serve our values since they are primary elements in our definition of what is good and desirable. Note that because of our systems perspective we see the whole as being more than the sum of its parts and thus we look to a composite value that is more inclusive than the greatest good of the greatest number. Note also that serving good does not *require* action (or nonaction), as do moral rules, and that the degree of encouragement is less than for the more fundamental moral ideals since minimizing harm (evil) tends to have higher priority than serving good. Preventing harm may justify causing harm, as with a surgical operation, but serving good does not normally justify causing harm. And, although serving good may justify failing to prevent harm, the justification must be clear. (See also the discussion of the whole-win attitude [Value 3] for explanation of what we mean by "good of the whole.")

----

2.   **Do unto others as we would have them do unto us.**

In acknowledging the usefulness of this principle — known by many as the Golden Rule, a principle shared in one form or another by most of the world's major religions — we also need to recognize that it has limited generality. Just as judges and police may be obliged to act toward others as they would not have others act toward them, the duties of OD-HSD consultants may require them to act toward others in ways in which they would not want others to act toward them as persons. For example, the OD-HSD role can require confrontation that is painful for others and that we might not want to deal with in our own lives, even though it is the right thing to do professionally.

----

3.   **Always treat people as ends, never only as means; respect their "being" and never use them only for their ability to "do"; treat them as persons and never as objects.**

This principle suggests an area in which OD-HSD professionals may be vulnerable. It is easy for us to slip into treating people as means to organizational ends and ignore the importance of their personal life purposes, thus treating them only as means. It is also easy for us to focus on people's positions — such as "CEO," "division manager," "engineer," "accountant," "clerk," or "employee" — and lose our sensitivity to the persons who occupy those positions.

----

4. Act so we do not increase power by the most powerful stakeholders *over* the less powerful.

We recognize that certain conditions may allow ethical justification for violating this principle. For example, as noted earlier in discussing justification for ethical violations, in order to achieve greater equity in power distribution in the longer run, it may be appropriate for us to facilitate a short-run increase in the power of more powerful stakeholders. Generally, however, when we are asked by managers to do things that will increase their power over their subordinates, we encourage them to support the empowerment of their subordinates, thus making more power available both to them as managers and to their subordinates — but it is power *with,* rather than power *over.*

Note: The principles outlined above tend to be more universally applicable than the ethical guidelines outlined in Chapter Five. However, many of the guidelines are also general, and their specificity is not apparent without the detail of their subpoints. The guidelines help make the ethical principles and the moral rules and ideals more concretely applicable to the conditions of our profession.

An Annotated Statement: Ethical Guidelines for Practice

▮▯▮

We commit ourselves to acting in accordance with the following guidelines.

I. **Responsibility to Ourselves**
   A. **Act with integrity; be authentic and true to ourselves.**

   _____

   To some extent, this element in our ethical position is related to a concern expressed during the early development of this Statement — namely, that in becoming a profession we risk losing our personal identity. Most of us seem to believe that such loss of self is not necessary and that, in fact, our personal authenticity is at the heart of our role. Furthermore, we believe that, by acting in accordance with this guideline, our professional identity can even enhance our sense of self.

   Another aspect of being true to ourselves is being true to those we identify as family (including husbands, wives, children, parents, brothers, and sisters). Rather than subordinating ourselves or our family lives to our professional lives, we seek to coordinate and align all of these interests as fully as we can. We recognize that sometimes subordination of one or more is necessary, but we seek to coordinate rather than subordinate. (See Guideline I-C about seeking to resolve conflicts in a whole-win way.)

B. Strive continually for self-knowledge and personal growth.

By this we mean being aware that:

- "What is in us" (our perceptions of ourselves in our world) and "what is outside us" (the realities that exist apart from our perceptions) are not the same.
- Our values, beliefs, and aspirations both limit and empower us.
- Our values, beliefs, and aspirations are primary determinants of our perceptions, our behavior, and our personal and professional effectiveness.

C. Recognize our personal needs and desires and, when they conflict with other responsibilities, seek whole-win resolutions.

Consistent with the definition given in the discussion of Value 3-b, a whole-win approach to resolving conflict means caring about others *as well as ourselves* and seeking to achieve results that work for everyone, individually and collectively. This may mean compromise, but our experience indicates that when people in conflict work together against their problems, rather than against each other, they are often able to create solutions that do not require anyone to give up anything he considers important. Thus we believe that resolutions with little or no compromise can often be found *if we believe they are possible.* (See also Guideline III-D.)

D. Assert our own interests in ways that are fair and equitable to us as well as to our clients and their stakeholders.

In doing this, we seek to guide ourselves by professional and social values as well as by narrower economic or commercial values. For example, in pricing the products and services we offer, the market's economic and commercial values may allow us to "charge what the traffic will bear," but our professional values may guide us to charge less. On the other hand, in view of our investment of time and energy in our products and services, fairness and equity to ourselves support charging a "reasonable price." For other examples, see the following guidelines: III–C–3 (about our responsibility to our clients), IV–B–1 (about our responsibility for granting use of our copyrighted materials), and V–C–2 and 3 (about aspects of our social responsibility).

II. Responsibility for Professional Development and Competence
 A. Accept responsibility for the consequences of our actions and make reasonable efforts to ensure that our services are properly used; terminate our services if they are not properly used and do what we can to see that any abuses are corrected.

Each of us accepts responsibility for being our own judge of "proper" use of our services. Among other measures, we include making every effort to ensure that our services are used to serve, rather than obstruct, movements toward peace, justice, freedom and responsibility, and all our other values. (See Belief 5-c about conflicts involving values and ethics.)

B. Develop and maintain our individual competence and establish cooperative relations with other professionals.

Viewed collectively, our profession potentially includes all practitioners who conceive of their field as Human Systems Development — ranging from development of individuals to transnational systems, including organizations and all other subsystems in between. All of us are committed to developing our professional competence within our particular areas of concentration and sufficient competence in other areas so that we can cooperate with other professionals, both within OD-HSD and outside of it, in serving our clients' specific needs in ways that are compatible with serving the global system. As Belief 5-d notes, we recognize that our accomplishments, individually and collectively, are interdependent.

1. Develop the broad range of our own competencies. These include:
    a) Knowledge of theory and practice in
        (1) Applied behavioral science generally
        (2) Leadership, management, administration, organizational behavior,

system behavior, and organization/
system development specifically

(3) Labor union issues, such as collective bargaining, contracting, and
quality of working life (QWL)

(4) Multicultural issues, including issues of color and gender

(5) Crosscultural issues, including issues related to our own ethnocentric tendencies and to differences
and diversity within and between
countries

(6) Values and ethics in general and
how they apply to both the behavior of our client systems and our
own practice

(7) Other fields of knowledge and practice relevant to the area(s) within
OD-HSD on which we individually
concentrate

b) Ability to

(1) Act effectively with individuals;
groups; and large, complex systems

(2) Provide consultation using theory
and methods of the applied behavioral sciences

(3) Cope with the apparent contradiction in applying behavioral science
that arises when our "science" is too
particular or too theoretical to be
applicable or when our real approach is intuitive and not clearly
grounded in science

(4) Articulate theory and direct its application, including creation of
learning experiences for individuals; small and large groups; and
large, complex systems

Those of us who are generalists —
with practices encompassing the entire
range of human systems development,
from personal to transnational systems —
need competency in all the areas mentioned above. Those of us with a more con-
centrated focus need greater competence
in our areas of concentration and only
enough in the other areas to be able to
communicate and cooperate with other
OD-HSD professionals. For example, a
person whose focus is on management consulting needs to know enough to be able
to cooperate with those whose focus is on
team building and vice versa. She also
needs to know something about the likely
effects of her work on the organization as
a whole. See also Guideline I–A about personal authenticity.

2. **Establish collegial and cooperative relations
    with other OD-HSD professionals. These in-
    clude:**
    a) **Using colleagues as consultants to pro-
          vide ourselves with feedback or sugges-
          tions about our own development and to
          minimize the effects of our blind spots**

One systematic approach to doing
this is called "peer review." It involves
meeting with a small group of other professionals every few years (usually every three
to five years) for an extensive review of
one's past and current practice and one's
future aspirations. In particular, it covers
such issues as difficulties encountered, par-

ticularly ethical dilemmas, and plans for one's own development. (See Guideline IV-A-1-c with regard to our reciprocal responsibility to support others in reviews of their practices.)

b) **Creating partnerships with colleagues to enhance our effectiveness in serving clients whose needs are greater than we can serve alone**

Among other things, this includes establishing clear, mutual understanding and agreement about our relationships with one another and with our client(s). Our guidelines for doing this are similar to those for contracting with clients, dealing with conflicts, and avoiding conflicts of interest. (See Guidelines III-C and D and IV-C, respectively.)

C. **Recognize our personal needs and desires and deal with them responsibly in the performance of our professional roles and duties.**

Among other things, this includes avoiding actions or statements that might foster perceptions that our self-interest conflicts with our client's interest, as when strong emotional or romantic attachments might be perceived as affecting our professional judgment. In this example, we emphasize *perceptions* of conflict because, even though conflict may not exist in reality, the perception of conflict can significantly affect our ability to perform as professionals.

D. Practice within the limits of our competence, culture, and experience in providing services and using techniques.

   1. Neither seek nor accept assignments outside our limits without clear understanding by clients when exploration at the edge of our competence is reasonable.

   2. Refer clients to other professionals when appropriate.

   3. Consult with people who are knowledgeable about the unique conditions of clients whose activities involve specific areas in which we are inexperienced or not knowledgeable:

      a) In special functional areas (such as marketing, engineering, or R & D)

      b) In certain industries or institutions (such as mining, aerospace, health care, education, or government)

      c) In multicultural settings (such as when we practice in settings in which there is significant diversity in the race, ethnicity, or gender of the people involved)

E. Practice in cultures different from our own only with consultation from people native to or knowledgeable about those specific cultures.

For professionals whose practice extends (or may extend) to one or more other cultures, some of the guidelines in this Statement of potential relevance include Guidelines II–B–1–a–4 and 5, III–B–1–c and d, V–B, and V–C–5. In this connection, it is important to note that the limits on one's ability to practice in different cultures not only extend to crosscultural settings involving different countries but may also apply to multicultural settings—such as those involving diversity of ethnicity, race, or gender — or to different functional areas and industries (as referred to in Guideline II–D–3 above).

Consultation with someone who knows the culture may be brief if we are confident that our own cultural orientation will not cause undesirable effects for the client system or for the larger system within which it functions. We recognize, however, that our own cultural conditioning may blind us to such effects, and so we undertake sufficient consultation to protect ourselves, our clients, and their stakeholders. This applies particularly when our practice is in other countries than the one(s) within which we were raised. It may also apply to practice across the boundaries of different subcultures within our native country, as when a professional from the Northeastern United States practices in the Deep South or vice versa.

III.   Responsibility to Clients and Significant Others
   A.   Serve the long-term well-being of our client systems and their stakeholders.

Although our contracts often have a short-term focus, we try to keep both the short and long term in mind and encourage our clients to do the same. For example, a client may be responding to pressure to meet short-term profit goals in ways that are likely to incur severe long-term costs. We will be alert to long-term considerations and seek to serve them as well, as long as we can do so within the area of our contract. If we cannot do so with integrity, we will seek to renegotiate the contract or, if that is not possible, explain our reasons and withdraw if we can do so responsibly.

1. Be aware of the beliefs and values relevant
    to serving our clients, including our own, our
    profession's, our culture's, and those of the
    people with whom we work (personal, orga-
    nizational, and cultural).
2. Be prepared to make explicit our beliefs,
    values, and ethics as OD-HSD professionals.
3. Avoid automatic confirmation of predeter-
    mined conclusions about the client's situation
    or what needs to be done by either the client
    or ourselves.
4. Explore the possible implications of any OD-
    HSD intervention for all stakeholders likely
    to be significantly affected; help all stake-
    holders while developing and implementing
    OD-HSD approaches, programs, and the like,
    if they wish help and we are able to give it.

For example, if possible we will (1) work
with labor unions and workers' representatives
as well as managers if the client system is unionized and (2) provide help in minimizing loss
to those stakeholders who suffer loss, as in the
case of down-sizing and cutting back, in order
to serve the greatest good of the whole. (See annotation following Value 3-b in Chapter Four
about whole-win attitudes.)

In our work with organizations, a special issue comes up when those organizations
have labor unions or other worker organizations. Because we see our role as serving our
client systems and their stakeholders, we have
obligations to those unions or worker organizations and their representatives. For example,
an OD-HSD professional would not participate
in an attempt by management to get rid of an

existing union or to keep a union out of a client organization if there is any indication that the people within the organization might want it. In contrast, in an organization without a union, one consequence of the OD-HSD professional's work may be to create conditions under which people would not need a union to serve their interests so that efforts to organize one would not be effective. And, to take this a step further, in an organization with a union, OD work may contribute to making a union unnecessary and lead to the dissolution of an existing one. This can create a paradox—namely, the presence of the union is necessary for creating the conditions under which it seems unnecessary. One possible solution may lie in a shift in the union's role from being more of an adversary to being more of a cooperator, as in the Quality of Working Life (QWL) activities of many unions. Experience suggests that in such cases the adversarial role does not cease when collective bargaining matters are being dealt with, but collective bargaining works more smoothly by virtue of the parties being better able to understand one another's interests. And, when the parties mutually agree on areas in which they will cooperate, their cooperation produces benefits that could not have been accomplished without the union.

---

5. Maintain balance in the timing, pace, and magnitude of planned change so as to support a mutually beneficial relationship between the system and its environment.

B. Conduct any professional activity, program, or relationship in ways that are honest, responsible, and appropriately open.

By *honesty* we mean speaking the truth about what we think and feel, and by openness we mean speaking the whole truth. As professionals, we are committed to honesty and have a strong preference for openness as well. However, most of us qualify our commitment to openness depending on conditions, such as the usefulness of what is being expressed. For example, leveling about something a person or system cannot change may be unnecessarily destructive and harmful, and leveling beyond a system's ability to cope with the information may be destructive. In such situations, being less than fully open may be appropriate.

In addition to being open in our outward expression, we also seek to be open in our inward receptiveness to influence from those affected by our work.

---

1. **Inform people with whom we work about any activity or procedure in which we ask their participation.**

   a) **Inform them about sponsorship, purpose and goals, our role and strategy, costs, anticipated outcomes, limitations, and risks.**

   b) **Inform them in a way that supports their freedom of choice about their participation in activities initiated by us; also acknowledge that it may be appropriate for us to undertake activities initiated by recognized authorities in which participants do not have full freedom of choice.**

For example, it may be appropriate to require managers with low interpersonal competence to participate in activities that will help them develop that competence. If they are unwilling, their freedom could still be respected by allowing them to choose a job that does not require such competence.

c) **Alert them to implications and risks when they are from cultures other than our own or when we are at the edge of our competence.**

This is particularly necessary when we work with people from other cultures who look to us as "experts." We must be particularly careful that they do not attribute to us expertise that is not appropriate for their cultural conditions.

d) **Ask help of the client system in making relevant cultural differences explicit.**

Work with the people of the client system in making relevant cultural differences clear so that by virtue of their participation in identifying such differences they will be alert to the difficulties inherent in them during our work together.

2. **Seek optimum participation by people with whom we work at every step of the process, including managers, labor unions, and workers' representatives.**

For example, when asked by senior level managers to do development work at lower levels of an organization, do so only with participation by managers at intervening levels, if possible.

3. **Encourage and enable people to provide for themselves the services we provide rather than foster continued reliance on us; encourage, foster, and support self-education and self-development by individuals, groups, and all other human systems.**

    In brief, our role obliges us to work ourselves out of a job whenever possible.

4. **Develop, publish, and use assessment techniques that promote the welfare and best interests of clients and participants; guard against the misuse of assessment techniques and results.**

    For example, guarding against misuse means that in consulting on the use of an assessment technique for selecting people for promotion, we need to pay attention to the effects on those *not* selected (and also on the organization as a whole) as well as to the effects on the people selected.

5. **Provide for our own accountability by evaluating and assessing the effects of our work.**
    a)   **Make all reasonable efforts to determine if our activities have accomplished the agreed-upon goals and have not had undesirable consequences; seek to undo any undesirable consequences, and do not at-**

tempt to cover them up; use such experiences as learning opportunities.

b) Actively solicit and respond with an open mind to feedback regarding our work and seek to improve our work accordingly.

This responsibility to our clients is linked to our professional responsibility to share information about the effects of our work so as to enable others to practice more effectively (as Guideline IV–B–2).

---

6. Cease work with a client when it becomes clear that the client is not benefiting or the contract has been completed; do not accept or continue work under a contract if we cannot do so in ways consistent with the values and ethics outlined in this Statement.

Withdrawing from an engagement can be especially difficult when it threatens our economic security. For this reason, it is important that we work together as a profession in providing ways and means of supporting individual professionals who act on their ethical obligation to withdraw.

C. Establish mutual agreement on a fair contract covering services and remuneration.

1. Ensure mutual understanding and agreement about the services to be performed; do not shift from that agreement without both a clearly defined professional rationale for

making the shift and the informed consent of the clients and participants; withdraw from the agreement if circumstances beyond our control prevent proper fulfillment.

2. Ensure mutual understanding and agreement by putting the contract in writing to the extent feasible, yet recognize that:

   a) The spirit of professional responsibility encompasses more than the letter of the contract.

   b) Some contracts are necessarily incomplete because complete information is not available at the outset.

   c) Putting the contract in writing may be neither necessary nor desirable.

Opinions differ regarding the desirability of always putting the contract in writing. All seem to agree that clear, mutual understanding and agreement are essential, but many do not consider writing a necessary means to that end, although it may help sometimes. Their experience is that emphasizing the written contract when mutual exploration is the essence of the psychological agreement may do more harm than good. In such cases, they consider a verbal agreement preferable and believe that having a written contract, which would have to be changed as the work progressed, would unnecessarily formalize and rigidify the relationship.

---

3. Safeguard the best interests of the client, the profession, and the public by making sure that financial arrangements are fair and in

keeping with appropriate statutes, regulations, and professional standards.

D.   Deal with conflicts constructively and minimize conflicts of interest.

1.   Fully inform the client of our opinions about serving similar or competing organizations; be clear with ourselves, our clients, and other concerned stakeholders about our loyalties and responsibilities when conflicts of interest arise; keep parties informed of these conflicts; cease work with the client if the conflicts cannot be adequately resolved.

When our primary employment is with an organization other than our client, such as when we are employed by a university or a consulting firm, we are alert to conflicts between the interests of our employing organization and our client. We will avoid such conflicts if possible or, if they arise, deal with them in accordance with the guidelines in this Statement. For example:

- University-based consultants may feel conflict about publishing data generated while serving clients
- Consultants employed by private firms must recognize potential conflicts involving *all* their firm's clients and not just their own clients

---

2.   Seek to act impartially when involved in conflicts among parties in the client system; help them resolve their conflicts themselves, without taking sides; if it becomes necessary to change our role from that of impartial con-

sultant, do so explicitly; cease work with the client if necessary.

3. Identify and respond to any major differences in professionally relevant values or ethics between ourselves and our clients; be prepared to cease work, with explanation of our reasons, if necessary.

4. Accept differences in the expectations and interests of different stakeholders and realize that those differences cannot always be reconciled; take a whole-win approach to the resolution of differences whenever possible so that the greatest good of the whole is served, but allow for exceptions based on more fundamental principles.

5. Work cooperatively with other internal and external consultants serving the same client systems and resolve conflicts in terms of the balanced best interests of the client system and all its stakeholders; make appropriate arrangements with other internal and external consultants about how to share responsibilities.

6. Seek consultation and feedback from neutral third parties in cases of conflict involving ourselves, our clients, other consultants, or any of the systems' various stakeholders.

We recognize that perfect neutrality may not be possible, but we will seek third parties who approximate it.

E. Define and protect confidentiality in our client relationships.

1. Make limits of confidentiality clear to clients and participants.

In doing this, we recognize our responsibility for anticipating and avoiding morally hazardous situations. If we fail to tell people about the limits of our commitment to confidentiality, we can find ourselves being told things that put us in serious conflict between protecting our client's interests and respecting our commitment to confidentiality. Unlike priests and personal counselors, we seldom, if ever, can appropriately commit to unlimited confidentiality.

2. **Reveal information accepted in confidence only to appropriate or agreed-upon recipients or authorities.**

Implicit within "appropriate recipients" are professional colleagues when discussion with them is confidential and compatible with the interests of our clients and informants. In case of such discussion, we accept responsibility for ensuring the commitment to confidentiality by those with whom we share.

3. **Use information obtained during professional work in writings, lectures, or other public forums only with prior consent or when disguised so that it is impossible from our presentations alone to identify the individuals or systems with whom we have worked.**
4. **Make adequate provisions for maintaining confidentiality in the storage and disposal of records; make provisions for responsibly preserving records in the event of our retirement or disability.**
F. **Make public statements of all kinds accurately, including promotion and advertising, and give service as advertised.**

1. Base public statements providing professional opinions or information on scientifically acceptable findings and techniques as much as possible, with full recognition of the limits and uncertainties of such evidence.

We will work actively with prospective clients in helping them make informed choices, rather than being limited only by the commercial maxim "caveat emptor" (let the buyer beware), which puts all the responsibility on the buyer.

---

2. Seek to help people make informed choices when they refer to statements we make as part of promotion or advertising.
3. Deliver services as advertised and do not shift without a clear professional rationale and the informed consent of the participants or clients.

IV. Responsibility to the OD-HSD Profession
   A. Contribute to the continuing professional development of other practitioners and of the profession as a whole.
   1. Support the development of other professionals by various means, including:
       a) Mentoring with less experienced professionals
       b) Consulting with other colleagues
       c) Participating in reviews of others' practices

Among other things, this includes participating in such activities as the peer reviews described under Guideline II–B–2–a.

2. Contribute to the body of professional knowledge and skill, including:

a) Sharing ideas, methods, and findings about the effects of our work

b) Keeping our use of copyright and trade secrets to an appropriate minimum

We recognize that developing some materials requires a substantial investment of time, money, and effort and therefore appropriately deserves legal protection of the rights associated with those materials (or other properties). However, we seek to make our materials as readily available to one another as we can, consistent with ensuring a fair return to ourselves for our efforts. (See Guidelines I–C and D about our responsibility to ourselves.)

B. Promote the sharing of professional knowledge and skill.

1. Grant use of our copyrighted material as freely as possible, subject to a minimum of conditions, including a reasonable price based on professional as well as commercial values.

2. Give credit for the ideas and products of others.

3. Respect the rights of others in the materials they have created.

C. Work with other OD-HSD professionals in ways that exemplify what the OD-HSD profession stands for.

1. Establish mutual understanding and agreement about our relationships, including pur-

poses and goals, roles and responsibilities, fees, and income distribution.

In reaching such agreements, we will respect all laws. The spirit of this guideline is intended to be consistent with the "good of the whole," including ourselves, our profession, our clients, and the larger society of which we all are members.

------

2. Avoid conflicts of interest when possible and resolve conflicts that do arise constructively (following guidelines similar to Guideline III–D).

D. Work actively for ethical practice by individuals and organizations engaged in OD-HSD activities and, in case of questionable practice, use appropriate channels for dealing with it.
1. Discuss directly and constructively when feasible.
2. Use other means when necessary, including:
   a) Joint consultation and feedback (with another professional as a third party)
   b) Enforcement procedures of existing professional organizations
   c) Public confrontation

In working for ethical practice within our profession, we accept primary responsibility for ourselves. When others seek to give us feedback (ideally in accordance with the above guidelines), our aim will be to understand their feedback (regardless of whether we agree with it or how we feel about it) and to respond nondefensively. After reaching such understanding, we will seek to work through any differences constructively in a win-win (whole-win) way.

Before we give feedback to others, we will first seek to understand how they perceive their situation. Then, if appropriate, we will give our feedback as constructively as we can in accordance with generally accepted guidelines for giving feedback — such as describing behavior without judging, being specific, not labeling, reporting our reactions, and suggesting alternatives (without advising). (For further discussion of guidelines for leveling, see Morton, 1966). We expect others to act with sensitivity to the consequences of their choices, and we respect their ability to accept responsibility for such consequences. Among other consequences to which we expect one another to be sensitive are those that affect other professionals individually and the profession collectively.

Ideally, our ethical problems with one another can be resolved at the level of direct discussion, as referred to in Guideline D-1 above. However, we recognize the possibility that other means, such as those described in Guideline D-2, may need to be used. (For further discussion, see Frontier Issues in Chapter Twelve about the profession's responsibility for monitoring the ethical practice of its members.)

E. Act in ways that bring credit to the OD-HSD profession and with due regard for colleagues in other professions.

1. Act with sensitivity to the effects our behavior may have on the ability of colleagues to perform as professionals, individually and collectively.

2. Act with due regard for the needs, special competencies, and obligations of colleagues in other professions.

3. Respect the prerogatives and obligations of the institutions or organizations with which these colleagues are associated.

V. Social Responsibility
  A. Accept responsibility for and act with sensitiv-
      ity to the fact that our recommendations and ac-
      tions may alter the lives and well-being of peo-
      ple within our client systems and within the
      larger systems of which they are subsystems.
  B. Act with awareness of our own cultural filters and
      with sensitivity to international and multicultural
      differences and their implications.
      1. Respect the cultural orientations of the in-
          dividuals, organizations, communities, coun-
          tries, and other human systems within which
          we work, including their customs, beliefs,
          values, morals, and ethics.
      2. Recognize and constructively confront the
          counterproductive aspects of those cultures
          whenever feasible, but be alert to the effects
          our own cultural orientation may have on
          our judgments.
  C. Promote justice and serve the well-being of all
      life on earth.
      1. Act assertively with our clients to promote
          justice and well-being, including:
          a) Constructively confronting discrimina-
              tion whenever possible
          b) Promoting affirmative action in dealing
              with the effects of past discrimination

For us, *affirmative action is positive, constructive action in support of those members of society who
need such support to make up for the effects of their having been disadvantaged or discriminated against by society.* For example, Head Start programs in the
United States for disadvantaged preschool children are a widely recognized, highly successful
attempt at affirmative action. We recognize that
some attempts have had negative effects, including reverse discrimination and preferences

whose effects have subtly disempowered blacks and perpetuated the implicit assumption of white superiority and black inferiority. However, by acknowledging such imperfections, we do not question the fundamental desirability of affirmative action. In fact, we consider it especially important and see among its primary goals (1) the educational and economic development of disadvantaged people (regardless of race) and (2) the eradication from societies of racial, ethnic, gender, or other forms of discrimination.

---

c) **Encouraging fairness in the distribution of the fruits of the system's productivity**

We see our roles as primarily helping people become conscious of the issues of fairness and justice and facilitating *their* dealing with them. In doing this we seek to be clear about what *we* consider fair and just, but our role is primarily facilitating our clients' determination of what fairness and justice mean for them. In cases in which our ethical standards are seriously violated, we may feel obliged to withdraw.

In this aspect of our work, we recognize that differences in people's access to information, knowledge, power, and ability to deal with injustices are conditions that affect what we do and how we do it. We are prepared to act affirmatively in order to support the empowerment of those who do not have what they need to obtain justice for themselves. At the same time, we are aware that our action may not be seen as serving the client's interests and, as a result, might jeopardize our ability to

serve the client in other ways. We recognize the inevitability of this dilemma and
seek to resolve it as ethically as we can.

---

2. Contribute knowledge, skill, and other resources in support of organizations, programs, and activities that seek to improve
human welfare.
3. Accept some clients who do not have sufficient resources to pay our full fees and allow them to pay reduced fees or nothing
when possible.
4. Engage in self-generated or cooperative endeavors to develop means for helping across
cultures.
5. Support the creation and maintenance of cultures that value freedom, responsibility, integrity, self-control, mutual respect, love,
trust, openness, authenticity in relationships,
empowerment, participation, and respect for
fundamental human rights.
D. Withhold service from clients whose purpose(s)
we consider immoral, yet recognize that such service may serve a greater good in the longer run
and therefore be acceptable.

For example, some OD-HSD professionals
might consider producing and promoting the use of
cigarettes or the manufacture of certain offensive
weapons immoral purposes, but they could still work
for clients who do these things as long as they thought
it would serve the good of the whole. However, we
are aware that by allowing this kind of behavior we
risk the error of rationalizing activities that we consider truly unethical, and we seek to avoid such error. (See the section above on "Justification of Moral-
Ethical Violations.")

E. Act consistently with the ethics of the global scientific community of which our OD-HSD community is a part.

Among other things, this involves committing ourselves to the "Hippocratic Oath for Scientists, Engineers and Technologists" developed by the Institute for Social Inventions:

I vow to practise my profession with conscience and dignity;
I will strive to apply my skills only with the utmost respect for the well-being of humanity, the earth and all its species;
I will not permit considerations of nationality, politics, prejudice or material advancement to intervene between my work and this duty to present and future generations;
I make this oath solemnly, freely, and upon my honour ("In the News," 1988, p. 1).

Finally, we recognize that accepting this Statement as a guide for our behavior involves holding ourselves to standards that may be more exacting than the laws of any countries in which we practice, the ethics of any professional associations to which we belong, or the expectations of any of our clients.

Bibliographic References

Adler, M. *We Hold These Truths: Understanding the Ideas and Ideals of the Constitution.* New York: Macmillan, 1987.
Frankel, M. S. *Values and Ethics in Organization and Human Systems Development: An Annotated Bibliography.* Washington, D.C.: American Association for the Advancement of Science, 1987.

Frizell, N., and Gellermann, W. "Integrating the Business and Human Dimensions of Management and Organization Development." In S. Mailick, S. Hoberman, and S. Wall (eds.), *The Practice of Management*. New York: Praeger, 1988.

Gellermann, W. "Values and Ethical Issues for Human Systems Development Practitioners." In R. Tannenbaum, N. Margulies, F. Massarik, and Associates, *Human Systems Development: New Perspectives on People and Organizations*. San Francisco: Jossey-Bass, 1985.

Gert, B. *Morality: A New Justification of the Moral Rules*. New York: Oxford University Press, 1989.

"In the News." *Professional Ethics Report*, 1988, *1* (3), 1.

Kiefer, C., and Stroh, P. "A New Paradigm for Organization Development." *Training and Development Journal*, 1983, *37* (4), 26–35.

Morton, R. "'Straight from the Shoulder'—Leveling with Others on the Job." *Personnel*, Nov.-Dec. 1966, pp. 65–70.

Simmons, J., and Mares, W. *Working Together*. New York: Knopf, 1983.

Tannenbaum, R., and Davis, S. "Values, Man, and Organizations." In W. Eddy and others (eds.), *Behavioral Science and the Manager's Role*. Washington, D.C.: NTL Institute for Applied Behavioral Science, 1969.

PART THREE

██████████████████████████████████

Cases and Commentaries

███

An important component of the project on OD-HSD values and ethics was the development of case scenarios illustrating critical value conflicts and ethical issues in the profession, followed by discussion and analysis of the scenarios either at panels convened at OD-HSD professional meetings or by invited commentators. The cases were prepared by project staff in consultation with the project's advisory board, using materials drawn from published literature and from critical incidents and statements of concern describing ethical issues in OD-HSD submitted by practitioners, researchers, and clients in response to a public solicitation.

Decisions to develop particular cases were based on the following criteria: (1) the seriousness of the problem raised, (2) the frequency with which it occurs in OD-HSD research and practice, (3) the likely impact of the outcome on organizational members and the organizational unit, and (4) the clarity with which the value conflicts and ethical dimensions of the case could be articulated. Each case concluded with one or a series of questions intended to focus attention on key issues.

Once a final version of the case was prepared, it was distributed to participants in an OD-HSD project panel approximately four to six weeks prior to the scheduled meeting. Two of the cases were not discussed at panels but were sent to selected commentators for their assessment. Panelists as well as invited commentators were chosen to represent a diversity of perspectives. They included OD-HSD researchers, consultants and teachers, behavioral scientists outside the OD-HSD field, and philosophers doing work in applied and professional ethics. All case respondents were asked to make explicit any assumptions they made about the facts of the case; be clear about what values, principles, or ethical reasoning helped shape their perspectives on the issues; discuss issues raised by the cases but not referred to in the questions that followed the scenario; and recommend ways of dealing with the ethical issues, referring where appropriate to "A Statement of Values and Ethics for Professionals in Organization and Human Systems Development," April 1985 (see Appendix C for this version of the Statement). At the panel, the case commentators were each given ten to twenty minutes to present their responses, after which those attending the session were invited to offer their reactions to the cases (which were distributed before the session began) and to engage in discussion with the panelists.

Subsequent to the panels, the respondents were asked to submit revised responses for review by the project's staff and advisory board. Authors were then sent reviewers' comments and asked to take them into account when preparing their manuscript for publication in this book.

The Cases

Twelve cases were developed as part of the project. The six appearing in Chapters Six through Eleven were selected by the coauthors for analysis because they reflect a broad range of value conflicts and ethical issues in OD-HSD. Where appropriate, the analyses by the authors draw on the material found in earlier chapters. When citing the Statement, the authors refer to the Annotated Statement in Chapters Four and Five. The analyses also include excerpts from the essays prepared by the invited commentators, who, when they mention the Statement, refer to the April 1985 version (see Appendix C), the one available at the time they wrote. While each case analysis has a primary author, each of the book's coauthors critiqued the work of the others.

Six cases also appear in Appendix D, along with selected remarks by the invited commentators. They are presented without detailed analyses so that others can use their analytical skills to identify the underlying values of the cases and to develop appropriate responses to the accompanying ethical issues. They offer the opportunity to stimulate discussion of values and ethics in OD-HSD in the classroom, at professional meetings, training seminars, or in similar settings, and we encourage such use by our readers.

Applying the Case Experience

Cases can function as a heuristic device by which professionals can evaluate their own values and those of their profession. We encourage readers to use the following cases and commentaries as well as those in Appendix D as resources in assessing your own values and developing or clarifying your own ethical position. Whether your role is as researcher, practitioner, teacher, or student, the cases are intended to provide a vicarious experience for the purpose of increasing your professional consciousness and enabling you to test the clarity of your personal values and ethical reasoning. Taken together, the cases constitute a collection of ethical concerns prevalent among OD-HSD professionals, the discussion of which can contribute to developing a widely shared set of ethical guidelines for the profession as a whole.

CHAPTER SIX

Negotiating
an OD Agreement:
The Ethics of
Contracting

ıııııııııııııııııııııııııııııııııııı

Roy Green and Joan Rosenbloom, two external OD consultants
with considerable experience in working with school administrators, have been contacted by Mark Shultz, the superintendent of a Supplementary Educational Services (SES) district,
to discuss a possible OD engagement. At their first meeting,
Shultz provides the two consultants with the following background information. SES districts carry out a variety of functions that local school systems often cannot perform effectively.
These functions include conducting surveys and research to establish program needs, teaching special education classes, providing instructional films, and coordinating educational televi-
sion in local schools.

Superintendent Shultz's SES district was established in
the early 1960s to serve a rural population extending over a large
geographical area with a relatively small number of school-age
children. The first superintendent of the district served continu-
ously until 1983 and had a staff of eight administrators, most
of whom were hired in the early days of the district. Seven of
them are still on the job. The SES district kept its largely rural
character until the early 1970s, when a newly completed major

highway network began to bring people from the nearby metro-
politan area into the region. By 1980 the SES district included
a substantial number of school districts that were distinctly
suburban in character. Shultz, who had previously served as
superintendent of a member school district, took office in 1984,
one year after the former superintendent retired. At that time
two new program administrators were added to the staff.

Shultz believes that in order to meet the changing needs
of the district his administrative staff will require substantial in-
service work, including clear delineation of goals for the district and the organization of staff activities. Shultz also expects
the staff's work in the future to require a more cooperative approach to decision making. He therefore wants Green and
Rosenbloom to work with the staff on goals clarification and
team decision making. The two consultants agree to do so in
principle, but first they want to interview all staff members and
then meet with Shultz and the staff together for a joint decision
about whether to proceed.

Green and Rosenbloom interview and observe the staff
over a three-week period. On the basis of their interviews and
observations, they both conclude that the SES district has a number of problems. Before contacting the superintendent again,
however, the consultants discuss between themselves two related
issues. First, how should they present their data and conclusions at the meeting with Shultz and the staff? Second, what
should they suggest as a proposal if a consensus emerges from
the meeting that the SES district should enter into an agreement for OD activity with Green and Rosenbloom? Both issues raise serious problems.

Green and Rosenbloom agree that, on the basis of their
interviews and observations, the staff members seem quite uncertain about their collective goals. Both consultants observe that
each staff member tends to concentrate narrowly on tasks within
his or her domain of responsibility and shows little concern about
how these tasks fit into a broader context. On the one hand,
it appears to Green and Rosenbloom that the staff could benefit
from focusing on goals clarification and team decision making.
On the other hand, the two consultants realize that they came

away from the interviews and observations with a sense of unease about the staff's willingness to work on such activities.

One of the newly appointed staff members, Jerry Gordon, discussed at length the relationship between Superintendent Shultz and the SES district Board of Education, a subject that Shultz had not even raised in his meeting with Green and Rosenbloom. According to Gordon, upon assuming office, Shultz took a number of steps designed to encourage greater board participation in the affairs of the district. However, these steps had resulted, said Gordon, in a situation in which on several occasions the board had sought to control program management. Gordon reported that at one point the board had sought to oust him but Shultz had refused to accede to its wishes.

Gordon's openness in talking to Green and Rosenbloom differed sharply from the way other staff members responded when they were interviewed. Looking back on those interviews, the consultants agree that, for the most part, it had been difficult to draw out staff members to talk about various aspects of their work and especially about their attitudes toward Superintendent Shultz. Although neither Green nor Rosenbloom can point to anything beyond subjective impressions, each considers it distinctly possible that relations between the staff and Shultz are beset by serious problems. The consultants, however, have no sense about the specific nature of these problems — for example, whether they relate to Shultz's leadership style, to conflicting agendas between him and the staff, to assorted festering grievances, or to fundamental differences over educational philosophy.

Green and Rosenbloom thus face difficulties about the appropriate stance to take in negotiating an agreement with the SES district. They concur with Superintendent Shultz's assessment that the staff needs help on goals clarification and team decision making. To serve that purpose Green and Rosenbloom could propose a series of workshops that they have conducted on many previous occasions. Their agreement with the SES district could be quite clear-cut, with little room for misunderstanding on either side. Green and Rosenbloom both feel, however, that the workshops might simply treat superficial symptoms of deeper problems for which far more extensive work would be appropriate.

The direct course, in view of the way the two consultants feel, would be to raise the deeper problems at their meeting with Shultz and the staff, and then propose more extensive work for dealing with them. On the basis of the impressions they have gathered over the past three weeks, however, it seems to Green and Rosenbloom that neither Shultz nor the staff are even ready to acknowledge the problems, let alone work to resolve them. Under these circumstances, they agree, the direct course would almost certainly fail. In their view, Shultz or the staff probably will not go along with the proposal for extensive work and, even if they both do, it will not be the kind of deep-seated support that meets a proposal that responds to a client's felt needs.

Green and Rosenbloom briefly consider not raising the deeper problems at all and proposing only the workshops on goals clarification and team decision making in the hope that, once under way, they can help Shultz and the staff move toward dealing with the deeper problems. They reject this approach, however, as essentially dishonest. It seems to them that OD professionals should not proceed with a hidden agenda. Green and Rosenbloom also consider suggesting a contract that calls for the series of workshops, but with a proviso that would allow for the possibility of a more extensive effort. They find, however, that they cannot phrase the desired proviso in a way that avoids the difficulties they would face if they directly proposed a major program. Green and Rosenbloom then discuss simply declining to enter into a contract with the SES district in view of the apparent attitude of Shultz and the staff. They are reluctant, however, to abandon the possibility of providing assistance: The SES district clearly needs help, and it seems to them that as OD professionals they should examine the situation long and hard before deciding that their efforts would not make a valuable difference.

The night before their meeting with Shultz and the staff, the two consultants still have not decided what to do.

Questions to Consider

1. Discuss the approaches to their negotiation problems that Green and Rosenbloom considered. Do you agree or disagree? Carefully consider the ethical and value judgments that entered into Green and Rosenbloom's reasoning.

2. In light of your views on values and ethics in the OD profession, discuss any other approaches to Green and Rosenbloom's problems that seem plausible to you.

3. Green and Rosenbloom considered it essentially dishonest to propose workshops on goals clarification and team decision making in the hope that once under way the two consultants could help Shultz and the staff move toward dealing with deeper problems. By contrast, no psychotherapist would undertake treatment by laying out a full diagnosis of a personality disorder and expect the client to contract to its treatment. Are there special features of OD consulting work that require a kind of full candor at the outset that does not seem mandatory for psychotherapists or other helping professionals?

4. Does the draft "Statement of Values and Ethics . . ." provide guidance with regard to problems that arise in negotiating an agreement? If so, which provisions are especially pertinent? Would you suggest any changes, additions, or deletions to make the Statement more helpful?

Comments by Robert F. Ladenson

As noted in Chapter Two, OD-HSD practitioners need to be aware that the contracting process is critical for the avoidance of morally hazardous situations in a consulting relationship. Negotiation of a consulting contract itself, however, may give rise to ethical issues. The four commentaries that follow analyze such issues in connection with the preceding case. The authors of the commentaries, however, focus on different ethical aspects of the case as most important. In this respect, the commentaries illustrate another point made in Chapter Two: namely, that the practice of OD-HSD consulting has an inherently interpretive character.

According to Herman Gadon, a psychologist and external consultant, the two consultants in the preceding case, Green
and Rosenbloom, face a problem of ethical choice with no solution. In Gadon's opinion, however, the two consultants created
the problem for themselves. As experienced OD-HSD consultants, Green and Rosenbloom should have been able, says
Gadon, to determine "pretty quickly" the hierarchical, rigid environment of the SES district and the absence within it of a "culture of openness and sharing." Gadon notes that in such an environment, "the opportunity to disclose information to a trusted
confidant will inevitably involve negative feelings toward those
in authority." In Gadon's opinion, Green and Rosenbloom made
"a basic and fundamental error" by not preparing Superintendent Shultz for this normal, expected aspect of the consulting
process. As a result of this error, says Gadon, the two consultants put themselves in a position in which "they will violate
an ethical obligation, and contractual one, no matter what they
do." According to Gadon, the "ethical obligation was to have
prepared Shultz for the potential consequences of the process
they proposed so that he could make an intelligent decision about
whether he would accept the risks involved." The contractual
obligation, on Gadon's account, "is to the staff to share with them
the results of the interviews and the decision to go ahead."

Gadon thus views the ethical problems that confront
Green and Rosenbloom as resulting from an error of judgment
for which they should "acknowledge the blame" — in short, from
a failure of competence. Such a viewpoint raises important systemic issues for OD-HSD consulting that reach well beyond
Gadon's specific critique of Green and Rosenbloom's performance. Gadon describes the circumstances in which OD-HSD
consultants create serious ethical problems for themselves through
failures of competence as "not an uncommon phenomenon." This
judgment, in turn, raises important questions concerning how
the community of OD-HSD practitioners acting collectively, as
well as individually, can take effective steps to reduce the level
of substandard consulting performance. An array of complex
issues present themselves in this regard concerning the pros and
cons of measures such as licensure, required continuing profes-

sional education, and the creation of ethics review boards within OD-HSD professional organizations. Gadon's perspective thus implicitly raises significant policy issues that the OD-HSD profession has not yet addressed in depth.

Like Gadon, Barbara Bunker, a psychologist at the State University of New York, Buffalo, finds Green and Rosenbloom's performance deficient in two critical respects. She believes that they should have done more preliminary work with Shultz and that they moved too rapidly into data collection. In regard to working more with Shultz, Bunker asks, "What kind of process has Shultz in mind? How would he react if . . . ?" Bunker maintains that "an exploratory, educative consultation with Shultz is in order before anyone else is involved." This last point of Bunker's relates to her views concerning Green and Rosenbloom's decision to interview the school district staff members. Bunker notes that collecting data in a system is an intervention. In her words, "[i]t raises expectations (or hackles) and begins a process." For these reasons, Bunker believes that consultants should not collect data in an organization without having a contract specifying to whom and when it will be fed back.

Bernard Mohr, an external consultant, analyzes the ethical issues that face Green and Rosenbloom from a markedly different perspective from that of either Gadon or Bunker. Although Mohr suggests that aspects of the two consultants' approach to negotiating a contract with the SES district may have contributed, in part, to creating their problems, he does not view Green and Rosenbloom's difficult situation as primarily one of their own making. Instead, Mohr regards it as a circumstance in which "one set of values squarely bumps up against another set of values." Mohr does not specifically delineate the conflicting values in this case, but the ones he probably would point to are apparent. The Statement strongly affirms the values of "authenticity and openness in human relationships" as central to OD-HSD consulting. With equal strength, the Statement affirms the values of "effectiveness, efficiency, and alignment." In the context of Green and Rosenbloom's situation, these two sets of values, which both exert a strong pull on most OD-HSD consultants, appear to pull in opposing directions.

Coming to terms with the above conflict necessarily involves broad issues related to the meaning of professional integrity for an OD-HSD consultant. Suppose that Green and Rosenbloom chose to share their impressions in a less than fully candid way with Superintendent Shultz and the SES district staff. Should one classify this choice as an ethically legitimate, though perhaps tactically debatable, decision about the usefulness in the circumstances of expressing certain aspects of their opinions? By contrast, should one view the choices in a far more negative way as the decision to engage in a form of deceitful conduct? As noted in Chapter Two, answers to these kinds of questions depend on how one conceives of the professional role in OD-HSD consulting—that is, it depends on how one interprets the basic values that underlie OD-HSD and shape its meaning. In his commentary, Mohr sketches out elements of such an interpretation in the form of general guidelines a consultant might use when confronted with a conflict between the values of openness and efficiency.

Michael Davis, a philosopher at the Illinois Institute of Technology, approaches the case from a perspective different from those of the other commentators. Davis views the contracting process in OD-HSD as the principal means of fixing what he terms a "focus of loyalty" for the consultant. In this regard, Davis notes an important aspect of OD-HSD practice by way of contrast with another profession—law. Davis points out that "[l]awyers generally know where their loyalty lies because their professional role is defined as serving the client within the bounds of law." By contrast, Davis observes, the Statement emphasizes what one might call a stakeholder orientation—that is, an outlook stressing the importance of balancing the legitimate interests and needs of all the individuals and groups, outside as well as inside the organization, affected by a consultant's activities. Given a stakeholder orientation, says Davis, the contract or, more exactly, the process of negotiation leading to the contract, assumes enormous importance for focusing the loyalty of a consultant so as to define for her a coherent professional role in the circumstances.

According to Davis, openness on the part of a consultant

during the process of contract negotiation facilitates the complex task of focusing loyalty while, at the same time, maintaining a stakeholder orientation. Applying this point to the case, Davis concludes that Green and Rosenbloom "must report their discoveries to Shultz and staff, making clear what seems to stand in the way of proceeding according to Shultz's proposal and what options remain." Whether or not one agrees with Davis's specific conclusions about this case, his commentary identifies an ethically critical aspect of the contracting process: A consulting contract must balance the legitimate interests and needs of all stakeholders in a way that, *at the same time,* defines a clear focus of loyalty for the consultant. Davis's commentary brings out some of the difficulties that may arise in negotiating a contract that satisfies both of these conditions.

Comments by Herman Gadon

Green and Rosenbloom are considering a number of options at the end of the case, "Negotiating an OD Agreement: Ethics and Values Issues." However, they have yet to ask themselves the right question: "How did we get into this situation?" They should not be there. Negotiation of an OD agreement is made with the person in the system who invites you in. In this instance it is Shultz, the person who first contacted the consultants. Initially he is the client. Identifying the client is the first critical step in negotiating an agreement. The client may change as a result of the negotiation. An OD agreement is always subject to renegotiation as a result of new informational diagnoses, but always with the client with whom the contract is in effect at the time. Green and Rosenbloom never seem to come to grips with this elementary requirement. It is a basic and fundamental error.

Clients have a right to be informed of the process that OD consultants will use and the likely consequences of using it. Then the client can make an intelligent decision about whether to go forward with it or negotiate a different arrangement. Green and Rosenbloom want to collect data from the staff, and they want to make the staff participants in the decision-making pro-

cess about how to respond to the data. To so involve the staff
would shift the client status to include the staff. Shultz had to
realize the implications of such a shift. Furthermore, the shift
ought not to be made without the staff, as a client, being informed of the process and its likely consequences and agreeing
to be included.

The implication of involving the staff as clients was no
mystery. In any system with a hierarchy that has not developed
a culture of openness and sharing, the opportunity to disclose
information to a trusted confidant will invariably involve negative feelings toward those in authority. Ventilation of withheld
feelings can be expected as part of the process. Those authorities have to be prepared to listen to such sentiments, to the extent that they exist, before progress can be made in problem
identification and problem solving.

Green and Rosenbloom, with considerable experience in
working with school administrators, should have been able to
determine pretty quickly how hierarchical the SES district was.
Therefore, they should easily have been able to walk Shultz
through a scenario that involved the staff in the process they
proposed.

Instead, what happened? It is apparent that Shultz was
not briefed about the consequences of the process. Instead, he
was asked to agree to interviews, which he did. He must have
believed that the interviews would provide only background
data, because Green and Rosenbloom agreed "in principle" to
"work with the staff on goals clarification and goal setting." This
apparently meant the introduction of workshops. The staff immediately became unsuspecting and involuntary participants.
There is nothing in the case to suggest that they understood the
implications of participating, and, as a result, agreed to do so.
It is therefore hardly surprising to find, after the interviews were
completed, that Green and Rosenbloom believe that "neither
Shultz nor the staff are even ready to acknowledge the problems, let alone work on them." Why should they? They never
contracted with the consultants to take this responsibility.

Furthermore, it is clear that the idea of goal setting and
values clarification workshops, which the consultants implicitly

promised, was a solution proposed prior to knowing the problem. Nor is it surprising to find that the interview data produced many problems — some serious — in addition to the need for work on goal setting and values clarification. These problems could have been anticipated by the OD consultants, and the consultants had an obligation to inform Shultz, before he agreed to go any farther, that they might arise. Then, if he had been willing, forewarned, to take the next steps, the staff, as an added client, needed to hear about the potential problems also. Green and Rosenbloom are reflecting "about the appropriate stance to take in negotiating an agreement with the S.E.S. District" after they have finished the interviews. If they had asked themselves that question on their first meeting with Shultz, I doubt that they would be facing the difficult choices presented in the case.

What should Green and Rosenbloom do now? First, they must acknowledge to themselves that their own errors of judgment have put them in a position in which no matter what they do they will violate an ethical obligation, as well as a contractual one, to either Shultz or the staff. The ethical obligation was to have prepared Shultz for the potential consequences of the process they proposed to follow so he could make an intelligent decision as to whether he would accept the risks involved. The contractual obligation is to the staff, to share with them the results of the interviews and to involve them in the decision to go ahead.

Given the dilemma, Green and Rosenbloom must first explain to Shultz what predicament they have created for him, for themselves, and for the staff. This would include presenting scenarios of likely consequences if the information were shared in a joint session with the staff and the likely consequences if it were not shared. These scenarios must take into consideration the likelihood that the staff will feel that the contract with them was broken, creating disappointment, lowered morale as a result of violated expectations, and lost respect for both Shultz and the consultants if Shultz then decides that he does not want to publicly expose himself or the staff to the interview data and its implications. Green and Rosenbloom cannot force him to do so. On this sad note, the relationship between Green and

Rosenbloom, Shultz, and the staff would terminate. Having been properly briefed, if Shultz made the decision to continue with the open meeting, he would do so with a different understanding and contract from that with which he had started. Under the new arrangements he would unmistakingly and explicitly share decision making with the staff.

In reviewing the options that Green and Rosenbloom considered, one cannot help but respect their dedication to an ethically guided decision. Their error resulted from their inability to see themselves as the cause of their dilemma. This is not an uncommon phenomenon. Without an awareness of the part one has played in creating a problem in a client system, one cannot acknowledge it. Without acknowledgment of this hard reality, it is impossible to make an adequate diagnosis of the problem. Without an adequate diagnosis, no solution will be appropriate. Even after consultants recognize that they have created a serious problem in an organization, some still may not be able to admit responsibility. Yet the first and foremost ethical obligation of an OD consultant is to accept responsibility and be held accountable for it.

Comments by Barbara Benedict Bunker

Negotiating an OD agreement is seen by most OD consultants as a crucial and mutually self-revelatory process in which much is learned about you by the client and about the client by you. The process of contracting should be ongoing throughout the life of a contract. Especially at the beginning, it may need to occur in smaller rather than in larger increments.

In this case, for example, I believe that Green and Rosenbloom moved much too quickly to data collection (interviews). They were apparently focusing on the question, Is what the client wants right for the organization? This is certainly an appropriate question. I will return to it shortly. However, they skipped an issue that has priority in this case.

The question that I think deserves attention is, Is the client going to like what he says he wants when the consultation process begins to deliver it? More specifically, Shultz's description of a "more cooperative approach to decision making" can be construed in the consensus model or as consultative (the CEO gets input but retains power to decide). Green and Rosenbloom know that the majority of persons on Shultz's staff have been with the district for a long time. They are apt to be conservative about change. What kind of process has Shultz in mind? How would he react if . . . ? In other words, I think an exploratory, educative consultation with Shultz about process and outcomes is in order before anyone else becomes involved.

I have experienced situations in which the chief executive of a company hired consultants out of a "fix them" attitude toward the employees. The consultant was expected to implement solutions that would treat the chief executive preferentially. It is easier to work first with the CEO alone than with him in a group later on. The consultants need to be clear with Shultz about how much responsibility they are willing to assume. There are a number of types of contracts concerning responsibility. Sometimes it may be appropriate to become an extra pair of hands and "do it for the client." My hunch here is that exploring these options will open up important issues in the client-consultant relationship, giving both parties more freedom of choice—including the freedom to decide not to proceed.

On a more individual level, there are different interpersonal styles and preferences in creating new relationships. They are also part of the contracting process. For example, in meeting someone who is a candidate for a position, one style is to act as if the outcome will be positive and the person will be hired. Often this approach is used because there is a desire to create and get a feel for what a working relationship would be like. However, this style can also create collusive pressures on both parties not to raise issues that might prove difficult and lead to the decision not to hire the person. There are different forms of colluding with the agenda setter. It is not possible in this case to know what the interpersonal dynamics are, but how they are handled becomes ethically important in creating a good contract.

In terms of these early contracting issues, I do not believe that consultants should go into an organization and collect any data without having a contract that states to whom and when it will be fed back. Collecting data in a system is an intervention. It raises expectations (or hackles) and begins a new process. In this case, it could be seen as a mirror of how the superintendent expects to work with his staff. Thus, it is an important step in the process of the system, not a discrete diagnostic consultant expedition.

The other set of issues that need addressing are those concerning the previously mentioned question, Is what the client wants right (and/or possible) in this system, and who decides that? Certainly these consultants need more information to prepare a good work process. It is unclear in this case which staff members were told about the consultants' role and why they were being interviewed (which could account for some of the withholding reactions while being interviewed). It does not sound as if staff were asked directly about their views regarding the need for more goal clarity and team decision making or which goals for joint work might be useful.

I think the decision to abandon workshops as the initial project is a correct and ethical move on Green and Rosenbloom's part. To proceed with Shultz's idea in the face of strong data about the lack of felt need for change appears inappropriately risky and may leave the system worse off. Green and Rosenbloom use the word "dishonest," but a more appropriate word is "risky." The situation becomes dishonest when the consultant does not apprise the client of the risk. Part of the risk is that if people go through a pro forma exercise that deals only with the surface of problems, skepticism about the usefulness of such processes may increase, thus making it harder to generate motivation for other change efforts.

A theme running through these reactions and the questionable analogy sometimes drawn between consultation and psychotherapy involves how much of the consultants' initial thoughts and hunches get shared with clients. First, there is the question of how much of the expert role the consultant chooses to take. The espoused theory in OD is that OD consultants are process experts but do not give expert advice. In actual practice, consultants with an experience base on which they have reflected often draw on that experience for their clients' use. In addition, some OD technology—for example, sociotechnical analysis and total quality control approaches—involves processes that put us in teaching roles. The implicit idea in some psychotherapy of the need for therapists to withhold (because they already "know") so that the client can experience the full process of self-discovery seems spurious to me. There is a regrettable tendency on the part of many consultants not to express enough of what we are experiencing early in a consultation. The fear is that of getting bounced out of the situation by being too forthright. The testimony of risk takers often is that the experience of high risk—that is, "saying it like it is"—has greater payoff than the more conservative strategy.

Comments by Bernard J. Mohr

I experience many ethics and values issues as two-horned dilemmas, neither side of which is a particularly comfortable place to be sitting. However, in the exploration of such less-than-comfortable positions, the greatest amount of personal learning and self-development and, I might add, a certain amount of anguish, takes place. So while I occasionally envy those of my colleagues who have been able to reach a point in their personal and professional lives where issues of ethics and values fall clearly and cleanly into place and actions are taken unequivocally, for myself, the resolution of these issues, as difficult a process as it is for me, leads me to articulate more clearly my philosophy of practice as a professional in this field. My only two wishes are that the process of resolving ethical and value issues would be less energy-consuming and that, with the benefit of hindsight—that is, more data—I will more and more frequently say yes, that was the best decision for *all* concerned.

With this as a preface, the reader might easily conclude that he or she is reading the thoughts of someone who is wishy-washy at best or, worse, simply incapable of translating his beliefs and values into daily practice. In my own defense, I would counter that I do indeed hold strong values related to organization consultation work and I consider myself an ethical person. So why do I have difficulty determining what action to take in the face of ethics/values issues? For me, the answer has to do not so much with the problem of moving from a philosophical stance into practice per se (although that, too, can be problematic) but more with determining what to do when one set of values squarely bumps up against another set of values, when one ethical position seems to contradict another ethical position. This is the situation, I believe, that faces our two external OD consultants, Green and Rosenbloom. Herein I attempt to identify the values and ethics that appear to be "bumping up against each other."

Green and Rosenbloom are considering three alternative courses of action, and for each we are told of a presenting dilemma. Let us review each alternative, its presenting dilemma, and the values and ethics context within which it lies.

Alternative Course of Action 1. Propose a series of workshops aimed at responding to the client's presenting problem with the hope that the other issues will surface and an opportunity to work on them will be created.

The presenting dilemma here is that such an intervention might well treat the symptoms rather than the deeper problems, unless, of course, the workshops facilitated a deeper understanding and energy level to work on those problems — in which case the consultants might be guilty of working with a hidden agenda. On the other hand, if the workshops do not address the deeper issues, are our consultants violating a prohibition against shorter-term, quick-fix solutions that do not lead to longer-term system health? Furthermore, if they move ahead in any direction without informing the client of their concerns, are they operating in a collaborative and open mode as espoused in our field of consultation? Truly our consultants are caught in a situation in which values and ethics seem to be bumping up against each other. In this, as in each of the proposed alternatives, there is no easy solution. However, it may be useful to determine what underlying assumptions or hidden dynamics are contributing to this dilemma.

As experienced consultants, and with access to wider system information than is possessed by any individual member of this system, Green and Rosenbloom need an alternative perspective on their problem of "now that we have this 'new' information about the system, what do we do with it?" In this not unfamiliar situation, my own response is to ask myself a few basic questions as a way of trying to generate a new perspective and thereby move off the horns of this dilemma. Specifically, I would ask myself, What data do I really have? What personal desires to be seen as "incisive" and as "the expert diagnostician" are driving me, and how do they conflict with my data? The question here revolves around my ability to separate my own needs (and I would be foolish to deny their existence) from the needs of the client system. My belief that this may be an issue in this case rests on my own experience that unclear group goals and ineffective team functioning are hardly ever caused only by simple information lacunae or minor skill deficiencies. More frequently these behaviors are symptomatic of deeper issues of the sort that have been sensed by Green and Rosenbloom. If this can be accepted as an operating assumption, then I would ask myself, Why am I surprised to get this "new" data, and why is it that my contracting process appears to have left out provision for the possible reporting of such data? This would raise the further question, Have our two consultants been working with an agenda hidden from the client and themselves from the start by not confronting these issues at the stage of initial contracting? These questions then lead me back to asking again, Where do the data stop and where do my own needs and projections take over?

Since, like our consultants, I would want to respond to the expressed need of the client, Shultz, and avoid working with a hidden agenda, I would strive to let my actions be guided by the principle of "helpful, informed choice" (Argyris, 1970). It is my belief that OD consultants are obligated to provide their client systems with information about available options, possible costs and benefits associated with these options, resources available to the system in applying these options, and, very importantly, a process for the client system to analyze and act on this information. Control of the depth of an intervention should always be a matter of informed choice, and it should always

be a decision made in partnership between the client and consultant. In this case, the consultants are talking as if they have
full responsibility for these decisions. While this may be the case
in a therapeutic situation, an OD consultation presupposes a
more collaborative stance (based on the presumption of basic
organizational health). Therefore, I think Green and Rosenbloom are responsible for creating a forum, a process, that allows informed choice to take place between both parties in such
a way that neither party feels backed into a corner.

Alternative Course of Action 2. Raise the possibility of
deeper problems with Shultz and his staff and propose a more
extensive intervention to deal with the situation.

The presenting dilemma here is that if they take an open,
"share all the data" approach, they may violate an implicit contract they have with Shultz to work on only the issues of goal
clarity and team decision making. (Of course, we do not specifically know whether their contract with Shultz allows for the
investigation and feeding back of data relating to issues between
Shultz and his team, but we can make the inference that it does
not since Green and Rosenbloom are having so much trouble
with this alternative.)

Additionally, if they take this alternative, are they pushing the client system further than it is ready to proceed at this
point, since the majority of Shultz's subordinates, and Shultz
himself, have expressed no particular desire to deal with these
deeper-level issues? Naturally, if they avoid sharing their data,
they find themselves back in the predicament posed by alternative 1.

Again, the development of an alternative perspective as
a function of some self-directed questions may lead Green and
Rosenbloom out of their quandary—or it may not. The questions I would ask myself in this situation, in addition to those
asked in the previous alternative, include: Who is the client and
does it make a difference what actions I take? If I see the client
as being the total system or "the relationships" between system
members (a la Warner Burke), do I have a different point of
view than if I see only Shultz as the client? And if I see only

Shultz as the client, what are my obligations to him versus my obligations to the rest of the system? Is there a need to collect more data to confirm or disconfirm the impressionistic data held by Green and Rosenbloom, and, if so, what is the appropriate contract for the collection and feeding back of such data?

My own bias in this case is to fall back once more on the admonition by Argyris (1970), that the role of the OD consultant is to provide valid data to the system, within a process that supports free choice, and in such a way that system energy is mobilized to deal constructively with the data. If this is an acceptable position, my responsibility becomes one of expertly designing a process and mechanism that meet not just one but all three of Argyris's criteria. This is not an easy task to accomplish, but it will at least provide a framework for further action.

Alternative Course of Action 3. Propose a series of workshops with a provision that would allow for the possibility of a more extensive effort.

This alternative presents many of the same dilemmas as those attached to the previous options. Additionally, it raises the possibility that such an intervention, although intended to respond to the client's presenting problem, may indeed be doomed from the outset if the underlying dynamics (in which the presenting problems are situated) are not dealt with from the beginning. On the other hand, this may be a case of a system needing to experience some small successes with the consulting team before it is ready to undertake a larger, more significant commitment.

In addition to addressing the previously mentioned questions, I would want to ask myself to try and resolve this dilemma: Can a process be designed in which "helpful informed choice" takes place at the same time some constructive work is done to move the situation forward even if the client decides to go no further? And who is to judge "real worth" and who is to make this decision — myself, the client, or some other combination?

A Final Nonalternative. Each of the foregoing alternatives has some viability, whereas the alternative of simply disengaging from the client system is not, in my opinion, a viable alternative.

It is not a viable alternative because an intervention has already begun (the data collection); and even though this was done under the guise of an exploratory review, the reality is that the system has already been changed by even this limited external contact. To disengage completely at this point would, I believe, violate our values regarding collaborative decision making, our values regarding our obligation to feed back data we collect, and our value of being helpful.

It would also be an action whose premise is the naive notion that a client system is not "ready" unless the level of energy to move ahead is shared equally throughout the system and there is widespread agreement on the problems from the outset. In fact, I believe that the role of the consultant is sometimes to work on these very issues of "unreadiness" by helping the system make an informed and free choice about its future.

The field of OD has many good values, which in turn suggest what is or is not ethical behavior. Unfortunately, when values "go bump in the night," thorny issues of what constitutes ethical practice are raised. I have tried to show how some of the value dilemmas might be approached (I hesitate to use the word "resolved" because that makes it sound too simple) and correspondingly how some of the ethical issues would be impacted. I consider the discourse around such case studies as these essential to a heightened sense of clarity about ethics and values issues, and I welcome comments on what is written here.

Comments by Michael Davis

Perhaps the best way to think about this case is as a problem of loyalty. To whom do Green and Rosenbloom owe primary loyalty? To themselves? To their profession? To Shultz? To the SES district? To the district's administrative staff? Problems of loyalty arise for most professionals now and then. But, as I understand "A Statement of Values and Ethics . . . " (See Appendix C), such problems are built into the OD profession to an unusual degree. Resolving such problems must be a normal part of OD work. The problem Green and Rosenbloom face in this case may be more complex than those most OD professionals must solve, but it is not otherwise different. Seeing how normal the problem is, I think, is almost the last stage in seeing how to resolve it. But the place to begin is with another profession. Consider the law.

Lawyers generally know where their loyalty lies because their professional role is defined as serving the client within the bounds of the law. If a lawyer cannot in good conscience do what a particular client wants done, she may refuse the case (provided she is not drafted by a court or bar association). But once she accepts the case, her profession requires her to ignore the welfare of nonclients, including her own, insofar as their welfare conflicts with her client's. If the law requires her to do something for a nonclient — say, give due notice — she will do that not because it benefits the nonclient but because the law requires it. Part of being a lawyer is focusing one's loyalty on the client subject to the requirements of law. Though lawyers do sometimes find their loyalty divided — for example, when the corporation they represent is sued by the stockholders who legally constitute the corporation — divided loyalty is generally avoided when at all possible. For a lawyer, acting with one's loyalty divided is both rare and regrettable.

For OD professionals, however, that seems not to be true. The theme of "A Statement of Values and Ethics . . . " is that an OD professional has a more or less equal duty to "the client, the organization, its members, other stakeholders, the OD-HSD professional, the OD-HSD profession, society and . . . life on earth" (see Preamble, Appendix C). That will be true no matter who calls in the professional, pays his salary, or sets the agenda. Part of being an OD professional is the state of divided loyalty. "Client" does not indicate a special focus of loyalty — only the source of employment.

For most professionals, such unfocused loyalty would be disastrous, at least in terms of how their roles are traditionally conceived. Imagine what lawyering would be like if lawyers had to show the same concern for all "stakeholders" in a case. OD avoids such disasters by making the contract of employment — or,

more exactly, the process of negotiation leading to agreement
on the contract—central to its work. The contract itself is the
means of focusing loyalty, of creating a role the OD professional
can fill. If a contract cannot be written that protects the welfare
of all stakeholders, an OD professional must decline employment.

Declining employment is difficult for most professionals.
No doubt some of the difficulty is a combination of instinctive
kindness and greed. Few of us can easily turn away someone
asking help. And most professionals are, like others who earn
a living by what they do, naturally uncomfortable turning away
someone with money in hand. But much of the difficulty is, I
am sure, simply that professionals generally like doing what they
do. Applying one's skills even when one can do no good is a
constant temptation.

Though declining employment is difficult for most professionals, it is more difficult for an OD professional. The Statement requires the OD professional to be candid with all participants in the consulting process. So, for example, even if
Rosenbloom and Green decide not to negotiate an agreement,
they will have to tell Shultz and his staff much of what they would
tell them if they were going to undertake negotiation. They cannot, as a lawyer might, avoid the confrontation by declining
employment for some such polite reason as "other commitments."
They will have to tell all participants in the consulting process
that what is needed is a major program, not the minor one Shultz
wants. And they will have to explain why.

I must admit to doubting the wisdom of such a requirement when an OD professional wishes to decline a consultation. It makes declining too hard and so increases the temptation to accept and hope that things will work out. If Green and
Rosenbloom must let the cat out of the bag no matter what,
why, they may wonder, disappoint Shultz and his staff? Surely,
they can do something for the district.

Though I admit to doubts about requiring so much candor, I must also admit sympathy for the ideal of human relations that motivates the authors of the Statement to impose that
requirement. A profession that makes its goal "a widely shared

learning and discovery process" naturally tries to avoid conduct that might lead to misunderstandings. If Rosenbloom and Green declined without explanation, one inference would be that they had given the SES district a clean bill of health. Candor will prevent such misunderstandings.

Green and Rosenbloom seem to be pretty clear-headed about what they can and cannot do. They conclude that they can do something if they are less than candid but, apparently, only if they are less than candid. They reject that approach because "OD professionals should not proceed with a hidden agenda." This seems to me to be exactly the right reason to reject that approach, although I think it would not necessarily be a particularly good reason for a lawyer to refuse a client or a psychotherapist to refuse a patient. OD professionals should not proceed with a hidden agenda because such an agenda would be inconsistent with the process of negotiation by which they come to have a focus of loyalty. Absent a contract, to whom would they owe loyalty should Shultz's interests turn out to be in conflict with his staff's, or the staff's with the SES district? These are, of course, much the same questions with which I began. But now, I think, it is plain that, absent a contract covering the matter, these are questions for which an OD professional — as OD professional — can have no answer. For an OD professional, entering into a contract with a hidden agenda would be like setting sail on the open sea without a compass — that is, something not to be done except in the most pressing of circumstances, of which this case is not an example.

So, Green and Rosenbloom must report their discoveries to Shultz and staff, making clear what seems to stand in the way of proceeding according to Shultz's proposal and what options remain. They should do so in the hope that Shultz and staff will make the right decision once they have all relevant information before them, but with the understanding that Shultz and staff are not likely to thank them for their candor or give them an opportunity to show what they can do.

CHAPTER SEVEN

⬛⬛⬛⬛⬛⬛⬛⬛⬛⬛⬛⬛⬛⬛⬛⬛⬛⬛⬛⬛⬛⬛⬛⬛⬛⬛

Confronting
a Clash
of Cultures

⬛⬛⬛⬛⬛⬛⬛⬛⬛⬛⬛⬛⬛⬛⬛⬛⬛

Alan Greer is genuinely excited about his visit to Cornea, a Pacific Island country. He is part of a six-member team organized by the United Nations at the invitation of the government of Cornea to assist the country in its efforts to move toward an industrialized economy. The team includes an economist, two civil engineers, a city planner, and two management consultants, one of whom is Greer, a specialist in Organization Development.

The UN team is met at the airport by Bennie Perot, a European-trained social scientist of French descent who is deputy director of the island's economic development program. He is the government official responsible for coordinating the UN team's collaborative effort with government and local business. Cornea has little industry and, according to UN criteria, is undeveloped. However, two years ago, rich nickel and copper deposits were discovered and, recognizing the potentially high payoff, government officials began preparations for developing these resources. The government's use of the UN team marks the first involvement of outsiders in its economic development.

The first meeting of government and business officials and

the UN team focuses primarily on determining the agenda for
the eight-week period that the team will be in the country. A
prime concern for Greer and his management colleague, Klaus
Hammel, is to gain insight into the local business culture and
the organization of work in various businesses. Toward that end,
they set forth several necessary procedures, including interviewing a select sample of management and nonmanagement employees, individually and in groups, and surveying a larger sample of all employees in key businesses. Perot says that his office
will make the necessary arrangements.

To cover as much ground as possible, Hammel and Greer
agree to divide the work load evenly, carry out their work independently, and review their activities at the end of each day.
Accompanied by a member of Cornea's economic planning
group, Greer enters the country's only glass-manufacturing plant
and meets with top executives to discuss plans for interviewing
and surveying employees. Greer finds the executives very receptive — perhaps too receptive, he thinks. They are eager for Greer
to begin his work. But their attitude changes when Greer assures them that information gathered from workers during his
investigation will be held in strict confidence. The business's top
executive, Aklee Mota, observes that such a procedure is contrary to their expectations and unacceptable. Mota explains that
in Cornea employees are expected to respect the authority of
their superiors without dissent. Not only do the executives expect Greer to reveal any information he uncovers that may suggest "disloyalty," but all interviews are to be conducted in the
presence of one of the company's top executives.

Greer is stunned by Mota's declaration. How can he expect to elicit candid responses from employees in the presence
of their superiors? More important, the notion of acting as a
company agent committed to revealing evidence of a dissident
point of view is, in Greer's mind, inconsistent with his responsibility to respect the autonomy of individuals and represent himself honestly to those from whom he seeks information. After
the meeting ends, Greer informs his government aide that he
will have to speak with Perot before he can proceed.

Greer conveys to Perot his concerns about proceeding with

his survey under the conditions stipulated by Mota. In a cordial manner, Perot explains that Greer's "Western ways" are simply not appropriate in his country. He notes further that for employees to be interviewed by Greer in the absence of their superiors would be a sign of disrespect for the latter and that workers would experience great discomfort if placed in such a position. In Cornea, lines of authority are well established and embraced by all citizens. Perot assures Greer that there will be no difficulty in obtaining candid interview responses.

Greer returns to the plant, still somewhat uneasy about his situation. He is resigned to continue but will be alert for any developments that might hamper the conduct of his investigation or his ability to act responsibly.

At the outset of his first interview, which involves a middle-level manager at the plant, Greer explains the purpose of his visit and stresses the importance of the interview. He also notes that the manager's participation is to be voluntary and that he is free to refuse to answer any of the questions. At this point, the company executive sitting in on the session interrupts to assert that all employees will willingly participate and respond to all questions. For Greer, who has always been sensitive to the possibility of subtle coercion in organizations and feels strongly about the importance of informed consent and free choice, this is another startling development. Greer presses the matter further, explaining to both the executive and the manager the importance of allowing the respondent free choice in deciding if and how to respond. But Greer soon realizes that he is making little headway. In fact, in the manager's case it becomes obvious that the notion that he has a right to make an independent decision is quite disconcerting to him.

That evening, Greer telephones Perot and expresses his doubts about continuing with his assignment. While he wants to contribute to Cornea's economic development, he will have great difficulty reconciling his professional responsibilities and personal values with the political and social conditions of the island. Perot emphasizes to Greer that, as a skilled social scientist, he is important to Cornea's future. The best way for Greer to help the country is to recommend ways to improve the island's economy, thereby enhancing the quality of life for all its citizens. "Surely," Perot asks rhetorically, "you would not abandon us in our time of urgent need?"

But Greer has deep concerns about whether he can proceed in a way that is ethically responsible. And, perhaps even more important, he is skeptical about how widely any economic gains will be distributed among the population in this politically autocratic country. Moreover, he recognizes that by continuing his work he will be perpetuating a system of authority that, in his mind, contributes to the exploitation of people. Admittedly, those in subordinate positions appear comfortable with their lot. Indeed, Greer cannot detect any visible tension. But does this make it right? How, Greer wonders, can Perot, who was educated in Europe and has excellent credentials as a social scientist, accept things as they are?

Questions to Consider

1. If you were in Greer's position, would you continue with the project?

2. What action, if any, would you take to ensure that the people you interview are not exploited as a result of your work?

3. In the face of the cultural differences you may experience, how can you or any OD consultant or researcher balance your own values and ethics against those of host countries that are so different from your own? What guidelines might be applicable in such situations?

4. What other ethical or value issues are suggested to you by this case and what guidelines would you propose for dealing with them?

Comments by William Gellermann

At the end of this case, Greer sees his situation as allowing him little or no choice. His unnecessarily limited perception of his ethical problem can be analyzed in terms of the five-step model presented in Chapter Three.

Step 1a: Ethical Violations? Justified? He wants to avoid violating his ethics about "perpetuating a system of authority that . . . contributed to the exploitation of people" and apparently sees no ethical justification for doing so (inferred from his wondering how Perot could accept things as they were).

Step 1b: Values Conflict? He values contributing to Cornea's economic development, which he thinks he might be able to do; but that desire is in conflict with the value he places on the fair sharing of economic gains among the population of the country, which he assumes would be unlikely to happen.

The limits of his approach seem to prevent him from seeing any need for further thought about his situation (of the kind outlined in Step 2). Therefore, he seems on the verge of a decision to withdraw from the project (Step 3).

The five-step model can also be used to show how Greer might have more clearly defined his problem and then developed a more thoughtful solution to it. As you can see, the approach quickly takes him away from a view of withdrawal as his only alternative. (Note that the model's use is not strictly linear, since the flow of thinking moves among the steps as one thought suggests another within the general five-step framework.)

Step 1a: Ethical Violations? Justified? This situation has potential for violating the ethical principle, "Act so I do not increase power by the most powerful stakeholders over the less powerful," but such violation, which may be necessary in the short run, could still be ethically justified because of the longer-run opportunity for enabling the more powerful stakeholders to give up power *over* people in exchange for a substantially greater amount of power *with* people. (See the "Ethical Principles" section of the Statement in Chapter Four.) Further analysis is needed (Step 2), but, initially, the problem can be seen as more than just violation of an important ethical principle that would require withdrawal.

The Cornean situation provides an opportunity, in the longer run, for OD-HSD consultation to "encourage fairness in the fruits of the system's productivity" (Statement Guideline V–C–1–c). In the short run, it seems justifiable to violate that ethic on the grounds that such encouragement would be likely to jeopardize the whole project and thus do more harm than good. Such justification, however, would be contingent on commitment to act on that ethic as soon as doing so becomes reasonable.

Step 1b: Values Conflict? In this situation, among the primary values are Cornea's economic development, fair apportionment of the fruits of that development, and freedom and self-control for the Cornean people. It may take time to make noticeable progress on the latter two and, as a result, value conflicts are likely, relative to perpetuating both an unfair distribution of income and a system that appears to inhibit freedom and self-control. As with Step 1a, this analysis indicates the need for the fuller analysis of Step 2.

Step 2a: Vision, Facts, and Assumptions. The purpose and vision of the UN project team are not clear. Nor are they clear for Greer's part of the project (although we are told that the prime concern he shares with Hammel is "to gain insight into the local business culture and the organization of work in various businesses"). It seems unlikely, however, that Greer's vision for his part of the project can be aligned with the quest for a good life that is general to the purpose and vision of OD-HSD generally — namely, "to promote a widely shared learning and discovery process dedicated to the vision of people living meaningful, productive, good lives in ways that simultaneously serve them, their organizations, their societies, and the world" (Preamble to the Statement).

In working with Cornean government and business leaders, Greer would need to be alert to his ethnocentric tendencies, particularly in defining what is meant by "people living meaningful, productive, good lives" in ways that are guided by Cornean definitions and not only by his own.

In accordance with Statement Guideline II–E, Greer should seek consultation from at least one person who is "native to or knowledgeable about" the Cornean culture—probably Perot, at least for now—in order to help him differentiate facts about Cornean culture from his assumptions about it. Among other things, he needs to understand with much greater clarity the nature of the relationship between managers and employees in Cornean business so that he can "act with sensitivity to international differences, his own cultural filters, and their implications" (Guideline V–B). A primary "fact" in his present situation is that he and Hammel have eight weeks to "gain insight into the local business culture and the organization of work in various businesses" and, within that limited contract, he should be able to make a positive difference consistent with his and the profession's ethics and values.

Step 2b: Review Ethical Problem. On review, Greer could more clearly see his problem: namely, it deals almost exclusively with his ability to make a positive difference on the immediate results of the UN team's work during the next eight weeks. Those results will probably be in the form of written and oral reports with recommendations and perhaps some personal relationships on which subsequent work can be built. Viewed in that more focused way, rather than in terms of whether he can ethically participate in a project to "perpetuate an authoritarian system" and contribute to the "exploitation of people," his problem virtually disappears. He can almost certainly participate without facing serious ethical problems.

Step 2c: Choose "Best" Option. The "best" option at this point seems to be for Greer to continue with the project, doing the best he can to conduct interviews in ways that give him as much information as he can gather under the circumstances and that are consistent with protecting the confidentiality of the interviewees, if confidentiality can be promised. He can try to arrange confidential interviews with clear understanding by everyone of any limits on that confidentiality, but, if senior managers are not agreeable, he can continue the interviews with awareness of the possible limited value of the information.

The goal of "sharing the fruits of the system's productivity" can be seen as a longer-term objective; it is probably unrealistic for Greer to expect to do much toward that end in the short run.

Step 2c: Another Thought About "Best" Option. As noted under Step 2a, Greer can develop a conscious relationship with Perot in which Perot would serve as consultant in helping Greer understand the Cornean culture in general and the business culture in particular.

Step 2a: Another Thought About Facts and Assumptions. Does Perot know other people within Cornea who share the OD-HSD perspective, such as OD-HSD professionals or people in allied social or behavioral science fields? Or does he know people in other professions, educational institutions, government, religion, business, and so on, who might have insight into what is going on in the country generally and in business particularly?

Step 2c: Another "Best" Option Idea. Another element within Greer's "best" option might be to network with people in Cornea who seek change similar to the kind he thinks is likely to be good for Cornea. They could help him keep his Western biases from distorting his perceptions. They could help clarify a Cornean purpose and vision for the change process and recommendations for the report that are appropriate for Cornea. And, even more important, if such people exist, they might well play a primary role in the change strategy by forming an internal network of Corneans actively involved in the change process.

Step 2a: Another Thought About a "Fact." To what extent do such people, if they exist, already constitute a network?

Step 2c: Another "Best" Option Idea. Greer's short-term objective is a report by the UN team to Perot and the Cornean government (and implicitly to those business executives whose cooperation would be required). Based on what he now knows, that report would probably include an indication of the general direction for the change effort and recommendations for initial activities that would give the Corneans (and the UN team) the kind of additional experience and information they need to plan further action. If possible, he should interview enough senior people on this trip so that he can be reasonably sure that the general direction and recommendations will be acceptable to them.

Step 2a: Another "Fact"? Are there any business organizations within Cornea that *do* function in ways close to those that Greer and Hammel think are most likely to be effective? If so, that should help them in communicating with the Cornean leaders, since the report can refer to people and organizations with which they are familiar.

Step 2c: Revised "Best" Option. At this point, the best option seems to include several measures: continue the project with recognition that its immediate goal is a report with recommendations for further action; use the interviews to get as much information as reasonably possible (on a confidential basis, if possible but, if not, with everyone involved aware of the fact); recognize that more equitable sharing of system productivity is unrealistic in the short run, but not in the longer run; use Perot as a consultant on Cornean culture; network with Corneans who share Greer's vision and values, asking them for help in interpreting the findings and devising the report; aim at strengthening that network as a source of positive change within Cornea; and interview key government and business leaders to ensure acceptability of the recommendations (and, if possible, to give those leaders a sense of ownership in the recommendations).

Step 2d: Analyze Consequences. The short-term consequences are likely to involve strengthening the ability of people already within Cornea to bring about positive change. At the least, any changes resulting from the consultation process could strengthen Perot's position; and, if others with shared values exist, their positions could be strengthened, too. Government leaders and business executives would also be strengthened. In the short run, the changes will have limited effect on middle managers and workers, although a pilot project might have positive effects for a few. Because the system is apparently highly authoritarian and rigid, it will take time to develop mutual understanding and trust between the external consultants and those within Cornea who are responsible for the change process.

Short-term increases in power of senior managers might occur in the short run but would be justified based on longer-term possibilities already described. A withdrawal by Greer from the project could lead to resistance by Cornean leaders to assistance from outsiders in the future, thus causing more harm than good.

Step 2e: Any Ethics Violations? There are no violations besides those already discussed. This five-step approach has identified ways of avoiding such potential violations — namely, confidentiality — or ethically justifying violation — namely, making powerful people even more powerful over the less powerful in the short run in exchange for the opportunity to replace power *over* with power *with* for everyone in the longer run.

Step 2f: Improve? One improvement comes to mind. If possible, a draft of the report should be reviewed with Perot and a few of the other internal people — if Greer is able to find any — as a means of making sure they accept it, with the intention of giving them ownership in it, and as a test of its acceptability to the other recipients. These Corneans might also suggest revisions that would make the report both better and more effective.

Step 3: Decision, Step 4: Action. Act as planned above, but with readiness to change the plan as the situation evolves.

Step 5: Reflection. In the course of reflecting on his action, its consequences, and the thinking that preceded it, Greer's understanding of his situation will continue to evolve. For example, he will better understand the nature of Cornean culture and business culture in particular, whether there are individuals or organizations within Cornea who are aligned with OD-HSD's vision and values, and the extent to which a network of support already exists within Cornea. That understanding will also clarify the extent to which the abstract OD-HSD vision is appropriate for the people of Cornea. As the situation evolves, Greer will be able to act with greater understanding, and thus the risk of ethical violation will decrease. Of particular importance in this respect are the Statement's Guidelines V–B–1 and V–B–2:

1. Respect the cultural orientations of the individuals, organizations, communities, countries, and other human systems within which we work, including their customs, beliefs, values, morals, and ethics.
2. Recognize and constructively confront the counterproductive aspects of those cultures whenever feasible, but with alertness to the effects our own cultural orientations may have on our judgments.

In thinking about the above demonstration of the five-step model's use, it is important to recognize that the model is not intended only as a list of questions to be asked. Neither is the Statement intended simply as a list of do's and don't's. Rather, in combination, they provide a frame of reference for meaningful thought relative to evolving situations in the course of professionals' lives whenever their ethical sensitivity tells them something may be "wrong."

Primary determinants of an OD-HSD professional's ethical sensitivity are his or her own purpose and vision and the values implicit in them. Clarity about them would have helped Greer deal with his ethical problems more readily, because they would have given him a context for thinking about his problems in a more meaningful way. If purpose and vision are well conceived, they provide perspective for the choices we make in our quest for a good life.

If Greer had had a more fully developed ethical sensitivity, it would have alerted him much earlier to potential ethical problems. In fact, at the very beginning of his involvement in

Cornea, he violated an ethic that could have helped him avoid the morally hazardous situation in which he later found himself. That ethic commits OD-HSD professionals to "practice in cultures different from our own only with consultation from people native to or knowledgeable about those specific cultures" (Guideline II–E). In addition, he violated the ethic that says to "develop the broad range of our own competencies, including knowledge of theory and practice in . . . cross-cultural issues, including issues related to our own ethnocentric tendencies and to differences and diversity within and between countries" (Guideline II–B–1). Greer had not only ethical but also competency problems.

If Greer had had even minimal knowledge about theory and practice in cross-cultural OD-HSD and awareness of his own ethnocentric tendencies and of the profession's ethics related to cross-cultural practice, he would have been alerted to the need for preparing himself to deal with the reality of Cornea's culture and its people. Ideally, he would have found a consultant knowledgeable about Cornea before he went there.

As just noted, the Statement encourages OD-HSD professionals to recognize that competency is an ethical responsibility. Greer violated that standard by not preparing himself for cross-cultural work. Another flaw in his competency can be inferred from the case's description of the UN "team," which appears to have been little more than a collection of individuals. As an OD-HSD professional, Greer could reasonably have been expected to help those individuals become a team by, among other things, helping them identify their common purpose and vision for their work with the Corneans. A common purpose and vision, even if only short-range, might have helped Greer avoid the problem he found himself facing at the end of the case. It also would have made the agenda setting and the subsequent work of all the team members more effective.

As for Greer's concern about the authoritarian system, most OD-HSD consultants work with organizations that are more or less authoritarian. The potential for ethical violation lies not simply in the act of working with an authoritarian system; rather, it involves the principle, "act so we do not increase power by the most powerful stakeholders over the less power-ful." In fact, OD-HSD practice may increase that power in the short run and thus be an ethical violation. But doing so would be ethically justifiable if, in the longer run, those with power to delegate authority and support the empowerment of the people who work for them can be encouraged and enabled to trans-form their power from power *over* to power *with*. Such transfor-mation can create a whole-win solution to the problem of power because it makes more power available to everyone, including the organization.

Additional Comments

At the fifth OD World Congress in 1985 at Zeist in the Netherlands, about thirty people met in small discussion groups to discuss "A Clash of Cultures." Several of the participants were asked to think about their responses to the case and then, fol-lowing the group discussions, to prepare written responses en-compassing both their own ideas and those of their group.

Those who responded were: Ian Barber, an internal con-sultant raised in England, living and working in Spain; Donald Cole, an external consultant raised, living, and working in the United States; Pessy Krausz, an external consultant raised in England, living and working in Israel; Matjaz Mulej, an ex-ternal consultant and professor at the University of Maribor raised, living, and working in Yugoslavia; John Nirenberg, raised in the United States, living and working in Singapore as a professor at the National University of Singapore at the time he responded to this case (he acknowledges the assistance of Yue Wah Chay, Geok Theng Lau, William Koh, and Ching Ling Tan, all of whom were tutors in the School of Manage-ment at the National University of Singapore); Hugo Prein, an external consultant and professor at the University of Utrecht living and working in the Netherlands; and Zofia Rummel-Syska, an external consultant and professor at Warsaw Univer-sity raised, living, and working in Poland.

Excerpts from their responses are presented below. They are of interest not only because of their content but also because of the different cultural orientations reflected in them. The first sets of responses were to three questions asked at the end of the case. The last response dealt with an issue not touched on by the other respondents — namely, how the evolution of the OD-HSD profession can affect practitioners differently and how the stage of a practitioner's evolution can affect his or her ethical orientation to a situation such as the one described in the "Clash of Cultures" case.

1. If you were Greer, would you continue?

Barber: The first question I would want to answer in deciding whether to continue is, who is the client? — not only as a person or group but also in time. Is it the government in the short term or the entire population in the longer term? If my client is the population in the longer term, I would try to continue and make a long-term commitment after explicitly defining both the client and the scope of the project. If, in the short term, the government is the client, I would not be prepared to work with it. This is an example of Assumption 5e of the Statement (1985) (see Appendix C), in that by refusing to work I might cause my clients to reconsider the conditions under which they will allow me to work.

Krausz: While I accept Greer's hesitation, the arrangements and method of interviewing could be such that everyone involved could gain short-term insight into past, present, and future aspirations, expectations, skills, and needs. Therefore, I would continue.

Mulej: Greer has only eight weeks, and his task may be limited to gaining insight into organizational relations in Cornea's few factories in order to prepare a subsystemic model (he is a subsystem of a multidisciplinary team!) from his viewpoint. Due to development problems, political issues will contribute to the complexity of his situation, but probably not until the later evaluation of the findings and elaboration of the model for Cornea's development. The model will have to be elaborated in a shared effort by the international team and Cornea's team in order to build bridges from an "imported model" situation to an "our own model" situation and from a multidisciplinary elaboration to a (much more wholistic) interdisciplinary one.

Nirenberg and others: As a member of the UN mission, Greer must first live up to the expectations of that role, which include, in part, his behaving consistently with the UN *Universal Declaration of Human Rights* and with the OD Statement (1985). In fact, the Statement says that "in general we accept as a guide the United Nations' *Universal Declaration of Human Rights,*" and the "specific fundamental rights we value include rights to life, liberty, and security of persons; freedom of thought, conscience, and religion; freedom of opinion and expression; and freedom of choice."

The proposition that one should respect cultural differences should not be used as an excuse to turn a blind eye to exploitation and totalitarian practices. This Greer refuses to do, and he therefore finds himself in an intolerable situation from which he wishes to extricate himself. Given the constraints Greer faces, he still has a few options worth pursuing before he decides to quit. He could seek approval to use a pilot study, become a participant observer, or attempt to obtain the support of the UN mission to apply pressure from the government agency to overcome the limits established by the company's management. If the culture of Cornea is such that all alternatives fail, and if there are no prospects that Greer's service could be performed according to standard OD professional practices and his code of ethics, which includes the maintenance of respondent confidentiality, he should withdraw. The fact that the business leadership would like to maintain its power is not enough to discourage attempts to perform a professional function according to its established standards. (*Note:* As stated earlier, the Statement does not require total confidentiality; it requires only that the limits of confidentiality be defined and protected.)

Prein: I would continue, but not in the way Greer did. I think he is behaving too arrogantly, as if he alone knows right from wrong. In a way, he is thinking for the managers of Cornea in the same way that they think for their employees. He is also behaving too rigidly — using such usual "Western" procedures as interviewing and surveying — measuring only the formal structure. Surely there are informal structures and mechanisms by means of which people in such a bureaucratic/hierarchical situation try to make conditions more livable for themselves (as in World War II Holland during the German occupation). It seems to me that the case fundamentally involves conflict between, on the one hand, a *collectivist* culture, in which the elder member of the family or the higher manager is considered the representative of the family or organization, and, on the other hand, an *individualist* culture — such as the U.S. culture from which Greer himself comes — which places higher value on individual autonomy. The differences in opinion about such sociocultural issues do not justify Greer's ending his assignment. Rather, he should change his strategy.

Rummel-Syska: (*Note:* Rummel-Syska's responses to this case were written in the context of conditions in Poland during 1985–1987. In late 1989, she asked that the following be added to her comments: "In June 1989, rapid changes have started in Poland . . . We are a society in transition . . . Values, rules of behavior, norms will change . . . Now we are on the way to real European Democracy, personal responsibility, independence, more truth, sincerity . . . and there is no system to blame anymore . . . People cannot change in one day . . . Polish organizational culture is in transition from authoritarian to democratic, from bureaucracy to natural open system and behavior will change." Her original comments, with slight editing, appear in the sections below, beginning with the following excerpts.)

As I understand the case, Greer's situation can be described as an apparent ethical dilemma involving a choice between doing what he is told to do while holding the system responsible for improperly using his expertise and withdrawing because he feels personally responsible for ensuring that his expertise is used properly.

In Poland, specialists in different fields face situations similar to that of Greer. They work under the basic rule that the task must be done without regard for results, immediate or longer-term, and they hold the system responsible. Engineers agree to use bad materials, architects design poor housing, publishers print inferior books. They are conscious of this, but they seldom say no. They do not "search for excellence"; rather, they seek task accomplishment without looking at the quality of results. This phenomenon, now quite common in Poland, stems from our centrally planned economy. The most important thing is to fulfill the plan because otherwise people will not be paid.

So what should Greer do? Some might contend that although he may produce a poor project, he should not withdraw because the system is responsible. It seems to me that this opinion was expressed by some of the Polish participants in the World Congress discussion. In my opinion, Greer must resign and say no if he does not have a strong conviction that his project will do more good than harm.

An OD consultant must be sure that the effect of his work will be to help his client system and, at the same time, do no harm. Greer must learn more about the culture of the island, particularly about how the authorities work. He should try to do what reasonably can be done, using strict methodology as much as possible. To withdraw simply because he cannot proceed as he would prefer, specifically with regard to confidentiality, would, in my judgment, be wrong.

2. What action would you take, if any, to avoid exploitation of your interviewees?

Barber: In order to avoid exploitation, there are two possible courses of action, which are not mutually exclusive:

- Spend time talking to senior management, trying to convince them that it would be advantageous to interview the staff in private. Maybe the suggestion of a pilot study could achieve the desired result.
- Contract nonconfidentiality with all the interviewees. Know-

ing that their comments may be used to their disadvantage, the employees would be free to choose the level of honesty they wish to employ in their answers. Senior management must understand, however, that this contract may lead to a distorted view of the situation. But under no circumstances would I "reveal any disloyalty," although under the conditions described, I find it hard to believe that any would manifest itself.

Krausz: I would take the following steps:

• Encourage top officials to participate in and take responsibility for helping design employee questionnaires, encourage them to help analyze the findings, and involve them in drafting the final report
• Try to draw management into helping with interview arrangements—for example, reviewing questions, making practical arrangements, timing, ordering interviews, and generating enthusiasm
• Suggest that questionnaire results—perhaps without identifiers—should be readily accessible to all, thus eliminating fears as to what will be done with the information

Bearing in mind that Greer could detect "no visible tension," and people "appeared to be happy" with their lot, Greer could seek to foster unity between people's present acceptance of their situation and future questioning of it, with the possibility of continuing meetings of a cross-section of staff and management. If Greer could provide a positive experience of this during his eight-week intervention, then continuation might be possible. By this means, one might deal with the possibility of exploitation, although, of course, much depends on how we define "exploitation." To me, exploitation exists when people are used to others' advantage with little or no regard for their own good. In that sense, exploitation seems to exist in Cornea. However, the people there seem not to experience it. Careful use of the survey approach, I suggest, may help people become more sensitive to their own needs and desires and less vulnerable to exploitation; but I stress that it must be *careful* use. Within eight weeks it is unrealistic to expect much change. We need to be careful about not presuming too much about what is "good" for the people of Cornea.

Mulej: Greer should prepare three sets of actions:

- To coordinate his own work and the work of other members of the international team
- To implement shorter-term action for his own eight weeks in Cornea
- To help initiate longer-term activity by the Cornean people (political leadership, management, and others) toward more creative cooperation for the development of their own country, their organizations, and themselves

To make management and government personnel easier to approach, Greer should point out that the term *management* should be understood to mean "management of the entire process of planning, designing, supplying, manufacturing, marketing and monitoring of the products" rather than "subordination and management of people." With this understanding, the interviews will concentrate on problems in employees' own processes of work and mutual cooperation and on problems of work life rather than on opinion about their bosses' behavior. Greer cannot proceed or prevent misuse without such information because without it the influential people would quite probably feel attacked by his work.

Greer's short-term action during his eight-week visit might include generating the cooperation of Cornea's leaders in designing the questionnaires because influential people tend to develop adversarial attitudes if they are not, or do not feel, considered equal members of the influencing team. I believe that such preparation would help Greer prevent a misuse of the information from his interviews.

Nirenberg and others: Greer could seek approval to use a pilot study in which some employees would be given an opportunity to speak candidly without the presence of management. He could then compare the results of the groups to see if significant differences do exist and then seek to change the process to a confidential one if in fact the data gathered are likely to contribute to better understanding of the development needs of the country. If management is unconvinced of the wisdom of such a program, Greer could try a different method of data gathering whereby he becomes a participant observer and works side by side with the employees, gathering his data by observing their behavior. Naturally, in his report he would have to insist that individuals remain unidentified.

Prein: I would give less emphasis to the interviews, using them only for "harmless" data, and more to informal data-gathering procedures, including:

- Talking with Perot about how to handle this ethical problem, how he understands it, how he lives with it
- Trying to find the informal structure and mechanisms in the culture of Cornea and, as an OD consultant, strengthening those mechanisms
- Using a local specialist to find adequate ways of handling these problems

Rummel-Syska:. There are topics that people may discuss freely in the presence of their managers and those that they cannot. In my opinion, Greer may ethically attempt to find out how openly people will speak in the presence of their managers. My experience in Poland is that subordinates complain openly of many bad working conditions in front of their managers, and, in turn, their managers complain in front of their bosses because none of them feels responsible for their situation. Everyone blames "the system." Quite often, low work productivity is not the fault of the system, but for workers and managers the system becomes an easy scapegoat.

3. How can you or any OD-HSD consultant or researcher balance your own values and ethics against those of host countries that are different from your own?

Barber: There are, in my opinion, certain issues that are negotiable even though the local culture may apparently demand them. I say "apparently" because I feel that we make many assumptions about cultures, both our own and others, that may not be justified. In some cases, it is undoubtedly necessary to revise our value/ethical orientation to enable us to work in the host culture. For example, consultants such as Greer, who value independence, autonomy, and personal responsibility, will need to accommodate their sense of what is "good" and "right" to the reality of cultures, such as Cornea's, in which unequal distribution of power and differences in levels of independence are generally accepted, if they want to be effective in such cultures. This accommodation process is generally slow and sometimes painful, often involving pitfalls resulting from the mistaken belief that we understand the new values. We must "feel" the new values — as they are felt by members of the new culture; and, generally speaking, that process of feeling cannot be accelerated.

Another extremely important factor is the recruitment of local help, native to both the country and the company. After initial discussions we and they both may have to question some of our assumptions and values. These people will be very useful in helping us diagnose the current situation because our more deeply entrenched values are likely to keep us from seeing things accurately without their help.

The major ethical questions one usually has to face are whether to work within the host culture or try to change it, and, if change is favored, how and how much? Cultures change when a critical mass of people within the society find an alternative more acceptable than the current situation. Therefore a consultant may offer, explain, or propose behavioral or attitudinal alternatives for people in the host culture to consider.

Krausz: During our discussion of this case at the OD World Congress, widely differing attitudes prevailed between OD practitioners from Iron Curtain countries and those from the West, with the latter being more uneasy about Greer's role. One way OD consultants can balance their values and ethics with those of their host country could be by increased sensitivity training for themselves — "Healer, know thyself." Another ethical solution would be to enable those in the host country to channel local energies positively while teaching them the skills with which to judge for themselves what is for their good.

Mulej: Greer is obviously bringing ethics and values of the (more or less) twenty-first century to a country with eighteenth-century ethics and values. In his terms, he is right; in Cornea's terms, futuristic — and so are all OD consultants and politicians who forget about development economics and related history. In such cases, troubles are unavoidable.

The following considerations seem to have been neglected by Greer:

1. New values and ethics need a new economic base.
2. Industrialization demands new ethics and values, which will approach the modern "Western ways" only gradually; mentality does not change overnight or by a political decree (even one that is progressive, logical, and theoretically justified); Cornea will require a long time to change its economic base, values, ethics, and the behavior of its citizens.
3. It is necessary to study any country thoroughly before one goes to work in it, allowing time to check previously acquired information at the beginning of a mission.
4. One must understand the education of people generally as well as that of political and managerial personnel.
5. One should not try to change all of a given culture at once.
6. One should proceed carefully and pragmatically, half a step at a time, to avoid losing ground.
7. One must find and clearly express strong arguments for people to perceive their needs, possibilities, shared values and knowledge (old and new), shared priorities and corresponding possibilities, the resulting long- and short-term objectives, the resulting necessary activities, ways of doing them, and the likely positive and negative results. (If people do not coauthor and own these elements in managing their future, they will most probably not trust and accept the changes that consultants help introduce into their countries.)

Nirenberg and others: This case raises two vital issues of concern to OD practitioners in cross-national settings. First, what exactly is culture? And what does it mean to respect a culture?

I believe attempts to resolve these issues will lead us to an impasse based on the politics of development. The industrial form of organization wrenches apart preindustrial cultures; efficiency and productivity are demanding taskmasters. The status quo is challenged and "culture" changes, as it is itself a mechanism of adaptation to new conditions faced by a group of people.

To "respect" a culture leads us into another disturbing impasse, this one over whether there is, or should be, a valid set of universal principles and whether we as "outsiders" have the right to advocate them. For example, while I recognize Sudan's right to exist, I find it difficult to "respect" a culture that performs clitorectomies, especially when the practice results in the deaths of 20 percent of the female subjects each year.

It seems then that we have a fairly difficult struggle ahead in our attempt to resolve these issues while striving to provide a single workable statement of values appropriate for the practice of OD-HSD worldwide.

Prein: In working with another country/culture, an OD consultant has to be aware of cross-cultural differences in values and beliefs. That is why it is so important for OD consultants to obtain consultation from someone who knows the local culture.

In preparing for an engagement in another country, I think OD consultants should seek to be clear about the purposes and goals of their engagement and the host country's norms. They should not undertake a consultation if they do not think they can serve the purposes and goals with integrity and in ways that respect the host country's norms. This does not mean that they have to agree with or even like the norms; it means only that they can tolerate the norms as a means of serving goals they value. To some extent, this can involve letting the goals (ends) justify the means. And that is acceptable as long as the conflict with one's own values and ethics is not too great.

If the differences between the norms of the host country and the consultant's own values are too large, an important contribution of the OD consultant would be to make the differences explicit, demonstrating to the client what his value system is and with what consequences, positive and negative, it operates. The client may become more aware of his own value system by experiencing differences with the system of the OD consultant. The OD consultant needs the skills of a "relative outsider" who can see and hear with new eyes and ears and offer her observations without labeling the client as "bad."

Rummel-Syska: According to Kenneth Boulding (1985), there is not so much difference between cultures as people tend to believe, and resolutions of any differences are attainable. In analyzing the "Clash of Cultures" case, I think we need to keep that thought in mind. OD professionals have to be aware of their specific cultures and be careful not to invade the cultures of others, which we called "cultural or intellectual imperialism" during our OD World Congress discussion group.

The Polish attitude during the panel discussion revealed to me that we — Polish OD consultants — are much more autocratic and intolerant than are Western European and American OD consultants. (*Note:* Remember that this was written in 1985. See Rummel-Syska's observations at the beginning of her initial comment.) Polish participants tended to assume that universal norms are obligatory, ignoring specific attitudes, approaches, and behaviors in other cultures. That is, "People must behave as they are told, even against their will, and in the long run they will get used to it and see that the idea was right." This Polish approach probably stems from our political experience, in which all main decisions are imposed by force at the government level and reach even to schools, nurseries, family groups, and so on. But in my opinion, our experience after World War II is not an example to follow. I was astonished to find during the World Congress panel session how arbitrary we have become in our relations with people.

4. How does the evolution of the OD-HSD profession affect the way practitioners react to a situation such as the one in the "clash of cultures" case?

(*Note:* In his response to this case, Cole raised this question, one not covered by other respondents. His response is presented separately below.)

Cole: All professions pass through at least three different stages on their way to becoming a true profession, and the field of Organization Development is no exception. While these stages are evolutionary, at any one time there are likely to be people in the field from all three stages; and the particular stage in which they find themselves helps explain their reactions to situations such as those described in the "Clash of Cultures" case.

The first stage of any profession is best characterized by the "pioneers" — people like Florence Nightingale and Dorothea Dix. In OD we sometimes call them the "gurus" or the "grand-fathers." These are people who recognize a need and move to fill it. Because the field has not yet been invented, they practice out of "good intentions," intuition, and a body of knowledge that they make up themselves or draw from other disciplines and other professions. If they are successful, a body of knowledge and skills begins to develop and the field enters the second stage.

Stage Two is a methods-based stage where what has been found to work in some situations is applied in a relatively routine, undifferentiated way to most situations. T-Grouping was such a technology. At one stage in the development of OD, T-Groups tended to be routinely applied to most problems that were pointed out to OD consultants. This is understandable because at that time this was one of the few generally accepted methods that OD consultants possessed.

Stage Three begins with the development of a code of ethics and the development of various options for interventions. An emerging profession eventually begins to think not just in terms of means (the how) but also in terms of the ends (for what purpose, such as influencing the "bottom line"). Eventually, enough technology is invented so that a differential diagnosis is possible, with some situations receiving one set of procedures and other situations receiving another set. The profession eventually becomes the artful application of a growing body of knowledge according to the guidelines contained in the code of ethics. Because the means by which the profession is to be practiced have been defined by the code of ethics and a body of knowledge and skill, the profession can begin to police its boundaries and define who is ethical and competent and who is not.

If we can discuss "A Clash of Cultures" from the perspective of a stage-two professional — that is, a technician — and from the perspective of a stage-three professional, the case may become less difficult and complex.

In my opinion, Greer is a stage-two professional. Management has decided that a favorite OD procedure is inappropriate for its company and its culture. Deprived of a favorite procedure, Greer does not know what else to do but quit. It would not be ethical to promise that a conversation would be confidential when in fact it would not. But while confidentiality may be desirable, it is not always essential. A skillful OD consultant in Greer's position might turn these monitored interviews into conversations about sensitive subjects that could provide a greater level of mutual understanding between the two parties.

An old adage says, "You have to meet the client where he (or she) is." Stage-Three professionals are able to begin where the system is because they are more ends- and values-oriented and have a wider range of technology to employ, albeit under the guidance of their ethical standards. Stage-Two professionals have a difficult time doing this because they are more technology- or means-oriented. Their technology is limited, however; for problems beyond the scope of their limited repertoire, they either have little to offer or use inappropriate means.

CHAPTER EIGHT

▌▐▌▐▌▐▌▐▌▐▌▐▌▐▌▐▌▐▌▐▌▐▌▐▌▐▌▐

Doing Action Research: The Conflicting Roles of Researcher and Consultant

▌▐

As the panel session at her professional association meeting con-cludes, Sandra Kohl is pleased with her presentation. For several months, she had anticipated this opportunity to present her preliminary hypotheses on the effects of corporate culture on organizational performance, and her confidence is reinforced by the positive reaction to her work by those attending the session. As an assistant professor of management at an elite univer-sity, she has devoted much of her early career to the study of organizations. The development of several testable hypotheses is an important milestone.

As she leaves the session room, Kohl is approached by someone who had attended the panel. Mark Watson identifies himself as a vice president with Compucare, a computer hard-ware firm, and she accepts his invitation to discuss her work in greater detail over lunch. During their conversation, Wat-son refers to his company's unsettled and ill-defined corporate culture in an industry characterized by severe growing pains. As a result of these conditions, the company is experiencing strained management-worker relations and a high attrition rate among technical employees. Watson believes that if the firm is to survive in a volatile industry, it needs to "get its act together" and foster a corporate environment that will promote employee loyalty and increase production output. He asks Kohl if she would be interested in applying some of her ideas on corporate culture to Compucare.

Watson's offer takes Kohl by surprise. She has little consulting experience because she has thought of herself primarily as a scholar committed to increasing the body of knowledge related to organizational behavior. Yet, she reasons, this might be a welcome opportunity to gather valuable data, test her hypotheses, and offer assistance to a company requesting her help. She expresses her willingness to pursue the matter further, and Watson indicates that he will discuss their conversation with company officials and get back in touch with her.

Several weeks later, Kohl is in a meeting at Compucare headquarters to discuss with company officials the terms of her contract. Present at the meeting, in addition to Watson, are Compucare's CEO, Max Winters; the company's chief financial officer, Jack Parsons; and assistant corporate counsel, Barbara Clawson. Because of her relative inexperience in corporate consulting, Kohl is a bit uneasy in the company of these executives, but she is able to communicate the essence of her research in a way that they appear to understand. Like Watson at the panel session, the other company executives respond very favorably to her research idea. Winters voices the opinion that her investigation and subsequent findings could be just the tonic the company needs to cure its current malaise. Kohl neither encourages nor challenges the CEO's observation.

The executives agree that Kohl will have access to internal memos and to all company employees through surveys and/or interviews. Kohl insists that when employees are informed of the nature of her research, it should be made clear to them that their involvement is entirely voluntary and that all identifying data gathered during the course of the study will be held in confidence. For her part, Kohl agrees to share the findings of her research with the company and, where appropriate, to assist the firm in implementing intervention strategies that her research indicates would help solve its problems.

The final issue to be resolved is the study's timetable. Both Winters and Parsons, perhaps feeling the heat of the company's current difficulties, suggest a six-month time frame. Kohl explains that such a brief period is impossible, given her duties at the university and the nature of the research process. She considers suggesting at least a two-year study but suspects that her suggestion would be rejected. Instead, she proposes a twelve- to fifteen-month study as the absolute minimum required for the research. With obvious reluctance, company executives accept her timetable.

Kohl employs a number of data-gathering techniques during the early stages of her research. Using questionnaire surveys and individual and group interviews, she begins to develop a profile of employees, both management and nonmanagement, at Compucare. She identifies three general groups of employees. One consists of people who are generally supportive of the company's leadership and hopeful about the firm's future. Another group contains employees who are simply "hanging on," waiting for a better opportunity to surface elsewhere. And a third group complains about uncaring and poor management by top company officials. Kohl hypothesizes that the problems lie partly in poor communication among different levels of the company and in the absence of mechanisms for employee participation in company decision making. More involvement in company affairs, she hypothesizes, would improve employees' morale, increase their sense of loyalty to the organization, and help develop a corporate culture based on shared values, expectations, and commitments. Given her earlier contact with top management, she has no reason to believe that they will not be receptive to proposals for increasing employee participation.

At one of Kohl's interviews, an employee named Marlene Woods complains of sex discrimination against her by the company. Based on her investigation of the matter, Kohl is convinced that Woods and other female employees have been subjected to discriminatory treatment with regard to promotions. As a strong advocate for women's rights, Kohl is sympathethic to Woods's complaint. Woods asks if Kohl would be willing to help her by discussing her case with the company's assistant corporate counsel as a preliminary step to gaining redress. Although personally supportive, Kohl worries that if she were to take an active role in this case it would distract from her research tasks. Moreover, if her role in this case were to become widely known, she fears that other disgruntled employees would seek her help with their grievances. After all, Kohl reasons, her role is that of researcher, not therapist or advocate. Nonetheless, Kohl is troubled. Delaying action on Woods's behalf until the research is completed seems inconsistent with her strong personal position. She agrees to consider the matter and talk with Woods again in a few days.

During the course of the investigation, Kohl experiences considerable difficulty in gaining the agreement of minority employees to be interviewed. Despite her pledges of confidentiality, she has had little success in gaining their cooperation. She suspects that this reluctance is due to their suspicions about what use the company might make of the information. She realizes that her research findings will be compromised if she cannot assess the opinions and attitudes of minority employees through in-depth interviews.

Kohl casually mentions this to Watson in response to one of his inquiries about the progress of her work. He offers to ask Winters to send a memo to all minority employees encouraging their participation. Kohl is concerned, however, that such a memo from the company's chief officer would create subtle and irresistible pressure on those employees to participate, a situation that would conflict with her stated position that all participation be completely voluntary. As a scientist, however, she is committed to producing valid and reliable results, which at present are threatened by the low participation rate of minority employees. She tells Watson that she would like some time to consider his offer.

As they are about to part company, Watson mentions that he is considering several changes in personnel and that he would like to learn her opinions of some of the employees she has encountered during her work at the company. He asks her to call his office to arrange a meeting and then excuses himself in order to go to his next appointment. Kohl is startled by his request,

especially since he was present at the meeting at which agreement was reached that no identifiable information would be
made available to company personnel. How can Kohl disclose
such information without violating the confidentiality of those
participating in the research? She must admit to herself, however, that she has learned a great deal about employees' skills
and attitudes. And she has, after all, been invited into the company to help solve its problems. By not sharing her knowledge
with Watson, will she not add to the risk that the company's
problems might be exacerbated by poor personnel decisions?
As a scientist, she appreciates the importance of basing decisions on the most complete and accurate knowledge available.
How can she deny that opportunity to Watson? She continues
to ponder her predicament as she enters her car for the return
trip to the university.

   In a meeting with Winters and Watson at the six-month
point in her investigation, Kohl proposes to introduce on a pilot basis three different strategies, closely monitoring the effects
of each. One strategy calls for the creation of new channels of
communication between top management and middle management and between the latter and lower-level employees. Another
creates new structural linkages between management and lower-
level employees to facilitate greater participatory decision making
by employees at all levels. A third strategy establishes task forces
of representatives from all employee groups in order to improve
communication and encourage employee contributions to company policies and practices. When pressed by Winters and Watson about the possibility that any one of the three strategies is
more likely than the others to be effective, Kohl takes the position that until all three are tested there is no valid basis for making such a judgment. When asked how long the testing process
will take, Kohl states that she expects to present the results of
her analysis in six to seven months. Winters and Watson are
obviously dismayed over Kohl's projected timetable and conclude the meeting abruptly by suggesting that she get on with
the task.

   Three months later, one of the intervention strategies employed in two of the company's units is yielding clearly positive

results. The verdict is not yet in on the other two interventions. Kohl, in her role as scientist-researcher, urges company officials not to leap to premature conclusions but to permit her analysis to continue further. Two more months pass, with very little change in the effects of the three intervention strategies. Kohl plans to introduce some minor changes in two of the strategies that will test the hypotheses she has developed on the basis of her analysis subsequent to their original implementation. She believes that a few more months of observation and data analysis will produce sufficient evidence for evaluating her hypotheses. She is excited about the likely impact this work will have on her career, as her next year at the university is the one in which she becomes eligible for tenure.

Compucare executives, however, have their own agenda to attend to and are growing impatient with Kohl's cautious and deliberate approach. Six months after the interventions were implemented, it is quite evident to them that the effects of one of the interventions are dramatic and compelling. In their minds, there is no need for further testing. Kohl argues otherwise, but in a moment of candid self-reflection, she wonders whether she is unfairly emphasizing her research objectives at the expense of Compucare's welfare and her responsibilities to the company.

Questions to Consider

1. Did Kohl make the goals and methods of her research sufficiently clear at the meeting convened to negotiate the contract? Do you believe that clarity or lack of clarity regarding contract terms would have made a difference with respect to the ethical dilemmas Kohl experienced? Whose responsibility — the client's or the OD professional's — is it to ensure the preparation of a contract that is adequately clear, comprehensive, and specific? How can the formalized structure of a contract be balanced against the flexibility that may be required once research is under way?

2. What action would you take in response to Woods's claim of unfair treatment in promotion decisions and her request for your help?

3. How would you respond to Watson's offer to help increase the involvement of minority employees in your research interviews by having Compucare's CEO send a memo encouraging them to participate "for the good of the study and of the company"?

4. How would you deal with Watson's request that you meet with him to share your evaluations of company personnel with him?

5. In this case, how would you balance your research responsibilities with those that accompany your consulting or helping role? What guidelines might be useful in helping OD professionals sort out and effectively discharge their responsibilities when their roles as researchers and consultants conflict?

6. What prerogatives and responsibilities does the client have in situations in which the requirements of sound research clash with the organization's more pressing, practical needs?

Note: This case was originally presented at a panel at the annual meeting of the American Psychological Association, Los Angeles, August 1985. Participants in the panel who prepared written commentary on the case for this book included the late Fred R. Berger, a philosopher at the University of California, Davis; Leonard D. Goodstein, a psychologist and consultant; Rodney L. Lowman, a psychologist and director of the Career Development Laboratory, Houston, Texas; and Joan Sieber, a psychologist at California State University, Hayward.

Comments by Mark S. Frankel, Including Comments by Fred R. Berger, Leonard D. Goodstein, Rodney L. Lowman, and Joan Sieber

This case highlights some ethical concerns for OD-HSD professionals who assume the dual role of researcher and consultant, a not uncommon feature of OD-HSD work and one experienced by other professions as well. Ideally, OD-HSD consulting rests on a solid base of knowledge and experience, and it is undoubtedly appealing to both professional and client to contribute to the advancement of knowledge in ways that also produce practical solutions to organizational problems. But as the case illustrates, one must not be blind to the pitfalls — ethical and pragmatic — associated with such an outwardly appealing arrangement.

Given the dual role assumed by Kohl, I found it useful to approach the case initially from the perspective of the moral rule that one should fulfill one's responsibilities. In this instance, Kohl's responsibilities derive from two sources: her professional role, which in this case is both consultant and researcher, and the agreement (contract) she reached with Compucare about their working relationship.

As an OD-HSD consultant/researcher, Kohl can look to the Statement for insight into the responsibilities that accompany her professional role. In addition to specifically enumerated responsibilities in the Statement, a central theme throughout the document is that OD-HSD professionals should promote values within the organization that enable people to live "meaningful, productive, good lives" (see Preamble, Chapter Four). This places an affirmative responsibility on the part of OD-HSD professionals that may be breached if, in a specific situation, they fail to act in a manner that reinforces important core values of the profession.

The agreement, or contract, that Kohl and Compucare negotiated constitutes another source of Kohl's responsibilities, as well as those of the company. In principle, a contract not only clearly defines the expectations and responsibilities of the covered parties but also takes into account unanticipated events; contracting becomes "an ongoing process for the checking of expectations and not merely for articulating the initial set of expectations" (Goodstein). Although such a contract can have legal force, for our purposes it also constitutes a promise, made voluntarily on the part of those involved, to fulfill certain expectations and responsibilities. To break such promises may in certain circumstances be a violation of a basic moral rule.

In addition to viewing the case from the perspective of one's moral responsibilities, the case also offers several valuable lessons on avoiding "morally hazardous situations." As noted

in Chapter Two, OD-HSD professionals often find themselves
in complex and ambiguous circumstances that can heighten the
risk of errors in judgment, at times confronting the professional
with difficult moral choices that increase the likelihood of morally
unjustified behavior.

To assist in guarding against such situations, OD-HSD
professionals can appeal to several sources of guidance. There
is the original contract, which can clarify for all parties the nature of the working relationship and the prerogatives and responsibilities of the principals and thus help avoid those morally
hazardous situations that can be anticipated.

Another source of guidance is clarity about the values that
one brings to the assignment. Indeed, an explicit purpose of
the Statement is "to guide us (OD-HSD professionals) in making more informed ethical choices" (see Nature and Purposes,
Chapter Four) by offering them the cumulative and collective
wisdom of the profession on matters of professional and moral
significance. Recognizing that "conflicts involving values or ethics
[are] inevitable in our practice" (Belief 5-b), the Statement also
encourages OD-HSD professionals to "Identify and respond to
any major differences in professionally relevant values or ethics
between ourselves and our clients" (Guideline III–D–3). The
message is clear: reflecting on the values underlying one's work
and on potential ethical problems prior to commencing work
can help one avoid morally hazardous situations later. This message is reflected in the five-step model presented in Chapter
Three as well.

A third source of guidance is an understanding of one's
professional competence and the existing (technical) practice
standards promulgated by the profession. The Statement is quite
clear that OD-HSD professionals should "practice within the
limits of our competence, culture, and experience in providing
services and using techniques" (Guideline II–D). Recognizing
the limits of one's professional competency is critical in guarding against agreeing, either knowingly or unwittingly, to perform work for which one is inadequately prepared with regard
to either knowledge or skills. Admittedly, this matter is somewhat complicated for OD-HSD professionals and their clients

because of the absence of generally accepted professionwide practice standards by which one's competency can be measured. As a consequence, the responsibility for ensuring congruence between one's competency and the projected work rests heavily on the shoulders of individual OD-HSD professionals. (As described under Guideline II–B–2 in the Statement, one approach to ensuring that one does this responsibly is peer review.)

Anticipating Conflicts and Clarifying Values Up Front. Although a dedicated scholar, Kohl has "little consulting experience" and the offer of a consulting engagement by a Compucare official takes her "by surprise." Unfortunately, she seems "singularly unaware of the cultural values she brought with her — the value placed on pure truth and knowledge in the academic culture — and how they conflict with the cultural values of the business world — action and pragmatism" (Goldstein). Because of her failure to anticipate and understand such differences and to negotiate with Compucare officials a strategy for resolving them prior to commencing her work, she increased her risk of exposure to morally hazardous situations.

For example, there is obvious strain between Kohl and company executives over the timetable for introducing and evaluating intervention strategies. The company has little patience for the deliberate schedule that Kohl advocates. But while she voices outward concern about drawing "premature conclusions" that may ultimately not be well founded, in a "moment of candid self-reflection" she questions her own motives; perhaps she is "unfairly emphasizing her research objectives at the expense of" Compucare. All professionals must be alert to the possibility of self-deception, which may prompt decisions that adversely affect their clients or that use them to further ends without their full understanding and consent. Certainly, the OD-HSD field is "beyond the early days in which 'anything went' and university researchers . . . could use organizations as their personal laboratories to explore various constructs of theories of change" (Lowman).

While a contract setting out the expectations and responsibilities of all parties cannot eliminate the possibility of self-deception and the morally hazardous situations it can create, it is a "process of mutual education" (Sieber) that enables those involved to shape priorities and design appropriate strategies up front, so that each is alert to subsequent behavior that may be inconsistent with the original understanding.

Kohl also appears to have a conflict in her own mind regarding Watson's request that she share with him her opinions of employees who may be involved in personnel changes. She views her promise of confidentiality to employees, so essential to her research, as conflicting with a goal of her consulting—that is, to enable the company to make decisions based on the best knowledge available. This instance points out the importance of being clear about one's own values and ethics. What are Kohl's priorities? How can she balance the values associated with her researcher role with those of a consultant? It is a bit risky, morally speaking, to consider this matter subject to the ebb and flow of the project and to people's reactions as the work proceeds.

If, as it appears, Kohl considers the promise of confidentiality essential to the research, which is the basis on which she intends to assist Compucare, there seems to be no justification for wavering on the matter. She has a moral responsibility to keep her promise to employees *and* to Compucare, and the latter commitment "could be met only by fully conducting the research with its observance of strict confidentiality" (Berger). For researchers who take on a consulting role, morality may require that they proceed only if clients are "willing to provide guarantees of the most essential requirements for the integrity of the research project" (Berger). The point is that one must be as clear as possible about the values, and the priorities assigned to them, that underlie one's work upon entering into the initial contract. If Kohl had referred to the Statement's provision on confidentiality, which stipulates that the OD professional should "define and protect confidentiality" (Guideline III–E), it might have helped reduce the moral ambiguity that she experienced and the hazards that accompanied her uncertainty about her obligations.

Treating Competence as a Moral Responsibility. The OD-HSD Statement attaches considerable ethical importance to competency, and understandably so. Incompetence can lead to errors in judgment, exposing clients to serious risks. "In the simplest rendering, this case represents an ethical violation of a professional practicing outside her area of competency. It is only a slight exaggeration of analogy to compare Kohl's behavior to that of a medical laboratory researcher who has developed a new artificial organ and who then decides experimentally to implant it in a live patient with no prior surgical or clinical experience" (Lowman). While one can draw from the case the conclusion that Kohl was not adequately prepared to apply her research to the organizational culture at Compucare, it is not so clear that she should bear the full weight of responsibility for the problems caused by this lapse.

As a member of a profession that disapproves of accepting work outside of one's competence, she is justified in turning to the profession for guidance on how to apply her skills in an effective and responsible manner. "[W]ithout rules of practice, there will be far too many cases of the type described here in which organizational intervention projects are driven by the needs (and, regrettably, the incompetence in intervening) of the researcher, not the needs of the organization" (Lowman).

While the absence of professionwide standards of practice does not absolve Kohl of her responsibility to practice within the limits of her competence, it is important to recognize that individual professionals and consumers of their services should be able to rely on the professional group for guidance and support. It is the profession, more than any single professional, that is best prepared to shape the cumulative, collective expertise and wisdom of the profession into standards of practice and conduct. And it is the profession, more than any individual, that can commit adequate resources to support professional competence on the one hand and to monitor, evaluate, and respond to deviations in professional performance from agreed-upon technical and ethical standards on the other. (With respect to tech-

nical competency, however, this task is made more difficult by
the absence of professionwide competency standards in OD-HSD.)

Taking Sides: A Third Role? Finally, there remains the
dilemma that Kohl experiences when confronted with evidence
of sex discrimination by Compucare. She worries that taking
the matter to company executives will disrupt her research; in
any event, she never agreed to assume the role of advocate. "An
interventionist (much less a researcher) should not confuse roles
by becoming an advocate for worthy causes, even those [that]
match [her] values" (Lowman). Yet, Kohl is obviously distressed
by what her investigation reveals about the company's treatment
of women.

Although, from the perspective of ethics as morality,
preventing harm, such as that resulting from sex discrimination, is not universally required, the OD-HSD Statement creates a professional duty to "constructively confront discrimination whenever possible" (Guideline V–C–1–a). While urging
professionals to help different parties within a system "resolve
their conflicts themselves, without taking sides," the Statement
recognizes that this may not always be possible. It acknowledges
that "if it becomes necesary to change our role from serving as
impartial consultant, do so explicitly; cease work with the client,
if necessary" (Guideline III–D–2).

The moral choice for Kohl, then, is not whether to stand
clearly in opposition to sex discrimination at Compucare: her
personal values as well as those of her profession clearly signal
that she should. Rather, to avoid taking action that might be
injurious to the company, its employees, and her research, she
must consider carefully how to devise a strategy that enables
her to "constructively" shape remedies for grievances brought
to her attention. (The substeps outlined for problem analysis
in the five-step model described in Chapter Three might help
Kohl devise such a strategy.)

CHAPTER NINE

▌▐▌▐▌▐▌▐▌▐▌▐▌▐▌▐▌▐▌▐▌▐▌▐▌▐▌▐▌▐▌▐▌▐

Alerting Clients
to Risks

▌▐▌▐▌▐▌▐▌▐▌▐▌▐▌▐▌▐▌▐▌▐▌▐▌▐▌▐▌▐▌▐

Comtex Inc. is part of the fast-changing and highly competitive telecommunications industry. While the opportunities for
growth in both the domestic and international markets are considerable, so, too, is the competition. To prepare for the decade ahead, Comtex's CEO, Tom Lang, instructs key company
staff to review all business operations and offer their recommendations on how to increase the firm's competitive position.

Coordinating the review are Janet Street and Richard
Korner of the company's internal OD department. Street is
twenty-eight years old and beginning her second year at the company. Korner is two years away from retirement, after having
worked for Comtex in several capacities for thirty-two years.
The review is conducted over a six-month period and includes
a careful evaluation of personnel records, company policies and
procedures, economic trends, production data, and interviews
with a sample of employees, some individually and others in
small groups.

On the basis of the six-month study, several steps that
Comtex can take to improve its competitive position are identified. Some of those steps, however, would result in hardships

for many people. Certain work changes and recommended reorganization would lead to personnel reductions in some divisions of the company. A shift in the company's production line to enter new markets would require closing plants in two communities, which would cause serious economic repercussions. And contracting out some of its production work, while resulting in substantial savings, would mean terminating contracts with several small suppliers that have relied on their business with Comtex for a major share of their revenues during the past five years.

Street believes that the recommendations in their report to Lang should be linked to a series of proposals for ameliorating the above adverse consequences. After all, she tells Korner, "We have a responsibility not only to inform management of the risks of implementing our recommendations but also to ensure management's commitment to do all that it can to reduce the costs associated with their effects."

Korner, however, disagrees with Street's latter claim. In his judgment, the influence of their recommendations would be seriously undermined if linked to proposals for ameliorating their adverse impact. "Our chief responsibility is to the company," he tells Street, "and whatever concerns we might have for others should not divert us from that primary obligation." The final decision, he reasons, is management's, and he believes that it is not his or Jan's responsibility to "ensure management's commitment" to anything regarding the future direction of the company. Furthermore, he sees no practical way to do so even if there were such a responsibility on their part. After all, he asks Street, "Can one be held responsible for making something happen without the authority or power needed to accomplish it?"

Street considers Korner's position far too limited. She argues that, as the source of the recommendations and as two of those likely to be involved in their implementation, she and Korner cannot simply "hope" that the company takes appropriate ameliorative action. They must urge it to do so!

Questions to Consider

1. If you were in the position of the internal OD consultants, how would you define your responsibility?

2. In recommending interventions, what responsibilities should OD consultants assume for alerting their clients to the risks associated with various options? Is there a responsibility to recommend ameliorative action in response to the risks?

3. If the client adopts a recommended intervention with risks to third parties, what responsibilities, if any, does the OD consultant have toward those at risk?

Note: This case was presented and discussed at the June 1985 Annual Meeting of the Association for Creative Change in St. Paul, Minnesota. Panelists who prepared written commentaries on the case are Beverly P. Brown-Hinckley, manager of organization effectiveness at the Procter & Gamble Company in Cincinnati, Ohio; John C. Bryan, president of Bryan* Weir-Bryan Ltd., a personal and organizational consulting firm; Jerilyn Fosdick, president of Fosdick and Company, an organizational consulting firm; and Stanley R. Hinckley, Jr., president of Hinckley and Associates, an organizational consulting firm. Excerpts from their prepared texts follow.

Comments by Mark S. Frankel

As discussed in Chapter Two, the idea of a moral code of conduct advances the notion of a core set of rules that forbids various kinds of behavior either causing harm to others or increasing the likelihood that others will experience harm. While the rules are not absolute, they may not be violated without sufficient moral justification.

Such a moral code, with its core set of rules (outlined in the Statement under "Moral Rules and Ideals") has clear implications for the moral responsibilities of OD-HSD consultants, whose decisions and actions may affect the well-being of others. If, in the case under consideration, harm comes to persons as a result of actions taken by Comtex based at least in part on advice from Street and Korner, should they be held responsible for causing harm? Do they bear any responsibility for not doing enough to prevent the harm from occurring?

Street holds that they have a "responsibility . . . to ensure management's commitment to do all that it can to reduce the costs" associated with the effects of whatever action Comtex takes. Korner, however, admits to no such responsibility, claiming that their "chief responsibility" is to the company and that they would be in default of their obligation if their attention were diverted to the possible outcomes for others. Furthermore, he argues that the responsibility claimed by Street is severely weakened by their lack of authority or power to follow through.

From the perspective of the moral code of conduct, the distinction between *causing* and *preventing* harm is important. While there is a basic moral rule to avoid causing harm to others, there is no rule that says one is obligated to prevent harm, although that is a moral ideal. From the perspective of OD-HSD professionals, that ideal is given added force since the Statement is explicit about the moral ideal to "prevent . . . harm" (see "Moral Rules and Ideals"). Hence, the Statement encourages Street and Korner to do what they can to protect Comtex employees, suppliers, and the larger community from the potential harms associated with their recommendations. If they do not "protect from harm," the Statement *encourages* them to have a clear moral justification but does not *require* such justification. (See annotation following "Moral Ideals," Chapter Four.)

The employer-employee relationship, like that between the client and the professional, is a fiduciary one in which the employee has a duty to promote the best interests of the employer. On its face, the relationship carries with it certain employee responsibilities due to the employer but not to others. These duties derive from the employee's role in relation to the employer, and the norms in force are related to that role. But professionals, whether self-employed or under salary, have different obligations or duties to their clients based on or derived from professional norms.

Strain in the employer-employee relationship is likely to occur in organizations employing professionals because organizational duties and professional duties often come into conflict. Bureaucratic organizations require predictable behavior and loyalty. Yet professionals typically expect to be given considerable autonomy, subject only to the limits of their expertise, and contend that they should be permitted to act on their sense of professional or social responsibility. Hence, conflicts between role-related obligations to employers and universal obligations to third parties are a perennial issue in professional ethics. Ultimately, one's role-related responsibilities "must be limited by universal responsibilities to others" (Bayles, 1989, p. 111). In principle, the moral code of conduct and its core set of rules and ideals offer a basis for determining what "universal responsibilities" ought to apply when considering one's obligations to third parties. But the moral rules offer little guidance in resolving concrete ethical dilemmas. However, professional norms, by specifying and reinforcing the moral rules, can serve as a basis for defining one's obligations to others. As Bayles (1989, p. 22) observes, "Professional norms that are specifications simply make universal norms more concrete by indicating a type of situation a professional encounters."

The Statement offers more concrete guidance for Street and Korner in helping them resolve the conflict between their obligations to Comtex and their responsibilities to third parties. For example, in detailing the responsibilities of OD-HSD consultants to "clients and significant others," the Statement declares that they should "explore the possible implications of any OD-HSD intervention for all stakeholders likely to be significantly affected" (Guideline III–A–4) and "inform people with whom we work (this would presumably include fellow company employees and suppliers) about any . . . costs, anticipated outcomes, . . . and risks" associated with the planned intervention (Guidelines III–B–1 and III–B–1–a). Moreover, commentary accompanying the Statement states that OD-HSD professionals should "help in minimizing loss to those stakeholders who suffer loss" (see Guideline III–A–4–a–2).

The Statement also recognizes, however, that there will be "differences in the expectations and interests of different stakeholders" and that "those differences cannot be reconciled all the time" (Guideline III–D–4). In such instances, one's responsibilities to the various stakeholders must be weighed against one another and defined as precisely as possible so that when the violation of moral rules or ideals or professional norms is necessary, its moral justification is clear.

Comments by Beverly P. Brown-Hinckley

Four assumptions were made, based on a review of the case: (1) The internal consultants who will have responsibility for coordinating the effort were not involved with management during the discussions or diagnosis that resulted in the proposed intervention. (2) This organization—like many others—is male dominated and technology driven, and as such, the organization's culture contains biases that limit its ability to utilize effectively and value the contributions of women and the role that staff consultants play in changing organizations. Different biases may also exist relative to men in staff roles who are close to retirement. (3) Internal consultants experience little choice in terms of whether they accept the project as defined by management. As a result, they feel little ownership for the project. (4) Neither consultant has a broad base of support or influence within the organization.

Several key problems emerged as the case evolved; they were primarily related to consultant responsibility and consultant ethics/values. They are as follows:

1. Even though management commissioned the study and requested that the internal consultants make recommendations, there was no indication from the client regarding what action would result from the study. Management should have realized that a study of this nature could result in the need for massive organizational change, or raise expectations—or anxieties—within the work force, and/or affect the community in which the company does business. Before beginning the study, the consultants were responsible for making management aware of the possibility that data could emerge that would lead to negative consequences. Additionally, it is important for them to work with the client to legitimize their role in assisting the organization to address effectively the data and plan any ameliorative actions that might be required. Failure to do this places the consultants in a precarious position once they realize that their recommendations will have a negative impact on the organiza-

tion. At this point they are caught in a dilemma: They don't have a legitimate vehicle or agreement with management for making proposals for ameliorative actions; and, from an ethical standpoint, they cannot make their recommendations without also recommending steps to nullify the negative impact. (See Guidelines II–A through II–C, Appendix C.)

2. Given that they did not establish an agreement with management on their role in planning ways to address the outcomes of the study, the consultants should have developed an alternate strategy that would have required that they meet regularly with management throughout the diagnosis. The purpose of such meetings would have been to keep management informed of the trends and/or key issues that were emerging and to make any appropriate "in-flight corrections." This strategy might have alleviated the potential for "surprising" management at the end of the study with recommendations intended to respond to adverse consequences. It might also have provided an opportunity for management and the consultants to predict jointly the outcomes of the study and develop ameliorative actions together.

3. The dissension between the two consultants threatens to undermine their effectiveness and their relationship at a time when it is important for them to work as a united front. The fact that they differ over how to present the data they have collected is primarily a situational issue. There are more fundamental issues related to how they each view the organization and their individual careers and responsibilities, which have much more bearing on their relationship and their behavior in this case. For example:

- How does a relatively new female staff person gain visibility and credibility with management and be seen as a competent contributor in a male-dominated, technology-driven organization?
- Why should a person who has held different roles in the organization and is close to retirement take the risk of antagonizing management about something that he believes has a low probability for success and for which he claims no responsibility?

- How can the differences between a new and relatively inexperienced staff person who is trying to make an impression
  in the organization and a skeptical, nearly retired staff person who has learned that you "don't make waves" be managed? How do you balance the personal and professional
  risks each perceives?

These issues raise ethical dilemmas for all OD-HSD consultants.
How should they behave when (1) the action that is required
of them professionally is incongruent with their personal values
or (2) their personal values differ from those of their professional
colleagues?

    4. The fact that Street and Korner are internal (rather
than external) consultants presents additional problems:

- They have very little leverage and/or power to make things
  happen within the organization. Internal consultants usually
  make things happen by networking with others and relying
  on their own personal (rather than role-related) power and
  on their ability to influence others in ways that mobilize their
  support.
- They have little or no choice about whether they accept
  management-defined projects, since they are paid to be the
  organization's consultants. They rarely have the option to
  say no to management without experiencing professional
  consequences.
- The resources (salary, credibility, access to management,
  monies to support interventions, and so on) are all controlled
  by management.
- They are probably viewed as being in the most expendable
  role in the organization—one that contributes least to the
  bottom line.

These matters make it even more difficult and risky for internal consultants to be "bearers of bad news" and step outside their
defined roles to recommend needed ameliorative action. In addition, if they attempt to recommend ameliorative action, they
may weaken their ability to make a positive difference in the

future, and that may be ethical justification for not taking the risk.

1. If you were in the position of the internal OD consultants, how would you define your responsibility? The internal OD consultants' responsibilities can be defined as follows:

a. Be clear about the objectives and expectations of management/client and determine what would constitute successful completion of the project. A clear contract (written agreement) is important.
b. Legitimize their role in assisting, advising, and recommending changes to management that are required to achieve the best results.
c. Keep the client informed of trends or key findings at strategic points throughout the diagnosis, not only at the end.
d. Make it clear to the client, early in the process, that the intervention may:
   - Surface recommendations that will have negative repercussions
   - Be risky
   - Raise expectations and/or anxieties within the organization
   - Require management to do things differently
   - Have an impact on productivity and morale

Whatever data the consultants have about what will or might happen as a result of the intervention should be shared early in the process.

e. Recommend ameliorative actions if implementing the outcomes of the diagnosis will have a negative impact on the organization, its processes, and its people.
f. Make every attempt to address the differences between them in a way that doesn't discount or disempower either of them personally or professionally.
g. Share all of the information with the client honestly and completely.

2. In recommending interventions, what responsibilities should OD consultants assume for alerting their clients to the risks associated with various options? Is there a responsibility to recommend ameliorative action in response to the risks? This is a fundamental ethical responsibility for all consultants. To do less is an abdication of their responsibility, dishonest and, therefore, unethical. (Refer to Guideline II–B, Appendix C.) Consultants are required to recommend ameliorative action when the known or suspected risks associated with their recommendations will result in jeopardizing the effectiveness of the client, the client system, its processes, its people, and/or other stakeholders. They cannot be held fully responsible for the decision that is ultimately made by the client, but they are ethically bound to provide the client with as much information as is available to assist the client in making the most knowledgeable and best decision possible, including possible ameliorative action. Consultants should bear this responsibility even when there is little organizational support and when the decision is potentially risky.

Consultants also have a social responsibility to ensure that their actions and recommendations minimize the negative effect on the lives and well-being of individuals within the client system. Therefore, they should make their recommendations as strongly as they can.

3. If the client adopts a recommended intervention with risks to third parties, what responsibilities, if any, does the OD consultant have toward those at risk? Since internal consultants can't fully control what the client decides to do, their options become more limited and more risky. They still have the responsibility to continue to influence the client's decision by:

a.   Using solid data that may leverage and align support and action from others in the organization who will be affected
b.   Showing corollaries between this intervention and others where similar risks are involved
c.   Using their personal power and influence with others in the organization who may have more credibility with the client or more formal power in the organization

d. Proposing potential interventions that diminish the negative effects of the intervention

To do nothing would mean that the consultants were colluding with the client in activities that they consider unethical
and socially unjust. A more drastic response might be to decide consciously to leave the organization or the client system
and communicate formally to the organization and management
the reasons for their departure. This option should, of course,
be the last resort after all other efforts have failed. It should be
a part of every consultant's repertoire of behaviors, and they
should be willing to use it when nothing short of colluding with
unethical practices can be done.

Comments by John C. Bryan

Though the case presents questions regarding the responsibilities of the two internal OD consultants, broader value issues must be considered in order to assess their responsibilities.
The case raises three questions for consideration. I shall address
each in turn.

*1. If you were in the position of the internal OD consul-
tants, how would you define your responsibility?* As internal OD
consultants, Street and Korner have at least three roles to fulfill:
consultant to management, organization member, and member of the OD profession.

As internal consultants and project coordinators, Street
and Korner are responsible for enabling management to make
effective and informed decisions. This means informing management not only of what alternatives are available but also of
the risks, costs, and potential benefits of each. (See Guideline
II–B, Appendix C.) It also means enabling management to articulate its values and assess its decisions in the light of those
values.

As organization members, internal consultants have not
only the right but also a responsibility to articulate their values
and seek to influence organization culture. The obligation to

act in accord with one's own values, personal and professional, may require one to forsake or temporarily set aside the role of impartial consultant. (See Guidelines II–I–1 and II–I–2, Appendix C.) I concur with Korner that the final decision belongs to management.

An internal consultant's membership does not stop at the boundary of her immediate client system. Street and Korner are not only members of Comtex; they are also members of the OD profession and of the larger society of which Comtex is a part. This broader membership brings with it a social responsibility to be aware of the potential impact of one's professional recommendations on the well-being of individuals, client systems, and the larger systems of which they are a part. (See Guideline IV–B, Appendix C.) I concur with Street that as "the source of the recommendations" the consultant has a responsibility to inform the CEO of potential adverse consequences and alternatives for ameliorating them.

2. In recommending interventions, what responsibilities should OD consultants assume for alerting their clients to the risks associated with various options? Is there a responsibility to recommend ameliorative action in response to the risks? The primary responsibility of an internal OD consultant to management is to facilitate maximum effectiveness in decision making. The assumption is that the more or better informed management is, the better its decisions will be. If management is not aware of risks, costs, and options, its capacity to make good decisions is greatly diminished.

Increasingly, organizations are becoming aware that they exist in relationship to a wide variety of stakeholders and that their long-term growth and well-being are significantly influenced by how well they nurture and maintain those relationships. In this particular situation, Comtex's decisions have potential impact for current employees, for at least two communities where plants are now located, and for several long-term suppliers, as well as for managers and owners. Attending to those impacts and their potential influence on Comtex's future health and relationships is the responsibility of management. Enabling management to be aware of those potentials, both positive and negative, and to make informed decisions is the responsibility of the OD consultants.

Korner maintains that "the influence of their recommendations would be seriously undermined if linked to proposals for ameliorating their adverse impact." I do not think the issue here is to make *influential* recommendations so much as to make thorough, well-informed ones. Discussions about ameliorative action are particularly important, and OD consultants have an ethical responsibility to see that such actions and the values underlying them are given as full a consideration by management as the consultants can promote. (See Assumption 2–a, Appendix C.)

3. If the client adopts a recommended intervention with risks to third parties, what responsibilities, if any, does the OD consultant have toward those at risk? Street and Korner are at least responsible for informing management of the risks and of available ameliorative action. In this instance, they are also responsible for ensuring that workers' representatives are appropriately involved in the decision-making process. (See Guideline II–B, Appendix C.) That they have any responsibility to third parties beyond this is not clear to me. It would indeed be difficult to maintain client-professional confidentiality if any further direct action were taken with third parties. (See Guideline II–K–2, Appendix C.) Perhaps the ultimate act of responsibility is to refuse to participate in the project, to withdraw one's professional services. As an external OD consultant, termination of a contract is not quite the same as it would be for an internal consultant. Korner is two years from retirement. Street is at the beginning of a career. It seems to me that the degree of value conflict would need to be quite high to warrant such withdrawal of professional services.

Comments by Jerilyn Fosdick

1. If you were in the position of the internal OD consultants, how would you define your responsibility? My overall responsibility would be to serve the organization as a whole, including all levels and all relationships. This view is grounded in systems theory and has a humanistic value base. Responsibility would not be restricted to enhancing profitability but would also involve helping the company to be ethical in its practices and fair in its dealings with others and to recognize its moral obligations to the people who constitute the company and contribute to its success. (See Assumption 2, Appendix C.)

The moral responsibility of the company to its stakeholders emanates from its capacity to affect their well-being. My moral responsibility to the company is a reflection of my capacity to influence its operation (Ladd, 1982). Unlike other business consultants, OD practitioners have a professional duty to work for outcomes that are beneficial for both the client organization and the persons affected by its decisions.

Street's belief that she and Korner should assume responsibility for "ensuring management's commitment" is correct in its emphasis but exaggerates the consultants' authority. Overall, OD consultants are obligated to formulate alternative courses of action that best serve the interest of those concerned and to communicate their views clearly and assertively. As Korner notes, however, they must also recognize the complexity of the situation confronting them and the number of others who have a legitimate voice in determining a course of action. In the Comtex case, Korner and Street have an obligation to identify the negative consequences of any actions they considered and to suggest means for mitigating them. However, they must also recognize that their ideas may be disregarded or modified by management. (See Guideline II–B, Appendix C.)

2. In recommending interventions, what responsibilities should OD consultants assume for alerting their clients to the risks associated with various options? Is there a responsibility to recommend ameliorative action in response to the risks? Alerting clients to the potential risks of various intervention options is an essential responsibility of the OD consultant. The scope of this duty is constrained only by the capacity of the consultant to foresee and understand such risks. Not to inform clients of known or likely negative consequences is professionally irresponsible.

Recommending courses of action to mitigate risk is also an important responsibility. Some recommendations will eliminate risks for the client company and its immediate stakeholders, while others reflect the needs of those not party to the deliberations.

An obvious responsibility of OD consultants is to serve the best interests of their clients, which includes providing expertise that the client lacks. Adequately discharging this responsibility involves minimizing obvious and immediate threats to the success of a recommended strategy and calling attention to long-term risks that may not be immediately apparent. In the Comtex case, for example, dramatic measures to reduce costs and enhance profitability may have important unrecognized implications for the company's reputation, the morale of its employees, its public relations, and its overall corporate image. It is always in the client's best interest to present recommendations for decreasing the negative impact of an otherwise desirable course of action.

The consultant also has an ethical obligation to attempt to safeguard the rights and well-being of parties jeopardized by a recommended course of action who are not able to defend their own interests. This responsibility is rarely identified in a consultant's job description but is a central part of our professional ethic. The consultant may find it difficult to serve equally all these masters — company, employees, suppliers, community — and must establish priorities based on the specifics of the situation. In the Comtex case, we would assume that the company is going to choose a course of action that will enhance its chances for survival and profitability; so Street and Korner do not need to make that issue their highest priority.

Their first concern should be to urge management to identify its responsibility to the employees. This takes priority because of the closeness and interdependence of the historical relationship between management and workers. The consultant's second priority is to encourage the company to recognize its obligations to deal with the impact of the change on suppliers and the local community. Overall, the company has a responsibility to recognize and address the consequences of its actions for each of its stakeholders, and the OD consultant has an obligation to facilitate this process.

3. If the client adopts a recommended intervention with risks to third parties, what responsibilities, if any, does the OD consultant have toward those at risk? The immediate obligation of a consultant when third-party interests are in jeopardy is to be certain that the client understands the situation. When the client fully appreciates the nature of the risk and still chooses to proceed, the consultant has a duty to advocate for those threatened and to attempt to influence the client to adopt a strategy that eliminates or reduces the risk.

Depending on the severity and nature of the risk, the consultant also may have an ethical responsibility to disclose the risks either to the parties involved or to others, such as the press or government agencies. There are times when not disclosing known risks is an act of complicity or collusion. The OD consultant must live with the personal and professional consequences of his decision to disclose or stay silent in such instances. Such decisions are painful because they involve choosing between evading responsibility for an unethical act and betraying the trust of one's client.

Comments by Stanley R. Hinckley

In commenting on this case, I have assumed that Lang included no line managers among those "key company staff" he asked to review all business operations. Also, it is not clear who, besides Street and Korner, were involved in the study. We do not know what expertise and viewpoints were represented on the "study team." More importantly, the lack of line manager involvement increases the possibility that no line people will feel ownership in the report. A line-staff conflict over the report and its recommendations thus becomes likely. In my experience, it is much more difficult for staff people to present their conclusions and recommendations in ways that match the language, perspective, and orientation of top management than it is for line managers.

Consultants' Responsibilities to Management. The consultants' responsibility is to summarize the results of the review and to present a report that allows management to make the best possible — that is, well-informed — decisions. To fulfill this responsibility, the consultant must advise management of (1) the short- and long-term risks associated with the various choices and (2) the options available about how to manage those risks. It also means designing the report and the meeting in which it is presented so that top management has a real opportunity to identify and examine their own values that are relevant to the decisions they must make. Street is right in telling Korner that their responsibility is "not only to inform management of the risks of implementing our recommendations," but she makes a mistake when she adds, "but also to ensure management's commitment to do all that it can to reduce the costs associated with their effects." Their responsibility is to give management all the relevant information (including ways to manage and reduce the risks), but there is no way they can "ensure management's commitment."

Consultants' Responsibilities to Each Other. An obvious interpretation of Street and Korner's attitudes and values is that Street's career depends significantly on her ability to develop and maintain the trust and respect of top management. I would recommend to her that she pay close attention to where she stands with management and recognize that her future depends on the competence with which she carries out her assignments. Her visibility and influence in Comtex with top managers and other key people are important to her career. Korner, in contrast, has "given up" on any future improvement in his career and has adopted the organizational stance of "don't rock the boat." The Statement (Guideline III–C, Appendix C) provides guidance for the process they need to follow in order to work through their differences. Street and Korner need to participate in confronting the issues between them and in doing effective problem solving to develop a plan they can both support.

Consultants' Responsibilities to Stakeholders. I believe that we hold, as basic values, justice and the right of all people to have access to all information that is likely to affect them. Since the report has been prepared for top management, it belongs to them and they have "first rights" to decide how the information will be used. One of their rights and responsibilities is to determine when and how to share with the affected employees, suppliers, local communities, and other stakeholders. This raises a critical issue in the practice of Organization Development: When does being "loyal" become collusion?

For the internal OD staff, they must maintain the confidentiality of their report until top management has digested it and decided on a course of action. If Street prevails and the report includes advice on how to ameliorate the effects on stakeholders, that advice probably would — and should — address the best time to sit down with the affected parties and the type of communications, proposals, and negotiations that might be most productive. The advice can and should be framed in terms of what is likely to be best for Comtex's long-term well-being. Then top management's course of action would include their decisions about whether to take that advice.

If the report does not include such advice, or if top management adopts a course of action that involves violating the values of the OD consultants, a serious dilemma arises. This resulting dilemma provides a strong argument for including such advice in the report and presenting it to management in a carefully designed meeting.

The dilemma relates to the question, Who is the client? Obviously, top management is the client for the study and the report. But, as OD staff for Comtex, Street and Korner must consider the whole Comtex system their ongoing client. This includes the relevant parts of the larger system of which Comtex is a part: their customers, suppliers, the families of employees, plant communities, and other stakeholders. Street and Korner must decide at what point their loyalty and commitment to the good of the total system takes precedence over their loyalty to top management. If the OD consultants do everything possible to persuade management to act for the good of the total system and fail, I believe they must consider "violating the trust" of top management — their implicit contract with Lang. They would risk being seen by the top as untrustworthy, incompetent, and unprofessional. These are real and serious risks that internal consultants often must face. They must be evaluated consciously and thoroughly.

Should they decide that they must breach the assumed confidentiality of their report, they will have to work with others in the system to persuade top management to reconsider and choose a different course of action. Their goal becomes to attempt to effect a major change in the values, policies, norms, and/or distribution of power in the system that includes Comtex and all its stakeholders. Such strategies not only risk the loss of one's job but also involve another ethical dilemma: One's behavior may cause permanent damage to top management's view of Organization Development and all OD practitioners, resulting in a violation of Guideline III–B of the Statement (Appendix C).

The alternative to what some might call a revolt against top management is to collude with management in the violation of one's own values. There may be times when one decides that collusion is the best course, but I firmly believe that this choice should be made only in full awareness. The possibilities of being pressured or falling into unconscious collusion with those in power are rampant in our field. To do so is, I believe, a sign of incompetence as a practitioner.

There are many strategies available for being true to one's own values that are only moderately risky relative to losing the trust and confidence of top management. Among my first choices for steps to take, once it is clear that management is not going to handle the situation in a manner I would consider ethical, would be to talk confidentially with some of the key people in the affected plants and divisions and help them consider how they might influence upper management to handle the cutbacks and shutdowns in ways that are best for the total system, including the long-term interests of Comtex. Once the word begins to spread internally, some suppliers, families, and community members are likely to hear about it. Although top management might be furious about the "leak," they might be forced to reconsider their strategy and choose a healthier and more productive one.

If this strategy does not work, a riskier step would be to "blow the whistle" with a leak to the press. Other strategies are available across a spectrum of risk and perceived "disloyalty" to the top. What one chooses to do depends finally on one's values, one's commitment to those values, the degree of one's aversion to collusion, and how much it would "cost" if one's job with the company were lost.

CHAPTER TEN

Facing Racism
and Sexism
in Organizations

▌▌▌▌▌▌▌▌▌▌▌▌▌▌▌▌▌▌▌▌▌▌▌▌▌▌▌▌▌▌

The Blite Corporation is a predominantly white organization with more than 8,000 employees. Of its 1,500 managers, 110 are black. The company is considered by the community in which it operates to be a corporate leader in promoting good race relations among its employees. Hiring and promoting women and members of minority races have been stated company goals for more than a decade, and all managers are evaluated according to their success in achieving their particular numerical targets. Despite this apparent success, the company vice president responsible for affirmative action, Norman Baylor, is disturbed by comments from both white and black managers indicating that neither group is satisfied with the quality of race relations at the company.

Baylor decides to engage the services of Ken DeForest, an external OD consultant who has done prior work for Blite on issues unrelated to race, to assist in investigating the matter. At their first meeting following a lengthy telephone conversation, Baylor and DeForest agree that as his first steps DeForest will gather information and prepare a preliminary diagnosis of race relations in the company before a decision is made on what further involvement by the consultant might be appropriate.

DeForest and Baylor also agree that before any attempt is made to engage in companywide data collection, a smaller, representative group of managers will be selected as an advisory committee to meet with DeForest. The purpose of such a meeting is to provide DeForest with insight into what managers think about the company's race relations record, help him construct a questionnaire and interview schedule, and enlist the cooperation of other managers for the full intervention. Priority will be given to making the group balanced according to race and sex, and then other factors such as age, department, managerial responsibility, and so on, will be considered. In consultation with DeForest, Baylor selects the group's members and invites them to participate. Included with his memorandum of invitation is a letter from Blite's president, Howard Stone, affirming his support for the study.

Eleven of the twelve managers invited to the meeting attend the session with DeForest. After presenting some background information about himself, DeForest distributes a brief open-ended questionnaire designed to give him some initial insight into the group's opinions regarding race relations in the company. The only demographic data requested relate to the race and sex of the respondents. He informs the participants that everything they say at the session will be held in strict confidence and that the questionnaires should be completed anonymously. Time is then allotted for questions about the project. After a lunch break, DeForest leads a two-hour discussion of race relations at Blite. The meeting adjourns at mid-afternoon and another session is scheduled for later that week.

That evening DeForest begins to review the questionnaire responses. To his amazement, in both substance and tone they are dramatically different from the comments made at the meeting's afternoon discussion, which, despite acknowledgment of a few problems, indicated that overall relations are good. Some of the problems identified by black managers include inadequate commitment of company resources to improving race relations, insufficient number of blacks in managerial positions, insensitivity of individual white managers to racial tensions, and a less than fair apportionment of the economic gains achieved by the company. White managers complain of reduced promotional opportunities for white employees, diminished power for whites, too many company resources expended in support of race relations programs, and the advancement of blacks not sufficiently prepared for higher-level responsibilities. Overall, blacks are less likely than whites to believe that Blite has done enough to improve race relations and more likely than their white counterparts to be concerned about the quality of race relations at the company. Furthermore, although not specifically questioned about it, the female managers volunteer the opinion that women, regardless of their race, are not fairly represented in management positions.

The responses reflect a considerable amount of built-up hostility by both black and white managers. Yet none of this was readily apparent to DeForest during the afternoon session. He decides to discuss the matter with the group at the next session.

All twelve invited managers are present at the second meeting. DeForest expresses his surprise at the questionnaire responses. The differences of opinion within the group are greater than he had expected, given the flow of the group's earlier discussion. At this point, a black manager, who was the lone absentee at the first meeting, interrupts. He voices his skepticism of the effort to be undertaken by DeForest. He argues that if the company were seriously interested in improving race relations and gaining the frank opinions of black employees it would have hired a black consultant; what makes DeForest think that blacks will sufficiently trust him with their most candid opinions on race relations?

At this moment, a white female manager rises to express her concerns about the intervention's intended impact on company employees. On the one hand, she believes that female employees are often shortchanged in their efforts to obtain managerial positions at the company. She blames this in large part on sexist attitudes held by the company's top executives, all of whom are male. In this sense, she can identify with blacks as victims of white male power. On the other hand, however, she views the company's efforts to improve race relations and to create more opportunities for blacks as a threat to advancement by white females. Will DeForest's work contribute to what she perceives as the decline in the influence of and opportunities for white female employees?

A white male manager then interjects his opinion that the notion of racial tension at Blite is blown out of proportion. He feels that blacks under his supervision are treated fairly and that he and his black subordinates often joke about racial matters. Throughout the company, he continues, blacks have achieved improved employment status over the past ten years. In fact, in his opinion, some very competent whites have been passed over because of company efforts on behalf of black employees.

DeForest decides to announce a break for lunch in order to assess the morning's events. Several things are becoming clearer to him. For example, despite marked improvement in race relations, Blite still experiences racial problems that adversely affect the company's operations and productivity. Sexism is also a problem perceived by some female managers. He is pleased that these problems have been brought to the surface, for only now can they be confronted directly and alternative responses be assessed.

Yet, in order to get to the core of these problems, DeForest needs to elicit the candid opinions of the employees who will participate in the data-gathering phase. But can he, as a white male, expect to gain the confidence of black and female employees? He is aware of behavioral research findings indicating that, on the subject of racial dynamics, the race of the investigator influences the type of information gathered and the interpretation given to it. Although he has never considered himself racially biased or paid much attention to those research findings, DeForest wonders if, in denying any racial prejudice, he is also denying the possibility that others, especially blacks, might still mistrust him because of racial difference. Perhaps he is not as open to that possibility as he needs to be. But if this is the case, what can he do about it? He cannot halt the process at this point, and he surely cannot change his racial origins.

DeForest's concentration is interrupted by a phone call from Agnes Sanderson of Blite's legal department. She expresses a concern that, despite the company's record of achievement in hiring and promoting minorities, the data gathered by DeForest could be used to support future equal employment opportunity (EEO) legal actions against Blite. She wants to be sure that the legal department will have the opportunity to review all survey instruments and interview schedules and, if warranted, require that items be altered or eliminated entirely. DeForest explains that he will be delighted to have the department review his materials prior to their use but that he, in consultation with Baylor, must be the final judge on what is retained or omitted. They end their conversation with an obvious difference of opinion on the matter.

When DeForest and Baylor originally discussed the intervention, DeForest mentioned that undertaking efforts aimed at improving race relations in a company with a predominantly white work force would undoubtedly precipitate a higher than ordinary level of tension. He wanted Baylor to be alert to that possibility, but now the reality of that message is causing him to reassess his own plans. He wants to do what he can to help reduce racism and sexism among company employees. He also wants to be fair and perceived as such by the people with whom he will be working. But will his own race and sex be a handicap in achieving those objectives? Is his competency compromised by his race? And how can he convince the legal department that his work is intended to improve race relations, not generate racially based legal claims against the company? He realizes that whatever action he takes, including withdrawal from the project, can affect future race relations at Blite. He needs more time to evaluate his options.

Questions to Consider

1. What should DeForest do to lessen his uneasiness about the effect of his race and sex on his work at the company? Specifically, what are his obligations to himself, the company, individual employees, and the OD profession?
2. Although DeForest does not intend his work to result in legal action against the company, he is not able to promise that it will not do so. And, if employees file complaints,

he might well be caught in the middle. What should he do with regard to the legal department's demands?

3. What special challenges to the values and ethics of the OD profession are raised by work on racial matters? How should individual practitioners and researchers prepare themselves for such work? Does the draft Statement (Appendix C) offer any help?

4. When an OD consultant works with an organization in which people are clearly discriminated against because of race or sex, particularly with regard to their representation at higher levels of management, does he or she have an ethical obligation to do anything about it when the matter is not part of the original contract? Elaborate on the reasons for your position, including, if appropriate, any guidelines for taking action.

Note: In asking people to comment on this case, we sought a diversity of points of view. Those who responded were: Lee G. Bolman, lecturer on education, Graduate School of Education, Harvard University, and external consultant; Ophie A. Franklin, executive director, International Center for Integrative Studies/The Door—A Center of Alternatives, New York; William Gellermann, external consultant with multicultural experience but not expertise; Bailey W. Jackson, lecturer on education, School of Education, University of Massachusetts at Amherst, external consultant with multicultural expertise; Patricia H. Werhane, Wirtenberger Professor of Ethics, Department of Philosophy, Loyola University, Chicago, author of *Persons, Rights, and Corporations,* editor of *Employee Rights and Responsibilities Journal.* Excerpts from their comments follow.

Comments

Prologue

Gellermann: The following comments identify and clarify most of the key issues raised by this case, but it is important to note that such comments can only suggest the depth of the issues related to the role of OD-HSD consultants in dealing with racist — and sexist — beliefs and attitudes within their client organizations and within the larger society of which both they and their clients are members. As I see it, a primary barrier to real depth is that labeling the problem as "racism" or "sexism" tends to give the illusion of understanding it; for me, labeling or identifying the problem is only the beginning of the quest for understanding. The following comments help us go farther into that quest, but I want to stress that they only suggest the depth of our need for understanding. For the purposes of this book, that is all right, since it leaves the responsibility for plumbing that depth with you, the reader.

During the 1960s, when the civil rights movement in the United States was high in the consciousness of American society, one of the civil rights leaders said, "If you're not part of the solution, you're part of the problem." The problem still exists, and I think the basic idea is correct: Your willingness — whether black or white, male or female, minority or majority — to acknowledge, first, that you *may* be part of the problem and then, after reflection, to recognize the extent to which you *are* part of the problem, are both necessary steps toward solution. I hope you will reflect on what your own response to the case suggests about both of these questions and then read the following comments with those reflections in mind.

Without such acknowledgment, any of us would be unable to solve the problem. And that inability suggests another aspect of the problem — namely, that those of us in the "superior" role are likely to feel less intensely about our need to acknowledge the problem, our place in it, or the urgency of solving it. The core issue is one of values. Do those of us with power under the present system care more about "justice for all" or about preserving the benefits the system gives us? For me, preserving the benefits of a narrowly defined "good life" at the expense of justice is immoral in that it pays for the good life of some at the expense of good life for others.

In dealing with this issue, however, we also need to be careful not to be drawn into the psychological "game" of "victim and victimizer." In my opinion, that game has an essentially disempowering effect on the victims because it tends to create a view of them as powerless. In one version of the game, victims (for example, blacks) hold victimizers (for example, white males) responsible for the victims' problems. For those who buy into that game, the victimizers are expected to feel guilty (because of the past sins of white males) and therefore accept full responsibility for solving the victims' problems. As I see it, that game is a waste of energy. It is more productive for everyone, victims and victimizers, to see the victims as having the power to solve their own problems and to hold them responsible for doing what *they* can do in their "quest for a good life," since that is the essence of empowerment. This does not mean blaming the victims for their oppression; nor does it absolve white males from responsibility for doing what *they* can do. It does mean, among other things, respecting people's dignity and integrity and supporting them in their efforts to empower themselves rather than emphasizing their powerlessness and other people's abuses of power.

One possible consequence of the victimization world view was suggested by Shelby Steele, a leading black academic. While appearing in a PBS documentary about racial tensions in New York City, he said "blacks are too burdened by their own sense of victimization to have the confidence necessary to succeed in the mainstream business world" (Klein, 1990, p. 36). In considering that idea, we need to be aware that Steele's views are controversial in the black community; rather than joining in the argument, it is better for us to concentrate on whether such an idea can be useful in helping blacks empower themselves. For example, if some blacks do feel the burden of victimization in a way that undermines their self-confidence, then our role can be to help them (1) acknowledge the benefits of *holding on* to that "burden" (such as the power it can give and the community feeling it can give with others who share that burden) and (2) identify the benefits of *letting go* of the burden (such as the release of energy that they can then use in empowering themselves).

Bolman: In any situation in which serious intergroup conflict is, or might be, present, it is difficult if not impossible for a member of either group to be equally credible and trust-worthy to both parties. A white male such as DeForest, who contracts to work on a project involving "race relations" and then wanders into a thicket of race and gender issues without any apparent awareness of the credibility problem, is probably naive about issues of race and gender, and perhaps about basic dynamics of intergroup conflict as well. He is, apparently, in beyond his level of competence, and that is a basic violation of almost any code of professional ethics.

The case is vague about what skills and experiences DeForest does have, and it says nothing about the nature of his prior OD work for Blite. The case suggests that there is substantial conflict simmering beneath the surface at Blite. Was DeForest unaware of this?

Some information that would be helpful is unspecified in the case: Is Baylor black or white? What skills and experience does he have in dealing with these issues? The most reasonable inference from the case seems to be that he is white and not very sophisticated.

Had I been DeForest, when I was first contacted about working on race relations at the company I would have asked myself two questions: (1) Do I have the appropriate skills and experience to undertake such a project? and (2) Whom could I engage as a co-worker to create a team that is balanced in race and gender? I would not undertake the project without a black colleague (preferably a black woman, since the case at the outset appears to present issues of both race and gender), and I would not do it at all unless I felt it was within my area of expertise.

Franklin: Confronting racial problems in organizations requires understanding a complex system of internal and external boundary management controls, value conflict controls, and belief system maintenance behaviors that take into account the socialization processes and world view perspectives of the consultant, the client system, and the environment in which the change is to occur. Traditionally, the client system's environment, which tends to make the client system a microcosm of the environment's culture, has mitigated against resolution of racial conflict. When attempts to intervene in organizations are by consultants whose sociopolitical world views are consistent with those of the institution seeking change, the similarities of those views make it difficult, if not impossible, for such consultants to contribute significantly to the resolution of racial conflict.

Just as the presence or absence of people of color in the institution can blur the boundary between persons and roles (such as the blurring of access to manager roles for black persons), the same kind of blur is present and working in the unconscious behavior of the white consultant as a defense against anxieties about his or her own survival in working with the institution. For example, truly understanding the situation might lead to the conclusion that a black person might better serve in the consultant role. Survival in this context is multidimensional and includes the socially acceptable behaviors that support and condone racism in the institution. The threat to identity experienced by one group (white) as the result of the presence of the other (black) race has its origins in the fantasies and assumptions that are learned from the consultant's earlier experience in the culture.

In order to grasp fully the implications of this threat to white identity, it is necessary to view racism as a peculiar psychopathology that is characterized by the almost complete absence of ethical or moral development and an almost total disregard for appropriate patterns of behavior where people of color are concerned (Wright, 1975); all these elements are supported, encouraged, and reinforced by the culture. This behavior is made acceptable by a set of psychodynamic justifications that include projection of blame, delusions of grandeur, denial of reality, perceptual distortion, phobia regarding differences, rejection of constituted authority if possessed by blacks, and an inability to accept democracy and racial oppression as conflicting ideals (Hillard, 1978).

Managing the dilemma in the intervention, and indeed in the Blite Corporation, requires a dialectic between the black and white managers that is reflected in the composition of the intervention team. Parity and equity of presence, authority, autonomy, and power are essential to interventions confronting problems of race. Any attempt at intervention by a lone white (male or female) consultant into a conflict where whites are dominant is likely to involve a contradiction of consciousness that colludes in maintaining a dependent relationship by the black out-group to the white power structure. This dependent relationship is mirrored in the structure of the intervention, which makes the black managers and staff dependent on the self-awareness, expertise, technology, and benevolence of the lone white consultant.

In such a design, there exists a three-tiered manifestation of the presenting problem (for example, race conflict and power inequities)—at the boundaries between the society and the institution, within the institution between its leadership and its management subsection, and within the intervention between its white leadership and the black subgroup of managers and staff. The ethical dilemma posed as a consequence is whether the intervention is or should be designed to examine white racist behavior (for example, integrating blacks into a white system and keeping it a white system) and to develop appropriate accommodation. To examine out-group liberation as an option raises still another dilemma: namely, who is the client when the intervention is being paid for by the white institution?

Werhane: I first want to discuss some issues related to Baylor's approach to the situation and suggest what he might have done *before* he decided to bring in a consultant.

Baylor perceived dissatisfaction about race relations in the company on the part of black and women managers and some whites as well. Given this perception, Baylor was faced with a number of problems, including:

- Are the stated company goals for hiring and promoting women and minorities publicly known to all employees? Are these goals specific enough so that they are achievable in practice? Are these goals perceived by white employees and managers as unfair to them?

- Are Baylor's perceptions of unrest among women and white and black managers correct?
- Can the racial problems at Blite be solved without appealing to an outside consultant? Should they be?
- If an outside consultant is brought in, what is his role? How will that person be perceived by the unhappy managers of both races and sexes?

Given the tense racial situation, Baylor — and the Blite Corporation — should have taken a number of steps before bringing in an outside consultant. While outside consultants are useful because they often introduce a balanced and more objective perspective to a problem, a prior internal self-study and critique can often bring to light information and issues that a consultant as an "outsider" can not readily discover. Therefore, an internal self-evaluation is an appropriate starting place for problem analysis.

Having made the decision to hire a consultant, a number of other steps should have been taken before the consultant was given the task of data collection. These include:

- Carefully select the kind of consultant for this job; should the consultant be a woman or a minority, or can a white male accomplish what Blite needs?
- Ascertain consultant competence for this job before it is begun.
- Decide on the consultant's role and authority.
- Prepare the company and its employees for the consultant's intervention.

In addition, the consultant — in this case, DeForest — could have recommended that an internal self-evaluation be conducted before work was begun.

1. What should DeForest do to lessen his uneasiness about the effect of his race and sex on his work at the company? Specifically, what are his obligations to himself, the company, individual employees, and the OD-HSD profession?

Bolman: I would suggest that he meet with Baylor, discuss what he has learned so far, and say to Baylor, "We have verified your concern that there is a problem. I think that you need to engage a consulting group with specific expertise in these issues. That team should be balanced in both race and gender. I think this is a set of problems that goes beyond my expertise, and I should probably withdraw from the consultation. I would be happy, however, to assist you in finding consulting help and to work with the new consultants to help them enter Blite."

It is, of course, not always easy for external consultants to withdraw from a consultancy for fear of losing the relationship with the client and the revenues involved. But at the heart of an effort to develop a code of ethics is the recognition that the ethical choice is not always easy and not always in the short-term interest of the professional. It seems to me that it is essential for us to commit ourselves to a standard of being honest with ourselves and our clients when we are underqualified and there are other professionals with substantially greater expertise than our own in the issues that are central to the consultation.

Franklin: The strategy I envision, as it would apply to the Blite situation, is one that would call for the exercise of internal task maintenance by DeForest, especially in times of stress, that would enable him to experience the issues emotionally before cognitively translating them from the perspective of the black and female out-groups, while simultaneously internalizing the reality that keeps these out-groups from acting assertively in support of their own interest. More generally, "out-group" can be used to describe any group of persons integral to the social process but kept outside of its primary social system, rather than peripheral or marginal to it, with the latter implying possibilities for moving into the mainstream of that system. The latter implies some element of choice of movement in the system. In contrast, emotionally experiencing the out-group position is to experience the devastation implicit in a culture of silence and powerlessness (Freire, 1970).

Evidence supporting the interpretation that blacks at Blite are an out-group can be found in the case's reference to "minority," "predominantly white," "the community," and so on, all of which define reality from the world view of the white controller perspective. Further, DeForest misses what for me seems to be the classic upper-level interpretation of the problem at Blite—namely, that "racism, a behavioral system whose goal is to establish, maintain, expand and refine White supremacy, . . . is the priority value" (Welsing, 1974), whether explicitly or implicitly stated. The goals to which DeForest targets this intervention are secondary at best, in that profit, wealth, and improvement in race relations and/or efficiency are not more than unconscious manifestations of the unarticulated primary task. Had DeForest not been intimately involved in the benefits of the hidden agenda (white supremacy), he might well have capitalized on the opportunity to include in his intervention strategy a black co-consultant to help him deal with his and the institution's blind spots. This is not intended as an indictment of DeForest but rather as a documentation of a system whose domination pervades all human activity despite personal motivation, competencies, and interests. It therefore requires careful scrutiny in dialogue with others outside the system and a negotiation of terms of mutuality.

White supremacy, by implication, prescribes how people of color are to behave. Imposing white-prescribed behavior tends to trigger unconscious collusion by blacks (and other people of color) in the distorted reality of the white supremacists' perspective, thereby causing blacks to internalize that reality into their world view and their behavior in a way that confirms white fantasies of superiority. DeForest would need to be able to recognize the fantasy, the collusion, and the behavioral manifestation of that collusion while experiencing the associated emotional messages in order to address adequately both sides of the issue.

What DeForest does in these circumstances will almost certainly have serious ethical consequences. On the one hand, adherence to the world view of the white supremacist perspective exacerbates the problem by forcing on the black out-group an identity that reinforces both its sense of separateness and powerlessness and its culture of silence (passive aggression) as a tactic of survival. On the other hand, applying strategies that address the world view of the black out-group will tend to separate the consultant from his own racial reference and is likely to lead to his denunciation by some, if not all, white managers and perhaps to his inability to continue working with Blite.

To create a balanced intervention system, Baylor and DeForest must provide a supportive climate for study for all stakeholders and their respective visions of reality. I would do this by including primary out-group representation with equal status on the intervention team, which, in the Blite case, includes blacks and whites, men and women, and managers and staff. In the selection of black representation, it is imperative that world view as well as skin color be considered in order to compensate for past histories of abuse and intimidation in the work setting. Trappings of subgroup identity, be they skin color, hair texture, costume, or whatever, are not sufficient to effect results that fully serve social justice.

Jackson: First, let us focus on what DeForest should have known and done prior to entering into this contract. DeForest seems to have a number of blind spots that have contributed to his being in this dilemma. Here are just a few:

- The apparent assumption that he is working in an acultural profession
- The apparent assumption that one can be "color blind" or not racially influenced or prejudiced in this society
- A lack of appreciation for the impact of racism on the way situations are read by blacks, Asians, Hispanics, and Native Americans

Most OD-HSD practitioners fail to recognize that the profession is heavily influenced by a white male view of the world. We fail to pay attention to who writes the books and articles we read, who develops the models we use, and who conducts the research to which we refer. We do not seem to recognize that these people, predominantly white and male, view the world through a set of glasses that are influenced by their race and gender. As a result, we have a profession that is, by default, significantly influenced by a white and male view of organizations. That view influences what we see when we diagnose organizations, what we prescribe for these organizations, and the strategies we use when we are consulting with organizations.
Our inability to grasp this awareness and integrate it into

our consciousness is related to our view that the white and male perspective is the normal perspective of the world; we do not recognize it as uniquely white or male. For example, we see our theories, techniques, and models as being for and dealing with "organizations," not *white male* organizations. If DeForest had understood this limitation in the thinking and practice of OD-HSD, he might have been more sensitive to the biases inherent in the strategies and models he chose to follow.

DeForest does not seem to understand that his view of the Blite Corporation could be influenced by his racial and gender identity. This blind spot, coupled with the lack of sensitivity to race and gender issues inherent in the profession, put him at a distinct disadvantage as a resource in this situation.

It also appears that DeForest does not understand that there are blacks, Asians, Hispanics, and Native Americans who will distrust him just because he is white. Not understanding this reflects a serious lack of awareness about racial issues and the manifestations and effects of racism on individual perceptions — especially for someone who has accepted responsibility for a project dealing with race relations.

Given the stage of DeForest's relationship with the Blite Corporation, short of referring the client to someone more competent to handle this contract, DeForest could try the following:

- Get a nonwhite OD-HSD consultant who has experience in this area to work with him. He should pay attention to the groups within the organization and how that profile can be best reflected in the consultant staff regarding gender, race, age, and so on.
- Get good representation on the advisory committee of the various racial groups. Develop a relationship with the committee that will allow him to use it as a checkpoint for any racial biases that might be operating in the effort.

DeForest's obligation to himself is to increase his consciousness of the impact that race and racism, as well as other forms of social oppression, have on organizations. His obligation to the Blite Corporation is to be honest about the limitations resulting from his white male biases.

Werhane: Although DeForest's race and sex tend to bias Blite's women and minorities against him, he has made too much of this, and he appears naive about discrimination problems. His commitment as an OD-HSD consultant is to take as unbiased and fair an approach to this problem as is possible, and he should demonstrate that commitment in his actions. If DeForest is relatively unbiased in his treatment of the managers at Blite, while being aware of his own race and sex, this will become apparent as he works with these people. If he cannot behave with such awareness, he should resign from this job. In any event, he should not brood over the fact that he is a white male, since he can do nothing about that. His job is to demonstrate that his race and sex make no appreciable difference in his approach to the subject.

Gellermann: DeForest is at a branch in the road of his relationship with Blite (and in his "quest for a good life"). He can become part of the problem or part of the solution. The Ethical Guidelines in the Statement say that he should "practice within the limits of his competence" (Guideline II-D) and know enough about "multicultural issues, including issues of culture and gender" to work with other OD-HSD professionals who have the necessary expertise (Guideline II-B-1-a-4). But *he seems not to know that he does not know* — namely, that he is outside the limits of his competence and he needs help — although it may be dawning on him. In his position, I would work with Baylor to engage one or two additional consultants for our consulting team so that it will better reflect Blite's race and gender mix and simultaneously add multicultural expertise. Then, among other things, I would recommend to the team that we encourage Baylor to create an affirmative action steering committee with which we could work (including Baylor as a member). And I would urge that the committee be reasonably representative of all the relevant interests within Blite — genders, races, higher- and lower-level managers, workers, and so on.

Not only would such actions effectively serve the client's

needs, but they also are consistent with the ethics in the Statement (Appendix B), particularly the following:

• Establish collegial and cooperative relationships with other
  OD-HSD professionals, including (a) using colleagues as
  consultants to provide ourselves with feedback . . . and to
  minimize the effects of our blind spots and (b) creating partnerships with colleagues to enhance our effectiveness in serving clients whose needs are greater than we can serve alone
  (Guideline II–B–2).
• Act assertively with our clients to promote justice and well-
  being [and] . . . promote affirmative action in dealing with
  the effects of past discrimination (Guidelines V–C–1 and
  V–C–1–b).

2. What should DeForest do with regard to the legal department's demands?

Bolman:. I think DeForest was right not to concede immediately to all of Sanderson's requests. If I were involved in
this consultation, I would first need to collect more information. Is Sanderson expressing a legitimate company concern,
or is she a nervous loose cannon? I would want Baylor's perspective on the meaning of Sanderson's request, and I would
want to understand Sanderson's concerns as well as I could. I
would be willing to work with her to find a way to proceed that
met both our concerns. Consultants and lawyers both provide
counsel to organizations, and both have a responsibility to use
their expertise in the overall best interests of their client. Line
management has to decide what role it wants the legal department to play. If management decides that it is more concerned
with avoiding lawsuits than with working on issues of affirmative action, I would give them my judgment about the consequences of such a course and tell them that such a direction
would suggest to me that I should withdraw.

Jackson: DeForest had a responsibility to: (1) advise Baylor of the possible consequences of embarking on a change effort
of this type and (2) encourage Baylor to meet with the legal

department and hear its concerns. DeForest also should be prepared first to explain to Baylor why the data he is collecting are necessary and how they will be used and then to offer suggestions on how the objectives of the effort can be accomplished without putting the corporation at risk and to be available to the legal department to help formulate ways of doing so.

Werhane: DeForest must work with the legal department at Blite, but with Baylor in charge and not the legal department. DeForest should be clear about the legal implications of any study he undertakes so he can tactfully but firmly defend his intervention procedures. Baylor needs to smooth DeForest's relationship with the legal department so DeForest can get on with his task in a way that is acceptable to Baylor, the legal department, and himself.

Gellermann: The Statement gives guidance: "Act with due regard for the needs, special competencies, and obligations of colleagues in other professions. Respect the prerogatives and obligations of the institutions or organizations with which these colleagues are associated" (Guidelines IV–E–2 and IV–E–3). However, achieving a mutually acceptable solution with Sanderson may be difficult because the legal tradition from which she comes has tended to be adversarial (win-lose). If she and I cannot easily resolve our differences, I would involve Baylor. Guideline III–D–3 may also become relevant (although at this moment it seems unlikely): "Identify and respond to any major differences in professionally relevant values and ethics between ourselves and our clients; be prepared to cease work, with explanation of our reasons, if necessary."

3. What special challenges to the values and ethics of the OD profession are raised by work on racial matters? How should individual practitioners and researchers prepare themselves for such work? Does the draft Statement (Appendix C) offer any help?

Bolman: Racial issues, as they present themselves in the United States, are an example of a more general phenomenon:

politics between groups that differ in both culture and power. Whenever a group with one culture (that is, values, beliefs, lifestyles, language, faith) has more power than another group with a different culture, both intergroup conflict and oppression are likely. The groups may be defined by race (as in the United States or South Africa), by religion (as in Northern Ireland or the Middle East), by language (as in Canada), or by any other dimension on which two groups can differ. The combination of differences in both culture and power is likely to produce oppression of the subordinate group. The consultant who is more closely tied to the dominant culture risks allying with injustice; the consultant who is more closely tied to the subordinate culture risks being powerless. A consultant on either side of the interface risks misunderstanding and being misunderstood by the members of the other group.

How does a consultant become skilled in dealing with issues of race and gender? First, the consultant should be aware of major theory and research around intergroup conflict in general and around race and gender issues in particular. Second, the consultant's training should include opportunities to explore one's own culture and attitudes and to learn about the culture and attitudes of others who are members of different groups. Third, the consultant should work in training and consulting events that deal with these issues, at first under the supervision of more experienced professionals.

The draft Statement (Appendix C) does refer to these issues at several points. It enjoins the consultants to recognize the equal worth of human beings, regardless of differences in race, gender, creed, socioeconomic status, or sexual preference. It requires of the consultant a "professional level of competence" in "multicultural issues, including issues of color and gender." It also states that professionals must recognize the limits of their "competence, culture, and experience" in providing services. I support the standards that those statements set. Currently, the primary question for me concerns not those standards but whether most practicing consultants meet them.

Franklin: As for the OD profession and its "Statement of Values and Ethics . . . ", the profession needs to decide what it stands for with regard to social justice in all aspects of human activity, including economics, education, entertainment, labor, law, politics (meaning relations between people), religion, sex, and war as it relates to white supremacy, and then to have the moral mental courage to make that position more explicit than in the April 1985 version of the Statement (Appendix C). For the profession to make a strong stand will be difficult if not impossible because the vast majority of practitioners are part of the white supremacist culture. However, the OD profession as a subculture may reduce the effects of white supremacist mentality and thus enable OD to achieve a more liberated and assertive position of influence. Is this possible?

Jackson: As stated above, the primary challenge to the profession is to become more sensitive to the racial and gender bias inherent in the theory and practice of OD. In addition, the profession also must become more sensitive to the impact that racism, sexism, and other forms of social oppression have on the client-consultant relationship and on the conception and implementation of the change effort. The profession must be more forthcoming with a position of advocacy for social justice and the elimination of social oppression. Such a statement would let consultants know that work in organizations that does not serve a social justice agenda and/or engages in activities that actively or passively support forms of social oppression are not consistent with the goals and values of the profession.

Individual practitioners and researchers must involve themselves in consciousness-raising and skill-building programs that will fill the current void in OD education and training programs with regard to the impact of race (and other social group identities) and racism (and other forms of social oppression) on the profession, the practice of the profession, and the practitioner. Specifically, practitioners must add the following competencies to their existing profile:

- Commitment to social justice, against social oppression, and the full appreciation and inclusion of the widest range of social group diversity available in a given situation.

- Personal awareness of the influence of one's own racial perspective (and the influence of one's other social identities, such as gender, class, age) on one's view of the world; also, personal awareness of how racism (and other forms of social oppression, such as sexism, classism, ageism) influence one's view of the world
- Knowledge about the history of racism (and other forms of social oppression) in the country and the immediate environment of the client system; knowledge of the cultural attributes of the members of the client system
- Skills and experience applicable to working racial agendas in organizations

There would need to be some changes and additions to the existing draft Statement to provide useful guidance for DeForest or any OD consultant in a similar situation. While there are important provisions that would be supportive of any effort that has already been mounted to address racial issues in an organization, there is not much in the draft Statement that directly suggests to OD practitioners that they should aggressively pay attention to the points cited above. I believe that provisions that address these four points might be a beginning.

Assuming that generic statements about the worth, empowerment, and rights of human beings will include all human beings is a faulty assumption. Unfortunately, our concept of who is human rarely includes Asians, blacks, Hispanics/Latinos, Native Americans, women, the elderly, members of the lower classes, and other oppressed groups. Those of us who are white, male, and so on, are usually the ones we implicitly think of when we use the term *human*. Until this changes, we cannot continue to rely on statements of this type.

Finally, most of the language in the draft Statement that might have anything explicitly to do with "racial matters" is embedded in the section on "cross-cultural" interaction (for example, Guidelines II–D and IV–D, Appendix C). While these discussions are important for those working outside the United States, they do not sufficiently address the issues for those of us who, like DeForest, are working on multicultural issues in organizations like Blite.

Werhane: The draft Statement offers general guidelines for consultants. An OD consultant in DeForest's position should evaluate his own position on race relations. If consultants are truly aware of their biases and treat the managers and other employees with whom they deal fairly, confidence will develop between them in whatever intervention project they attempt to institute. In the Blite case, this will take time, particularly for DeForest, who, with Baylor's help, must establish himself as a trustworthy person.

Having properly prepared himself, DeForest can then evaluate the race relations and affirmative action policies at Blite. Following the above outline of the steps that Baylor should have taken, DeForest should conduct discussions with Blite employees about values and about affirmative action and race relations policies. With managers at Blite he should develop suggestions about the improvement of these goals and policies. Often policies developed by employees and middle management are easier to implement than are those dictated by management, even if those newly developed policies are identical to those previously in place.

Gellermann: For me, racial issues offer OD professionals a special challenge—namely, to reframe their collective purpose to encompass a Human Systems Development perspective as well as the more familiar OD perspective. From the HSD perspective, OD professionals can view their individual efforts as contributing to achievements by their profession on a scale that individual professionals could not undertake. On matters such as racism and sexism, their ultimate client, if they and their profession accept the challenge, is the entire society within which their client organizations (such as Blite) are subsystems.

The Statement can help. Work on racial issues on the scale of an entire society is consistent with the vision expressed there. It involves a variation on "Think globally, act locally"—namely, "Think societally, act locally." Most OD professionals would concentrate on racial matters within their client systems—business, government, schools—but by viewing their individual efforts as contributions to a national effort, they may see additional opportunities for coordination that will enable them to produce results greater than the sum of the parts. (And their professional associations might provide additional coordination and leadership.)

The Statement offers further help with guidelines relevant to issues related to race in the area of "Social Responsibility" (Guideline V). They deal with our responsibility for being sensitive to "multicultural differences, our own cultural filters, and their implications" (Guideline V-B), including: (1) Respect the cultural orientations of the individuals, organizations, communities, countries, and other human systems within which we work, including their customs, beliefs, values, morals, and ethics; and (2) Recognize and constructively confront the counterproductive aspects of those cultures whenever feasible." They also support acting "assertively with our clients to promote justice and well-being," including constructively confronting discrimination and promoting affirmative action (Guideline V-C-1). (See also the Statement's section on values for a discussion of what we mean by "justice.") The Statement also recognizes that "our action may not be seen as serving the client's interests and, as a result, might jeopardize our ability to serve the client in other ways. We recognize the inevitability of this dilemma and seek to resolve it as ethically as we can." (In case of such a dilemma, the five-step model may help. See Chapter Three.)

4. When an OD consultant works with an organization in which people are clearly discriminated against because of race or sex, particularly with regard to their representation at higher levels of management, does he or she have an ethical obligation to do anything about it when the matter is not part of the original contract?

Bolman: Should doctors mention a condition they notice, even though they were consulted about something else? If we ask an attorney to draw up a will and she notices that our proposed arrangement, though perfectly legal, would have very adverse tax consequences, should she say anything? I think the answer has to be yes in all such cases. Presumably, all professionals are held accountable for a standard of care, which includes a responsibility to alert our clients to something that we notice even though they might not.

Moreover, it seems to me that an OD consultant is responsible both to the organization and to the people whose lives are significantly affected by it. If I see injustice or any other form of ineffectiveness in my client organization, I feel a responsibility to communicate what I have seen and what I think it means. The organization always retains the right to choose not to deal with those issues, but I have an obligation to try to ensure that it is aware of the problem and that it makes an informed choice.

An example is a client who planned to use only male trainers for a management development effort because "most of the participants are male, and they won't accept women." I felt it was my responsibility to question the assumption that the male participants would never accept women and note that such an assumption was likely to become a self-fulfilling prophecy. My advice had not been solicited on that question, and initially it did not seem to be appreciated. Yet I thought it was important for me and for the client that I raise the issue. (The client eventually decided to use women. The women did, at times, have to work harder to gain credibility, but overall they did as well as the men.)

It has often been my experience that clients do not react with immediate enthusiasm when I initiate unsolicited discussions of race or gender, even though I try to raise those issues in a way that is as nonpunitive as possible, with minimal blame directed at the client organization.

Franklin: Preparation for this challenge requires an enlightened practice inspired by new learnings that include contributions from theory, logic, and world view targeted at *counter-racism.* Few if any of these learnings will be found in the annals of white scholarship and none in the discipline of white behavioral science. However, an abundance of information in other areas of scholarship has been made available by researchers expert in their fields. I would recommend as a starting point the works of Frances C. Welsing, Joseph Ben-Jochanon, Martin

Bernal, Ivan Van Sertima, Frantz Fanon, Chancellor Williams, Paulo Freire, George G. M. James, John Henry Clark, and Asa Hillard, among others too numerous to mention.

As indicated earlier, I believe that to avoid the issue of white supremacy is to relegate oneself to permanent status as a mid-level OD practitioner with limited capacities to confront issues of threats to identity (one's own or others') and probably incapable of interventions that help institutions grapple with the complexities of freedom, justice, and equality. Similarly, issues of gender and age are different in their oppression only in that the dynamics and practices perfected on the racial out-groups are turned inward toward subsectors of the supremacist culture and mirrored in the self-destructive behavior of the oppressed.

Jackson: In this case the consultant has not only an ethical responsibility to raise this finding but also a contractual obligation to do so. If a consultant is engaged in a consulting relationship intended to enhance the functioning of the client system, notices a situation such as the one described herein, and does nothing about it, he or she would be committing an act of gross negligence.

It is unfortunate that many, if not most, OD consultants would have to ask themselves this question. For many OD consultants, it is possible to consider themselves successful at enhancing the health of an organization without paying attention to how the organization is managing diversity or dealing with prejudice, discrimination, harassment, and other forms of social oppression. This should not be. Somewhere in our conception of organizational health there must be a recognition of the necessity for social justice, the effective management of work force diversity, and the appreciation and full utilization of the available multicultural perspective.

Werhane: In general, while discrimination is obviously wrong and should be corrected whenever and wherever it occurs, OD consultants cannot decide in advance whether they have an obligation to correct discriminatory actions in every company with which they consult. Sometimes the task of the consultant in a particular company is both important and altogether distinct from this sort of personnel problem. Sometimes, too, if trust in an OD consultant is developed in another situation, he or she may then be in a position to comment on discrimination in that company and perhaps be asked to work with management on their discrimination problems. As an OD consultant, one should take a stand against any unfair practice; but this does not preclude working in a company in which discrimination occurs without necessarily being obligated to solve that problem.

Gellermann: Viewed in the context of the challenge I mentioned in response to the previous question, OD-HSD professionals have the opportunity to commit themselves to serving justice. Given the potential for constructive change represented by their unique abilities, we could even say that they and their profession have a moral responsibility to make such a commitment. If they do so, then, in my view, they have a moral obligation to confront discrimination constructively, regardless of the specifics of their contracts. (As mentioned earlier, the Statement is explicit about this in Guideline V-C-1.) Furthermore, as most OD-HSD professionals know, a sound case can be made for acting affirmatively to end discrimination based on organizational values (profitability, productivity, efficiency, and so on) under most, if not all, conditions. However, as Franklin noted in one of his comments, those values may be secondary. If so, OD-HSD professionals need to understand why and be prepared to deal with that fact. Most importantly, the *moral* reason for serving justice is that it is the good and right thing to do, whether or not it serves the organization's values. This does not deny that the organization's values must be considered in order for the professional to be effective in serving justice within the organization. It does mean that OD-HSD professionals need to be clear about the conditions under which they are prepared to risk rejection by their clients or to refuse or withdraw from work with a client because such work would be inconsistent with their values and ethics (Guideline III-B-6).

CHAPTER ELEVEN

⁨▌▮▌▮▌▮▌▮▌▮▌▮▌▮▌▮▌▮▌▮▌▮▌▮▌▮▌▮▌▮⁩

A Conflict
of Basic Values?

⁨▌▮▌▮▌▮▌▮▌▮▌▮▌▮▌▮▌▮▌▮▌▮▌▮▌▮▌▮⁩

In 1982 Federal Dynamo Corp., a large industrial concern employing over 50,000 people, and Local 141 of the IUEW negotiated as part of their collective bargaining agreement a far-reaching quality of working life (QWL) program. The program called for setting up QWL committees in every unit of every division in the corporation in which bargaining unit employees worked. Federal Dynamo put its two internal OD consultants, Mort Brown and José Frias, to work full-time on implementing the QWL program. It also retained two external consultants, Lucille Grossman and Joyce Carter. The four consultants were to work as a team to help set up and coordinate every aspect of the program.

The corporation and the union both saw the QWL program as a major vehicle for implementing a basic organizational change. After years of stability, Federal Dynamo faced increasingly stiff competition. Over the long stable period, the work force at all levels had become accustomed to working in accordance with set routines. The new competitive environment, however, demanded that employees develop the ability to handle new kinds of situations with much less supervisory guidance than in the past.

In its first two years of operation, the program had its

ups and downs. Some QWL committees functioned effectively, while others never really got off the ground. Nonetheless, the corporation and the union agreed to continue the program in the 1984 collective bargaining agreement. In large measure this reflected their strong belief in the necessity for organizational change as much as it indicated satisfaction with the progress of the program. By the spring of 1985, however, the program had become increasingly accepted by the bargaining unit employees. The biggest obstacle to success at this point lay in the attitude of the lower-level managers, who, for the most part, resented the QWL committees. They neither participated in the program nor made any effort to follow up on the various ideas the committees developed.

Everyone involved in implementing the program recognized the problem, but no one seemed ready to confront it. Finally, on a Monday afternoon, toward the end of a monthly meeting of the QWL program steering committee, Dave Mulligan, a union vice president, put the issue on the table. "We all know what's holding back this program," he said. "It's the attitude of the first and second levels. We're not going to go forward until the company kicks them in the butt. They have to get the message that unless they can work with the QWL committees they won't go anywhere in the Federal Dynamo Corporation."

A vaguely uncomfortable silence fell over the steering committee for a brief time after Mulligan had spoken. Some desultory comments then followed to the effect that he had raised a tough issue that the steering committee would have to face at some point. No one, however, pursued the matter, and the meeting ended. The next day, though, Brown, one of the internal OD consultants, drafted the following memorandum:

TO: Joyce Carter, José Frias,
Lucille Grossman
FROM: Mort Brown
DATE: August 13, 1985
SUBJECT: First- and Second-Level Manager
Participation in QWL
Dave Mulligan raised a problem at the last
steering committee meeting that won't go away by

itself. If QWL is going to change this organization
in a big way, we have to get first- and second-level
managers much more involved in the program, and
we have to do it soon. I suggest that the four of us
meet next week on Friday, August 23, at 2:00 P.M.
in my office and begin to discuss this problem seriously.

Meanwhile, I want to share with you my immediate reaction to what Dave said yesterday. I'm
certain that the steps he proposed just won't work.
I can understand his frustration. We all sense it.
But if the theory we've based our program on has
anything to it, the first and second levels will never
get involved, *in the way we would like,* as a result of
cracking the whip over them. First of all, QWL proceeds from a holistic approach to organizations, an
approach that emphasizes taking into account the
interests and needs of every stakeholder in an organization. Our QWL program holds out the promise of greater autonomy for the bargaining unit employees. If the program works, they will have a
much greater voice in the day-to-day management
of their units than they've ever had. But what happens to the first and second levels if their success
in the organization gets tied directly, through promotions and raises, to an evaluation of how they
participate in QWL? They will experience a loss
of authority in their relations with their people and
no corresponding gain in the influence they exert
when dealing with their supervisors. I don't see how
the first and second levels can develop any sense
of ownership in regard to QWL under this circumstance.

Second, as Ouchi emphasized in *Theory Z,*
the kind of change we're after requires *consistent* adherence to an organizational philosophy that serves
as the basis for "uniting the activities of employees
through a common understanding of values and

goals" (1981, p. 112). How can this idea of a common understanding enter the picture if the organization makes QWL participation purely voluntary for one category of employees but coerces another group into participating? I agree that we have to do something soon to get the first and second levels on board. But we can't use theory X to create a theory Z organization. It won't work.

Two days later, Grossman and Frias each responded to Brown's memorandum with the following memoranda of their own:

        TO: Mort Brown, Joyce Carter,
                  José Frias
   FROM: Lucille Grossman
   DATE: August 15, 1985
SUBJECT: First- and Second-Level
                  Management Participation in QWL
      I agree absolutely that we can't ignore the problem of first- and second-level participation in QWL any longer. A meeting at 2:00 on Friday the 23rd to discuss this issue is fine. I can see already, however, that I come to the problem very differently from Mort. To begin, I'm uncomfortable with the a priori tenor of his memorandum. Strong salary and promotion incentives cannot work, he says, to motivate more first- and second-level involvement in QWL. Why not? According to Mort, they can't work because his pet theory tells him they can't. Shouldn't we ask about what experience tells us? I don't know of any hard empirical data that settles the issue, but I see plenty of evidence in the world of how applying pressure to people can start a process that results in attitudinal changes. In the 1950s we used to hear that civil rights laws won't work because "you can't legislate a change of heart." Well, we've got civil rights laws now and a very

changed society as a result. Mort cited Ouchi's *Theory Z*. It's very interesting to note that Ouchi also says the following: "In one type Z company with which I am familiar each plant holds a monthly beer bust at the end of the working day. . . . *Any manager who regularly fails to take part in the beer bust will fail to achieve success and continued promotion"* (my underlining) (1981, p. 68).

Mort has gotten ideals and reality mixed up. Ideally, the first and second levels should become involved in QWL by way of a voluntary process that strongly reflects concern for them and provides the kind of support that will help them deal with aspects of the program they may find threatening. Such an approach, however, might take years to implement. Meanwhile, we have an organization facing a radically altered environment in which it probably won't survive unless major internal change occurs soon.

I think that many OD professionals don't like to face up to the fact that our basic values don't always coincide. We have to make trade-offs, in this instance, between humanistic and economic values. Ideally, the problem of first- and second-level participation should be worked out in some other way than using salary and promotion incentives in a manner that smacks of coercion. Speaking realistically, however, organizational change has to come, and it has to come soon. A less than ideal approach to dealing with the first- and second-level managers may be unavoidable.

TO: Mort Brown, Joyce Carter,
           Lucille Grossman
FROM: José Frias
DATE: August 15, 1985
SUBJECT: First- and Second-Level Management Participation in QWL
         1. I am available for a meeting on Friday, August 23, at 2:00 P.M.

2. I discussed Mort's memo with Lucille. I think she's right in arguing that theoretical grounds alone don't rule out the possibility of success in using strong salary and promotion incentives to bring about greater involvement in QWL on the part of the first and second levels. Unlike Lucille, though, I don't see that we face a situation in which we must choose between basic values. Mort says that we should take all stakeholders into account. I agree. He then complains, however, that the bargaining unit employees will realize a gain in autonomy from QWL but that the first and second levels will not. I disagree.

Last fall I took a continuing education course in social philosophy in which the instructor distinguished between two senses of autonomy. In the first sense, autonomy means having the right to decide what to do in regard to a given situation. In the second sense, people gain in autonomy to the extent that they become more capable of independent thought. It seems to me that QWL is mainly about promoting autonomy in the second sense but not in the first. Maximizing autonomy in the first sense, the right to decide what to do, would create utter chaos in an organizational context.

As far as I'm concerned, it is reasonable to proceed on the assumption that, even if motivated extrinsically at the outset, most of the first and second levels will benefit from their involvement with QWL, specifically by becoming more autonomous in the second of the above senses. For this reason, they will gain from the program no less than any other category of stakeholder. It may well be that a fair number of first- and second-level managers will have to make some difficult adjustments in the short run that they may resent. On the other hand, is there any rational alternative? Everyone in the organization will have to make similar adjustments.

If most of them can't, the organization will surely decline, and there may not be jobs for anyone.

By Friday morning, Joyce Carter had read and thought about the three memoranda she had received from her OD colleagues in the QWL program. She spent the morning drafting a memo herself, which she then put in the mid-afternoon interoffice mail:

TO: Mort Brown, José Frias, Lucille Grossman
FROM: Joyce Carter
DATE: August 16, 1985
SUBJECT: First- and Second-Level Management
             Participation in QWL
             Lucille and José may be right in saying that putting a little heat on the first and second levels will get them more involved in QWL. I'm troubled, however, by José's memorandum. He seems to argue that it's all right to put pressure on the first and second levels to participate more in QWL *because the participation will be good for them.* This strikes me as paternalistic thinking that anyone committed to the basic values of OD ought to avoid. Taking human dignity seriously, at a minimum, involves refusing to compel behavior of adults on the ground that, although they don't realize it, the behavior makes them better people. José acknowledges that QWL may present some real problems for the first- and second-level managers. He goes on to say, however, that in his opinion most of them have what it takes to cope with the problems, and that, in any event, as he sees it they have no real choice anyway, at least insofar as they're rational. I, for one, feel pretty uncomfortable deciding what other people can or can't cope with, and what they have to agree with ultimately if they're "rational." I feel a lot better leaving other grown-up individuals to make these kinds of decisions for themselves. This

doesn't mean that we can't work actively to secure greater participation in QWL by the first and second levels. If we have a deep commitment to the values of OD, however, our efforts have to reflect respect for human dignity and sensitivity to the psychic needs of everyone involved in the program.

I think Lucille came closer than José to defining our problem accurately. In saying this, I don't mean to concede yet that we can make QWL work in a reasonable time only by "getting tougher" with the first and second levels. On the other hand, should that be the case, then we really do face a tragic choice between basic values. Unlike Lucille, though, I'm not at all sure where I would come out on such a choice. In any event, I agree that we need to discuss this subject a lot more. I can make a meeting on Friday the 23rd at 2:00 P.M.

The four consultants met as planned on August 23 at 2:00 P.M. There was a vigorous exchange of views, but at the end of the discussion everyone remained basically at the point at which he or she had begun.

Consider the Following

The OD consulting team comes to you for advice. They want you to suggest a way of involving the first- and second-level managers in the QWL program that (1) does not take an excessively long time given the need for organizational change at Federal Dynamo and (2) is consistent with the basic values of OD, such as dignity, autonomy, and equal concern for the interests of all the stakeholders in an organization. The four members of the team concluded that their inability to reach agreement stems in part from a lack of consensus among themselves about the basic values of OD. For this reason, they want you to state your own conception of these values clearly and to relate this conception explicitly to your proposal with respect to getting the first- and second-level managers more involved in QWL.

Note: This case was originally presented for discussion at the OD Network Conference, San Francisco, October 1985, at which Jeanne Cherbeneau and Robert Tannenbaum were present. The comments by Robert F. Ladenson and Dorothy M. Tucker were prepared at a later time.

Comments by Robert F. Ladenson

The four consultants in the preceding case found it difficult, at least for some time prior to exchanging their memoranda, to discuss among themselves the continued noninvolvement of the first- and second-level managers in the QWL program at Federal Dynamo. The memoranda exchange was prompted by blunt and, apparently, unexpected words on the part of union vice president Mulligan at a monthly QWL steering committee meeting. Prior to that time, the consultants seem to have largely evaded the topic. Did the problem stem from mistakes of a strategic nature made at an earlier stage when first implementing the QWL program within the organizational structure of Federal Dynamo? Or did the difficulty lie primarily with the consultants themselves and their personal interactions with one another? Or, finally, did it have more to do with factors intrinsic to the issues they had to resolve?

The following commentaries express different points of view concerning the issues of this case. According to Dorothy M. Tucker, a psychologist and external consultant, the four consultants "seemed to ignore fundamental requirements for implementing change." She observes that none of the consultants "objected to the imposition of the QWL program on the company." The case does not indicate, says Tucker, "that any attempt was made to 'sell' the program to various staff levels." In this regard, Tucker says that "[a] move to engage the first- and second-level supervisors in learning the 'why' of the program with explicit rewards tied to their support" could have been made. In Tucker's judgment, however, "from the beginning the program was imposed rather than sold."

Robert Tannenbaum, emeritus professor of the development of human systems in the Anderson Graduate School of

Management, University of California at Los Angeles, and Jeanne Cherbeneau, president of Cherbeneau and Associates, a management and organization development consulting firm, both view the four consultants as beset by problems of group dynamics. Tannenbaum regards the correspondence of the consultants through memoranda, rather than interacting face to face, as an indication of "probable hostility." He notes phrasing in several memoranda that, in his judgment, raise the issue of whether the expressed differences of the consultants "are simply vehicles for expressing deeper interpersonal feelings they may or may not be aware of." Tannenbaum asks whether the consultants "know themselves reasonably in depth" and whether they ever openly but caringly confront one another in the interest of facilitating better self-understanding?

Cherbeneau views the four consultants as beset by problems in the area of group dynamics revealed principally, in her opinion, by the exchange of memoranda. According to Cherbeneau, the consultants made a significant mistake by defining their respective differences as conflicts of values. Such a characterization, says Cherbeneau, has a tendency to create "dysfunctional emotional investments in a given position that so often interfere with hearing and appreciating others' positions, as well as being able to find workable solutions." Based on her reading of the four memoranda, Cherbeneau maintains that the consultants could have equally well framed their disagreements in much less emotionally laden terms — specifically as differences concerning either theoretical questions or pragmatic judgments. Such, in turn, might have led the consultants, Cherbeneau believes, "to a more accurate focus for discovering solutions."

In his case commentary, Robert Ladenson, a coauthor of this book, views the consultants' exchange of memoranda quite differently than does Cherbeneau. Ladenson reads the memoranda as containing important preliminary efforts by each consultant to probe his or her own thoughts about critical, though infrequently explored, aspects of OD-HSD in the context of working through a specific problem. Ladenson considers it appropriate to characterize the disagreement among the consultants as involving differences of opinion about questions related

to fundamental values. Indeed, he regards such a characterization as essential for understanding the nature of the disagreement. Ladenson believes that OD-HSD practitioners continually face the issue of how to integrate reflective and critical
consideration of values questions more effectively into the diverse
aspects of their professional lives.

Comments by Dorothy M. Tucker

The QWL program at Federal Dynamo is in a stage of
confusion and consequently is unable to meet its goals. The four
consultants who were assigned to design and implement the program seemed to ignore fundamental requirements for implementing change. For example, they did not measure staff and
management willingness to change, and they apparently did
nothing to build themselves as a team.

To me, the consultants seem primarily responsible for the
ineffectiveness of the QWL program. Their inability to determine accurately and comprehensively the needs of the corporation and to evaluate the responsiveness of the QWL program
to the corporation's values, mores, standards, and behavioral
attitudes contributed to its ineffectiveness.

Confrontations between management and the consultants
might well have been avoided by:

- Conducting a comprehensive needs assessment survey prior
  to QWL implementation
- Implementing a management communications program between top and lower-level managers prior to the QWL implementation
- Administering a survey for the purpose of measuring task
  behavior and attitudes about change
- Developing an alternative plan in the event that the first plan
  failed or became impossible to manage—for example, management by objectives measures and administrative systems
  applicable to and responsive to program, staff, corporation,
  and individual needs

These actions probably would have revealed the disfavor
in which the lower-level managers held the program and helped

maintain a dialogue throughout the project. Data generated would have identified the feelings and perceptions of production staff as well as lower- and top-level management toward change.

Though lower-level management was afraid of change and worked actively to discourage the QWL program, they did take action to use some of the program variables to their benefit. However, values differed at all three levels of staff hierarchy within the company, and these differences should have been exposed, treated, and neutralized by the consultants. Since they were not, the problems became an issue and began to tear at the very fabric of company morale and management systems.

There are recognized rules of thumb that are applicable here—most notably, Shepard's (1973) aphorisms for change agents:

1. Never work uphill.
2. Don't build hills as you go.
3. Work in the most promising area.
4. Don't use one when two could do it.
5. Don't over-organize.
6. Don't argue if you can't win.
7. Keep an optimistic bias.

Had the lower-level managers applied these rules to the QWL program, the results would have been different.

There existed a real problem of "ownership." It is interesting to note that none of the consultants objected to the imposition of the QWL program on the company. As "experts," I would have expected them to raise that issue at an early stage. There are data confirming that the program was implemented with the company as a whole. However, there are no data on whether any attempt was made to "sell" the program to various staff levels.

In reviewing comparison data, Blanchard (1983) points out that selling means explaining "why." If the organization is trying to get workers to move to a more mature position and to get managers and first-line supervisors to support such a move, they should be aware of the life cycle of such movement. In the present situation, for example, first- and second-line supervisors did not support the program. If they really do not want to do it, situational leadership theory says the organization should use its authority and give specific instructions and directions for behavior acceptable to the company. And indeed, as Brown suggested and Grossman and Frias advocated for different reasons, that was the approach they recommended. Only Carter believed that such an approach was demeaning. In short, it appears that from the beginning the program was imposed rather than sold.

A move to engage the first- and second-level supervisors in learning the "why" of the program with explicit rewards tied to their support (as Brown and Grossman suggested), or at least some subtle expectations of reward ("What you learn will help you move up in management"), would have been an appropriate response to this dilemma.

It is interesting to note Grossman's comment concerning the difference between "reality and idealism" as they relate to how some OD practitioners view the world. Life theory (Consultation Skills Laboratory, 1984) makes the point that when a strength is overplayed it becomes a weakness. Being idealistic is a strength until it is overplayed. Then it becomes impractical, unrealistic, and ambiguous. Eventually, others come to distrust the judgment of one who is seen as overly idealistic, a point OD practitioners need to keep in mind.

My response to Carter's argument is that upholding and supporting the freedom and dignity of others is a strength; but to let someone die while you wait for them to really "want" medicine is ludicrous. If Carter's position involved the more directive approach to "selling" described above, I see no reason it could not be pursued. Contrary to Brown's position that first-line supervisors would lose authority, they in fact could be shown how the program could enhance their effectiveness. Grossman incorrectly advocated that pressure alone will get their support. Although Frias was on point, I find his rationalization tortuous.

Relating back to the basic theory and data on attitudes and attitude change by Fishbein and Ajzen (1975) is helpful. Attitudes have emotional, cognitive, and behavior elements. Changing any one creates dissonance and the motivation to change the others. To change the behavior of supervisors toward QWL, one needs to change how they feel or what they know about the program. Attitudes also change when needs or goals change. In short, there are many approaches available to the consultants that would help save the QWL program. A strong "sales" job is not inconsistent with OD values. However, OD consultants can "oversell" and promise more than they can deliver, mostly out of ideals that are unrealistic.

The QWL program's lack of success can be traced to the consultants' inability to analyze satisfactorily the values and management systems of the corporation before QWL implementation. Their lack of consensus and ability to work harmoniously as a team also reduced their effectiveness. Before working with managers, I would want to work with the consultants on the issues of how they work with one another.

Comments by Robert Tannenbaum

The First Two-and-a-Half to Three Years of the Program. The program was established to deal with the "new competitive environment." There is no indication that it was designed to underscore or move toward "OD values." Neither at the outset nor later did the consultants make their own—possibly conflicting—values known to the client system. (See Guideline II–D, Appendix C.)

The four consultants—two internal, two external—were "to work as a team." During the early period, what was done to develop the consultant team? Did they ever deal with their own value differences or those between them and the purposes of the program? (See Guideline II–F, Appendix C.)

Both the corporation and the union knew from the beginning that employees would have to develop the ability to handle new kinds of situations *with much less supervisory guidance than in the past.* Certainly well-trained and experienced OD consultants should have been aware of the implications of this for all existing supervisors—particularly for the lower-level managers. But apparently they were not—that is, not until nearly three years later. In my judgment, this represented an important consultant competency deficiency. (See Guidelines I-B and I-C, Appendix C.)

After nearly three years, the lower-level managers "neither participated in the program nor made any effort to follow up on the various ideas the committee developed." Why did they not participate? What opportunities had been provided them to do so? Had the consultants ever been concerned about them, their roles, and the impact of the program on them? (See Guideline II-B.)

Espoused Values Versus Values in Use. The case reveals a number of instances reflecting discrepancies between the espoused values and the values in use by the consultants:

- In coming to "me" for advice, they want a way of involving the first- and second-level managers that is "consistent with the basic values of OD, such as dignity, autonomy, and concern for the interest of all the stakeholders in the organization." These seem to be their values; yet their actions, stated and inferred, have not been consistent with them.
- Brown states in his memorandum that "QWL proceeds from a holistic approach to organizations . . . that emphasizes taking into account the interests and needs of every stakeholder in an organization." And yet, in the past, he apparently has not done so with respect to the lower-level managers. Similarly, Carter states that "our efforts have to reflect respect for human dignity and sensitivity to the psychic needs of everyone involved in the program."
- At the end of the August 23 meeting, "everyone remained basically at the point at which he or she had begun." Apparently, openness and change are for clients and not for consultants.

Psychological Avoidance of Conflict and Risk. Many consultants have deep fears of behaving toward others in ways that might trigger the others' anger or their own. Some are aware of this in themselves; others are not. I do wonder why the consultants in this case did not "see" the growing resentment of the lower-level managers toward the QWL committees, or, if they did so, why they did not confront these feelings. Why did not one or more of them ever raise this issue before the program steering committee, instead leaving it to Mulligan to do so? And after Mulligan raised the issue himself in a monthly meeting, why was the matter not then pursued? Why did the consultants later primarily express their points of view (including their differences) to each other by means of correspondence rather than one on one or in a meeting of the four of them?

To me, the interconsultant memos indicate some deeper feelings, indirectly expressed. Grossman refers to Brown's "pet theory." "Mort has gotten ideals and reality mixed up." And "many OD professionals don't like to face up to the fact that our basic values don't always coincide with the way the world is." Frias says that Brown "complains." Carter feels that Frias's position reflects "paternalistic thinking that anyone committed to the basic values of OD ought to avoid." I do wonder whether the memos disclose basic value differences between the consultants or whether their expressed differences are simply vehicles for expressing deeper interpersonal feelings (such as anger or hostility) of which they may or may not be aware.

I do not, offhand, agree with the consultants' conclusion that "their inability to reach agreement stems in part from a lack of consensus among themselves about the basic values of OD." Our OD values support continual striving for self-knowledge and personal growth (see Guideline I–D, Appendix C) and actively soliciting and responding to feedback regarding our work (see Guideline II–M–2). It seems to me that these consultants do not know themselves reasonably in depth; and I doubt that they have ever openly but caringly confronted one another in the interest of facilitating better self-understanding as a part of their own "team work."

Conclusion. I would not at the outset give advice to the consultants on the "apparent" problem about which they have approached me. I would not state my conception of the basic values of OD; nor would I offer a proposal to get the first- and second-level managers more involved in QWL. I would, instead, suggest working directly with the consultants for at least a few sessions, at first for diagnostic purposes but later to assist them in confronting within themselves and between themselves the issues that have reduced their effectiveness as consultants. If this process yields positive outcomes, then the consultants (perhaps with some support and input from me) can then proceed to deal with the noninvolvement of the supervisors and with other unfolding issues of their consultancy.

Comments by Jeanne Cherbeneau

This case is an excellent example of the confusion frequently experienced when attempting to decipher the "real" issues involved in a situation in which "differences" clearly exist. The thesis of this commentary is that it is not sufficient to identify only the *content* of the differences in order to work toward ways of managing or resolving differences constructively and effectively.

I will explore here the importance of how we think about differences. Further, I will demonstrate how identifying the type of conflict and related factors can lend clarity to the order (that is, first order, second order) of the various issues and, consequently, lead to a more accurate focus for discovering solutions. This approach frequently can reduce the dysfunctional emotional investments in a given position that so often interfere with hearing and appreciating others' positions as well as with being able to find workable solutions.

I believe that sometimes we unnecessarily create emotionally laden conflicts by labeling what are sound, theoretical behavioral principles as "values," when in fact they can be one and the same. For example, the "value" of free choice or self-determination is exemplified in the theory and practice of involving people in problem solving and decision making. We know from experience and research that such involvement tends to lead to more accurate identification of core problems and to more feasible and effective solutions. This is achieved by virtue of the broader sense of ownership and increased accuracy of information (that is, information is obtained from people closest to the source) engendered by a participative process. Ideally, all people with relevant information and decision-making authority have had opportunities to offer input into and agree on both the problems and the solutions.

What one person argues to be an intrinsic "value," another person perceives as simply pragmatic — that is, it "works." While on the surface this case appears to illustrate conflicts in values and ethics, there are in fact several different types of conflict operating: conflicts in theory, conflicts in objectives, and conflicts in strategies or methodologies. Again, clarity about the kind of conflict at issue can lend focus for resolution. Additionally, these conflicts frequently are not disagreements about values per se but disagreements over which values should reign when a situation makes given sets of values mutually exclusive. In other words, everyone may share the values, but a choice must be made to honor or act on one value or another. This dilemma is referred to by Gellermann (1985b) as a "meta-value" — that is, a value concerning consciousness of values, valuing values, and addressing value scales of importance.

This case also demonstrates a related factor that does not appear to be so much an issue of values as it is an issue of group development and group competence — that is, the consultants' abilities as a group to resolve or manage effectively conflicts of all types.

Definition of Terms. If we refer to the definitions of values and ethics contained in Chapter Three, values are defined as those qualities or things — such as behaviors, results, beliefs, and attitudes — that are considered desirable, important, or worthy. Ethics refers to standards of conduct that guide our behavior. Values are more fundamental, intrinsic, and worthy of esteem for their own sake and provide the implicit foundation for ethics.

Objectives or desired outcomes refer to goals or *ends* — what is desired to be achieved — while strategies, methodologies, or interventions refer to *means* — how to achieve given objectives. Objectives and methodologies may be values in the sense of *intrinsic* worth, being desirable for their own sake. They are generally the specific applied results or actions under consideration.

They may or may not take into account or be based on or guided by an intrinsic value or set of values. In other words, objectives and methodology *do not necessarily* reflect deeper beliefs about what is "right" or "wrong" from an ethical perspective.

Theory refers to one's assumptions and beliefs about something — for example, assumptions or beliefs about human or group behavior. Theory, too, may reflect one's intrinsic values and may or may not be supported by research data. It should be noted that many of us in the applied behavioral sciences tend to refer to even human behavioral theory that is well-grounded in empirical research as "theory" because so many variables can affect the predictability, consistency, and sameness of behavior. That is, while solid research-based theory may be useful in guiding us in our understanding of and approaches to our work with people and organizations, we allow for the unpredictable or unexpected and for the possibility that we may not be in a position to know all the factors influencing a potential outcome. One unknown factor can shift dramatically the outcome of an intervention, not to mention the effectiveness of the approach. Consequently, given the complexity of our work, we try to be aware that we are making theory-based intervention choices not on the basis of "all things considered" but on considering all the things we know and that "theories are neither true nor false, only useful or not."

Case Analysis. An analysis of the positions held by the consultants in this case reveals that various types of conflicts are operating. Brown, for example, by stating that they should not "crack the whip" by tying effective involvement to performance appraisal, pay, and promotion, is saying that he does not believe that to be an effective strategy for increasing effective managerial involvement. The issue, therefore, is not that the objective of increased managerial involvement is not shared but that the means for achieving it is not shared.

On the other hand, when Brown describes his rationale for why the strategy will not work, he reveals a number of additional objectives, which for him appear to be of a first-order nature. For example, he states that "the kind of change we're after requires *consistent* adherence to organizational philosophy" and a common understanding of values and goals. He further believes that managers will feel they have lost their authority and ability to make choices and will not gain influence or a sense of ownership.

These points essentially are objectives, or desired outcomes, that may or may not be shared at either a first- or second-order level by the rest of the consultants; that is, they may not believe that managers *must* have a choice, feel some ownership, gain influence, and not lose a sense of their authority. These points are also theoretical *assumptions* about what will influence the effectiveness of the QWL effort and to what degree. While Brown raises multiple objectives/values issues — autonomy, free choice, independence, influence, stakeholder orientation, system effectiveness and efficiency, a holistic systemic view, quality of life, process and results, system development and growth — the critical question is what objectives, assumptions, and values are shared with others at what level.

Everyone might be able to agree on the values/objectives in and of themselves, yet they could have very different views as to what is essential or most important, either from the perspective of personal *integrity* and *ethical behavior* — for example, the idea that utilizing only strategies that support certain values is a "standard of conduct" — or from that of *effectiveness* — assumptions about what will or will not work. In this case, Grossman, Frias, and Carter do not share Brown's theoretical assumptions about conditions necessary for QWL efforts to work. Notably, the fact that they are all seeking strategies that will work is a shared intrinsic value.

Grossman not only fails to share Brown's theoretical assumptions; she also proceeds to define an order of importance of the values/objectives he has identified. To her, organizational survival — namely, what works to achieve managerial involvement and does so *immediately* — seems to be more important than adhering to all of the other stated values/objectives.

Carter, on the other hand, places greater importance on the values/objectives stated by Brown and shares Grossman's self-defined pragmatic or "realistic" values/objectives. As a consequence, Carter experiences more internal conflict about both strategy and a process for determining which values/objectives are essential. In her view, there is a painful potential for having to make a "tragic choice"—the existential meta-value choice required when one is faced with an ethical dilemma of conflicting values.

While Frias shares Carter's and Grossman's values/objectives with regard to organizational survival, he differs from Brown in assumptions about the effect of the proposed strategy. This makes it possible for him to share Brown's, Carter's, and Grossman's values/objectives and yet not share Brown's concerns that the proposed strategy either will be ineffective or fail to maintain other values/objectives, such as autonomy or a stakeholder orientation. For him, neither a values nor an ethics conflict exists. He also identifies an order of priority by placing the long-term positive effects ahead of short-term negative reactions.

Carter supports several of the values/objectives stated by the rest of the group—for example, being sensitive to human needs, respecting human dignity, and supporting free choice—and goes on to project what might be regarded as a more "ethical" issue or standard of conduct—that is, that one should not be paternalistic. She feels that Frias's thinking about what was good for managers and his judgments about the managers' abilities to be rational and cope were a demonstration of "paternalistic" values and behavior. She shares, then, the broad value of human dignity but disagrees with Frias's ways of thinking about it.

Conclusion. A number of points can be extracted from this case. One point is that the identified differences, for the most part, can be viewed just as easily as differences in objectives, strategy, and theory as differences in values. As proposed at the beginning of this analysis, the benefit in viewing these differences from this perspective is twofold. First, it helps clarify what, in fact, the differences are, as well as where there is agreement. This clarity should lend some assurance that the "real" problems/differences are being addressed, which also should support the quest for accurate and workable solutions.

The second benefit is a point of semantics related to the fact that the concept of "values" tends to connote and be associated with personal integrity, identity, and worth. As a consequence, these fundamental beliefs are "near and dear to the heart" of a person, and there is significant emotional investment in maintaining them. The potential for emotional volatility is high when these values are questioned or threatened. To talk about alternative objectives, theory, and strategies tends to be less emotionally laden and, consequently, provides for a greater possibility of thoughtful consideration of alternative points of view.

A related example of the problem of labeling differences as "values differences" is the tendency to label negatively the person with whom one disagrees. Grossman demonstrates this tendency by referring to Brown as too idealistic, and Carter demonstrates this tendency by referring to Frias as paternalistic. One has to ask what purpose labeling serves except to create defensiveness on the parts of Brown and Frias. One might just as easily view Frias's thinking as a thoughtful attempt to analyze the proposed strategy from the perspective of who benefits or not and how, and to identify real or perceived sources of resistance and potential for success or failure. Brown might be viewed as simply trying to assess what will be effective and consistent with certain values.

To take this point a step further, one might negatively conclude that it is more important to Carter and Grossman to represent themselves as having "better" values than Brown and Frias than it is to optimize the possibilities of finding solutions by avoiding stimulating defensiveness. But what purpose does it serve to draw this conclusion about Carter and Grossman except to then stimulate defensiveness on their part? The perpetuation of this vicious and debilitating cycle is self-evident.

Again, if differences are viewed more from the perspective of what we are trying to achieve and what "works" rather than in terms of what is "right" or "wrong," the potential for challenging or threatening another's sense of integrity, identity, and meaning is reduced. And the opportunities to unite around objectives and workable methodologies are increased.

In sum, the question raised here is not about the value of identifying "values" but about the value of labeling them as such when trying to resolve or manage differences.

A final point relates to the inability of this group of consultants to manage their differences effectively. While this, too, might be labeled a "values" issue related to individual and group "competence," it might more effectively be considered a professional area for personal growth and development of skills. My approach as an external consultant would be to start by focusing on the group's gaining skills in managing their differences (an objective/value of encouraging "independence").

As the group becomes better able to sort out differences and agree on objectives, strategies, and values, some of the workable approaches they might consider include the following:

- Utilize a process that engages the first- and second-level managers in doing their own analysis and drawing their own conclusions about the benefits of the QWL effort. Top management at some point might be involved in this by meeting with groups of the managers and also sharing their hopes for the outcomes of the QWL program, their support of it, how they see the managers' roles and the benefits of the effort for the managers. If this is not feasible for logistical or time reasons, videotapes or memos from top management might be utilized. The positive effect of either "live" or written communication would be influenced, of course, by the degree to which it is presented as information sharing and experienced by the managers as a sincere concern for the common good and for them as managers, as opposed to a "like it or not" mandate.
- Build in various reward and recognition mechanisms—for example, awards dinners, bulletins, prizes, and so on—highlighting successful ideas that have been generated and acted on by QWL committees in concert with their managers.
- Build into performance reviews accountability for efforts to improve morale and productivity, with involvement in the QWL effort one of many possible ways to achieve higher

levels of morale and productivity. Results would be evaluated as well.

These strategies would be intended to take into account the "values" of theoretically sound, effective, and workable strategies as well as desirable objectives.

More important than these intervention suggestions, however, is supporting the consulting group in getting "unstuck" and acquiring the skills to be more effective in problem solving and understanding and managing their differences. When they have improved these skills, they will be better able to move themselves, others, and the organization toward positive action rather than inaction (another value/objective).

Comments by Robert F. Ladenson

This case involves an exchange of memoranda among four consultants in which each of them expresses his or her point of view about a problem on which the consultants, working as a group, have not yet made headway. One might thus view the consultants as primarily facing group process issues related to the nature of their interaction with one another. To focus on process issues rather than on the substantive opinions expressed in the memoranda would necessarily involve the omission of essential aspects of the disagreements among the consultants.

One may describe those disagreements alternatively as involving four consultants or as involving four *viewpoints*. Under the latter description, instead of identifying each viewpoint by the consultant who advanced it, one could do so by substituting numbers: (1) for Brown's viewpoint, (2) for Grossman's, (3) for Frias's, and (4) for Carter's. Such a method of identification serves the purpose of calling attention to substance as well as process. Each of viewpoints (1) through (4) in all likelihood contains a portion of the truth but not all of it. The viewpoints, however, are not easily reconciled. One may, without difficulty, imagine another case in which a single consultant, instead of a four-person team, experiences in some measure the attractive pull of each viewpoint and thus feels a need to reconcile them in her own mind.

The following discussion thus goes a step or two further, exploring the substance of viewpoints (1) through (4) for the purpose of uncovering possibilities of resolution in areas of apparent conflict or, as it may turn out, deeper layers of complexity. Such an exploration makes explicit the crucial respects in which the points of comparison and contrast between the four viewpoints raise questions concerning fundamental values.

Viewpoints (1) and (2), on first impression, concern a factual issue, the efficacy of means that include a substantial element of compulsion to achieve the end of ultimately reducing the role of compulsion and, more generally, of command in organizational life. Resolution of this issue, however, follows neither in fact nor in principle from the results of empirical OD-HSD research. By its very nature, such research seldom, if ever, allows for closely controlled studies. Accordingly, in a great many instances OD-HSD research yields results, or theoretical conclusions, subject to diverse interpretations depending on a wide variety of factors, including, to a large extent, an interpreter's deeply held values.

Such would be the case, in all likelihood, with respect to any specific study purporting to settle questions about the effectiveness of compulsion as a means to realize participatory, democratic ends in the context of organizational life. That is to say, a person's values generally would affect how he interprets such a study. For this reason, the difference of opinion between proponents of viewpoints (1) and (2), if pursued beyond the statements expressed in the memoranda, would lead in reasonably short order to basic questions of value, albeit possibly couched as assertions about human nature and motivation.

Suppose, for example, that a supporter of viewpoint (1) is presented with an empirical case study in which the use of compulsion apparently brought about an organizational change characterized by increased participatory decision making. Almost certainly she would either find grounds for doubting the results reported in the study or contend that those results, even if accurately reported, do not compel her to reject viewpoint (1). She might, for example, distinguish between evanescent, short-term gains and stable, long-term progress derivable through compulsion with respect to democratic, participatory organization change. Having drawn this distinction, she could go on to concede the former as possible but continue to insist on the impossibility of the latter. In the final analysis, however, it seems that such insistence would stem from her views about human nature, which, in turn, embody her conception of the most important values in human life.

Returning to the proponents of viewpoints (1) and (2), Brown and Grossman, how might they resolve their differences of opinion? The preceding analysis suggests that disagreement, or at least an absence of agreement over significant values issues, underlies their differences about the effectiveness of compulsion as a means to secure a higher level of participation in the QWL program on the part of the first- and second-level managers. One may view their exchange of memoranda, however, as an important first step for both consultants in a dialogue through which they can identify and clarify for themselves the basic values behind their respective points of view. Accordingly, it seems that such a dialogue should continue. Both consultants should strive continually to reflect on their values, articulate them clearly for the purpose of furthering the dialogue process, and listen to one another's words in a careful, open way. By doing so, it is probable that both consultants will arrive at a deeper and more precise understanding of their respective schemes of values.

Furthermore, in response to the critical pressure each brings to bear on the other's viewpoint in the dialogue process, they each will probably reshape their value schemes by introducing into them subtle yet significant distinctions. Such, in turn, may create greater room for compromise and accommodation, especially in light of the increasingly felt need· on all sides to arrive at agreement on a strategy concerning how to proceed.

How should one understand the contrast between viewpoints (3) and (4)? The main point of disagreement between these viewpoints concerns which of two kinds of freedom counts for more in connection with values issues related to the question of how to increase the involvement of the first- and second-level managers in the QWL program. One may refer to the two kinds of freedom as "external" and "internal" freedom.

The principal impediments to an individual's realization of *external freedom* emanate from sources external to that person — specifically, from the actions of other human beings. One distinguishes different varieties of external freedom by the nature of the human actions constituting the restriction or limitation in the circumstances. For example, prison inmates lack one kind of external freedom possessed by "free" individuals — that is, those residents of a state or nation who are not imprisoned. These latter residents, however, lack another variety of external freedom — namely, freedom from the threat of punishment for violating the law.

In contrast, the essential impediment to free action from the standpoint of *internal freedom* consists of factors internal to human individuals, factors such as ignorance, closed-mindedness, low self-esteem, or debilitating emotional problems. The boundaries of freedom in the internal sense thus expand for human beings to the extent that they develop intellectually, emotionally, or along other significant dimensions. Viewpoint (3) treats internal freedom as most important in connection with the values at stake in deciding how to deal with the first- and second-level managers. In contrast, viewpoint (4) maintains the primacy of external freedom.

A policy of compelling the first- and second-level managers to participate in the QWL program for the purpose of promoting their development in major areas of personal growth amounts, in effect, to limiting their external freedom in order to expand the realm of their internal freedom. Viewpoint (4) characterizes such an approach as paternalistic. This characterization, however, raises many issues requiring further analysis. One needs to look closely at the idea of paternalism, analyzing its constituent elements so as to provide guidance about the circumstances in which the idea applies, and locate with precision the morally objectionable features of practices and policies appropriately described as paternalistic.

The idea of paternalism has one of its clearer applications in the case of actions by a governmental body that limit the external freedom of individuals for the sake of making them more free from the internal standpoint. A question thus arises of the degree of analogy between actions limiting external freedom for the sake of expanding internal freedom in the context of the relationship between governors and governed, on the one hand, and the relationship between employer and employee on the other. This question, in turn, presents further complexities. The employer-employee relationship, on first impression, has a voluntary aspect that is lacking in the relationship between a government and the individuals over whom it exercises power. Nonetheless, it seems that the idea of voluntariness admits of degrees, which, in turn, raises yet further questions about how to determine such degrees in the context of the employer-employee relationship and how to compare them with the presumably more clear instances of paternalism involving the relationship between governors and governed.

The above issues are extremely difficult to resolve. One needs to approach them in a highly theoretical way. Insofar as they concern matters about which most individuals tend to have few firm intuitive convictions, one also needs to approach these questions with a great tolerance for intellectual ambiguity — that is, with the ability to suspend judgment for considerable periods of time. The contrast between viewpoints (3) and (4) thus provides a good illustration of one way in which differences over questions of values present issues that fully engage the intellect as well as the emotions.

Each of the four consultants in this case wants to generate increased participation by the first- and second-level managers in the QWL program at Federal Dynamo, but in a manner that is consistent with major values of OD-HSD, as affirmed in the Statement. The four consultants diverge, however, over their interpretations of these values. To reach a working agreement about how to proceed, the consultants need to deal with issues of both process and substance. The process issues involve such matters as identifying barriers to communication among themselves, removing these barriers, and facilitaing effective group action. The content issues concern interpretation of critical OD-HSD values, such as freedom, autonomy, empowerment, and democratic decision making. This case provides an indication of the intellectually complex and subtle questions that confront reflective OD-HSD practitioners in attempting to understand the nature of their profession's most important values.

CHAPTER TWELVE

Looking Ahead: Frontier Issues for Human Systems Development Professionals

Frontier Issues are a class of issues that deserve special attention because they involve matters at the growing edge of the profession. Other issues dealing with the context and content of the profession's ethics have been discussed in earlier chapters, and in some cases that discussion has touched on Frontier Issues. But because of their importance to the profession's growth, they deserve the fuller attention they receive here. In most cases, these issues are new.

Note: This chapter was written by William Gellermann from the perspective of his membership in the OD-HSD profession and is addressed to other members of the profession, since, he feels, "the issues are most meaningfully framed and discussed in such a context. By doing this, I do not mean to exclude readers who are not OD-HSD professionals. Quite the contrary, I invite you to listen in on our dialogue."

Like Chapter Four, this chapter includes material derived from a chapter in *Human Systems Development* by Tannenbaum, Margulies, Massarik, and Associates (Gellermann, 1985b), which can in turn be traced back to earlier versions of the Issues Discussion.

All references in this chapter to the Statement are to the latest version in Chapters Four and Five unless otherwise specified. In combination, Chapters One, Four, Five, and this chapter comprise the latest Issues Discussion.

Frontier Issues

1. Are we a "profession?" Do we want to become one? If so, what kind? Throughout this book, it has been assumed that OD-HSD is a profession, or at least that it is well along the way to becoming one. This assumption is based in part on the results of a survey in mid 1989 that suggested that many practitioners think of OD as a profession and consider themselves professionals (see Appendix A).

However, some people, including Peter Block, an outstanding speaker and writer on the practice of OD, have raised questions about the desirability of becoming a profession. (Note: Block did this in personal conversation about a draft of an article based on this book that was written for the *OD Practitioner* [Gellermann, 1990].) Block sees common purpose and vision as primary. His concern is that in institutionalizing ourselves as a profession we could destroy our ability to serve our purpose because institutionalization tends to mean such things as setting boundaries and standards and concentrating on public relations. Those functions could become primary for "the profession" and self-defeating for our common purpose, particularly by excluding outsiders. Function rather than purpose could become primary.

Block said, "Dialogue is the solution because there is no answer." I asked, "But what is the question?" And he said that he thinks dialogue about purpose is the answer to an ethical existence. I asked if that meant he thought dialogue about values and ethics was inappropriate. He said, "No. Dialogue about values and ethics is important, but it requires a context of common purpose to give it meaning." He said, "What we are seeking is some vehicle for social action and service — a vehicle for volunteerism." He stressed that we need to make it easier to help people *in* rather than to keep them *out*. He concluded that what we need has something to do with our spirit.

All those ideas seem reasonable, except for the initial assertion that we are not a profession and should not become one. On first thought, it seems clear that we are in the process of becoming a profession whether we like it or not, and the question is what kind of a profession do we want to be? I agree that dialogue is the solution and that there is no "answer." As I see it, we are involved in a continuing quest for good life, and the lives we live as professionals, individually and collectively, are a continuing answer to that quest; hence no single "answer," but rather a *continuing lived answer.*

In that connection, I think it is useful for us to live as a professional community — a community whose members are bonded together by a common purpose (an expression of the spirit of our community) and within which we reflect on how we are living our quest. In particular, we need dialogue about what we want our lives to be (our common quest, our common purpose and vision), what's currently going on (current reality), what we can do as next steps in moving from where we are to where we want to be (action plans), and, particularly, the standards of importance (values) and standards of behavior (ethics) we choose to guide us along the way.

There seems to be general agreement on the importance of a common purpose for our community, as expressed in the Statement: "to promote a widely shared learning and discovery process dedicated to the vision of people living meaningful, productive, good lives in ways that simultaneously serve them, their organizations, their societies, and the world" (see Chapter Four).

If we can establish substantial consensus on that or on some other common purpose, we will have taken a major step toward establishing ourselves as a *community* of professionals. In fact, we may be able to avoid the problems Block cites by thinking of ourselves as a "professional community" rather than as a "profession." However, a better solution to those problems may be to see ourselves as a profession — most OD-HSD practitioners seem to think that way anyway, and both the Statement and later sections in this discussion of Frontier Issues refer to us as a profession — but to be clear that for us *profession means community.* In contrast, we also need to be clear that being a profession does not mean the emphasis on functions (boundary setting and public relations) and the kinds of institutions (organizations, associations, and so on) associated with such other professions as medicine and law. If we can be clear about that, perhaps we can avoid the traps associated with becoming institutionalized. In fact, our best protections from falling into those traps are the consciousness of process and ability to communicate about process that are so important to the work we do with our clients.

2. Who are "we"? The current Statement refers to us as "a global professional community." For those professionals who have met one another at international conferences it is gradually becoming clear that "we" are, in fact, *global, professional,* and *a community.* That sense of community is still emerging, and for many of us it has just barely begun, but it seems a logical (as well as a psychological) next step in our own development as a human system.

Our profession began as a scattering of individual practitioners who worked almost exclusively as internal consultants to organizations. We then expanded to include external OD consultants who were generally independent and to some extent competitive. This combined group of internal and external OD consultants met annually at conferences of the U.S. OD Network, the OD Division of the American Society for Training and Development, the OD Institute, the Gesellschaft für Organisationentwicklung (German-speaking consultants), and several other national groups. Other regional groupings of consultants—national, subnational, and in certain large cities—began to emerge in the United States and other parts of the world. At the same time, teachers from colleges and universities began to emerge in professional groupings, such as the Academy of Management's Organization Development and Organizational Behavior Divisions and the Organizational Behavior Teaching Society.

Eventually the people in these various groupings began seeing themselves as a "profession" that needed to do the things required for really becoming a profession. These necessary steps included establishing a widely shared body of knowledge, clarifying professional competencies, and agreeing on ethical standards, all of which are currently in progress. Though the annual professional meetings were initially national, beginning in the United States and then in such countries as South Africa and Mexico, they have now become multinational—including Europe, Central and South America, the Western Hemisphere, and Southeast Asia, among other regions—and transnational—including gatherings of professionals from countries all around the world, such as the annual meetings of the OD Institute and the International OD Association.

The profession seems to be on the verge of transformation from a worldwide network of independent individual practitioners to a global community of interdependent professionals who, by virtue of their competence and their consciousness, will be able to take on challenges that would have been inconceivable as long as they viewed themselves primarily as individuals. (Note: For a discussion of the variety of professionals who might be included within the OD-HSD professional community, see the section in Chapter One headed "The Field of Organization and Human Systems Development.")

3. Is it possible to develop general agreement on values and ethics among OD-HSD professionals throughout the world, particularly given the fact of major cultural differences? Geert Hofstede (1980) has reported the results of a study of 116,000 employees of a single, multinational corporation in forty countries around the world. Based on statistical analysis of the data, he identified four primary dimensions that he used to describe and differentiate the cultures of those forty countries.

The dimensions are: Power Distance (the degree to which unequal distribution of power in institutions and organizations is accepted); Uncertainty Avoidance (the degree to which uncertain, ambiguous situations are threatening and people seek to avoid them); Individualism-Collectivism (the degree to which people are expected to take care of themselves and their immediate family or, at the collective extreme, they expect their relatives, clan, organization, or other in-group to care for them in exchange for absolute loyalty to the group); and Masculinity (the degree to which people hold masculine values, such as assertiveness and acquisition of money and things, and lack of concern for people and the quality of their lives).

To illustrate what those dimensions mean more specifically, consider these differences in attitudes of people who are low and high on the Power Distance dimension (Hofstede, 1980, p. 46):

Low	High
a. Inequality in society should be minimized.	a. There should be an order of inequality in which everyone has a rightful place.
b. All people should be interdependent.	b. A few people should be independent; most should be dependent.
c. Hierarchy means inequality of roles established for convenience.	c. Hierarchy means existential inequalities.

Or on the Individualism dimension (p. 48), consider the following:

Low	High
a. Identity is based on the social system.	a. Identity is based on the individual.
b. "We" consciousness is primary.	b. "I" consciousness is primary.
c. Belonging to organizations is emphasized; membership is the ideal.	c. Individual initiative and achievement are emphasized; leadership is the ideal.

In spite of methodological criticism of his study (Goodstein and Hunt, 1981; Hofstede, 1981), Hofstede's results clearly suggest that substantial cultural differences exist along the four dimensions he identified. And, more important for our discussion, his results indicate that certain values that seem central to OD-HSD may be more reflections of the U.S. culture that gave birth to the field than they are a sound basis for establishing a global perspective for the field's values and ethics.

That the United States differs from other cultures is indicated by the following results reported by Hofstede (1980, p. 49): on Power Distance, the United States ranked below average (fifteenth out of forty countries, with forty being the highest ranking), but not as low as several other wealthy countries: on Uncertainty Avoidance it ranked low (ninth); on Masculinity it ranked above average (twenty-eighth); and on Individualism-Collectivism it was the single most individualistic country of all those studied (fortieth).

Two alternatives for dealing with cultural differences in developing professional ethics on a global scale seem reasonable. The first can be called the *pluralist alternative:* that is, one in which countries or clusters of countries with similar cultures develop common statements. Ideally, all of those statements would follow a similar format so that similarities and differences could be readily identified. The second alternative can be called the *universalist alternative:* that is, one in which a substantial consensus is developed around a single common statement throughout OD-HSD's global professional community, but with recognition of and allowances for cultural differences.

The way the second alternative might come about can be illustrated by the contrast between the primary "I" consciousness of individualist cultures and the primary "we" consciousness of collectivist cultures. OD-HSD tends to transcend that apparent conflict by viewing it not as *"either* I *or* we" but as *"both* I *and* we." And within the "both-and" perspective, the orientation is to find or create whole-win solutions that coordinate serving the good of the individual and the collective, rather than subordinating one to the other.

By choosing the "both I and we" orientation toward who we are, we transcend the apparent polarity of individualism and collectivism and acknowledge the possibility that individual uniqueness can be enhanced by membership in the collective. We are not required to make that choice, but freedom allows us to make it. I believe that such a choice is particularly necessary for members of the OD-HSD profession in order to realize our highest potential, as individuals and as a professional community. For example, it is possible for us to think of ourselves as:

- Persons first, then members of our national professional communities, and, finally, members of our global professional community
- Members of the global OD-HSD professional community first, then members of our national professional communities, and, finally, persons
- Persons first, then members of the global OD-HSD professional community, and, finally, members of our national professional communities

For me, the third alternative, which focuses first on personal identity, then on global identity, and finally on national identity, is preferable. (This preference, however, may reflect my development within the conditions of U.S. culture.) In any case, it is important to understand that by personal identity I include that which some people call "higher self." In other words, it is that which is at the core of personal integrity. I believe that if we all ground ourselves in such a personal identity, we root ourselves in the common ground of all human life. I do not know exactly what it means to "root ourselves in the common ground," but I believe the OD-HSD profession is particularly well qualified to facilitate a widely shared learning and discovery process that seeks to establish such meaning.

The belief that there is a ground common to all human life is especially important when we practice in cultures other than the one(s) within which we were raised. Cultural relativism tends to treat all cultures as equally "right" and to require outsiders to live within the constraints of the cultures where they live. One of our colleagues, an American who has practiced in the Far East, expressed his difficulty with cultural relativism in these words: "If I live in [another country], should I be a cultural prisoner — an alien forever . . . a socially neutered respectful observer? . . . I believe I am a World citizen with the right to express myself on any issue anywhere." Relativism certainly offers pragmatic guidance on how to act, but it is not necessarily *right* if we accept the idea of a ground common to all human life. As just noted, the OD-HSD profession has unique contributions to make in the quest for such common ground, which is, in my judgment, primary in our collective "quest for a good life."

In any case, we can expect the discovery or creation of our global professional community to be an exciting process. We can undertake it as a contribution by our profession not only to our own development but also to global peace and to the constructive resolution of differences throughout the world.

4. Who is our client? To whom are we responsible and for what? Though these questions have been in the consciousness of Organization Development professionals for a long time, they take on new significance as the profession expands its scope to encompass all human systems. This issue was raised in a note criticizing an earlier version of the Statement: "The whole Statement is written as though 'the client' is the organization or system as a whole. In fact, there is always a particular client within the system — the head of the outfit, the board of directors, or the director of personnel. An ethic of consulting must deal with that special relationship . . . It's important to think through the balance between working for one's particular client and for the system as a whole."

There is an apparent paradox in that criticism. Usually individuals and occasionally groups employ our services, and we are accountable to them as well as having an ethical obligation to them. At the same time, we commit ourselves to "serve the long-term well-being of our client systems and their stakeholders" (Guideline III–A). Our specific ethical obligation to those who employ us is somewhat ambiguous in the Statement because its reference to "client" can be read as referring to those who employ us or the system or both. That ambiguity is intentional since our mission involves serving both. Serving our employers' special interests is both practical and ethical — practical in that we cannot continue to serve a system without serving our employer's interests, and ethical in that when we contract with an employer we are ethically bound to fulfill that contract. But we need to be careful that in acting under that contract we do not do things prohibited by our ethics, including acts that would harm the system.

Answering the question "Who is our client?" requires a broader perspective than one focused only on the person(s) with whom we contract. We are *system* development consultants and *the system is our client*. In the same way that physicians serve the health of their patients and do not limit themselves to responding only to what the patients want them to do, we have a broader responsibility. To the extent we realistically can, we have an ethical responsibility to serve the long-term, interdependent interests of the system and its stakeholders, as noted in the preceding paragraph. If the special interests of those who employ us conflict seriously with those of the whole system or any of its stakeholders, we are faced with a dilemma; the Statement gives some guidance, as in Guideline III–D, regarding conflicts of interest. Again, though, such dilemmas involve considerations that are both practical (doing what it takes to continue serving the system) and ethical (doing things that are consistent with serving our employer, the whole system, and its stakeholders).

The Statement acknowledges that we "accept differences in the expectations and interests of different stakeholders and realize that those differences cannot be reconciled all the time" (Guideline III–D–4). That gives us some room for making the practical adjustments necessary to serve those who employ us. However, we are also accountable to our consciences and we have a duty to our profession, whose ethics focus on the good of our client systems and all their stakeholders. And, finally, it is important to recognize, as noted earlier, that many of us believe that ultimately our client is the world.

5. To what extent do the aspirations of OD-HSD professionals include serving "the well-being of all life on earth"? A questionnaire survey in 1983 asked about "helping organizations align their purposes with the welfare of the earth and all its people" (Gellermann, 1984b). Responses were strong and varied widely, ranging from "I like the idealism there. Who knows where the aim for the stars will take us?" and "Yes. Definitely," to "Pretentious and irrelevant do-goodism," "Come on! I for one have no messianic complex," and "too grandiose." In addition, others noted that we have a responsibility to serve

all life and not just human life, so the Statement was changed
to read, both more simply and more comprehensively, "the well-
being of all life on earth."

The issue is still open. The primary question seems to
be: Does OD-HSD as a profession have a global aspiration?
In view of the fact that we work with human systems, we are
working with open systems and they are, therefore, ultimately
subsystems within the global human system. Therefore it can
be argued that a global perspective is essential, even from the
limited point of view of our clients' interests. Although our organizational clients may not see the connection, it is appropriate for us to take a leadership role in relating the organization's
interests to those of the global system whenever we can do so
effectively. This does not mean, though, that it is necessary to
stress that connection with all clients under all conditions. However, it is important to recognize that OD-HSD professionals
are uniquely qualified, by virtue of their membership in a global
professional community, to maintain a global perspective and
assert it whenever it might make a positive difference.

*6. Can the OD-HSD profession-as-a-whole contribute to
developing the whole system composed of all human life on earth?*
This issue is similar to but different from the issue just discussed about the extent to which we aspire to serving "the well-
being of all life on earth." That issue focused primarily on our
relationship with our client organizations and other human
systems, by putting our service to them in the context of whether
that service is good for "the well-being of all life on earth." In
contrast, this issue focuses on all life on earth *as a human system*
and suggests that the OD-HSD profession-as-a-whole has the
potential for facilitating the development of that system in a manner analogous to the service OD professionals give to their organizational clients.

The OD-HSD profession has the potential for becoming
a significant subsystem within the macrosystem comprised of
all human life on earth. If the profession will develop itself as
a global professional community and apply to itself the kinds
of developmental approaches it encourages its clients to use, it
seems reasonable to conclude that it can contribute to improv-

ing the quality of all human life by improving that life's ability to function as a human system. Among other things, this will involve supporting the creation of a global vision, with which some professionals are already involved, through a project called "Global Cooperation for a Better World," headed by the wife of the secretary general of the United Nations, Mrs. Marcela Perez de Cuellar. It is also likely to include, among other contributions, ways of helping our clients throughout the world in:

- Clarifying their values and ethics in ways compatible with achieving and maintaining a sustainable global society
- Enhancing whole-win, cooperative aspects of their cultures
- Increasing their ability to function democratically both internally and externally, enabling the members of their client systems to participate in making decisions about system functioning, on the one hand, and enabling the client systems to participate in decisions by the more inclusive systems of which they are members, on the other

In doing this, cultural differences will need to be acknowledged and honored to as great an extent as possible. In cases of conflict, however, OD-HSD professionals will ideally guide their action by asking, "Is it good for the world?"

7. To what extent, if any, is the profession responsible for monitoring entry to the profession and the practice of its members? In Chapter One, monitoring practice and practitioners was identified as one of the primary elements in the emergence of a full-fledged profession. We also noted opposition among OD-HSD practitioners to our becoming a profession because of the possibility that we could become a regulatory clique that controls entry and practice as have other, more well-established professions such as medicine and law. That opposition is based in part on grounds that we may overly institutionalize and rigidify ourselves. There are also concerns that we could become monopolistic and exploitative, as Shepard (1983) noted in describing the typical evolutionary pattern of professions. It is important that we acknowledge those possibilities and, at the same time, be clear that we can develop ways of avoiding them *if we choose to do so.*

In the first chapter we also made the point that "as societies become more dependent on professional services, it is vital
that professions and professionals be held accountable for their
conduct and for their commitment to public service" in exchange
for the public's trust. But it was also noted that law is a severely
limited social tool because it tends to focus on prohibiting socially harmful behavior and is relatively ineffective in encouraging
behavior that serves the common good. The more the professions can monitor themselves in preventing harm and encouraging their members to serve the common good, the less society needs to intervene. And the more individuals can monitor
themselves, the less their profession needs to intervene.

But it seems clear that the profession-as-a-whole will have
to act in the not too distant future; its primary choice is whether
to proact or react. Some may prefer to finesse the issues by acting as if we have no collective responsibility, but I find that position literally irresponsible and, therefore, unacceptable. In my
judgment, we cannot afford much longer to ignore the issues
of monitoring entry and practice or to treat them as if they are
of low priority. My preference is to anticipate probable difficulties, prepare for them, and then revise our preparations based
on our experience, rather than wait for difficulties to arise and
then react to them.

We have already touched on the issue of monitoring entry. I agree with Hinckley (1986), quoted earlier, that our profession, by definition, should be as inclusive as possible. But that
does not mean ignoring the issue of inclusion. Most of us, I
think, prefer to emphasize establishing ways of measuring or
otherwise identifying the competencies by which people can
qualify as "professional" and then making the necessary learning experiences available for all those who want to become
professionals. The section in Chapter One on "Body of Knowledge, Educating Practitioners, and Monitoring Practice and
Practitioners" has identified a number of efforts already under
way for doing both of these things.

The issue of monitoring practice and practitioners was
also touched on in the section to which we just referred. As that
section indicated, many professionals have taken individual

responsibility for monitoring their own practice by means of a peer review process. Some professional associations have established criteria for membership, including ACC, which includes participation in its peer review process as its primary criterion. In this connection, the demise of CCI, referred to in that section, suggests that support for voluntary peer review is relatively weak. To my knowledge there is no comprehensive, professionwide effort under way to provide for periodic reviews of our practice and our competence so that we can assure ourselves that as a profession we are maintaining ourselves at a professional level.

In my opinion, we have a collective responsibility to the public we serve to review our practice and our competence, although we may be reluctant to do so individually. Initiating such an effort is a primary responsibility of those with leadership power within existing professional associations. At the same time, I also acknowledge that those "leaders" can lead only where their members are willing to follow. I am convinced that what I am suggesting will not happen until a significant number of influential people ask for collective action toward creating a process for periodic review of our profession. I do not know what that process would look like, but I am confident that collectively we can design something that will work for us. As I see it, we need to use our individual freedom responsibly to create a system that enhances our ability to work collectively. It will mean that we give up some of our independence, which some of us are understandably reluctant to do, but, for me, that is the essence of maturing into interdependence. I particularly want to call on people throughout the global OD-HSD community to use their influence in creating a professionwide effort by, among other things, asking the leadership groups of their national or multinational associations to inform their members of the need for co-creating some means of periodic review of the "health" of our profession and enrolling them in the co-creation process.[1] (The remainder of this section discusses professional structures that might make such review possible.)

In discussing the status of OD as a profession, White and Wooten (1986, p. 193) quote the Society of Personnel Administration's definition of a professional as "a person who is in an occupation requiring a high level of training and proficiency. This person has high standards of achievement with respect to acquiring unique knowledge and skills. A person who is committed to continued study, growth, and improvement for the purpose of rendering the most effective public service. This level of training, proficiency, and ethical standards [is] controlled by the society or association of self-governing members. These people maintain and improve standards and criteria for entrance and performance in the field of work or occupation."

We may have a lot of people who meet the individual standards of being professionals, but we do not have control by a "society or association of self-governing members." We currently have a window of opportunity for proactively creating such a society or association before serious problems arise that could either damage us during our adolescence as a profession or mobilize us to react by forming the kind of association we need for dealing with matters that can only be handled collectively. White and Wooten propose one proactive alternative — namely, a hierarchical "National Organization Development Association," with national boards for education standards, ethics review, and examination and licensing, and similar boards for each state. Another alternative, which presently exists in nebulous form, is the Human Systems Development Consortium, to which many of the leading OD-oriented professional organizations in the United States have sent representatives in the past. The HSDC might, if it chose to recongregate, create the task forces necessary to enable the profession to set and maintain its education standards, monitor its practice and practitioners (perhaps using peer review or examination and licensing or some combination), and review its ethics. Such an organization would probably look less like a pyramid and more like a wheel, with the central consortium steering committee at the hub, the various member organizations as a ring around the hub, and then the various task forces in an outer ring. In any case, we now have a choice to proact or react, but that choice may not be ours much longer.

For now, the focus is likely to be on national associations,

such as the HSDC in the United States, or multinational associations, such as those in Europe, the Western Hemisphere,
and Southeast Asia. If we can develop such associations at the
national and multinational levels, however, the creation of a
global, transnational association, based on the same concentric
circle model, seems a reasonable next step.

In thinking about this whole issue of monitoring entry
and practice and creating structures to do so, it is important
to remember the points raised in discussing the first issue. Of
particular importance is keeping our purpose primary and not
letting functions and structures get in the way of our ability to
serve that purpose.

*8. To what extent, if any, is the profession responsible for
monitoring the ethical practice of its members?* The above discussion raises one last issue about monitoring practice and practitioners: namely, monitoring the *ethical* practice of our profession's members. This book and the Annotated Statement are
a means of providing the kinds of educational tools professionals
will need to enable themselves to practice ethically. But what
happens in case of violations? One option is to wait until they
occur and then react. However, many of us would prefer to anticipate possible violations by making our coping methods clear
before we need them, thereby reducing the likelihood of violations and preparing ourselves to deal with them effectively in
case they do occur. The Statement deals with this issue to some
extent in Guideline IV–D:

> Work actively for ethical practice by individuals and
> organizations engaged in OD-HSD activities and,
> in case of questionable practice, use appropriate
> channels for dealing with it.
>
> 1. Discuss directly and constructively when fea-
>   sible.
> 2. Use other means when necessary, including
>   a. Joint consultation and feedback (with an-
>   other professional as a third party)

    b. Enforcement procedures of existing pro-
        fessional organizations
    c. Public confrontation

Ideally, OD-HSD professionals will behave ethically. If they
have questions about one another's ethics, this guideline encourages them to deal with their questions "directly and constructively when feasible." Then, only if necessary, should they
use stronger means, turning first to consultation with a third
party to try to resolve their differences. In order to achieve
uniformity, it is probably desirable to develop professionwide
means of preventing violations (such as the Annotated Statement, cases, and issues discussions in this book). We will also
need professionwide means of responding to violations when the
means of response outlined in Guideline IV–D are inadequate.
The kind of organization suggested by White and Wooten or
an HSDC ethics task force of the kind suggested above are possible channels for response. Again, the question is, Can we mobilize our energy to deal with this need proactively or must we
wait until some kind of crisis requires us to deal with it reac-
tively? I would like to believe that the OD-HSD profession can
deal with this kind of issue proactively.

        In this connection, the caution raised by Kushner (1986,
pp. 127–129) in discussing the role of religion is helpful. He
says, "A religion which persists in understanding 'good' to mean
'unquestioningly obedient' is a religion which would make per-
petual children of us all. . . . Religion should . . . encourage us
to challenge its own positions critically not out of adolescent impatience with limits but on the basis of an informed adult conscience." Those ideas apply equally to the role of professions
in determining the ethics of their members. In other words, the
ultimate responsibility for ethical conduct lies with each professional, and the profession's responsibility is to encourage its
members to make their decisions on the basis of "an informed
adult conscience."

        One final point: It has been observed that "bad tends to
drive out good," as, for example, bad money driving out good in

the case of Gresham's Law of economics. The same can be said about "bad practice driving out good" in the life of a profession. If we do not collectively define what we mean by "good practice" and take collective responsibility for ensuring the prevalence of "good," then it is likely that "bad practice" will prevail. That seems particularly likely for the OD-HSD profession because of the competitive economic conditions within which most of us function. I hasten to add, however, that I believe it is possible to monitor "good practice" in ways that respect the individual responsibility of each of the members of our professional community.

9. Does the profession place high value on "democratic" decision making? The Statement refers to "appropriate" decision making (Value 3–c), which is a response to criticism of earlier versions that said we valued "democratic" decision making. Most practitioners who responded to the 1983 questionnaire (Gellermann, 1984b) accepted the word "democratic," but among them many wanted to recognize explicitly that democratic participation is not practical under all conditions. One person argued against that, however, by saying, "Don't qualify a true statement. Everyone knows that compromise is at times necessary or nothing." Another said, "'Placing a high value' does not mean a practicing professional will insist on democratic process as the only means in every situation."

Those who support using the word "democratic" are in agreement with Marvin Weisbord, a partner in a leading national consulting firm, who said in a keynote address to a U.S. OD Network conference, "The only thing we bring to the party that other specialists don't is a commitment to democratic processes for achieving desired results."

Comments from those who disagreed included: "The emphasis on democracy as an end is misplaced," "I don't think we are trying to make all organizations into 'democracies' and this statement creates that image," "Excludes many OD people," "Drop democratic decision making. It is not universally relevant to effective problem solving or decision making," "I don't like the statement — it commits to an ideology with which I am only sometimes aligned. But I'd rather have it stand than add anything to it."

The view of the people who would like to drop the reference to "democratic decision making" and shift the emphasis to "participation" and "involvement" may be summarized in the words of one respondent, who said, "Equating democratic decision making, which has a strong popular identity as a political process, with involvement and participation, is inaccurate and can create unnecessary resistance among clients . . . Participation and involvement are sufficiently justified by 'effective problem solving,' improved decision making, and 'organizational excellence' . . . Our democratic values should be secondary or, better yet, a nonissue."

Is it sufficient to drop the words "democratic decision making" and assume that their meaning is recognized by other words? I concluded that it was not; thus, although the reference to "democratic" decision making was changed, "democracy" was added so that it was explicitly recognized as a value. However, it is important to recognize that it may not be valued by all members of the profession. Part of the apparent aversion to "democracy" by some of us may come from confusing the vision of democracy with the current reality of political process in the United States and elsewhere. Disillusionment with that process can understandably leave people with doubts about democracy. For example, George Bernard Shaw has been quoted as defining democracy as "the substitution of election by the incompetent many for appointment by the corrupt few." However, if we view democracy as government of, by, and for the people, then, in spite of its current limitations, we can choose it as an ideal and work actively to make informed, competent, democratic participation possible, while, at the same time, recognizing its current inadequacies.

Even granting that possibility, however, some people rate other values more highly, such as excellence and efficiency. But many OD-HSD professionals believe it is possible to have excellence and efficiency with democracy and, in the long run, impossible to have them without it. (For evidence that supports the possibility of democracy coexisting with excellence and efficiency, see Mason, 1982; Simmons and Mares, 1983.)

Current reality may limit opportunities for democratic decision making, given the priority of the excellence and efficiency values, but we can still value democracy by encouraging participation and involvement in the present and striving to broaden democracy in the future. A central question is: *Are OD-HSD professionals willing to make democracy a primary value, even when some of their clients seem not to value it?*

10. To what extent is the profession responsible to labor unions, other worker organizations, and their representatives? One respondent to an earlier version of the Statement said, "It's important to recognize the 'cultural differences' between OD-HSD professionals (very individualistic) and many in the labor unions (more communal), [and] for OD-HSD professionals to acknowledge their own tradition and location in the struggle for control of the workplace." He adds, "I assume many . . . involved in this Statement want a more democratic form of business institution. That would seem to lead to a new approach toward the 'union' of workers . . . Union leaders are looking for new forms of conduct and it seems an appropriate time for us to do so as well."

This is a wide-open issue. OD-HSD practitioners hold widely differing positions: some pro-union, others anti-union, and most focusing on the ways in which specific unions and their representatives serve (or could serve) the greater good of the organization-system and its stakeholders. Of those concerned about how the union serves the good of the system, some are also concerned with how the system serves the good of the union as one of its primary stakeholders.

The Statement explicitly acknowledges the fact of labor unions and workers' representatives as people whom OD-HSD consultants are expected to inform and involve to the extent appropriate. (See Notes a and b under Guideline III–A–4.) This may create dilemmas in our work with unionized organizations when our employers object to our cooperating with the unions, but it is better to acknowledge such possible dilemmas than to ignore them.

The Statement also, through its expression of general agreement with the United Nations' *Universal Declaration of Human*

Rights, implicitly recognizes that "everyone has the right to form and to join trade unions for the protection of his interests" (Article 23, Point 4 of the declaration per Williams, 1981).

At the present time, it seems inappropriate for the Statement to refer to the responsibilities of OD-HSD consultants to labor unions and workers' representatives any more explicitly than it currently does. These groups are clearly stakeholders in many of our client systems, and as such are due the same consideration given to other stakeholders, including managers. Because we are frequently employed by managers in business systems, such a stance may seem wrong or at least controversial. However, if we accept the whole system as our client and commit ourselves to serving the interests of all its stakeholders, we have a responsibility to them. This does not deny the practical and ethical dilemmas mentioned earlier under Frontier Issue 3 in discussing the questions "Who is our client?" and "To whom are we responsible and for what?"

11. To what extent, if any, do we recognize responsibility for helping organizations and other human systems provide for the fair and just distribution of the fruits of their productivity among all of their stakeholders? As an example of this issue, consider a situation in which an OD-HSD professional facilitates an employee participation program that results in a substantial increase in productivity. Does she have an ethical responsibility for encouraging the fair and just distribution of that increase? Some people would not even consider the question. Others would say no. Still others would say that the employees who contributed to the increase should get some part of it, but opinions vary widely about how much they should receive and about the role of OD-HSD professionals in implementing the distribution.

The exact nature of this issue is still vaguely defined, since it can extend beyond concerns about sharing productivity increases to the question of how to establish equity in salaries, wages, and compensation generally. There are many organizations in which managers as well as workers feel they are not fairly treated by the existing compensation system, but feel powerless to change it. They talk as if they still want to contribute to the best of their ability, but their motivation must inevitably be affected negatively and with substantial loss in productivity, creativity, and satisfaction as a result.

This issue also extends beyond compensation to the question of how to establish fairness and equity for customers, stockholders, suppliers, governments, communities, and all of a system's stakeholders in sharing the fruits of its productivity. Equitable sharing is an ethical issue of primary importance for the OD-HSD profession; the Statement recognizes the promotion of justice as one of the profession's social responsibilities (Guideline V–C). However, as noted in the discussion under Guideline V–C–1, our role is more one of facilitating decisions about equity than of prescribing what is equitable.

12. For OD-HSD professionals who work with business organizations, how is profitability to be valued relative to other values? In an article about corporate moral development, Johnson & Johnson has been identified as one of the best examples of an ethical corporation (Reidenbach and Robin, 1989). Its credo shows a strong balance between concern for profits and concern for the interests of all stakeholders. That credo articulates the company's responsibilities in the following sequence: first, to its consumers ("doctors, nurses, patients, and mothers who buy our products and services"); second, to its employees; third, to all the communities with which it deals, "including the community of man"; and finally, to its stockholders. After listing these various groups in that order, the credo continues to say: "We have often been asked why we put the stockholder last . . . and our answer has always been that, if we do the other jobs properly . . . the stockholder will always be well served. The record suggests that this is the case." As part of the record, Johnson & Johnson's experience with the Tylenol crisis—in which some of its product was tampered with, resulting in massive, expensive recalls—illustrates how the credo was so much a part of the firm's way of life that its senior managers did not hesitate to recall regardless of cost.

Another perspective on the relative value to be given to

profit is offered by Russell Ackoff (1986) when he talks about profit as necessary for the survival of a business enterprise, but not the reason for it. As he says, profit is a requirement, not an objective; a means, not an end. He then expresses his conviction that those who manage corporations do so primarily to provide themselves with a quality of work life and standard of living that are good for them, rather than to maximize profit and growth. And, rather than apologizing for that objective, he contends that it should be extended to cover the quality of working life and living standard of all employees. He then puts quality of life and standard of living into perspective by emphasizing that they cannot be improved without making a profit, paying dividends large enough to attract and retain investors, increasing productivity, and providing for growth.

In combination, the Johnson & Johnson and Ackoff perspectives — the first with its focus on the degree of responsibility to some of the most important stakeholders in business, and the second with its focus on quality of work life and standard of living as primary values of senior managers and on profit as a means rather than an end — suggest ways of thinking about profit that may make decisions by OD-HSD professionals easier. These perspectives involve reframing our concept of "the bottom line" (profit) as primary, and seeing it as a means to serving other values, particularly the quality of life and standard of living values of senior managers. Within that new framework, it is much easier to think practically about how to serve those values as well as the other values we consider most important.

In the last analysis, however, our most difficult ethical choices will come down to acting in ways that are good and right because they are good and right, and not because they can be rationalized as being in the narrowly defined self-interest of the people with whom we contract. As the Statement notes, when we cannot act in ways that we consider ethical, we should withhold or withdraw our services (Guidelines II–A and V–D).

The importance of profitability is implicitly recognized in the Annotated Statement (annotation following the Preamble) with the following words: "Among other things, we seek to facilitate the development of human systems as healthy settings within which individuals can grow *in ways that enable those systems to survive and thrive economically so they can continue to be healthy settings"* (emphasis added).

13. Is it appropriate to found our value system on "happiness"? The introductory note in the Values section of the Annotated Statement (Chapter Four) says that "Our value system is based on: (1) life and the quest for happiness, (2) freedom, responsibility, and self-control, and (3) justice. When we give these values primary importance and then build on that foundation, these values have the priority that is implicit in our vision of 'people living meaningful, productive, good lives.'" In the discussion of that value, we identify happiness as meaning "whole lives well lived" in contrast to "the momentary satisfaction associated with satisfying momentary desires." And later, in the discussion of fundamental human rights, we quote Adler (1987, p. 59) as saying that *"the primary right is the pursuit of happiness, having its foundation in our moral obligation to make good lives for ourselves"* (emphasis added). We then call attention to the fact that the right is not to happiness, but rather to the *pursuit* of (or quest for) happiness—namely, people's opportunities-obligations to "make good lives."

Although we acknowledge that happiness is not a right, I contend that we value it above all other values. However, in my experience, we seldom, if ever, talk about it in our role as OD-HSD professionals. I think this is attributable, at least in part, to our work with profit-making organizations in which happiness tends to be regarded as irrelevant to, if not bad for, profits. As noted in the earlier discussion, profitability and happiness are not necessarily opposing values, although they may clash in specific short-term situations. In the long run, many of us believe both values are essential to the success of human systems, particularly businesses.

In order to make the case more completely for happiness as a primary value, we need to reflect on what we mean by it. Adler's ideas (1987) are helpful. He points out that "happiness is not only an ultimate good to be sought for its own sake, and never as a means to anything beyond itself. It is also the one complete good . . . When happiness is achieved, it leaves nothing more to be desired, for it involves the possession of all other goods" (p. 52).

Adler then looks closely at two different, though related, concepts of happiness. "One is the modern psychological conception of happiness as a feeling of contentment produced by the satisfaction we experience when we are able to fulfill whatever desires we happen to have at any moment in time. The other is the ancient ethical conception of happiness as a whole life well lived because it is enriched by the cumulative possession of all the goods that a morally virtuous human being ought to desire" (p. 52).

As noted earlier, it is the "whole life well lived" concept of happiness that we consider primary. Having said that, it will help to clarify what we mean by "well lived" in that concept. Again Adler (1987, pp. 54–55) is helpful by his differentiation between two kinds of desires. "One set of desires consists of wants human beings acquire in the course of their individual lives . . . Such desires differ from person to person . . . Another set of desires consists of the needs that all human beings share in common . . . [which] we normally speak of . . . as our natural needs." Then he describes how our desires can guide our lives by noting that "our needs are always right desires, desires for the real goods we ought to desire, whereas our wants may be either right or wrong desires." Adler illustrates how a "want" can be a "wrong desire" by referring to "individuals who want power or domination over others and are willing to infringe on the freedom of others in order to satisfy their desires" (p. 55). (Note the relevance of this want to our ethical principle about not acting in ways that "increase the power of more powerful stakeholders *over* the less powerful" and to the related discussion that suggests an ethical alternative that can increase the power available to managers by focusing on empowerment and power *with*.)

Based on these ideas, Adler asserts that a life "well lived" is guided by the prescription that "we *ought* to seek everything that is *really* good for us and . . . there is nothing else we *ought* to seek . . . Since happiness, ethically conceived, is the complete good of a whole life enriched by the cumulative possession of everything *really* good for us, the self-evident prescription just stated is equivalent to saying that we *ought* to seek happiness, that we are morally obliged to pursue it" (p. 57). For those of us who accept that idea, we believe that OD-HSD professionals "ought" to value happiness in the ethical sense of "a whole life well lived" and, therefore, believe that our profession's ethics "ought" to guide our behavior and our efforts to influence others' behavior in accordance with that value. We recognize that "ought" and "really good" are not always clear concepts in specific situations, but we accept responsibility for doing the best we can to act consistently with them. We do so not out of blind obedience to the tyranny of should or ought, but because we value happiness.

In the last analysis, we know we are living in accordance with that value, rather than just talking about it, when we meet the test for self-respect described by Nathaniel Branden in an audio recording (1985): "It has to do with knowing in the wee hours of the morning that: knowing the good, we have done it; seeing the beautiful, we have served it; knowing the truth, we have spoken it."

In short, our own happiness is in large part a function of the degree to which we are able to serve others' happiness as well as our own. And our ability to do that is in turn a function of our possession of moral virtue, defined by Adler (1987, p. 54) as "the settled habit or disposition of will to desire what we ought to desire." The discussion of values in the Statement is intended to help us do that.

When OD-HSD professionals talk about "quality of life" as a value, they are focusing on essentially the same thing as happiness. It contrasts with mechanistic values that ignore the quality of people's lives and treat people as objects to be used only in the service of system purposes without regard for their personal purposes. One manifestation of this value is the QWL effort by a number of organizations. It should be recognized, however, that when we refer to "quality of life" we mean all of people's lives and not only the parts they devote to work. We also mean *whole* life (from birth to death) and *all* life (not just the lives of our clients and their immediate stakeholders).

In order to understand more fully the happiness value, we also need to examine more closely two related values that focus on individual human beings.

- *Individuals are valued as whole persons, not only as employees or as means for achieving organizational results.* Tannenbaum and Davis (1969, p. 7) wrote of this when they referred to movement away from avoidance or negative evaluation of individuals and toward confirming them as human beings. Among other things, it means caring about them personally, including their concerns, hopes, desires, and fears, as well as their productive strengths and weaknesses. By recognizing the *whole* person, OD-HSD practice seeks to empower people to express their full potential in their jobs and their lives generally. For example, this is reflected when an organization supports a person's development even when it may mean the person's eventually leaving the organization.
- *Personal growth is valued as well as the growth of job-related competence.* Organizations may question whether it is their responsibility to encourage growth that does not directly serve their purposes, but OD-HSD practice tends to assume that without attending to people's full growth potential, the portion that is organizationally relevant is likely to suffer. There may even be a widely shared judgment that ignoring or hindering personal growth simply because it does not serve organizational purposes is morally wrong.

The place of happiness in the relationship between human systems and human beings may be described in the following parable:

A sinner is being shown heaven and hell. He sees two large doors and is led through one of them, which he assumes at first is the door to heaven because of the wonderful aroma of delectable foods that greets him. As he enters he sees a number of people sitting around a large round table. He notices that despite the wonderful feast in the mid-

dle, the people look emaciated and groan with hunger. Each has a spoon with a very long handle that
can reach the food in the middle. But because the
handles are so much longer than their arms, none
can get the food into their mouths. They suffer ter-
ribly from the unceasing hunger and frustration,
and the man realizes he is in hell. He is then led
through the other door to see heaven. At first he
sees what looks like the same situation — the same
delicious food, the same large table, people sitting
around it with long-handled spoons. But these people look cheerful and well fed, and they are chat-
ting and laughing. The man is puzzled and asks
what the difference is here. The reply: They have
learned to feed each other (Quoted in Wachtel,
1989, pp. 189–190).

Using the imagery of the parable, we could say that if
human systems and human beings could learn to feed each other,
we might change life on earth from hell for many to heaven for
all. And the OD-HSD profession, if we choose to do so, can
play an important role in achieving that transformation.

*14. Does ethics clarification have a place among the ser-
vices offered by OD-HSD professionals?* In the personal, group,
organizational, and system development that the OD-HSD
profession has offered historically, helping people clarify their
ethics and develop their ability to act in accord with consciously
chosen ethical standards has not been central to the practitioner's role. However, the need for such service has become increasingly clear recently, particularly in the United States, where
ethical problems in business and government have received a
great deal of attention during the late 1980s. Jerry Harvey, a
leader in the profession since its inception, was recently quoted
as saying that "the only emerging role that is available" for OD
consultants is one that "focuses on the moral, ethical, and
spiritual aspects of work" (Chase, 1989, p. 8).

Business in particular could benefit from the attention of

OD-HSD professionals because collectively we have an interest in the functioning of not only the whole business system but our individual client systems-organizations as well. By acting assertively to support the ethical leadership of industrial associations and professions related to business—such as the various science, engineering, and management professional associations and societies—the OD-HSD profession could enhance the forces that encourage individual business organizations to behave in ways that are good for their industries and society as well as their own interests. Given competitive market conditions, people who work for individual enterprises are under great pressure to behave in ways that serve the narrowly defined interests of their enterprises. Ethical leadership by industrial and professional associations can serve as a countervailing force to that of competition when it works against the good of society. And the OD-HSD profession-as-a-whole, in contrast to its individual members, is uniquely qualified to encourage such leadership.

15. To what extent, if any, do we recognize "love" as a dimension in the practice of OD-HSD? The Annotated Statement refers to "love" when it says that "the OD-HSD profession aspires to help people realize their highest potential, individually and collectively, by . . . supporting the creation and maintenance of a climate within which freedom, mutual trust, respect, and love prevail" (Belief 4-f). Those words are adapted from a policy statement developed by senior executives at Kollmorgen, a medium-sized electronics company (Kiefer and Stroh, 1983, p. 27). Many people in our field explicitly or implicitly refer to love. as in Tannenbaum's question, "Does this path have a heart?" However, as the Annotated Statement notes in its discussion of that belief, the reference to love is controversial, with some practitioners wanting to delete the word because it is "not necessary for organizational functioning," and others contending, "That's what OD is all about."

Given the systems perspective of our work, it is helpful to note Albert Einstein's view: "A human being is part of a whole, called by us the 'universe,' a part limited in time and space. He experiences himself, his thought and feelings as some thing separated from the rest — a kind of optical delusion of his consciousness. This delusion is a kind of prison for us, restricting us to our personal desires and to affection for a few persons nearest to us. Our task must be to free ourselves from this prison by widening our circle of compassion to embrace all living creatures and the whole of nature in its beauty. Nobody is able to achieve this completely, but the striving for such achievement is in itself a part of the liberation and a foundation for inner security." (Quoted in Pedrazzini and Gable, 1989, p. 3)

Answering the question, Does love have a place in our practice? requires us to ask ourselves further questions: What *do* we stand for? If love *is* important to us, what do we mean by it? These questions are not easily answered. In specifying what we mean by *love,* we can say that, among other things, we mean compassion (as in the Einstein quotation) and caring. In elaborating on these concepts, we will need to deal with the apparent contradiction between conditional and unconditional love, sometimes differentiated as the love of the father and mother. In commenting on how we can deal with that contradiction, one respondent to the Statement said, "It involves a dialectic between reason and feelings; a thesis, antithesis, and synthesis in which reason and feelings nourish each other." It is also helpful to note that such a dialectic will need to recognize differences in reasoning processes between males and females of the kind identified by Carol Gilligan, who discovered that "boys tend to apply abstract concepts like rights and justice to dilemmas, while girls [think] more about relationships" (Brown, 1987, p. 3). Love is clearly in the concrete realm of relationships and, though we do not have sufficient basis for generalizing, it is interesting to note that it has been men who have most strongly objected to acknowledging that love has a place in our practice, although many men have been equally as strong in support of its inclusion.

Our purpose at this point is not to resolve the issue, but only to identify it. For some of us, the answer is clear that love not only has a place in our practice, but is, in fact, at the heart of it. However, we also recognize that we still have much to do in clarifying what we mean by that.

16. To what extent, if any, is "beauty" among the most important of our OD-HSD values? This issue is at the horizon of our frontier issues. Its nature is suggested by Pedrazzini and Gable (1989, p. 16): "It has been suggested that aesthetics will be the ethics of the future. This idea makes a great deal of sense in a world of rapid change with the need for continual adaptation and evolution. This concept would make integrity, which is a biologically, and socially sound concept, the basis for ethics. Management is finding that those people who are congruent in their 'thinking, behaving, and believing' are the most successful in leading their organizations through change. There is a power in having integrated responses to situations [that] people can rely on. Responsibility flows from integrity. When human systems are integrated, they become able to respond as needed to achieve desired goals . . . The aesthetic perspective includes a world of 'other means' for which there is no verbal referent. The experience, like the image, is prior to the word and contains more knowledge. This perspective makes a unity of reason and intuition and provides the grounding for 'common sensing' and consensus." To make the link between esthetics and beauty explicit we need also to include the dictionary definition of *esthetic:* namely, "related to the beautiful as distinguished from the merely pleasing, moral, and [especially] the useful and utilitarian . . . [and] appreciative of, responsive to, or zealous about the beautiful" (Pedrazzini and Gable, 1989, p. 16).

From another perspective, the relationship of ethics to beauty may be described using a metaphor. A model for thinking about vision, current reality, and the process of bringing vision into being is described in Figure 4.

In the model, vision refers to an "image" in the mind's eye (including feelings as well as visual images) of a desired state. For an individual, it could be reflected in a person's answer to the question, What would your life be like if it were exactly the way you would like it to be? (as mentioned in our earlier discussion of empowerment). For organization members it could reflect their answer to the question, What would your organization be like if it were exactly the way you would like it to be? For example, at the individual level, Alexander Graham Bell

Figure 4. Living with Vision.

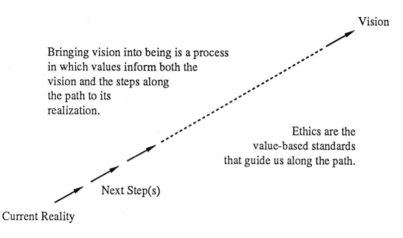

Vision

Bringing vision into being is a process
in which values inform both the
vision and the steps along
the path to its
realization.

Ethics are the
value-based standards
that guide us along the path.

Next Step(s)

Current Reality

Source: Adapted from Kiefer and Stroh, 1983.

was guided by a vision of the communication device we now call "the telephone." And, at the organizational level, in 1908, before we had satellites and transoceanic cables, a vision for the American Telephone and Telegraph Company was conceived as "a communication system that would enable anyone anywhere to communicate with anyone anywhere anytime." There may have been other dimensions to that vision, but that example illustrates how words can reflect a vision even when the technology for bringing the vision into being does not exist and when many people may believe that such a vision is impossible.

In thinking about vision, it is important to note that it reflects the esthetic perspective that Pedrazzini and Gable (1989) described as being one that exists "prior to the word" and, therefore, "contains more knowledge." In this connection, note also the relevance of the idea that "a picture is worth a thousand words."

According to the model in Figure 4, one need not know about how one is going to realize one's vision, but only to be clear about (1) one's "vision" (although it may change and become richer and more complex over time); (2) "current reality" (namely, that which is currently going on within and around one's self or one's organization or whatever social entity is involved in visioning); and (3) one's "next steps." With regard to "next steps," the meaning of that idea is well conveyed by Confucius's expression that "a journey of ten thousand miles starts with but a single step." One need not have a comprehensive plan for achieving one's vision, only a willingness to take each next step one at a time.

The place of values and ethics in the process of living with vision is also noted in the model: (1) values inform both the vision and the step-by-step process of realization, and (2) ethics, which are value-based standards, provide guidance for taking each step.

This discussion began by saying that a metaphor could be used to describe the relationship of ethics to beauty. If the life paths of individuals, from current reality to the realization of their visions, are conceived of as multicolored threads, then to the extent that those threads come together in the creation of the lives of organizations and other human systems, they can be conceived collectively as a tapestry. And, if that tapestry is esthetically satisfying, we can say that those lives are "beautiful" (as well as being "meaningful, productive, and good" in accordance with the vision described in the Statement). In that context, values and ethics have a fundamental place in determining the beauty of the tapestry; or, perhaps, beauty lies behind those values and ethics that "should" guide us in our "quest for a good life."

From another perspective, the metaphor is useful in thinking about our role as OD-HSD professionals and as a profession. If we conceive of human beings as the weavers of their own lives, we can conceive of ourselves as meta-weavers who help people learn to weave together in a way that creates a beautiful whole.

17. To what extent, if any, do we recognize "spirit" as a dimension in the practice of OD-HSD? Responses to the May 1983 Statement suggested including the following as one of the assumptions underlying the guidelines: "Human beings are . . . interdependent economically, politically, socially, culturally, and spiritually and are responsible for the choices they make within that context" (Belief 1-c). The spiritual reference was added because one person identified "starting a spiritual increment" as one of the central purposes of the profession and another person specifically suggested including *spiritual* in the words quoted above. In contrast, two people asked, "Is this a profession or a religion?"

Just as some people's experience with democratic political process can leave them with an aversion to democracy, the experience of others with established religions can leave them with an aversion to religion. Regardless of how practitioners feel about "religion," they may still be able to acknowledge that "spirit" is a dimension in the practice of OD-HSD, even if only in the sense of "team spirit."

As an example of how the issue of spiritual consciousness is becoming more visible, two highly experienced practitioners, Billie Alban and Sheldon Hughes, in a presentation to the New York OD Network (Diagonali, 1984), talked about their discovery "that managers are indeed looking for a deeper spiritual base upon which to build." They invited OD professionals "to be inspired, emboldened, and encouraged to infuse our training and consulting practices with our hearts, minds, and spirits." Even more significantly, an indicator of what is going on at this frontier is the transformational movement that treats "spirit" as primary. (For example, see Owen, 1987.)

The key questions underlying this issue are: Do we acknowledge spirit as an aspect of reality with which OD-HSD practice must deal? And, if so, how do we deal with it? As a first step toward answering these questions, Ken Wilbur's ideas are clarifying. Wilbur (1983, p. 70) says that we need to recognize that mind can adequately look at and map sense data because it transcends them; it can adequately look at and map intellectual data because they are its own creation; "but it cannot adequately look at and map spirit because spirit transcends it." The challenge for us as a profession is to find or create ways of gathering data about the realm of the spirit in ways that can be independently replicated by others and then interpreted in ways that allow for consensual validation, thereby enabling ourselves to move ahead together in serving our common purpose as fully as we are able.

One final point also needs to be made. The possibility that spirit may be at the core of our ability to act morally and ethically is suggested by Ralph Waldo Emerson (1988, p. 8): "The lessons of the moral sentiment are, once for all, an emancipation from that anxiety which takes the joy out of all life . . . It is a commandment at every moment and in every condition of life to do the duty of that moment and to abstain from doing the wrong. And it is so near and inward and constitutional to each, that no commandment can compare with it in authority. All wise men regard it as the voice of the Creator himself."

Harman and Rheingold (1984, pp. 109–110) express a similar idea in terms of its relation to our contemporary times: "The last great transformation of public beliefs regarding the proper source of values and guidance occurred nearly a thousand years ago, when the other-worldly perspective of the Middle Ages changed to the pragmatic, secular earth-oriented worldview that produced the Renaissance, the Industrial Revolution and the world we live in today . . . In the midst of the ruin of our former value systems, an old message is surfacing, stated in modern terms: *Guidance can be found, and the authority is the most trustworthy possible mentor — one's own higher self.*"

Conclusion

Building on the foundation of the generally agreed-upon values described in Chapter Four and the additional values suggested in this chapter, the OD-HSD profession appears now to be in a position to resolve constructively the issues that have been discussed in this and earlier chapters, as well as others that will emerge as the field continues to evolve in its collective consciousness of what it is. Even more important, the profession can be expected to continue defining and refining its mission in the world and, as a result, gain a heightened sense of itself as a global professional community. That mission seems likely to involve helping people achieve and maintain excellence as individuals, as organizations, and as other human systems — at levels far above most people's present levels of aspiration. Some people would even say that the highest level involves realizing, both in the sense of "becoming aware" and "bringing into being," the essential divinity that they believe exists within all human beings. Primary among the conditions that will make that highest achievement possible is the uniting of OD-HSD professionals throughout the world in a community committed to the realization of a common vision — namely, a vision that can be expressed as "people living meaningful, productive, good lives in ways that simultaneously serve them, their organizations, their societies, and the world" (from the Preamble of the Statement).

Notes

1. To personalize this request rather than simply leave it at an abstract level, I want to mention the names of people I think of within the international OD-HSD community who might help in initiating such action. In particular, I think of Marcel Bolle de Bal (Belgium), Ian Barber (Spain), Francois Breuer (Netherlands), John Bryan (Canada), José Campoverde (Peru), Amnon Caspi (Israel), Wojtek Daniecki (from Poland, though currently in the United States), Aldei Darveau (Canada), Karen Davis (United States), Jose De Anzizu (Spain), Guadalupe Martinez De Leon (Mexico), Herberto Diaz (Venezuela), Maurice Dubras (Canada), Louw du Toit (South Africa), Marvin Egberts (Netherlands), Claudio Fuchs (Chile), Uri Gluskinos (Israel), Yuri Hania (Soviet Union), Elisabeth Hermann-Belloso (Venezuela), Paul Iles (United Kingdom), David Jamieson (United States), Trygve Johnstad (Norway), Andrew Kakabadse (United Kingdom), Svein Kile (Norway), Kazuo Kohda (Japan), Pessy Krausz (Israel), Pierre Lacroix (Canada), Ralf Lampe (German Democratic Republic), Imre Lovey (Hungary), Catalina Martinez (Mexico), Antonio Solorzano Martinez (Venezuela), Ewa Maslyk-Musial (Poland), Willem Mastenbroek (Netherlands), Rauno Matikainen (Finland), Francisco Montes (Venezuela), Matjaz Mulej (Yugoslavia), John Nirenberg (moving to Australia), Jorge Parada (Mexico), Etty Paz (Israel), Pjotr Ploszajski (Poland), Arkadij Prigozhin (Soviet Union), Joop

Quint (Netherlands), Ananda Rao (India), Tony Roldan (Philippines), Zofia Rummel-Syska (Poland), Turid Sato (Norway), Johan Saulam (India), Klaus and Traudl Senkel (Federal Republic of Germany), Ken Shepard (Canada), Betty Smith (Canada), Bob Snipes (United States), Maria Stebelsky (Canada), Leopold Stieger (Austria), Andrezej Straszak (Poland), Gaby Szelei (Hungary), Perla Tayko (Philippines), Karsten Trebesch (Federal Republic of Germany), Alejandro Valadez (Mexico), and Nancy Westrup Villareal (Mexico). I know there are others I could have mentioned, but I decided to run the risk of leaving some people out, rather than finesse the problem of incomplete memory by not mentioning names at all.

In addition to asking each of these people to join in a call for action, I mention these names and countries so that readers will have a clear sense of how widespread the OD-HSD professional community could be if all its members were to ask: Who is in our networks? How are they interconnected? What might we do to transform ourselves into a true global, professional community? What are we willing to do to bring that community into being?

Background of the Values and Ethics Statement
▮▯▮▯▮▯▮▯▮▯▮▯▮▯▮▯▮▯▮▯▮▯▮▯▮▯▮▯▮▯▮▯

Beginning in 1981, a participative process for creating "A Statement of Values and Ethics by Professionals in Organization and Human Systems Development" was initiated. The Statement, which is the current outcome of that process, is presented in annotated form in Chapters Four and Five and, more concisely, in Appendix B. To provide perspective on that Statement and other events related to the process of developing heightened ethical consciousness and practice throughout the OD-HSD profession, this appendix describes the background out of which the Statement has emerged.

Recognition of the Need for an Ethical Position for the Profession

One of the widely recognized primary indicators of a profession's existence is an ethical position that is generally accepted by the members of the profession. Therefore, for those who want to support the emergence of OD-HSD as a profession, it has been important to acknowledge that a generally accepted ethical position has not existed, and then do what it takes to create one.

One of the earliest acknowledgments that there was no widely shared ethical position among OD-HSD practitioners was in a 1980 survey of OD practitioners. (Since the field at the time focused on *organization* development, it was known as OD; that is the reference used here.) That study concluded that OD was not a profession because it did not have a generally accepted code of ethics (Kegan, 1982). In response to that survey, Donald Cole, executive director of the OD Institute, drafted a first version of a "code" and published it in the June 1981 issue of the Institute's newsletter asking for comments. Among others, William Gellermann responded and Cole asked if he would draft a code for the Institute. Gellermann agreed to draft a "statement"; he believed that a "code" was too rigid to reflect the profession's stage of development. He also expressed the goal of implementing a participatory process for creating such a statement that would reach as many people in the profession as possible.

Key Events in the Evolution of the Statement

Following the publication of the first draft in June 1981, some of the key events in the evolution of the Statement have been:

September 1981. A second version was drafted based on replies to the first draft and ethics statements developed by the Association for Creative Change, the International Consultants Foundation (ICF), and the NTL Institute. The OD Institute published the second draft in its newsletter and asked for comments.

November 1981. A third version was drafted, again responding to comments and suggestions, and mailed to about fifty people, including all those who responded to earlier drafts and several people outside the United States. Again, the OD Institute newsletter published it and asked for comments. In addition to expressing support for the Statement process and making suggestions for improvement, several people expressed their desire for some kind of clearinghouse that would collect information about values and ethics of OD professionals.

February 1982. After extensive revision based on responses to the prior draft, a fourth version was developed. It also sought to integrate ideas from statements or codes of other organizations, particularly the American Psychological Association. This draft was accompanied by a questionnaire based on issues raised by responses to the prior draft, such as "Should we use the words 'profession' and 'professional'?" These materials were mailed to about forty people in the United States and thirty people in other countries. The OD Network in the United Kingdom and the OD Institute both published the Statement in their newsletters and encouraged responses.

March 1982. The board of the OD Network in the United States voted support for the process and identified Jeanne Cherbeneau and Frank Friedlander as liaison on professional values and ethics.

April 1982. Mark S. Frankel, then director of the Center for the Study of Ethics in the Professions at Illinois Institute of Technology, responded to the fourth version in a session he led at the OD Institute's Annual Information Exchange. During that session he offered the center's support for "a continuing effort on the part of OD professionals to increase their sensitivity to and understanding of ethical dilemmas associated with their work and to produce a more explicit document for professional educational and guidance."

May 1982. Frankel drafted a concept paper describing a proposal he was willing to prepare jointly with people in the OD profession. In it he described the project that was ultimately funded by the National Science Foundation and that, among other things, yielded this book and has laid the foundation for establishing a Clearinghouse on Information About Values and Ethics in Organization and Human Systems Development.

July 1982. A fifth draft was prepared and mailed, along with a questionnaire about issues raised by the fourth draft, to all people who had expressed interest in the process.

August 1982. Herb Shepard, then chair of Certified Consultants International, convened a meeting of leaders of various OD organizations in conjunction with that year's Academy of Management meeting. The group at that meeting was introduced to the Statement process and the clearinghouse concept. On the same day, Lynda McDermott and Don Warrick of the OD Division of the American Society for Training and Development hosted a dinner meeting for leaders in the OD field, including most of the people from the earlier meeting and a substantial number of others. At that meeting general support for both the Statement process and the clearinghouse was expressed by people who had attended the earlier meeting. The larger group expressed interest in receiving further information in preparation for a follow-up meeting of the Inter-Organization Group to be held in conjunction with the OD Network Conference in October 1982. The fifth draft and the questionnaire were mailed to all participants in both meetings. (The OD Inter-Organization Group later became the Human Systems Development Consortium, composed of leaders and representatives of OD-oriented groups, primarily in the United States.)

1983. After the meetings in 1982, most of the leading OD-oriented professional organizations, associations, and networks in the United States endorsed the Statement development process, and individuals and organizations in more than fifteen countries were participating. Among others, endorsements were given by leaders of ACC, the OD Division of ASTD, CCI, NTL Institute, the OD Institute, the OD Network, and HSDC.

In this connection, it is important to note that the organizational support has been for the Statement development *process* and not the Statement as such. It seemed unreasonable to expect the organizations to endorse the Statement until sufficient developmental work had been done to demonstrate substantial consensus among a significant number of practitioners. Each year since 1983 and continuing to the present, the OD Institute has published the Statement in its *International Registry of Organization Development Professionals and Organization Development Handbook.*

1984–1985. The HSDC and the Center for the Study of Ethics in the Professions (Illinois Institute of Technology) received the aforementioned National Science Foundation (NSF) grant ($90,000 to support working toward the institutionalization of the values and ethics of the OD-HSD profession by various means). As part of the project funded by that grant, numerous public announcements were made in OD-oriented journals and newsletters and responses were received from more than 300 people who wanted to be kept informed about the project. Case discussion forums on OD values and ethics were convened at the annual meetings of five of the leading OD associations in the United States and at the OD Institute's OD World Congress in 1985.

In addition to the Statement, an Issues Discussion was prepared as an essential companion document. When changes in the Statement were suggested by respondents, they were made if they seemed feasible; when they involved issues on which significant difference of opinion seemed likely, however, the differences were described in the Issues Discussion. In 1984, the first discussion was published in the *Organization Development Journal* (Gellermann, 1984b).

1986. The OD Network in the United States made copies of the Statement and the Issues Discussion available to interested members. CCI mailed the Statement to all its members along with requests for comments. As part of the NSF project, the Statement was mailed along with requests for comments to all people who had expressed interest in the project. And a workshop on values and ethics in OD was conducted at the United States OD Network annual meeting.

1987–1988. In 1987, an annotated bibliography on values and ethics in OD-HSD was published by the American Association for the Advancement of Science as a product of the NSF project. (Frankel had moved from the Illinois Institute of Technology to AAAS and transferred the project with him.) In both 1987 and 1988, half-day workshops on values and ethics were conducted at the annual conferences of the United States OD Network and the International OD Association and in 1988 at the annual conference of the Association for Creative Change. In addition, a full day session was done for the Annual Retreat of the Association for Creative Change/Canadian Association of Applied Social Scientists of Southern Ontario. During the course of those workshops, the workshop design and supporting materials were refined, and, more important, participants contributed to the Statement development process. Additional comments also came via the mail during both years and the Statement in Chapters Four and Five reflects that input.

1989. During mid-1989, a one-page Summary Statement and a questionnaire were mailed to the editors of the newsletters for all the regional OD networks in the United States. They were asked to send out these materials along with their newsletters; most of them did. Responses (n = 230) included: 215 considered OD a profession; 211 considered themselves members of the OD profession; 225 agreed that, among other things, being a profession requires clear ethics; 191 accepted the Statement as it was, but 57 had suggestions for improvement, and another 26 could accept it if certain changes were made. Primary conclusions drawn from those results were that (1) we are in fact moving toward a substantial consensus, but still have a way to go, and (2) a one-page summary, though widely acceptable, raises more questions than it answers, as indicated by the 57 suggestions and the 26 required changes (not to mention the one who could not accept any such statement and the 12 who answered "something else" rather than give any kind of acceptance or rejection response). For that reason, a Statement that is more concise than the Annotated Statement has been prepared (Appendix B). Both versions encompass many suggestions made in response to the questionnaire.

As noted under earlier events, leaders of several OD-oriented groups had endorsed the Statement development process but, except for the participants at the 1984 OD World Congress who also endorsed the process, there had been no direct feedback about support from the general membership of the profession. The response to the questionnaire indicated a lot of support from the respondents, but told us nothing about the nonrespondents.

To get more general support, the Business Meeting of the 1989 International OD Association Annual Conference in Irsee, Bavaria, was asked to endorse the process and did so unanimously. Also, participants at the 1989 OD Network Conference in San Diego were asked to endorse the process using a printed survey form. The results were as follows: 278 said they do endorse the process, 3 said they do not, and 4 gave no answer. It was also interesting to note that one of those who did not give his endorsement said that his reason was that the described process did not provide for face-to-face discussion, an approach that has not yet been used, except informally, but that does seem a desirable path to follow in the future.

Issues that Have Arisen in the Process
of the Statement's Development

As noted above, differences of opinion have surfaced as an increasing number of people have joined in the process of creating the Statement. For discussion purposes, three classes of issues can be identified.

- *Context issues:* Questions that do not involve the Statement directly, but are important because they establish a perspective for understanding the development of the OD-HSD profession and the Statement's content. For example: Do we consider ourselves a profession and professionals? What is our field? Who is an OD-HSD professional?
- *Content issues:* Questions that focus on matters central to our developing substantial consensus on what we say in our Statement, covering such things as what to include or exclude and what words or ideas best express what we mean.

For example: Are our ethics too culturally specific? Is our thinking oriented primarily to practice in the United States? Do we place high value on democratic decision making?

- *Frontier issues:* A class of issues at the growing edge of the profession's development that deserve separate attention from context and content issues. They involve questions that seem to be on the frontier of defining what the practice of OD-HSD is all about. To answer them requires going to a depth we are just beginning to discover. For example: Is it possible to develop general agreement on values and ethics among OD-HSD professionals throughout the world, particularly given the fact of major cultural differences? To what extent, if any, do we recognize "spirit" as a dimension in OD-HSD practice?

In Chapter One, content and context issues are discussed. Chapters Four and Five, along with all the case discussion chapters, deal with content issues. And Chapter Twelve focusses on frontier issues.

Conclusions

As indicated above, the process of creating the Statement has included drafting a version, sending it to people for comments and suggestions, redrafting based on the responses, and then repeating the process. To date, more than 500 people from more than twenty countries have participated directly in the process by indicating they can accept one or another version of the Statement and/or making suggestions for improving it. That process is expected to continue with increasing participation by people throughout the profession, ideally including increasing amounts of face-to-face discussion.

The number and magnitude of suggested changes have decreased during the last two years, but substantial changes are still being suggested, so periodic revisions may be needed for a few more years. In time it seems likely that the profession will achieve substantial consensus on the Statement and the Issues

Discussion combined. Many people accept the Statement as it is; others accept it as long as their positions are recognized in the Issues Discussion. In any case, both the Statement and the Issues Discussion should be viewed as evolving documents and not fixed and final, although, as substantial consensus is established, we can expect the number and magnitude of changes to decrease.

APPENDIX B

‖‖‖‖‖‖‖‖‖‖‖‖‖‖‖‖‖‖‖‖

A Statement of Values and Ethics by Professionals in Organization and Human Systems Development, June 1990

‖‖‖

Preamble

Organization and Human Systems Development (OD-HSD) is a professional network or community of professionals whose practice is based on the applied behavioral sciences, a human systems perspective, and both human and organizational values. As OD-HSD professionals we seek to promote and facilitate the process by which human beings and human systems live and work together for their mutual success and well-being. Our purpose is to promote a widely shared learning and discovery process dedicated to the vision of people living meaningful, productive, good lives in ways that simultaneously serve them, their organizations, their societies, and the world.[1]

[Note: This Statement is a concise version of the Annotated Statement in Chapters Four and Five. See also Appendix F for important information about how the Statement was developed.]

[Note: This statement may be copied for professional use without written permission. Please note that it is copied from W. Gellermann, M. S. Frankel, and R. Ladenson, *Values and Ethics in Organization and Human Systems Development: Responding to Dilemmas in Professional Life.* (San Francisco: Jossey-Bass, 1990.)]

Nature and Purposes

For OD-HSD to exist as a profession, substantial consensus[2] is necessary within the profession about its primary beliefs, values, and ethics. The process of co-creating this Statement is a means of establishing such consensus, but it is important to remember that *this Statement is not our primary objective. It is only a means to increase ethical consciousness and practice throughout our profession.*

This Statement is an *aspirational* guide, a specification of ideals toward which we strive.[3] For a more detailed description and explanation of our professional norms, see the Annotated Statement in the book by Gellermann, Frankel, and Ladenson referred to in the note on the previous page.

The purposes of this Statement are to (1) increase our professional and ethical consciousness and our sense of ethical responsibility, (2) guide us in making more informed ethical choices, and (3) help our profession function more effectively.

We intend this Statement as a resource to help us make responsible, informed choices about our behavior by helping us be clear about our:

- Vision, since it enhances our sense of common purpose
- Beliefs, since they affect our ability to see the truth
- Values, since they are the essential element underlying our choices
- Moral rules and ideals, since they are fundamental to our being responsible members of the human community
- Ethical principles, since they provide general guidance for our choices
- Ethical guidelines, since they provide more specific guidance in the kinds of situations we encounter as OD-HSD professionals

Using this Statement as a guide involves living consistently within its spirit and not just its words, particularly in ambiguous situations in which the good or right thing to do is not clear.

Because we view ethical practice as continuing and developmental, we encourage all OD-HSD professionals to use this Statement as a resource in (1) reflecting on their own values and ethics, ethical problems, and problem resolutions, and (2) communicating about the results of their reflection with other OD-HSD professionals and, when appropriate, with their clients.[4]

Beliefs

As OD-HSD professionals, we recognize the fundamental importance of the following beliefs, which guide our practice and provide context for our ethics. We believe that:

1. *Human beings* are
   a. Equally worthy regardless of race, creed, age, nationality, gender, ability, socioeconomic status, or any other attribute that distorts people's perceptions of their essential equality
   b. Rightfully entitled to equal opportunity in their lives
   c. Interdependent economically, politically, socially, culturally, and spiritually
   d. Rightfully responsible for taking charge of their own lives, functioning autonomously and interdependently, and for controlling and facilitating their own growth
2. *Human systems* — including individuals, groups, organizations, communities, countries, and transnational systems — are:
   a. Interdependent economically, politically, socially, culturally, and spiritually
   b. Unique configurations of human energy — derived from needs, desires, beliefs and values, purposes and visions, goals, talents, and resources — shaped by tensions among system, subsystem, and macrosystem dynamics
   c. Open systems whose actions influence and are influenced by a variety of stakeholders
3. *Human beings and human systems* are:
   a. Interdependent and therefore positively or negatively affect one another's lives, survival, productivity, and growth
   b. Interdependent with the earth's ecosystems
   c. Responsible for living in harmony with all beings so as to ensure a sustainable future.

Values

We acknowledge the following values[5] or *standards of importance* as the foundation of our ethics as OD-HSD professionals.

1. Fundamental Values
   a. *Life and the quest for happiness:* people respecting, appreciating, and loving the experience of their own and others' being while engaging in the search for and the process of co-creating "good" life
   b. *Freedom, responsibility, and self-control:* people experiencing their freedom, exercising it responsibly, and being in charge of themselves
   c. *Justice:* people living lives whose results are fair and equitable
2. Personal and interpersonal values (may also be larger system-level values)
   a. *Human potential and empowerment:* people being healthy and aware of the fullness of their potential, realizing their power to bring that potential into being, growing into it, living it, and generally doing the best they can, both individually and collectively
   b. *Respect, dignity, integrity, worth, and fundamental rights of individuals and other human systems:* people appreciating one another and their rights as human beings, including life, liberty, and the quest for happiness
   c. *Authenticity, congruence, honesty and openness, understanding and acceptance:* people being true to themselves, acting consistently with their feelings, being honest and appropriately open with one another (including expressing feelings and constructively confronting differences), and both understanding and accepting others who do the same
   d. *Flexibility, change, and proaction:* people changing themselves on the one hand and acting assertively on the other in a continuing process whose aim is to maintain or achieve a good fit between themselves and the external reality within which they live

3. System values (may also be values at personal and inter-personal levels)

   a. *Learning, development, growth, and transformation:* people growing in ways that bring into being greater realization of their potential, individually and collectively

   b. *Whole-win attitudes, cooperation-collaboration, trust, community, and diversity:* people caring about one another and working together to achieve results that are good for everyone (individually and collectively), experiencing the spirit of community and honoring the diversity that exists within community

   c. *Widespread, meaningful participation in system affairs, democracy, and appropriate decision making:* people participating as fully as possible in making the decisions that affect their lives

   d. *Effectiveness, efficiency, and alignment:* people achieving desired results with an optimal balance between results and costs, and doing so in ways that coordinate the energies of systems, subsystems, and macrosystems — particularly the energies, needs, and desires of the human beings who comprise those systems

Ethics: Principles, Moral Rules and Ideals, and Justifying Violations[5,6]

We commit ourselves to the following *standards of behavior.*

Fundamental Principle (elements of a meta-principle underlying all our ethics)

Act so that we would be willing to universalize the principles underlying our action and live with the consequences of our action if everyone else were to act in accord with its underlying principles.

Moral Rules and Ideals[7a,7b]

Morals (rules and ideals) are ethics aimed at minimizing harm or evil. We believe they are fundamental to living responsibly as members of the global human community.

1. *Moral rules.* Do no harm: do not kill, cause pain, disable, deprive of freedom, deprive of pleasure, deceive, cheat, break promises, disobey the law, or fail to do our duty.
2. *Moral Ideals.* Prevent (or do those things that will lessen) harm suffered by anyone: prevent death, pain, disability, deprivation of freedom, deprivation of pleasure, deception, cheating, breaking of promises, disobeying of the law, and neglect of duties.

Justification of Moral-Ethical Violations[6]

We recognize that violation of ethical standards (including morals) may be justified under certain conditions because such violation is required to minimize harm or to serve most fully the ideals represented by our values and ethics as a whole.

Justifying violation of morals and other ethical standards involves such considerations as: the standards violated; the harm avoided, prevented, or caused and the good promoted; the kinds of good or harm; their seriousness, duration, and probability of occurring; the number of people who will suffer or benefit; and the distribution of the benefit and suffering. In seeking to balance all of these considerations, we seek to serve the "greatest good of the whole," which includes valuing the "good of the individual" and respecting individuals' rights.

In considering possible ethics violations, we are guided by the following:

1. Do not violate moral rules without clear *moral* justification.[6a,6b]
2. Do not violate moral ideals, ethical principles, or ethical guidelines without appropriate,[6c] clear,[6b] *ethical*[6d] justification.[6e,6f,6g]

Ethical Principles

1. Serve the good of the whole.[7b]
2. Do unto others as we would have them do unto us.[7c]
3. Always treat people as ends, never only as means; respect their "being" and never use them only for their ability to "do"; treat them as persons and never as objects.

4. Act so we do not increase power by more powerful stakeholders *over* the less powerful.[8]

Ethics: Guidelines for Practice[5,6]

We commit ourselves to acting in accordance with the following guidelines.

I.   Responsibility to Ourselves
     A.   Act with integrity; be authentic and true to our-
          selves.
     B.   Strive continually for self-knowledge and personal
          growth.
     C.   Recognize our personal needs and desires and, when
          they conflict with other responsibilities, seek whole-
          win resolutions.
     D.   Assert our own interests in ways that are fair and
          equitable to us as well as to our clients and their
          stakeholders.
II. Responsibility for Professional Development and Com-
     petence
     A.   Accept responsibility for the consequences of our ac-
          tions and make reasonable efforts to ensure that our
          services are properly used; terminate our services if
          they are not properly used and do what we can to
          see that any abuses are corrected.
     B.   Develop and maintain our individual competence
          and establish cooperative relations with other profes-
          sionals.
          1.   Develop the broad range of our own competen-
               cies. These include:
               a) Knowledge of theory and practice in
                     (1) Applied behavioral science generally
                     (2) Leadership, management, adminis-
                          tration, organizational behavior, sys-
                          tem behavior, and organization/sys-
                          tem development specifically

      (3)   Labor union issues, such as collective bargaining, contracting, and quality of working life (QWL)

      (4)   Multicultural issues, including issues of color and gender

      (5)   Cross-cultural issues, including issues related to our own ethnocentric tendencies and to differences and diversity within and between countries

      (6)   Values and ethics in general and how they apply to both the behavior of our client systems and our own practice

      (7)   Other fields of knowledge and practice relevant to the area(s) within OD-HSD on which we individually concentrate

b) Ability to

      (1)   Act effectively with individuals; groups; and large, complex systems

      (2)   Provide consultation using theory and methods of the applied behavioral sciences

      (3)   Cope with the apparent contradiction in applying behavioral science that arises when our "science" is too particular or too theoretical to be applicable or when our real approach is intuitive and not clearly grounded in science

      (4)   Articulate theory and direct its application, including creation of learning experiences for individuals; small and large groups; and large, complex systems

2.   Establish collegial and cooperative relations with other OD-HSD professionals. These include:

    a) Using colleagues as consultants to provide ourselves with feedback or suggestions about

our own development and to minimize the
effects of our blind spots

    b) Creating partnerships with colleagues to en-
hance our effectiveness in serving clients
whose needs are greater than we can serve
alone

C. Recognize our personal needs and desires and deal
with them responsibly in the performance of our
professional roles and duties.

D. Practice within the limits of our competence, culture,
and experience in providing services and using techniques.

    1. Neither seek nor accept assignments outside our
limits without clear understanding by clients
when exploration at the edge of our competence
is reasonable.

    2. Refer clients to other professionals when ap-
propriate.

    3. Consult with people who are knowledgeable
about the unique conditions of clients whose activities involve specific areas in which we are inexperienced or not knowledgeable:

        a) In special functional areas (such as market-
ing, engineering, or R & D)

        b) In certain industries or institutions (such as
mining, aerospace, health care, education,
or government)

        c) In multicultural settings (such as when we
practice in settings in which there is significant diversity in the race, ethnicity, or
gender of the people involved)

E. Practice in cultures different from our own only with
consultation from people native to or knowledgeable
about those specific cultures.

III. Responsibility to Clients and Significant Others

    A. Serve the long-term well-being of our client systems
and their stakeholders.

        1. Be aware of the beliefs and values relevant to
serving our clients, including our own, our pro-

fession's, our culture's, and those of the people with whom we work (personal, organizational, and cultural).

2. Be prepared to make explicit our beliefs, values, and ethics as OD-HSD professionals.

3. Avoid automatic confirmation of predetermined conclusions about the client's situation or what needs to be done by either the client or ourselves.

4. Explore the possible implications of any OD-HSD intervention for all stakeholders likely to be significantly affected; help all stakeholders while developing and implementing OD-HSD approaches, programs, and the like, if they wish help and we are able to give it.

5. Maintain balance in the timing, pace, and magnitude of planned change so as to support a mutually beneficial relationship between the system and its environment.

B. Conduct any professional activity, program, or relationship in ways that are honest, responsible, and appropriately open.

1. Inform people with whom we work about any activity or procedure in which we ask their participation.

   a) Inform them about sponsorship, purpose and goals, our role and strategy, costs, anticipated outcomes, limitations, and risks.

   b) Inform them in a way that supports their freedom of choice about their participation in activities initiated by us; also acknowledge that it may be appropriate for us to undertake activities initiated by recognized authorities in which participants do not have full freedom of choice.

   c) Alert them to implications and risks when they are from cultures other than our own or when we are at the edge of our competence.

       d)   Ask help of the client system in making relevant cultural differences explicit.

2. Seek optimum participation by people with whom we work at every step of the process, including managers, labor unions, and workers' representatives.

3. Encourage and enable people to provide for themselves the services we provide rather than foster continued reliance on us; encourage, foster, and support self-education and self-development by individuals, groups, and all other human systems.

4. Develop, publish, and use assessment techniques that promote the welfare and best interests of clients and participants; guard against the misuse of assessment techniques and results.

5. Provide for our own accountability by evaluating and assessing the effects of our work.

       a)   Make all reasonable efforts to determine if our activities have accomplished the agreed-upon goals and have not had other undesirable consequences; seek to undo any undesirable consequences, and do not attempt to cover them up; use such experiences as learning opportunities.

       b)   Actively solicit and respond with an open mind to feedback regarding our work and seek to improve our work accordingly.

6. Cease work with a client when it becomes clear that the client is not benefiting or the contract has been completed; do not accept or continue work under a contract if we cannot do so in ways consistent with the values and ethics outlined in this Statement.

C. Establish mutual agreement on a fair contract covering services and remuneration.

1. Ensure mutual understanding and agreement about the services to be performed; do not shift

from that agreement without both a clearly defined professional rationale for making the shift and the informed consent of the clients and participants; withdraw from the agreement if circumstances beyond our control prevent proper fulfillment.

2. Ensure mutual understanding and agreement by putting the contract in writing to the extent feasible, yet recognize that:

   a) The spirit of professional responsibility encompasses more than the letter of the contract.

   b) Some contracts are necessarily incomplete because complete information is not available at the outset.

   c) Putting the contract in writing may be neither necessary nor desirable.

3. Safeguard the best interests of the client, the profession, and the public by making sure that financial arrangements are fair and in keeping with appropriate statutes, regulations, and professional standards.

D. Deal with conflicts constructively and minimize conflicts of interest.

1. Fully inform the client of our opinions about serving similar or competing organizations; be clear with ourselves, our clients, and other concerned stakeholders about our loyalties and responsibilities when conflicts of interest arise; keep parties informed of these conflicts; cease work with the client if the conflicts cannot be adequately resolved.

2. Seek to act impartially when involved in conflicts among parties in the client system; help them resolve their conflicts themselves, without taking sides; if it becomes necessary to change our role from that of impartial consultant, do so explicitly; cease work with the client if necessary.

3. Identify and respond to any major differences in professionally relevant values or ethics between ourselves and our clients; be prepared to cease work, with explanation of our reasons, if necessary.

4. Accept differences in the expectations and interests of different stakeholders and realize that those differences cannot always be reconciled; take a whole-win approach to the resolution of differences whenever possible so that the greatest good of the whole is served, but allow for exceptions based on more fundamental principles.

5. Work cooperatively with other internal and external consultants serving the same client systems and resolve conflicts in terms of the balanced best interests of the client system and all its stakeholders; make appropriate arrangements with other internal and external consultants about how to share responsibilities.

6. Seek consultation and feedback from neutral third parties in cases of conflict involving ourselves, our clients, other consultants, or any of the systems' various stakeholders.

E. Define and protect confidentiality in our client relationships.

1. Make limits of confidentiality clear to clients and participants.

2. Reveal information accepted in confidence only to appropriate or agreed-upon recipients or authorities.

3. Use information obtained during professional work in writings, lectures, or other public forums only with prior consent or when disguised so that it is impossible from our presentations alone to identify the individuals or systems with whom we have worked.

4. Make adequate provisions for maintaining confidentiality in the storage and disposal of records;

make provisions for responsibly preserving records in the event of our retirement or disability.

F. Make public statements of all kinds accurately, including promotion and advertising, and give service as advertised.

1. Base public statements providing professional opinions or information on scientifically acceptable findings and techniques as much as possible, with full recognition of the limits and uncertainties of such evidence.

2. Seek to help people make informed choices when they refer to statements we make as part of promotion or advertising.

3. Deliver services as advertised and do not shift without a clear professional rationale and the informed consent of the participants or clients.

IV. Responsibility to the OD-HSD Profession

A. Contribute to the continuing professional development of other practitioners and of the profession as a whole.

1. Support the development of other professionals by various means, including:

a) Mentoring with less experienced professionals

b) Consulting with other colleagues

c) Participating in reviews of others' practices

2. Contribute to the body of professional knowledge and skill, including

a) Sharing ideas, methods, and findings about the effects of our work

b) Keeping our use of copyright and trade secrets to an appropriate minimum

B. Promote the sharing of professional knowledge and skill.

1. Grant use of our copyrighted material as freely as possible, subject to a minimum of conditions, including a reasonable price based on professional as well as commercial values.

2. Give credit for the ideas and products of others.
3. Respect the rights of others in the materials they have created.

C. Work with other OD-HSD professionals in ways that exemplify what the OD-HSD profession stands for.
1. Establish mutual understanding and agreement about our relationships, including purposes and goals, roles and responsibilities, fees, and income distribution.
2. Avoid conflicts of interest when possible and resolve conflicts that do arise constructively (following guidelines similar to Guideline III–D).

D. Work actively for ethical practice by individuals and organizations engaged in OD-HSD activities and, in case of questionable practice, use appropriate channels for dealing with it.
1. Discuss directly and constructively when feasible.
2. Use other means when necessary, including:
   a) Joint consultation and feedback (with another professional as a third party)
   b) Enforcement procedures of existing professional organizations
   c) Public confrontation

E. Act in ways that bring credit to the OD-HSD profession and with due regard for colleagues in other professions.
1. Act with sensitivity to the effects our behavior may have on the ability of colleagues to perform as professionals, individually and collectively.
2. Act with due regard for the needs, special competencies, and obligations of colleagues in other professions.
3. Respect the prerogatives and obligations of the institutions or organizations with which these colleagues are associated.

V. Social Responsibility
A. Accept responsibility for and act with sensitivity to the fact that our recommendations and actions may

alter the lives and well-being of people within our client systems and within the larger systems of which they are subsystems.

B. Act with awareness of our own cultural filters and with sensitivity to multinational and multicultural differences and their implications.

1. Respect the cultural orientations of the individuals, organizations, communities, countries, and other human systems within which we work, including their customs, beliefs, values, morals, and ethics.

2. Recognize and constructively confront the counterproductive aspects of those cultures whenever feasible, but with alertness to the effects our own cultural orientation may have on our judgments.

C. Promote justice and serve the well-being of all life on earth.

1. Act assertively with our clients to promote justice and well-being, including:

    a) Constructively confronting discrimination whenever possible

    b) Promoting affirmative action in dealing with the effects of past discrimination

    c) Encouraging fairness in the distribution of the fruits of the system's productivity

2. Contribute knowledge, skill, and other resources in support of organizations, programs, and activities that seek to improve human welfare.

3. Accept some clients who do not have sufficient resources to pay our full fees and allow them to pay reduced fees or nothing when possible.

4. Engage in self-generated or cooperative endeavors to develop means for helping across cultures.

5. Support the creation and maintenance of cultures that value freedom, responsibility, integrity, self-control, mutual respect, love, trust, openness, authenticity in relationships, empow-

erment, participation, and respect for fundamental human rights.

D. Withhold service from clients whose purpose(s) we
consider immoral, yet recognize that such service
may serve a greater good in the longer run and therefore be acceptable.

E. Act consistently with the ethics of the global scientific community of which our OD-HSD community
is a part.[9]

Finally, we recognize that accepting this Statement as a
guide for our behavior involves holding ourselves to standards
that may be more exacting than the laws of any countries in
which we practice, the ethics of any professional associations
to which we belong, or the expectations of any of our clients.

Notes

1. The field we call Organization and Human Systems
Development (OD-HSD) is generally recognized by the name
Organization Development (OD). An increasing number of OD-
HSD professionals now conclude that Human Systems Development (HSD) is the most appropriate designation for our field,
since our potential clients range from individuals to the whole
world. With that expanded focus, the profession can, and some
professionals would say *must,* be oriented to whether or not what
we do is good for the global system as well as for our specific
clients. For most practitioners, especially those in OD and HRD,
this may not mean a change in the focus of their practice but
only a change in the context within which they view their practice. With such a perspective, the profession has the potential
for becoming a professional community whose collective action
will have global significance based on cooperative, collective action.

2. We recognize that technically there is no such thing
as "substantial" consensus; but for a group as large and diverse
as the OD-HSD profession, we find the concept useful, since
pure consensus is probably an unrealistic goal.

3. By providing a common reference for OD-HSD professionals throughout the world, we seek to enhance our sense of
identity as a global professional community. In this connection,

we recognize that since this Statement was initially developed within the United States, revision or adaptation may be necessary to make it relevant to other cultures.

4. We intend this current version of the Statement primarily as a stimulus for discussion within the profession. Its words are ones that we generally understand in our communication among ourselves. However, for communication with clients and others outside our profession, we probably need to revise the words in order to ensure that they can be readily understood by people who are not familiar with our jargon.

5. *Values* are standards of *importance* (desirability, worth, goodness, and so on). They are fundamental to the ethical concepts covered in this Statement. Those concepts are as follows:

- *Ethics* (including moral rules and ideals, ethical principles and guidelines), in contrast to values, are standards of *behavior* based on values.
- The *"fundamental principle"* is an adaptation of what Kant called the "categorical imperative," a principle about principles (a meta-principle).
- *Moral rules and ideals* are generally agreed-upon injunctions that seek to minimize harm or evil: *rules* focus on not doing harm oneself, while *ideals* focus on acting in ways that will prevent or alleviate suffering from harm or evil. Together, moral rules and ideals can be identified as basic to the existence of a viable, global human community.
- *Ethical principles* give more general guidance for action than do rules and ideals; yet, like them, principles tend to be shared with most individuals, professions, and other human systems that have reflected on their ethics.
- *Ethical guidelines* as outlined in this Statement focus more specifically on the conditions of OD-HSD practice than do the other ethical standards, although many of them are general and their guidance does not become specific until the level of their subpoints.
- *Moral-Ethical justification* allows for the fact that following the rules/ideals/principles/guidelines is not always moral or ethical and that it is sometimes necessary to justify violations. (See notes 6 and 8.)

6a. Generally speaking, violation of moral rules requires *moral* justification — that is, justification based on minimizing harm. For example, harming a few people (a moral rule violation) in order to minimize harm to a larger number would be moral justification, whereas harming a few to serve the good of a larger number would not. More concretely, laying off a large number of people (harm) to avoid laying off an even larger number (greater harm) would be a *moral* justification, whereas laying off a large number of people (harm) to make a larger profit for stockholders (good) would not be. That is why we can say, especially in the latter case, that an organization has a *moral* obligation to consider harm-minimizing alternatives such as attrition, retraining, and outplacement as means of staff reduction.

6b. Specifying that the justification must be "clear" means that it must be reasonable to rational people and not just a self-serving rationalization. A primary test of reasonableness is that the justification provides reasons that could be accepted by impartial rational people as a basis for advocating that the violation be publicly allowed. All rational people would not necessarily agree with the reasoning, but they would accept the idea that a rational person could use such reasoning.

6c. It is unreasonable to expect people to comply with moral ideals for all people all the time; therefore, justification cannot reasonably be *required*. Generally speaking, however, it would be *appropriate* to justify failure to prevent harm under conditions in which we might reasonably be expected to do so. For example, if we fail to prevent a large layoff when we might reasonably have been expected to do so, we will hold ourselves accountable for clear justification.

6d. In contrast to moral rule violations, violating moral ideals, ethical principles, or ethical guidelines involves *ethical* justification. That is, rather than justification being based on minimizing harm, it is based on a combination of minimizing harm and serving the good (as explicitly defined by our ethics and implicitly defined by our values).

6e. If rule violations are involved in violating an ethical guideline, our justification must be consistent with *moral* justification as well as with appropriate ethical justification. For example, an ethical guideline such as III–B–3, which directs us to "encourage and enable people to provide for themselves the services we provide rather than foster continued reliance on us" implicitly involves both the moral rule about not disabling and the professional ideal/value about encouraging people's development and growth. Fostering continued reliance (disabling) would require moral justification. At the same time, ethical justification for failing to encourage development would be desirable, though not required.

6f. When violations of our ethics involve situations that are unclear—that is, they are gray, rather than clear-cut black and white—we allow ourselves less clarity in our ethical justifications. However, we will be as clear as we reasonably can be. In other words, as noted earlier, we will seek to think in terms of "reasons that could be accepted by impartial rational people as a basis for advocating that such violations be publicly allowed." By that we do not mean that all rational people would necessarily agree with the reasoning; we mean only that all would accept it as being based on reason. For example, in justifying failure to encourage development, we might give reasons with which all OD-HSD professionals would not agree, but all would agree that the justification is based on reason.

6g. Although we neither expect nor require justification of all ethical violations, for reasons already noted, we acknowledge that we are responsible for making the judgments that lead to our failures to prevent harm or serve the good. And, generally speaking, if we fail to prevent harm or to serve the good under conditions in which we might reasonably be expected to do so, we will hold ourselves accountable for appropriate, clear, ethical justification.

7a. Moral rules and ideals need to be understood in the context of possible moral justification for violation, particularly those relative to "disobeying the law" and "failing to do our duty." There would be moral justification for disobeying bad laws or failing to do one's duty when obeying or doing our duty would be immoral (by causing harm or failing to prevent or lessen it). These two rules tend to be based on the assumption of a social context within which obeying the law and doing one's duty are consistent with minimizing harm.

7b. It is helpful to note the relationships among the moral rules (varieties of "Do no harm"), the moral ideals (varieties of "Prevent or lessen harm"), and the first ethical principle ("Serve the good of the whole"). The moral rules *require* us not to cause harm ourselves, and that applies to everyone. The moral ideals *encourage* us to prevent or lessen harm regardless of who causes it; but, in contrast to the moral rules, we cannot realistically be expected to do that with regard to everyone. And, finally, the affirmative prescription to "Serve the good of the whole" *encourages* us to act in ways that serve our values, since they are primary elements in our definition of what is good and desirable. Note that because of our systems perspective we see the "whole" as being more than the sum of its parts and thus look to a composite value that is more inclusive than the "greatest good of the greatest number." Note also that "serving good" does not *require* action (or nonaction), as do moral rules, and that the degree of encouragement is less than for the more fundamental moral ideals, since minimizing harm (evil) tends to have higher priority than serving good. Preventing harm may justify causing harm, as with a surgical operation, but serving good does not normally justify causing harm. And, although serving good may justify failing to prevent harm, the justification must be clear.

7c. In acknowledging the usefulness of the "Golden Rule," which is shared in one form or another by most of the world's major religions, we also need to recognize that it has limited generality. Just as judges and police may be obliged to act toward others as they would not have others act toward them, the duties of OD-HSD consultants may require them to act toward others in ways in which they would not want others to act toward them as persons. For example, the OD-HSD role can require confrontation that is painful for others and that we might not want them to "do unto us," even though it is the right thing to do professionally.

8. We may sometimes have to violate the principle about not acting in ways that increase the power of more powerful over less powerful stakeholders because those with whom we work are often among the more powerful members of our client

systems. But such violations may be ethically justifiable, particularly when they enable us to show those more powerful people how they can serve their organizational goals by supporting their subordinates' empowerment, which means a simultaneous increase in their power *and* that of their subordinates—but it is power *with* rather than power *over*. The justification for violating the principle in the short run would be that it keeps open the opportunity for us to exert our influence in the longer run, whereas not violating the principle could lose us that opportunity. As noted above, however, such justification must be reasonable to rational people and not just self-serving rationalization.

9. Among other things, this involves committing ourselves to the "Hippocratic Oath for Scientists, Engineers and Technologists":

> "I vow to practise my profession with conscience and dignity;
> I will strive to apply my skills only with the utmost respect for the well-being of humanity, the earth and all its species;
> I will not permit considerations of nationality, politics, prejudice or material advancement to intervene between my work and this duty to present and future generations;
> I make this oath solemnly, freely and upon my honour"

[Quoted in "In the News." *Professional Ethics Report,* 1988, *1* (3), 1.]

A Statement of Values and Ethics for Professionals in Organization and Human Systems Development, April 1985

Organization and Human Systems Development (OD-HSD)[1] is an emerging profession rooted in human values and relevant theory whose purpose is to help individuals, organizations, and other human systems achieve excellence.

Preamble

This Statement[2] is intended to serve as an aspirational guide, a statement of ideals toward which OD-HSD professionals can strive.[3] Its purposes are to

1. Increase professional consciousness and responsibility among OD-HSD professionals by
   - Stimulating a widespread discussion of values and ethics underlying OD-HSD practice
   - Highlighting and clarifying major differences in OD-HSD values and ethics and seeking to resolve them
   - Identifying those OD-HSD values and ethical guidelines which are generally accepted

2. Enable OD-HSD professionals to make more informed ethical choices about their practice by reference to a generally accepted set of guidelines[4]
3. Contribute to enabling the OD-HSD profession to achieve excellence in its own functioning

Our intention is to serve all of these purposes for OD-HSD professionals throughout the world to enhance their sense of membership in a global professional community.

Since this Statement has been developed from within the cultural perspective of the United States, as was OD-HSD itself, we recognize that it includes concepts, beliefs, assumptions, and values unique to that country's culture. We also recognize that practice according to the assumptions and guidelines outlined below may be precluded by certain cultural conditions. Our expectation is that discussion stimulated by this Statement will help us identify specific cross-cultural differences and similarities underlying the practice of OD-HSD.

Those who use this Statement should keep in mind that it is continually evolving and will change and grow as our profession matures.[5] Our ultimate goal is a widely shared learning and discovery process dedicated to the creation of professional excellence and lives that are fully worth living.

A basic assumption of these guidelines is that violating them might result in harm to the client, the organization, its members, other stakeholders, the OD-HSD professional, the OD-HSD profession, society, and/or life on earth.

The guidelines provide a reasonable standard for the protection of all those who are affected by the practice of OD-HSD. OD-HSD professionals are encouraged to share their ethical position with their clients; clients are encouraged to discuss that position with other OD-HSD professionals and, in case of questions or differences, work together on clarification and mutually satisfactory resolution.

Since we view ethical practice as a continuing, developmental process, we encourage OD-HSD professionals to (1) involve themselves actively in that process by becoming more sensitive to their ethical dilemmas (2) share the results of that process with other OD-HSD professionals[6] and, when appropriate, with their clients.

Assumptions Underlying These Guidelines

1. Human beings are
    a. Interdependent economically, socially, culturally, and spiritually and are responsible for the choices they make within that context
    b. Rightfully responsible for and capable of
        1) Making choices, taking charge of their lives, and functioning autonomously within a context of interdependence[7]
        2) Controlling their own growth and the pace of that growth[8]
    c. Inherently of equal worth as human beings, regardless of race, creed, age, nationality, gender, socioeconomic status, or sexual preference[9]
    d. Rightfully entitled to equal opportunity in their workplaces
2. All human systems — including individuals, groups, organizations, communities, and societies — are
    a. Interdependent, open systems whose actions influence and are influenced by a variety of different stakeholders; for example, the stakeholders of a business organization may include customers, managers, workers, suppliers, clients, patrons, investors, labor organizations, committees, communities, governments, societies, and ultimately the world
    b. Unique combinations of purpose, goals, resources, and needs that enable them to make unique contributions to the world; their purposes are to bring their contributions into being
3. A major aim of OD-HSD is to help the system become conscious of and able to fulfill its purpose by
    a. Enabling the system-as-a-whole and each part within it to
        1) Understand their purposes and interdependence with one another

    2) Review their purposes and revise them over time as conditions and their awareness of conditions change

    3) Clarify and refine their relationships so they can align themselves

  b. Helping individuals within the system to

    1) Accept responsibility for their lives

    2) Recognize both the extent of and the constraints on their freedom, their power to choose how they live their lives within the system, and the impact of the system on their lives

  c. Helping each higher-order subsystem (team, department, division, and so on) understand its purpose and interdependence and accept its responsibility for fulfilling its role within the system

  d. Providing for equitable distribution of the fruits of the system's productivity

  e. Creating and supporting a climate within which freedom, equality, mutual trust, respect, and love prevail

  f. Helping people align both individual and system purposes with

    1) The needs and purposes of all the system's stakeholders

    2) The welfare of all the people of earth, all living things, and their environment

4. A human system whose parts are integrated and consciously aligned with the system's overall purposes and its environmental context will function more effectively and efficiently because

  a. The system will avoid wasting energy on counterproductive behavior

  b. The environment will support the system if the system is aligned with the environment

  (*Note:* This does not deny the possibility of productive behavior by the system directed at changing the environment in order to achieve more enduring alignment.)

5. OD-HSD professionals

  a. Acknowledge the important and pervasive influence of values and ethics on the effectiveness and potential for growth of individuals, organizations, and society at large and consider them in the process and content of their OD practice

b. Place high value on

1) Individual dignity and worth and fundamental human rights[10]

2) The dignity, integrity, and worth of organizations, communities, societies, and other human systems

3) Quality of working life as part of system effectiveness

4) Authenticity in relationships and openness in communication[11]

5) Wide participation in system affairs, confrontation of issues leading to effective problem solving and democratic decision making[12]

6) Development of holistic ways of identifying and solving system problems

c. Realize that they are in a service profession in which they make available their expertise and personality, and are prepared to discuss the way they do this with colleagues and participants in the consulting process

d. Recognize the responsibilities of individuals to the groups, organizations, and other human systems of which they are members

e. Recognize that choices that may seem unethical in the short run may be ethical in the long run — for example, not responding to a request for a quick fix in order to allow conditions to emerge under which more authentic help is possible

f. Recognize that along with respecting the right of free choice goes the responsibility for discussing with clients the consequences of their choices and how those choices might be changed to yield different consequences

g. Recognize the need for balance in cases where the above values conflict and recognize further that practice according to the values and ethics described in this Statement may be precluded by certain cultural conditions[13]

Ethical Guidelines for an OD-HSD Professional

As an OD-HSD Professional, I commit to supporting and acting in accordance with the following guidelines:

I. **Responsibility for Professional Development and Competence**

   A. Accept responsibility for the consequences of my acts and make every effort to ensure that my services are properly used.

   B. Recognize the limits of my competence, culture, and experience in providing services and using techniques; neither seek nor accept assignments outside those limits without clear understanding by the client when exploration at the edge of my competence is reasonable; refer client to other professionals when appropriate.

   C. Strive to attain and maintain a professional level of competence in the field, including

   1. Broad knowledge of theory and practice in

      a. Applied behavioral science generally

      b. Management, administration, organizational behavior, and system behavior specifically

      c. Multicultural issues, including issues of color and gender

      d. Other relevant fields of knowledge and practice

   2. Ability to

      a. Relate effectively with individuals and groups

      b. Relate effectively to the dynamics of large, complex systems

      c. Provide consultation using theory and methods of the applied behavioral sciences

      d. Articulate theory and direct its application, including creation of learning experiences for individuals, small and large groups, and whole systems

D. Strive continually for self-knowledge and personal growth; be aware that "what is in me" (my perceptions of myself in my world) and "what is outside me" (the realities that exist apart from me) are not the same; be aware that my values, beliefs, and aspirations can both limit and empower me and that they are primary determinants of my perceptions, my behavior, and my personal and professional effectiveness.

E. Recognize my own personal needs and desires and deal with them responsibly in the performance of my professional roles.

F. Obtain consultation from OD-HSD professionals who are native to and aware of the specific cultures within which I work when those cultures are different from my own.[14]

II. **Responsibility to Clients and Significant Others**

A. Serve the short- and long-term welfare, interests, and development of the client system and all its stakeholders; maintain balance in the timing, pace, and magnitude of planned change so as to support a mutually beneficial relationship between the system and its environment.

B. Discuss candidly and fully goals, costs, risks, limitations, and anticipated outcomes of any program or other professional relationship under consideration; seek to avoid automatic confirmation of predetermined conclusions, either the client's or my own; seek optimum involvement in every step of the process by client system members, including managers and workers' representatives; fully inform client system members about my role, contribution, and strategy in working with them.

C. Fully inform participants in any activity or procedure as to its sponsorship, nature, purpose, implications, and any significant risk associated with it so that they can freely choose their participation in any activity initiated by me; acknowledge that their choice may be limited to activity initiated by recognized authorities; be particularly sensitive to implications and risks when I work with people from cultures other than my own.

D. Be aware of my own personal values, my values as an OD-HSD professional, the values of my native culture, the values of the people with whom I am working, and the values of their cultures; involve the client system in making relevant cultural differences explicit and exploring the possible implications of any OD-HSD intervention for all the stakeholders involved; be prepared to make explicit my assumptions, values, and standards as an OD-HSD professional.

E. Help all stakeholders while developing OD-HSD approaches, programs, and the like, if they wish such help; for example, this could include workers' representatives as well as managers in the case of work with a business organization.

F. Work collaboratively with other internal and external consultants serving the same client system and resolve conflicts in terms of the balanced best interest of the client system and all its stakeholders; make appropriate arrangements with other internal and external consultants about how responsibilities will be shared.

G. Encourage and enable my clients to provide for themselves the services I provide rather than foster continued reliance on me; encourage, foster, and support self-education and self-development by individuals, groups, and all other human systems.

H. Cease work with a client when it is clear that the client is not benefiting or the contract has been completed; do not accept an assignment if its scope is so limited that the client will not benefit or it would involve serious conflict with the values and ethics outlined in this Statement.

I. Avoid conflicts of interest.

1. Fully inform the client of my opinion about serving similar or competing organizations; be clear with myself, my clients, and other concerned stakeholders about my loyalties and responsibilities when conflicts of interest arise; keep parties informed of these conflicts; cease work with the client if the conflicts cannot be adequately resolved.

2. Seek to act impartially when involved in conflicts between parties in the client system; help them resolve their conflicts themselves, without taking sides; if necessary to change my role from serving as impartial consultant, do so explicitly; cease work with the client, if necessary.

3. Identify and respond to any major differences in professionally relevant values or ethics between myself and my clients with the understanding that conditions may require ceasing work with the client.

4. Accept the expectations and interests of different stakeholders and realize that their differences cannot be reconciled all the time.

J. Seek consultation and feedback from neutral third parties in case of conflict between myself and my client.

K. Define and protect the confidentiality of my client-professional relationships.

1. Make limits of confidentiality clear to clients/participants.

2. Reveal information accepted in confidence only to appropriate or agreed-upon recipients or authorities.

3. Use information obtained during professional work in writings, lectures, or other public forums only with prior consent or when disguised so that it is impossible from my presentations alone to identify the individuals or systems with whom I have worked.

    4. Make adequate provisions for maintaining confidentiality in the storage and disposal of records; make provisions for responsibly preserving records in the event of my retirement or disability.

L. Establish mutual agreement on a contract covering services and remuneration.

    1. Ensure a clear understanding of and mutual agreement on the services to be performed; do not shift from that agreement without both a clearly defined professional rationale for making the shift and the informed consent of the clients/participants; withdraw from the agreement if circumstances beyond my control prevent proper fulfillment.

    2. Ensure mutual understanding and agreement by putting the contract in writing to the extent feasible, yet recognize that

        a. The spirit of professional responsibility encompasses more than the letter of the contract.

        b. Some contracts are necessarily incomplete because complete information is not available at the outset.

        c. Putting the contract in writing may be neither necessary nor desirable.

    3. Safeguard the best interests of the client, the profession, and the public by making sure that financial arrangements are fair and in keeping with appropriate statutes, regulations, and professional standards.

M. Provide for my own accountability by evaluating and assessing the effects of my work.

    1. Make all reasonable efforts to determine if my activities have accomplished the agreed-upon goals and have not had other undesirable consequences; seek to undo any undesirable consequences, and do not attempt to cover up these situations.

2. Actively solicit and respond with an open mind to feedback regarding my work, and seek to improve it.

3. Develop, publish, and use assessment techniques that promote the welfare and best interests of client/participants; guard against the misuse of assessment results.

N. Make public statements of all kinds accurately, including promotion and advertising, and give service as advertised.

1. Base public statements providing professional opinions or information on scientifically acceptable findings and techniques as much as possible, with full recognition of the limits and uncertainties of such evidence.

2. Seek to help people make informed choices when making statements as part of promotion or advertising.

3. Deliver services as advertised and do not shift without a clear professional rationale and the informed consent of the participants/clients.

III. Responsibility to the Profession

A. Act with due regard for the needs, special competencies, and obligations of my colleagues in OD-HSD and other professions; respect the prerogatives and obligations of the institutions or organizations with which these other colleagues are associated.

B. Be aware of the possible impact of my public behavior upon the ability of colleagues to perform their professional work; perform professional activity in a way that will bring credit to the profession.

C. Work actively for ethical practice by individuals and organizations engaged in OD-HSD activities and, in case of questionable practice, use appropriate channels for confronting it, including

1. Direct discussion when feasible

2. Joint consultation and feedback, using other professionals as third parties

      3. Enforcement procedures of existing professional organizations

      4. Public confrontation

  D. Contribute to continuing professional development by

      1. Supporting the development of other professionals, including serving as a mentor to less experienced professionals

      2. Contributing ideas, methods, findings, and other useful information to the body of OD-HSD knowledge and skill

  E. Promote the sharing of OD-HSD knowledge and skill by various means, including

      1. Granting use of my copyrighted material as freely as possible, subject to a minimum of conditions, including a reasonable price defined on the basis of professional as well as commercial values

      2. Giving credit for the ideas and products of others

IV. Social Responsibility

  A. Strive for the preservation of fundamental human rights.[15]

  B. Be aware that I bear a heavy social responsibility because my recommendations and professional actions may alter the lives and well-being of individuals within my client systems, the systems themselves, and the larger systems of which they are subsystems.

  C. Contribute knowledge, skill, and other resources in support of organizations, programs, and activities that seek to improve human welfare; be prepared to accept clients who do not have sufficient resources to pay my full fees at reduced fees or no charge.

  D. Respect the cultures of the organization, community, country, or other human system within which I work (including the cultures' traditions, values, and moral and ethical expectations and their im-

plications), yet recognize and constructively confront the counterproductive aspects of those cultures
whenever feasible; be sensitive to cross-cultural
differences and their implications; be aware of the
cultural filters that bias my view of the world.

E. Recognize that accepting this Statement as a guide
for my behavior involves holding myself to a standard that may be more exacting than the laws of
any country in which I practice.

F. Contribute to the quality of life in human society
at large; work towards and support a culture based
on mutual respect for one another's rights as human beings; encourage the development of love,
trust, openness, mutual responsibility, authentic
and harmonious relationships, empowerment, participation, and involvement in a spirit of freedom
and self-discipline as elements of this culture.

G. Engage in self-generated or collaborative endeavors to develop means for helping across cultures.

H. Serve the welfare of all the people of the earth, all
living things, and their environment.

Notes

1. The field we call Organization and Human System Development is most generally recognized by the name Organization
Development since most of its practitioners focus primarily on
organizations. It is also known by the names change facilita-
tion, human resource development, Human Systems Development (because the profession works with such diverse systems
as individuals, families, communities, and even more inclusive
systems), and applied behavioral science (since the profession
bases much of its practice on applying the sciences of psychology, sociology, anthropology, and other behavioral sciences).

2. This Statement is built upon the foundation of several
previous statements and contributions, including those from the
Association for Creative Change, the Academy of Management,
the American Psychological Association, Certified Consultants

International, the National Organization Development Network, the Dutch Association of Organizational Experts en Advisors, the Gestalt Institute of Cleveland, International Consultants Foundation, the Organization Alignment Project of the Institute for the Study of Conscious Evolution, the International Registry of Organization Development Professionals, NTL Institute of Applied Behavioral Science, the OD Institute, the OD Division of the American Society for Training and Development, Organization Renewal, Inc., the International Human Resources Development Corporation, the Société Internationale pour le Développement des Organisations, OD Network-United Kingdom, Gesellschaft für Organisationentwicklung, Society for Applied Anthropology, a study group from Reseau OD Canada, the OD study group of SANNO Institute of Business Administration (Japan), the European Institute for Transnational Studies in Group and Organizational Development, the American Society for Personnel Administration, and the National Association of Social Workers. In addition, many other groups and individuals have contributed to its current state of evolution, including groups from Poland, South Africa, and Spain.

    3. This Statement is not intended as a *regulatory* code, buttressed by rules to govern behavior. (The profession does not presently have the monitoring and enforcement structure, with sanctions and supports, that such a code would require. Since there are so many associations of OD-HSD professionals throughout the world, a single, widely acceptable code and enforcement structure are unlikely in the near future and, even if they could be developed, at present there is no indication that professionals or their associations would want to develop them.) In contrast, this Statement is the beginning of an *educational* code, which seeks to describe and explain professional norms in a way that can be applied precisely in resolving the ethical dilemmas experienced by practitioners. Our expectation is that such a code, along with case studies and other educational materials, will be developed in time. (And, at least for the present, this seems to be where most professionals and their associations would like to concentrate their attention.)

4. OD-HSD professionals who also identify with an organization or professional association that has a formal code of ethics may use that code to guide their behavior. When the other code covers matters not covered in these guidelines or is in conflict with them, the people responsible for updating this Statement should be informed as a step toward resolving significant differences.

5. Among other things, as our knowledge increases so too will the precision of our ethical guidelines and principles.

6. In time, we expect OD-HSD professionals to share the results of their attention to ethical dilemmas so that we can accumulate the information (case studies and other educational materials) needed to create and maintain an educational code of the kind referred to in Note 4 of this Statement.

7. As much as possible, we proceed on the assumption that the ability to act responsibly, or at least the potential for it, exists. We recognize, however, that people may live under economic, social, and political conditions that severely limit their freedom in the exercise of that ability. We also recognize that some human beings may not act responsibly or be capable of making responsible choices. For example, emotionally disturbed people or persons whose life experiences have disempowered them — based on such conditions as poverty, discrimination, and oppression — need to be approached with sensitivity to and consideration for the effects of these experiences.

8. We generally believe that if people try to shift responsibility for their growth to others or if others try to take it from them, their growth will be fundamentally hindered. But we recognize that people can help one another by suggesting alternatives that enable them to reexamine and accept responsibility for their choices, and we consider such help an important part of our role. We also recognize that not all people are able to control their own growth, for such reasons as those mentioned in Note 7.

9. OD-HSD professionals recognize that people have different characteristics and competencies and may be valued differently by societies, but as human beings we view them as of equal inherent worth.

10. Specific fundamental rights we value include rights to
   a. Life, liberty, and security of person
   b. Freedom of thought, conscience, and religion
   c. Freedom of opinion and expression
   d. Freedom of choice

In general, we accept as a guide the United Nations *Universal Declaration of Human Rights.*

11. We recognize that there are conditions under which people cannot realistically be authentic and open. For example, conditions of dependence and oppression clearly would make such behavior dangerous if not suicidal. However, even when such behavior is not realistic, we value it and value changing conditions so that it can become realistic.

12. OD-HSD professionals recognize that democratic participation in decision making is not effective or practical under all conditions, but we are committed to bringing about the conditions that make such participation practical in all circumstances where it is consistent with human excellence.

13. When cultural conditions preclude following these guidelines, we accept responsibility for the consequences of our action or inaction and will seek to be clear about the guidelines we choose to guide our action in their place.

14. Consultation with someone who knows the culture may be brief if we are confident that our own cultural limitations will not have a negative impact on the client system or the large system within which it functions. However, we recognize that our own cultural conditioning may blind us to such negative impact, and thus undertake at least a minimal consultation.

15. See Note 10.

APPENDIX D

❚❙❚❙❚❙❚❙❚❙❚❙❚❙❚❙❚❙❚❙❚

For Further Study:
Cases and Commentaries

❚❙❚

Judging Success or Failure

The Barrington Company, a privately owned firm that is part of an industry experiencing economic stagnation due to more general national economic conditions, seeks ways to improve its competitive position within the industry and prepare itself for a predicted economic upturn in the near future. Lou Moss, president of the company, decides to contract with an OD consultant, Frank Karm, whose experience includes work for companies similar in size to Barrington, although in different industrial settings. Karm is asked to develop a strategy for increasing worker productivity.

After an initial diagnosis, Karm and Moss agree on a contract stipulating that Karm will work with the company in introducing a pilot "work restructuring" intervention into a single company plant. Once the pilot program is well established, Karm would then train personnel at that plant to help introduce

Note: References to the Statement in the commentaries of this appendix are to the 1985 version (Appendix C) unless otherwise identified.

and guide the intervention at other plant locations. In addition to the Midwest facility, where the pilot intervention is to be introduced, the company maintains plants in the Northeast and Southwest regions of the United States.

The work restructuring incorporates several new changes in work procedures and policies that require substantial worker retraining and introduces new compensation schemes to match the shift in work tasks and in workers' decision-making responsibilities. At a meeting of top company management, Karm identifies the goals of the intervention as (1) increased plant productivity and product quality, (2) improved employee morale, and (3) introduction of a pilot intervention that once firmly entrenched could be replicated in other company plants.

After about a year, the favorable impact of the intervention is widely recognized. Work quality and productivity have increased substantially and those involved in the pilot effort are quite proud of their apparent success and of the recognition that they are gaining from top company management. Moss and the firm's executive council express their commitment to guiding the diffusion of intervention components to the company's other plants. Following several sessions with personnel at the pilot site to prepare them for their role in facilitating the diffusion at the other plants, Karm and the Barrington Company part ways, each satisfied that the maximum effort has been made to ensure a successful diffusion of the intervention strategy. The fact that the expected upturn in the economy is now under way adds to their sense of optimism.

Several months later, however, it becomes apparent that the diffusion is not proceeding well. While still committed to the long-term goals of the intervention, managers at all levels of the company exhibit less concern for its practical implementation. There are two apparent reasons for this. First, when the pilot program was initially launched there was a sense of urgency about improving the company's competitive position in the industry. But with the generally improved economy and the company's improved financial position, the sense of urgency receded. And second, for those managers involved in the pilot intervention, the potential rewards for succeeding at a time of bleak economic indicators were high. But for managers at the other plants, which are contributing to and reaping the benefits of the improved economy, embracing new work restructuring at the present time would entail considerable risk. These managers view the intervention as ill-timed and potentially disruptive.

Despite the company's generally improved performance, employees involved in the pilot intervention experience frustration when diffusion of "their program" does not take hold in the other plants. In some cases, they consider their failure a personal defeat, which adds to the stress within the plant. This soon leads to a decline in the plant's productivity and work quality, and top management is concerned that such subpar performance will affect adversely the company's overall financial position. They turn to Karm for help in diagnosing this latest "problem."

After a preliminary diagnosis, Karm takes the position that he could not be expected to have anticipated the difficulties encountered after his departure. Furthermore, he does not feel responsible for the current difficulties since, in his judgment, they were precipitated by top management's unwillingness to achieve wider diffusion of the changes. Barrington's chief officers, however, are now less interested in incorporating work changes at the other plants and more concerned with improving the performance of their Midwest plant. They argue that Karm had given his trainees inflated expectations about their tasks and failed to prepare them for the resistance that they might face in the other plants. Moss claims that under their original agreement Karm had an obligation to ensure, as much as possible, the long-term success of the intervention at that plant, and the fact that the effort toward diffusion to other plants is stalled does not lessen that original obligation.

Questions to Consider

1. Given the conflicting claims over whether the intervention was successful, according to whom and by what criteria should an OD intervention be judged a success or failure? Should the contract between Karm and Moss have included criteria for evaluating the intervention?

2. What role should the OD profession play in establishing standards of practice and in resolving conflicting claims when adherence to such standards are questioned?
3. What are Karm's responsibilities, if any, to "ensure the long-term success of the intervention"? Karm contended that he "could not be expected to have anticipated the difficulties" that the intervention might encounter after his departure. Is this an acceptable rationale for delimiting responsibility or is it a rationalization for abdicating responsibility?

Note: The responses to this case are reprinted by permission from "Judging Success or Failure: Whose Responsibility?", *Journal of Religion and the Applied Behavioral Sciences,* 1986, *3* (3), 8–12. This case was originally discussed at a panel convened at the annual conference of the Association for Creative Change, St. Paul, Minnesota, June 1985. The commentators include Beverly P. Brown-Hinckley, manager of organization effectiveness at Procter and Gamble; John C. Bryan, president of Bryan*Weir-Bryan Consultants, Ltd.; Jerilyn Fosdick, president of Fosdick and Company; Stanley R. Hinckley, Jr., president of Hinckley and Associates; and Robert Terry, director of the Reflective Leadership Center, University of Minnesota.

Comments by Beverly P. Brown-Hinckley, John C. Bryan, Jerilyn Fosdick, Stanley R. Hinckley, Jr., and Robert Terry

Bryan: Throughout the case, issues of appropriate client and consultant roles (and therefore responsibility) are raised . . . Criteria for evaluation should be established during the contracting phase of an OD intervention. It is the consultant's task to enable the client to articulate the desired outcomes . . . and to establish realistic limits for the effort. Determining success or failure is the responsibility of the client. Enabling the client to establish meaningful goals and realistic limits is the responsibility of the consultant.

Fosdick: It is the client who makes the ultimate judgment about the success or failure of an intervention because [he] lives with it. . . . In an effort as complex as organizational change, it is highly desirable to establish jointly, explicitly, and early what the criteria are for judging success. If it is not written into the contract it should be written into the plan for the intervention — including any formal data-gathering processes necessary for the evaluation.

Brown-Hinckley: There were never any explicit agreements during the initial discussions, the roll-out of the pilot program, or prior to Karm's departure for any monitoring or follow-up to occur against the intervention's objectives. To have omitted this critical step in the intervention process was a serious [mistake]. Karm might have been able to avoid the resulting conflict and issues if he had addressed this matter earlier.

The client also has a responsibility in this area. It is difficult to imagine that an organization would engage a consultant for an intervention of this nature without a written contract or description of the project's scope and not do an assessment of the results achieved prior to the departure of the consultant. Given that client organizations usually have more power and control than the consultant with regard to resources and determining when to continue or end a project, perhaps the client in this case did not feel a need to "protect" itself against the possibility of failure. In any event, the primary responsibility for ensuring that the contract and monitoring process were in place largely resided with Karm.

Hinckley: The criteria for "successful completion" of the contract need to be specified, preferably in writing. They have to be developed through the joint efforts of Karm and the key line and staff people. But much more importantly, the *roles* of the consultant and key executives and managers need to be specified clearly at the beginning. The responsibility for getting clear roles established belongs equally to client management and to the consultant.

Fosdick: The evaluation process must include more than [the question] Did the effort succeed or fail? It must also ask why, what have we learned, and where do we go from here?

The conflicting claims over the success or failure of the intervention seem pointless and destructive. When Karm was called in the second time to assess what was occurring, he needlessly defended himself and also needlessly blamed top management for the situation. Karm initiated a win-lose conflict with his defensive posture. That turned a diagnostic situation into a personalized evaluation of success or failure with attendant blame and fault. The ensuing power struggle became an issue more of the consultant's professional and interpersonal competence than the success or failure of the work restructuring and the evaluation criteria for that.

Such defensiveness precludes or severely limits the learning opportunity (for himself and the company) and makes working together to improve the situation extremely difficult.

Bryan: Karm proposed the diffusion strategy and secured top management's agreement to it. There is no evidence that he went any further in preparing top management for their role in the anticipated diffusion. And the subsequent perception by those involved in the pilot that "their program" was not taking hold in the other plants suggests that Karm did not plan for securing support from other plant managers, nor did he prepare the pilot project personnel to do so.

Though a consultant cannot be expected to predict changes in management strategy, [she] can predict issues of role conflict and relationships among work units. . . . It is the consultant's responsibility to alert and prepare the client for *anticipatable* concerns. Karm did not meet this responsibility regarding the diffusion strategy.

Hinckley: When diffusion stalled and performance of the Midwest plant worsened, the "preliminary diagnosis" done by Karm led to his denial of responsibility and [the president's] blaming him. These behaviors seem strange if the relationship between them was a good one. We do not know the content of the diagnosis, but it must have included some indications of why the diffusion . . . slowed and why the Midwest plant was in trouble. If these data were gathered and analyzed by Karm alone, he made a serious error. The diagnosis should have been done jointly so that the client owned it. Then collaborative rather than adversarial planning would have been possible.

Brown-Hinckley: Management's involvement and visibility in the project were very low. Responsibility for managing it was shifted to Karm, who accepted it when he agreed to the terms initially identified. . . . This is a very dangerous position for any consultant, given that [he] is not part of the organization and has little direct power to make change happen. It also provides an excuse for clients to neither be involved nor feel any ownership and accountability for the process.

Fosdick: Karm has a professional responsibility to see that not only the commitment, but also the processes, structures, systems, and responsible people are in place that will support the long-term success of the intervention before he leaves. He is not, however, in a position of power (influence yes, power no) to ensure that these things happen. Nor is he in control of external forces [that] operate and affect the intervention.

Hinckley: A consultant cannot be held accountable for line management's behavior and actions, but can and should be held accountable for getting across to them the knowledge and information they must have for the change effort to be successful and permanent. A trap for OD consultants, which it is easy to fall into, is to accept, at least implicitly, too much responsibility for the success or failure of a change effort. This often comes about because (1) we feel relatively powerless to make things happen in the client organization and so are eager to take any responsibility that gives us the feeling that we are *in charge,* and (2) we want to position ourselves so that we can take the credit for real accomplishments. To be able to say only that we "provided some education and training" or "facilitated some groups" or "advised top management" as our part of a project leaves us feeling as an accessory or tool, not as a key player in an important and successful change project.

We should be held accountable for informing management of what we know about change projects. And we should attempt to convey that information to the highest possible level of management *and* to some critical mass of people throughout the system. My strong preference is to contract for working with the client system . . . to the end of the implementation and final evaluation phases of the change project. And this must include whatever is needed to help the upper levels of management determine (1) how to manage the "new" organization, how to support the change process, and how to evaluate its short- and long-term success, and (2) what new norms and behaviors they must develop.

Brown-Hinckley: When the situation had degenerated between the client and the consultant, the former still failed to realize or accept that without their involvement, leadership, and visibility the project was almost doomed from the very beginning. This was the client's share of the responsibility for the failure of the project. The consultant's share was in failing to identify the need for client involvement early and integrating it into the program and in assuming ownership for the program rather than having the client do so.

Hinckley: Karm should have known that [management] often lose[s] commitment, that expectations had been built and there would be serious repercussions if they were not met, and that management at all levels would have to learn and change if the project were to succeed in the long term.

For management's part, [it] should have recognized that [it] had made a long-term commitment to Barrington and to the people in [its] organization, and that abdication of that commitment and of the actions required to honor it was irresponsible and unethical.

We must do our best to lead key members of our client systems to examine thoroughly their own values, to not be "innocent," but to be responsible for the use of their own knowledge and skills, including that which we impart to them.

Terry: Consultants do not have, nor should they have, the power to decide the future direction or implementation of corporate goals. . . . Differential power means differential responsibility. . . . Organizational leadership's lack of responsibility in managing the overall change process was more prominent than the consultant's lack of follow-through. Basically, the consultant fulfilled his responsibility; management did not.

That is true on the face of it. However, I believe there is another level of responsibility that transcends the power disparity issue. Karm made a diagnostic error. He gave bad advice to top management that in the long run would lead to ordinary, rather than exceptional, organizational performance. What happened?

Karm accepted the goal of "increased worker productivity" as a given without reflection. Once this goal was set, the restructuring was an order. He pursued a traditional OD intervention approach — set goal, then restructure. He ignored two vital aspects of the diagnosis — vision and compelling interest. Did Karm have a responsibility to his client to question the stated goals and test the real compelling interest at stake in this situation? I say yes.

If he did so he would be moving from organizational development to organizational transformation. He would move beyond a narrow definition of his work to a broader one. Karm permitted Moss to accept slightly-above-average performance when he could have challenged Moss to envision his organization as an exceptional performer.

Moss and his team were willing to accept market forces as the prime determiner of success. . . . Excellent corporations, while impacted by market conditions, are not captured by the market. They are shapers, not just responders. Karm failed to provide consulting leadership for Barrington. Instead, he managed a fairly typical, if not uninspired, OD process. Do consultants have a responsibility to challenge and critique current organizational goals and to help evoke an alternative vision for an organization? Do they have a responsibility to offer leadership to leaders? I think so.

Hinckley: The OD profession, through one or all of its professional associations, should establish ethical standards. . . .

In reviewing my comments and "A Statement of Values and Ethics for Professionals in Organization and Human Systems Development" (April 1985), I find that there is an excellent match. If Karm had followed these principles and guidelines, he would have avoided most of the difficulties he experienced. Particularly relevant are the interdependence of all parts of a system [Assumption 3–a–1]; the long-term interests [Guideline II–A], the need for client involvement [Guideline II–B], the importance of fully informing the client [Guideline II–C], and the necessity of helping the client develop self-reliance and the internal capabilities to support the change effort [Guideline II–G]. A clear contract, preferably written, is described also [Guideline II–L–1 and II–L–2]. And the very important matter of Karm's responsibility to the people in the system is [made] clear [in] the section on Social Responsibility [Guideline IV–B].

Fosdick: It would be a positive contribution to the profession and the public if the OD profession had a formal review process to resolve disputes between clients and consultants. Consultants would then be accountable to an objective body, or supported by a body of peers when standards required interpretation or performance had to be evaluated.

Standards of practice should be established so members of the field can be identified, certified, [and] licensed. . . . However, [there are] many people who refer to themselves as OD consultants, yet . . . do not conform to any established criteria of educational achievement or experience (because there are none yet). As a result, efforts to determine a baseline common body of knowledge will be very difficult.

Brown-Hinckley: It would be very difficult to secure the compliance of all professionals to standards since the profession continues to evolve in so many directions. It would also be a monumental task to establish a widely accepted structure to make appropriate "judgments" regarding member adherence. As a group, we tend to be self-protective, nonconfrontive, and risk-averse when we observe unethical situations within our ranks. . . .

Short of licensing, the ultimate responsibility for adherence to standards rests with each individual practitioner and with [her] peers who must be professionally bound to the standards and to the resolution of conflicting claims.

Hinckley: I am not in favor of bringing in third parties to resolve disputes too early. Rather, I believe that we should require that all disputes and claims be subject to thorough discussion in a face-to-face meeting. If a satisfactory resolution cannot be achieved by the parties, then use of an outside party for consultation is a viable alternative. Of course, the legal system can be used by either party.

A Work System Design Contract

Ed Jones is hired by Joe Smith, a plant manager for XYZ Inc., to guide and facilitate the design of a new work system by utilizing sociotechnical principles and other applicable OD technologies. The design is to specify all roles, the structure, the interfaces with all relevant parts of the plant's environment, the information system, the decision-making system, and the reward system.

A design team is formed that includes four employees from each of three "classes" — that is, managers, production workers, and clerks. The management team members consist of the personnel manager, the operations manager, the day shift foreman, and the night shift foreman. The eight team members from the other two categories are all men in their mid fifties to early sixties who have each worked at the plant for more than twenty years. Two of the production worker team members are officers of the local union that represents the production workers. The clerks at this time are not organized. Two years earlier, an international union launched an organizing campaign but abandoned it because the clerks, who are mostly women, did not respond with enough interest to warrant further efforts.

Almost from the first meeting of the design team, the management members participate with substantially more assurance, initiative, and energy than their production worker or clerical worker counterparts. The union officials of the production worker union are less reticent than the others, but basically allow the management team members to take the initiative most of the time at working sessions. At one session, Walt Ames, the personnel manager, observes with evident satisfaction that the company and the union have gone for fifteen years without a strike. Not only that, he notes, but during the last fifteen years the company and union have succeeded in resolving every grievance before having to go to arbitration. The leaders of the production worker union face opposition in the upcoming election of officers from younger candidates who have committed themselves to take a more aggressive stance toward management.

When the team began its work, division management set forth criteria for a good design, including the following:

1. The design should specify "roles," not jobs, and all roles must be multi-skilled.
2. Every role should be focused on responsibility for business results and the design should assure individual "high commitment" to getting those results.
3. The basic design element should be "business teams," with each role being an important part of a team.
4. The design should not require the expenditure of additional wage dollars.
5. The design should not be limited by the existing union contract; a new contract would be negotiated soon, and whatever provisions of the contract were necessary to make the new work system succeed would be incorporated.

As the design work proceeds, it becomes clear to everyone that fewer employees will be needed in the new design, and that all employees will have to learn new skills — effective team work, problem solving, decision making, and so on — and take on much larger responsibilities than before.

Based upon his perception of the relationship between management and employees at XYZ Inc., Jones senses that over the previous ten years or so, an implicit psychological contract has developed between management and the workers, which can be summarized as follows:

Workers: We will do a reasonable day's work and take care of our jobs, putting in some extra effort when necessary, in return for good pay and freedom from strict management.

Managers: We will accept how you do your job, not be strict or demanding, and continue to pay you well, providing that results are adequate.

Jones comes to feel that management's decision that a new work system will be designed and implemented, and that it must meet the above criteria, is a unilateral change in this psychological contract, with no offer to collaborate with employees or union leaders to develop a new one.

Jones's contract is to assure management that the new work system is a good design, and to help the team develop a commitment to its success and move all the plant's employees to a state of optimism and readiness for implementation. But, as the design emerges, it is obvious that the workers and lower-level managers will be required to invest much more of themselves in their jobs, undertake to learn some new skills, and take on responsibility for "business results" without yet understanding what that might mean.

No one will be rewarded monetarily for the greater effort required by his new role, and everyone is threatened by the possible loss of his job. Efforts by the design team to create a new reward system are aborted when they conclude that the fourth management criterion provides no room to do this in a realistic or fair way.

Questions to Consider

1. Suppose Jones comes to believe that the new work design violates terms of the collective bargaining agreement between XYZ and the production workers. Discuss the various courses of action open to Jones.

2. Let us assume that Jones concludes that the new work design, though not necessarily in violation of the collective bargaining agreement, is nonetheless highly inequitable. Discuss the various courses of action he might take.

3. Discuss the implications for this case of the following pro-
    visions of the Statement (April 1985):

II. Responsibility to Clients and Significant Others
     A. Serve the short- and long-term welfare, interests,
         and development of the client system and all its
         stakeholders; maintain balance in the timing, pace,
         and magnitude of planned change so as to support
         a mutually beneficial relationship between the sys-
         tem and its environment.
 I. Avoid conflicts of interest.
     2. Seek to act impartially when involved in conflicts
         between parties in the client system; help them
         resolve their conflicts themselves, without taking
         sides; if necessary to change my role from serving
         as impartial consultant, do so explicitly; cease work
         with the client, if necessary.

Note: The three commentaries on this case were originally
presented at the 12th annual Organizational Behavior Teaching Conference, Charlottesville, Va., June, 1985. The commentators are Kenneth D. Alpern, a philosopher at DePaul University; Allan R. Cohen, professor of management at Babson
College; and Peter B. Vaill, professor of human systems at
George Washington University.

Comments by Kenneth D. Alpern

    Step back from the case a little and ask: What is the proper
framework or model for morally evaluating consultants in cases
such as the one before us? I will sketch very briefly three models
and mention reasons for rejecting the first two. Though I think
these first two models are incorrect, it is still important to identify them and understand why they are inadequate, for otherwise they will continue to exert undue influence in our thinking.

    Pure Contract or Instrument Model. The first model I will
call the Pure Contract or Instrument Model. In this conception

of consultancy, the consultant is thought of as hired by plant management to formulate a work design *for* them, within guidelines *they* have set, and in circumstances such that *they* have complete control over the decision to implement the work design. To view the consultant in this way is to view him as management's *instrument;* management sets a task and the consultant agrees to do it. The consultant's sole obligation and license is to do that task. Conceiving the consultant's task in this way, the only relevant moral or ethical evaluation of his performance would be whether he conscientiously fulfilled, or sought to fulfill, the terms of the contract in letter and in spirit. Any further moral evaluation, this model would have it, must be of the plant management; they are the ones who specified the guidelines within which the work design was to be formulated, and they are the ones who decide whether or not to implement it. If there is anything morally objectionable in the context or implementation of the work design, then it would follow that the managers, and not the consultant, are the ones properly held accountable. According to this model, the OD consultant only creates means for attaining certain ends. He does not decide on the ends and he does not decide which means will be used. He only makes certain things possible; he is not the agent, he does not *do* anything.

The consultant in the type of case before us can be viewed not merely as creating possibilities, but as creating power or giving it to others. Anyone who creates or passes on a power is at least to some extent responsible (in the sense of accountable and open to criticism) for seeing to it that the power is not misused. For example, a person who gives a gun to another person with good reason to expect that the gun would be used to seriously harm or violate the rights of others is prima facie to blame for that harm. A full, mature human being cannot claim to be insulated from moral evaluation merely because he was acting at another person's direction. Morally speaking, a person can never be purely an instrument.

Paternalistic Model. Recognizing that a person can never totally abdicate or cede moral responsibility can lead one to embrace a model for consultancy at the other end of the spectrum. I will call this model the Paternalistic Model.

According to the Paternalistic Model, the consultant is always responsible for the morality of his actions and must always seek to secure that the interests and rights of all parties are properly protected. In the case of the OD consultant to the XYZ plant, the Paternalistic Model would thus require that his work design should give proper place to the rights and interests not only of management, but of workers, clerks, and, indeed, of people outside the plant system, including consumers of the plant's products, and the public in general. (It should be noted that "A Statement of Values and Ethics . . . ," April 1985, appears at several places to require just such an extensive concern of the consulting professional.) Of course, there is unlikely to be a perfect harmony between the interests and rights of all parties. In such cases, the Paternalistic Model calls on the OD specialist, as does the Statement, to create a work design that produces the morally correct balance between those competing rights and interests. In essence, the OD specialist is to be the arbiter of morality.

The Paternalistic Model and the Statement can be appealing. There is a seductive "do-goodism" to their charge to the consulting specialist to ensure the morally best outcome. However, the Paternalistic Model and, in this regard, the Statement, are quite morally objectionable.

For one thing, the model implies that the consultant has no special obligation to management who hired him and to whom he contracted. Further, it may be objected that not only does the Paternalistic Model fail to recognize any special obligation to the contracting parties, but it fails to respect the autonomy of the persons it seeks to protect — that is, to respect their status as decision makers about their own interests and how to promote them. The workers, for example, may well find it insulting that others can decide for them what constitutes their own well-being. They may rightly object to the preemption of their own decisions and choices by those of the consultant. In addition, it is not unreasonable for the workers to be suspect and to take an attitude toward the consultant of: Look, *you* work for management. *Your* job is to see to *their* interests and propose a plan. We, for our part, will consider the plan you and management propose, and then we can all sit down and negotiate.

Toward an Intermediate Model. The goal in constructing an alternative model is to capture both proper concern for justice and the proper sanctity of contract. At the center is the question, Under what conditions may one morally contract to work at another's bidding, and under what conditions may/must one morally violate the terms of a contract conscientiously entered?

The following brief comments are meant as a practical guide for the consultant to a corporation. The first point to consider is that the consultant is aligning himself with those in power. The question then arises, Are others subject to that power being oppressed, or do they have effective means by which to formulate and promote their rights (and interests)? In the case we have been given, "others" include the unionized workers, the nonunionized clerks, and the public who may be affected by what goes on in the plant. Thus, the consultant should determine: Is the union leadership representative and effective? Do the nonunionized clerks hold any power in the system? Does the government or the public directly protect the public interest adequately? These are difficult questions to answer, but ours is a complex society, and we should not expect magically easy answers. In any event, if the answer to any of these questions is no, then by adding to the power of those who control the situation—whose aims conflict with those of the workers and the public—one is contributing to oppression and to that extent doing something morally objectionable.

When one contracts to serve the *interests* of management, one must be and remain assured that the *rights* of others will not be violated and that others affected have adequate means by which to protect their interests beyond their mere rights. (A consultant who contributes to the powers of others must be paternalistic with respect to the protection of rights and, with respect to interests, must not contribute to or make it an unfair fight.) One recognizes contract. But contract does not have absolute sanctity. One serves the interests of the client, but must not act so as to prejudice the rights of others or unfairly thwart others' pursuit of their own interests.

Comments by Allan R. Cohen

The situation Jones faces at XYZ Inc. involves a complex network of stakeholders with some overlapping and some competing interests. Stakeholders include top management, plant management, older and younger union members, clerical employees, supervisors, the personnel manager, and the members of the design team.

In such a setting, one of the first things with which Jones should have been concerned was the question of membership on the design team and its relationship to the interested constituencies. Having a design team that cuts across levels is a perfectly reasonable device for managing work system redesign, but issues of representativeness, autonomy, and balance all need to be considered. The case doesn't tell us who chose the members of the design team, but it is clear early on that the membership is not wholly appropriate. Important constituencies are left out or are underrepresented, and it is clear that members do not fully understand the function of their roles. Members of a design team need to think of themselves as communication links with other impacted parts of the organization, and need to address, from the beginning, questions of how free they are to use their own judgment versus the obligation to represent constituent interests.

Related to issues of membership are issues having to do with power balance among members. It is extemely difficult for parties of grossly unequal power to collaborate in problem solving, yet Jones does nothing to address power questions. If the process is to be fully collaborative in order to lead to widespread commitment, those members of the team who do not fully understand the issues or who feel blocked from free participation because of their position need as much education and support as it takes to enable them to make real contributions to the effort. Allowing management members to dominate the process sets the stage for future resentment and for potential undermining of any design team accomplishments.

The kind of changes envisioned require high commitment from members of the organization to make them work; they cannot be implemented in a way that reduces commitment. A new work system that calls for greater worker judgment, application of skills, flexibility, and the like, calls for more than just a good organizational design; it demands *processes* that generate higher commitment on the part of employees. Many factors in the case mitigate against such processes. The design team's process itself, as already discussed, does not even serve to gain the commitment of the worker members, let alone the wider work force. Management's design criteria are neither fully realistic nor appropriately comprehensive, since they tend to be solution oriented rather than diagnostic or boundary setting in character.

It is not necessarily wrong for management to insist that total wages not be increased by the new design, since it may be possible that a more engaging, sociotechnically designed work system could be far more productive with fewer people, but unless employees are guaranteed no loss of jobs as a result of the process, it is not reasonable to expect that they will be particularly cooperative in the implementation stage. The design criteria do not say that *individual* employees cannot be paid more for doing more responsible, skill-demanding work, but questions need to be addressed about what would then happen to employees made redundant. Is there other work for them? Would natural attrition and retirements solve the problem? What is the company willing to do to protect those who would not voluntarily be leaving?

Since we do not know the economic circumstances of this plant, nor the impetus for the work redesign, we do not know whether the plant is in competitive danger. Nevertheless, I do not believe that there is anything immoral or unethical about creating new ways of doing work that simultaneously reduce costs and provide more meaningful, interesting jobs for remaining employees. When the commitment of remaining employees is necessary to make the system work, however, then some form of employment security or planned attrition is necessary for effectiveness. It is not inconceivable that sufficient numbers of employees, including those at supervisory and management levels, might be reduced to allow for greater pay for those who remain, but the interests of effective groups need to be taken into account and protected in order not to produce backlash or undue resistance. Above and beyond whatever human considerations it wishes to take into account, management must deal with the concerns of such crucial parties if it is to realize any potential gains.

Of course, it is entirely possible that in the particular situation of XYZ's plant the new work system is not appropriate, and that possibility should be included in the design team's explorations. As a neutral outsider, Jones needs to be constantly helping both the team and the company address whether the proposed design will actually work to increase effectiveness in that particular setting; the system they are exploring does not work under every circumstance, and a good consultant will help the client understand this and diagnose the likelihood of success under existing circumstances.

In general, part of the obligation of an OD consultant is to help make issues explicit and consequences of various options visible. If a company, a manager, or a project group is making choices that are likely to backfire or lead to an inappropriate set of decisions, the consultant is obligated to raise those issues, implement whatever education is necessary to help clients make informed choices, and provide a counterweight to misplaced momentum (or lack of it). This is part of the consultant's obligation because presumably she brings to such change projects knowledge about organizational structure and processes that insiders may not have, or may not have yet acquired. If the consultant foresees a disaster in the making, it is incumbent on her to warn the clients in no uncertain terms and to make as explicit as possible the likely consequences of the choices being contemplated. That an existing implicit psychological contract between management and employees is being broken is, for example, not in itself immoral or unethical, but it is likely to lead to resistance and other kinds of difficulties if not attended to; Jones needs to help the organization pay attention to these possible consequences.

Similarly, the failure to take into account the impact of a new work design on existing supervisors is not unethical, but here, as in many situations, is likely to lead to undesired consequences. A consultant needs not be pro-union to point out to management that its behavior is likely to lead to greater militancy on the part of the union, nor need the consultant be pro-management to point out to union members the consequences of ignoring the impact of costs on competitive position and, ultimately, on jobs. It is the consultant's obligation to know something about organizations and the kinds of projects that he undertakes to help implement, but even with vast experience, perfect knowledge is never possible, since each situation will have its own twists. A consultant who is behaving ethically will pay careful attention to the specifics of a situation that he is in, not misrepresent his or her expertise or claim perfect results in advance, but will work hard to anticipate likely consequences of various choices and make them explicit to all the relevant parties.

Comments by Peter B. Vaill

Cases such as this one always pose the reader with a paradox: There are patently so many departures from sound professional practice on the part of all the case characters that it is difficult to see how reasonably intelligent and presumably responsible men and women could have gotten themselves into such a situation. Yet they did. The reader is implicitly invited by such cases (and it is important to say that most cases are of this paradoxical type) to then comment with twenty-twenty hindsight on why things proceeded as they did, and/or who should have done what along the way to make things turn out differently. A variation on the who-should-have-done-what-differently question is: What do I think I would have done had I been in such a situation?

I consider most such retrospective analysis relatively pointless — easy and superficially satisfying as it is to do — especially if one is irritated with a case character or event and wants to really "nail" the persons involved. The lifeblood of case method instruction in M.B.A. classrooms is this type of self-righteous fervor.

Yet, I am always reminded of a remark by the sociologist George Homans to a graduate seminar: "Whatever should have happened is what did happen"—thereby calling attention to the essence of the paradox. How is it that qualified people can behave stupidly and unconsciously? What is the nature of one's unfolding experience in organizational situations that seems to include the necessity for behaving in ways that one can later see, or that a case commentator can see, are stupid and unconscious? How did I get myself into that situation? cry the Joneses of our profession—which doubtless means all of us at one time or another.

In the next few paragraphs I am going to do a little of the twenty-twenty hindsighting, but to make a particular point that one does not often hear in discussions of ethics. In the final portion of these remarks I would like to turn my attention to what I consider the most meaningful question in the case: namely, what does Jones do now?

Retrospectively, there are a number of events in the case that portend a bad end for the situation. For instance:

1. Jones had a contract to produce a design, but he "should" have understood that he also needed a contract to facilitate a design *process.* Jones apparently overlooked this distinction, or was insensitive to it, which then resulted in his having no real role to play as group process issues began to multiply.
2. The lopsided composition of the design team and the demographics of it suggest the kind of interaction patterns that subsequently occurred: energetic initiation by the management side, relatively passive and probably increasingly resentful participation by the workers' side.
3. The superficiality of Ames's diagnosis of the amicable relations between management and the union suggests that management did not understand power relationships very well.

4. No one seems concerned about the unilateral imposition
    of the design criteria by division management, which fur-
    ther suggests that no one in the situation had grasped how
    thoroughly the success of the design process and the subse-
    quent design rested on participation, ownership, and com-
    mitment on the part of all concerned. If Jones's job was
    to "move all the plant's employees to a state of optimism
    and readiness for implementation," then it is difficult to see
    how he could not have perceived that the unilateral impo-
    sition of these design criteria virtually guaranteed suspi-
    cion, resistance, and feelings of having been exploited
    among lower-level plant people. But, apparently, he did
    not foresee such an outcome. He bought into a process that
    was practically certain to result in preventing him from
    fulfilling his contract.

5. The impossibility of some of the criteria and the improb-
    ability of others is troubling. Not only were the criteria im-
    posed, but, in retrospect, they are not even very good
    criteria. Where was Jones? Where were the other design
    team members?

6. Finally, there is some suggestion that Jones was having in-
    creasingly funny feelings about this whole process, and that
    is a good sign, for it means that he is not yet spiritually
    dead. Something is going wrong here, his gut seems to have
    been saying to him.

The reason I have been going over some of these relatively obvious defects and points of instability in the case narrative is not to suggest that anyone could or should have done
anything differently. We have no way of knowing whether that
was possible. Any claim to the contrary is overly facile and be-
side the point (which, by the way, is why practicing managers
have so little patience with academic analysis).

Instead, my point is an observation about the relationship between ethics and what we know about psychology and
the nature of social systems. What we can see happening in this
case is that management wanted something—a more effective
and efficient manufacturing process. In pursuit of this objec-

tive, they ignored much of what we know about the process of change, especially what we know about what causes resistance. When the resistance began to mount, management was in the position of choosing whether to cling to its business objective and escalate the "pressure" on the design team to produce a satisfactory design, or back off from the pursuit of the objective in order to consider what was happening in the situation that was causing so much difficulty. It appears—we do not know for sure—that management will attempt to force continued pursuit of the objective, which of course will lead to more conflict in an intensifying spiral, to the point where ultimately the abstract promise of the design will not be realized and there will be a whole set of labor-management issues to deal with that were not there before. Moral indignation will be at a fever pitch for every party to the situation, including Jones, who will be tempted to point the finger at someone else.

The moral I draw from this is that when you pursue your objectives stupidly, regardless of their merits, you ultimately end up in ethical dilemmas concerning the rightness of your original objectives and your rights to pursue them. This is why we need process consultants—to help action-takers pursue their objectives more wisely and sensitively, and thereby, we hope, avoid little tragedies such as this case reports, or bigger ones.

What does Jones do now? One might say he is so thoroughly compromised that about all he can do is retire from the scene. Perhaps he should give back his fee, too, although that itself is a debatable matter. Where do we draw the line between "acceptable ineffectiveness" and outright incompetence? In Jones's case, I think he should give back his fee for apparently failing even to try to deal with the group process issues as they arose. But that raises another question: If he admits to his incompetence by returning the fee, does he open himself to being sued for damages? The company has lost possibly millions of dollars, rather directly traceable to inaction on process issues by the design team. Perhaps Jones is a good deal more culpable in all this than most of us would like to think. It quickly becomes a complex legal question, one which the profession has not even begun to face up to, in my judgment.

There is something else Jones might do, though, to avoid all this legal messiness. He needs to start confronting issues with his client that he has been so far avoiding. Presumably the company still wants an improved design, and there has been at least a start on the design process, although it has not gone very far. Jones is now an involved party, and his capacity to help the design team out of the morass they are in will have to be as a contributor to the morass rather than as an independent consultant. He will have to be more assertive, more of a leader, more of a risk-taker if he is going to do anything at all.

The main issue Jones needs to confront is, What is a healthy design process and what relation does a healthy process have to the desired outcome of an effective design? Until the design team, and the management and labor systems surrounding it, shares some understanding of the answers to those questions, the process will not go well and Jones's effectiveness and possibly his integrity as a consultant will be continually compromised.

Whether Jones can initiate this new style, however, depends on whether he can acquire a new ethical sensibility, one he does not now possess. Such a sensibility has to do with being honest with oneself and with clients. The process by which a person who has been avoiding responsibility comes to accept responsibility and thus act differently is not a process that is well understood. Without a better understanding of the process of ethical enlightenment, so to speak, and how it can be fostered in men and women like Jones and his clients, there is really little point in discussing the ethics of action.

Confidentiality at What Price?

Captain Eric Davis is the head of the Organizational Effectiveness (OE) staff at a military base in the southwestern United States and ultimately responsible for his work to the base commander, Colonel Richard Abrams, who has been in his post for two years. At the request of one of the base's unit commanders, Major Scott McHenry, who has headed his unit for the last five years, Davis agrees to assess the unit's performance, provide McHenry with the results of the assessment, jointly plan any necessary changes, help him implement the changes, and evaluate the overall effort.

During the initial assessment phase, Davis and his staff interview over 100 personnel, review various reports, records, procedures, and policies, attend several command and staff meetings, and observe the day-to-day operations of the unit over a two-month period. This effort identifies both the unit's strengths and weaknesses. Among the more significant strengths are (1) a conscientious unit commander who cares for and supports his subordinates, (2) a highly qualified and motivated professional unit, which is fully committed to its assigned mission, (3) an excellent reputation, with a strong heritage and rich tradition, and (4) a high level of interpersonal trust. The most significant weaknesses include (1) a lack of appropriate state-of-the-art equipment, (2) a complex command and control system that at times results in conflicting communications, and (3) the negative impact on unit operations of the base commander.

The friction between Abrams and the unit derives from a difference of opinion about how the unit is to operate and who is to make operational decisions. As base commander, Abrams believes that it is his right and responsibility to make operational decisions for the unit. Members of the unit, however, are accustomed to receiving their direction from the unit commander. From their perspective, the base commander is unduly intrusive, eroding the initiative of the unit commander and instituting policies that preclude them from performing those activities that have been traditionally their own prerogative. McHenry confides to Davis that he is feeling conflicting pressures generated by his responsibility to obey his base commander on the one hand, and his sense of loyalty to his unit on the other.

As part of the assessment, Davis interviews Abrams to establish his perception of the unit's organization and performance. During the conversation, Abrams informs Davis in very specific terms of his negative feelings toward the unit and the unit commander. He tells Davis that he has the unit commander "on his list" and that he is "going to get him."

Davis and his staff present their findings to McHenry,

who then requests that plans be developed to correct the problems pinpointed by the assessment. Soon afterward, McHenry is relieved of his duties by Abrams and assigned to a base in New England. It is apparent that Abrams has taken steps to resolve his conflict with the unit in a manner consistent with his military authority. Prior to his departure, McHenry informs Davis that he intends to appeal the reassignment and, if necessary, to fight it all the way to the Department of the Army.

Davis is feeling a bit uneasy about this turn of events, primarily because he has firsthand knowledge of the base commander's intention to "get" McHenry. He knows that if he is called as a witness in any hearing, he may well be asked to divulge that information. The more he reflects on the situation, the more he becomes aware that he can be key to McHenry's defense.

Another matter that weighs heavily on his mind is that *his* efficiency report is prepared by Abrams. Revealing the information concerning McHenry could end not only his career but Abrams's as well. On the other hand, not divulging what he knows may mean the end of McHenry's career. Moreover, if he reveals the data to anyone outside the base OE staff, he will violate the profession's ethical principle (incorporated into army regulations) of promising confidentiality to participants. In addition to its impact on the immediate situation, such a breach of confidentiality could have a deleterious effect on the practice of OE generally.

While Davis struggles with this dilemma and attempts to sort out his own sense of right and wrong, he receives a call from McHenry, requesting a statement on his behalf for the appeal he is submitting to Washington. McHenry says he is hoping to have someone confirm the fact that he and Abrams were "at odds," and since Davis has closely observed the operations of his unit, McHenry believes he will have some data on the matter.

Genuinely confused by the situation, Davis calls his immediate OE supervisor, a senior OE consultant located at another military base, for advice. He advises Davis that per army regulation he is not compelled to divulge any confidential information collected during the OE effort or to reveal his sources. But he adds that the regulation has never been tested before in circumstances such as those Davis faces. His parting words are, "ultimately, it's up to you."

Questions to Consider

1. What difference would it make if Davis had specifically promised confidentiality to Abrams prior to the interview, as opposed to merely assuming that the conversation would be governed by the army's regulation on confidentiality in research?
2. Assume that McHenry had not requested a statement from Davis. Does Davis nevertheless have an affirmative duty to alert the proper army authorities of Abrams's vendetta against McHenry?
3. Davis recognizes the possibility that whether or not he agrees to provide McHenry with a statement, he may be ordered to testify at a subsequent hearing. Refusal to do so could subject him to contempt charges. If confronted with such a possibility, how would you advise Davis to respond?
4. Who is Davis's "client" in this case? Would your answer have any significance for how you would advise Davis regarding his responsibilities?

Note: The responses to this case are reprinted by permission from "Values and Ethics in Organization Development: The Case of Confidentiality," *Organization Development Journal* 1986, *4* (2), 14–20. This case was originally discussed at the OD Institute's Annual Information Exchange, Williams Bay, Wisconsin, May 1985. Robert Golembiewski is research professor at the University of Georgia; Daniel Kegan is an attorney and president of Elan Associates, Organizational Consultants.

Comments by Robert Golembiewski and Daniel Kegan

Golembiewski: "Confidentiality at What Price?" strikes me . . . as a useful vehicle for raising central issues about ethics, as well as about the level of "reasonably competent performance" associated with ethical provision of professional services, and especially for an "internal" OD resource.

The general focus of [my response] is on the OE consultant, Davis, and its organizing framework builds around the four questions with which the case concludes. My own perspectives will dominate, of course, and these are basically those of an "external" OD resource. My reactions thus at times may be a bit more adventuresome than those adoptable by some internal OD persons, whose fate typically will be more rooted in the client organization than mine when I consult.

Kegan: As I read this case again, two months after my first encounter . . . I found my perspectives and loyalties shifting. My initial reaction had autocratic, Theory X Base Commander Abrams wearing the black hat, professional Theory Y Unit Head McHenry in white, and the unfortunate OE practitioner Davis in gray — caught between the forces of good and evil.

On my last reading, I found myself more sympathetic [to] . . . Abrams. As I continued to analyze the facts of the case and to process my feelings and reactions, I turned to several sources for help.

I turned to "A Statement of Values and Ethics for Professionals in Organization and Human Systems Development (April 1985) . . . [and] with the facts, issues, and ethical questions of this case in mind, I found many of its provisions clearly applicable. However, rarely did the Statement provide answers [but] usually only confirmation that I had identified a difficult issue.

I consulted the American Psychological Association (APA) and the American Bar Association (ABA) publications. In consulting, my primary professional identity is as an organizational psychologist. As an attorney, I thought the ethical guidelines and principles of the [b]ar and of psychology might, by analogy, illuminate the lacuna[s] and shadows of organization development. Only after our May conference did [another] source become available to me — Lowman's *Casebook on Ethics and Standards for the Practice of Psychology in Organizations* (1985).

Golembiewski: Whether or not the degree of confidentiality is made explicit in the case strikes me as of no special moment. . . . Consultants have to respect their ethical moorings even when clients are vague or naive about them, and even when consultants "forget" to be explicit . . . or when clients misunderstand what should have been both obvious and elemental.

If the conditions of confidentiality are *not* made explicit, although [a]rmy regulations prescribe them, that implies [the] consultant's performance is deficient in one noteworthy regard. [The c]onsultant cannot simply count on sources knowing the rules of the game. . . .

I consider absolute confidentiality both improbable and unwise. "A Statement of Values and Ethics . . . " has it about right, I believe, when it advises [a] consultant to "make limits of confidentiality clear" to [the] client [Guideline II–K–1].

In what senses do I believe that confidentiality is prudently limited? In the case of [a] consultant's knowledge about an "immanent evil act," I believe, confidentiality cannot obtain. A consultant learning of an illegal act with serious and direct consequences for others should inform appropriate authorities.

Beyond such extreme cases, . . . I try to signal to clients my ideal about confidentiality in some such words: "We cannot go absolutely confidential under explicitly signalled conditions but, in general, I believe we'll both profit if you basically trust in my discretion concerning the possible use of any information. Generally, I'll try to check with you when I have the least doubt about using materials, or about whether and how the source might be disguised. But sometimes that will not be possible when I believe use of materials is prudent . . . If that makes you nervous, we can talk about why our trust level is not high enough. Maybe a consultative relationship is just not in the cards for us."

The usual notion is that confidentiality develops trust. And so it can, and does. My view does not deny this, but adds the crucial caveat that helping make desired things happen also can build trust. Here, discretion is a powerful supplement to general confidentiality.

Kegan: Clearly confidentiality arises — but confidentiality is actually two issues: confidentiality and privilege. *Confidentiality* is a person's promise, explicit or implicit, to hold certain information in trust and to use it only for the benefit of the confider. The good intentions and integrity of the trustee back his or her promise. *Privilege* is a legal rule — it permits certain types of people to refrain with impunity from divulging information otherwise lawfully demanded by a court.

Traditionally, priests, physicians, and attorneys have had such privileges. However, the *client* holds the privilege; a physician cannot lawfully refuse to divulge if the client waives the privilege. Recently, traditional areas of confidentiality have been narrowed — now a professional may be under an affirmative duty to warn a probable victim of the harm intended by the professional's client. Client communications to an attorney may be privileged. The rationale is that such protection encourages full disclosure of facts and permits a better defense. Before a client formally hires an attorney, while explaining the case, a privilege exists.

Golembiewski: Davis'[s] tussle with confidentiality seems to rest in substantial measure on what *he did not do, and reasonably could be expected to have done, or at least could have attempted to do.* Consider the situation in which Davis first learns that McHenry is on Abrams'[s] "list" and that the latter intends "to get" the former. Davis only stews about this information, apparently, when some such sequence [as the following] seems appropriate to me, even patent: Immediately, or early on, Davis should probe for clarity about specific meanings. No evidence of such a probing exists . . . Whatever the results of this probing, Davis should urge Abrams to meet with McHenry . . . *before* moving on to recommendations. No great risk inheres in Abrams'[s] possible disinclination to "go the last mile." So Davis might learn much, at little or no cost to [him]self. Indeed, this approach also might well build OE support for Davis, and hence be narrowly instrumental as well as reasonable praxis. If Abrams does not respond positively, were I Davis I could well say: "Unless you violently object, I propose to tell McHenry of our conversation and its contents." If Abrams does object violently, Davis might well pursue two simultaneous courses of action: report up the OE chain on Abrams'[s] recalcitrance as a major problem for the project and begin limiting the scope of the project to those areas specifically under McHenry's control. . . . Consideration also might be given to cancelling the project as envisioned more broadly.

Kegan: At the beginning of Davis'[s] interview with Abrams, did Davis clearly explain his professional obligations of confidentiality? Did Davis clarify the difference between professional confidentiality and legal privilege? Did Davis explain confidentiality and privilege in the [a]rmy context? Did Davis explain the purpose of the interview, who would have access to the data, and to whom the report would be made? The case is silent. APA Ethical Principle 9j states the ethical obligations of a researcher in a situation similar to Davis'[s]: "Information obtained about a research participant during the course of an investigation is confidential unless otherwise agreed upon in advance. When the possibility exists that others may obtain access to such information, this possibility, together with the plans for protecting confidentiality, is explained to the participant as part of the procedure for obtaining informed consent."

Golembiewski: Davis has a major responsibility to alert others about Abrams'[s] "vendetta." Early targets include Abrams, McHenry, and Davis'[s] immediate OE supervisor. Davis'[s] "affirmative duty" to alert other proper authorities clearly should be delayed, at the very least, until the initial probing contacts are made.

If probing does reveal strong evidence of a "vendetta," and if Abrams refuses to work on relationships with McHenry, Davis'[s] initial recourse is through the OE hierarchy. Hierarchies exist, in part, because subordinates can exhaust their own resources. To a sufficiently strong ego, utilizing the hierarchy does not signal "failure."

More heroic efforts by Davis . . . might be motivated by failures to make sufficient accommodations through the OE hierarchy or via McHenry. Generally, however, organizations that require heroic efforts associated with low or negative rewards will find that many useful things go undone.

Put in another way, Davis and the OE function are both poorly served by the Pontius Pilate attitude of Davis'[s] immediate [supervisor]. The issues clearly are *not* "all up to Davis," for their systemic character is obvious and their significance to the OE function is clear.

Kegan: McHenry has requested a statement from Davis confirming the conflict between McHenry and Abrams. Davis need not make such a statement. The OE study found a "negative impact on unit operation" due to the [b]ase [c]ommander. If the study findings were material, they could be subpoenaed by McHenry; Davis'[s] second statement is unnecessary. Statements could also be requested from other unit members and other base officers. Davis is not a source of such rare information that a breach of professional confidentiality is warranted.

Golembiewski: Davis should avoid testifying on two grounds. First, given a number of glaring deficiencies in reflecting reasonable competence . . . Davis'[s] testimony would amount to testifying against his vulnerable self about personal failures to attempt reasonable initiatives. . . . An ineffective attempt might be excused or even understood. But misfeasance in elementals presents more formidable challenges.

Second, Davis'[s] most reasonable basic strategy involves responding only to affirmative orders to testify . . . Even then, Davis should testify with great reluctance, citing the [a]rmy regulation about confidentiality concerning "research," even though the present case is not clearly "research." Davis should also preface each answer with his concern that his testimony might compromise future OE effectiveness.

Kegan: There are many stakeholders in this drama, including . . . Abrams and . . . McHenry and [his] unit, OE consultant Davis and the OE group, the OE profession, the OE supervisor, the new unit head, the army, and Davis'[s] family.

Davis recognized McHenry's loyalty to his unit, and his conflict with Abrams'[s] legitimate authority. This is a classic subgroup–deviant goals organizational issue. The case is silent on how the OE group perceived the situation and what they planned to do to correct it.

Davis and his OE group could be technically competent — or they could be quite incompetent. The case omits too many facts for an easy evaluation. However, Davis'[s] immediate supervisor appears derelict in his laissez-faire response to Davis'[s] request for clarification and help.

Golembiewski: When it comes to identifying the "client," Davis seems especially myopic, and gives little or no apparent attention to the "systemic" character of intervention so rightly and so frequently emphasized in "A Statement of Values and Ethics . . . " (Assumptions 2, 3a, and [3]b; 4a and [4]b; 5d). Davis assumes a "solid" and "permanent" client, a "narrow" definition substantially bounded by the interests of McHenry and his unit. This view of "client" was not optimum even at the onset of the intervention, and got progressively more deficient as time went on.

Davis'[s] view is myopic from several different points. First, it requires no special insight to anticipate Abrams/McHenry issues, *from the very earliest times,* in the contracting. After all, McHenry is "in the middle," and cross-pressures should be expected.

Second, at the very least, concern about expanding the definition of "client" should have been triggered by the admissions of McHenry and Abrams that turf problems existed between them, and perhaps more.

Third, Davis seems to have continued to the very end his narrow identification with McHenry's unit and, by implication, with the correctness of their apparent view that they had a historical right to be more self-determinative than Abrams preferred. Consider only a few possibilities that Davis might well have explored, and which the case implies he did not evaluate . . . Was the issue an insecure and status-anxious Abrams? Or do we see more the signs of a once-healthy but now overzealous need for unit self-determination that was nurtured by a succession of laissez-faire predecessors of Abrams? Numerous other possibilities occur to even inexperienced organization-watchers.

Fourth, Davis was not quick either to include the OE hierarchy as part of the appropriate "client system," or to make that point obvious to other elements of that system. This strikes me as most egregious on Davis'[s] part, for the "OE function" is [tacitly] a part of the context within which he functioned. In extreme cases, that OE hierarchy can provide shelter for operatives who are variously savaged by clients. To be sure, Davis was not well served by his immediate OE supervisor. But even that unsatisfying resort to the OE hierarchy came very late in the case and, moreover, does not exhaust the possible avenues of recourse even within the subsystem.

In too-great degree, then, Davis seems to have defined himself into a client relationship that isolated him both from support and restricted his range of alternatives for intervening. In that dual sense, Davis does not prudently reflect the systemic emphases in "A Statement of Values and Ethics. . . . "

Kegan: My using "A Statement of Values and Ethics . . . " to resolve the ethical issues of this case was akin to my experience eating Dunkin' Donuts—I feel addicted to more and yet feel unsatisfied. The current Statement presents few answers. "Reveal information accepted in confidence only to appropriate . . . recipients" [Guideline II–K–2]—but how is "appropriate" determined, and who defines it? "Seek to act impartially when involved in conflicts between parties" [Guideline II–I–2], but some value scheme always defines what is impartial. "Keep parties informed of these conflicts of interest" [Guideline II–I–1], but how then manage confidentiality?

"A Statement of Values and Ethics . . . " provides an aspirational and educational resource for professionals. What we need now are more actual cases published—on a regular and continuing basis. . . . These cases, together with a parallel commentary, can continue the development of our profession already enhanced by the Statement.

Freedom, Coercion, Responsibility, and T-Groups

Harry Goldfarb, a division sales manager with Ajax Corporation, receives an announcement from Pat Dean, the corporation's director of human resource development, about a week-long management development program. According to the announcement, the program will include exercises, lectures, T-Groups, and sensitivity training. The announcement states that the program will involve participants from different companies and will give them an opportunity to "see themselves as others see them." It states further that the program will "lead to greater self-awareness by providing participants with deeper insights into their implicit values concerning leadership and membership in an organization." The announcement comes with a covering letter signed by Fred Flick, CEO of Ajax Corp. Flick strongly urges all division managers "to take advantage of this marvelous opportunity, fully paid for by the Ajax Corporation."

Goldfarb is put off by the wording of the announcement, and the reference to sensitivity training makes him a little apprehensive. Goldfarb feels he can open up emotionally, but what he has heard about T-Groups and sensitivity training concerns him. He tells himself that if he is going to express personal feelings, he wants to be able to control the circumstances in which he does so. Goldfarb's first impulse is not to attend the program. He knows he does not like what he has heard about people being "torn apart" in T-Groups. Besides, for the past few months he has not spent enough time with his family. The covering letter signed by Flick, however, causes Goldfarb to have second thoughts. That afternoon he learns that the other four division sales managers at Ajax have already participated in the program.

The next day Goldfarb signs the card indicating that he will attend. Soon thereafter he receives more information. He learns that the program will take place the weekend after next at the Center for Holistic Development, located ten miles south of West Kishnev on a country road off Route 99, about forty-five miles from Goldfarb's apartment in the city. He also receives about one hour's worth of preprogram homework materials.

These include, for the most part, articles by prominent advocates of laboratory training that explain its principal features and underlying theory. The materials make no reference to any adverse effects that may result from participation in a T-Group. Nor do the materials cite any studies that raise questions about the effectiveness of sensitivity training. Goldfarb is put off again by much of the language in the homework materials. He finds phrases like "dynamic change process," "strategic models for human growth," and "synergistic, collaborative cultures" difficult to understand and remote from his role as division sales manager at Ajax.

The week of the seminar arrives. Goldfarb and the other participants arrive late Sunday and are told that the program will begin Monday morning. On Monday morning, the director of the center gives a short introductory lecture and then the participants are divided into T-Groups of ten members each. The trainer of Goldfarb's group, Perry Teller, gives a very brief introduction that describes the purposes of the T-Group in general terms. He says that the trainer's purpose is to "facilitate the group's process" and not to serve as its leader. He then ceases to speak.

A somewhat embarrassed silence follows. During the first hour a few group members make some halting efforts at breaking the silence, but the efforts do not go anywhere. The silence returns. Eventually several group members begin to complain about the situation. One expresses dissatisfaction that the group has not moved forward. Another says that he does not know what he is doing here. Several others complain about feelings of self-consciousness. Goldfarb does not say anything. He notes to himself that evidently the silence and lack of direction do not upset him as much as they upset some of the other group members. He does, however, find himself rather bored.

Finally, the group begins to discuss strategies for getting everyone to "unfreeze." Several proposals are presented and discussed, but the atmosphere seems charged with tension. Goldfarb finds this unsettling. Gradually, with some encouragement from Teller, the group shifts its focus to the responses of particular group members to the tense atmosphere. At first, the group members make rather detached comments about each other. After a while, the feedback becomes much more intense, and by the end of the evening session several group members have lowered some of the inhibitions that tend to keep people from talking frankly with one another about their behavior, and especially their feelings.

This is not so, however, for Goldfarb; he finds himself feeling remote from the group and uncomfortable in its presence. Something deep within him seems to have sent a message that this is not the time and place to open up. On the other hand, he senses that he is out of step with the group, but does not want to incur its disapproval, which he expects will be the result if he remains silent. He briefly contemplates going home, but it is already late, and he is exhausted.

By Tuesday afternoon, the members of the T-Group fall into a pattern of successively talking about themselves in a progressively intimate way against a background of silence and attentive listening by the other group members. Goldfarb waits for his turn with a sense of dread. Eventually the group concentrates its attention upon him. He does not want to say anything, but feels that he must in order to avoid criticism from the group. Finally he manages to talk a bit. He says some highly personal things, but struggles to retain control over what he says and how he says it. After what seems to Goldfarb an interminable period, the attention of the group shifts to someone else. The trainer compliments Goldfarb for "beginning to work through some very hard issues."

By end of the session on Friday morning, the group experiences a strong sense of emotional cohesiveness. Goldfarb does not share in it. He remains uncomfortable amid the group, and uncomfortable with himself about having spoken as he did about his emotions.

Consider the Following

Discuss this episode from the standpoints of Teller (the trainer) and Dean (the director of human resource development). Identify and discuss the professional value and ethical issues from each of their perspectives, especially regarding freedom, coercion, and responsibility.

Discussion by William Gellermann

(*Editors' Note:* Our intention in these appendix cases has been simply to reproduce them and the comments, with minimal additional comment from us, the editors. However, some editorial remarks are necessary here, because while the first commentary on this case has a particularly unfavorable orientation toward T-Groups*, the other two commentaries focus primarily on the case and therefore do not provide an alternative positive view about T-Groups. To correct that imbalance, Gellermann has prepared the following comments so readers will have a more balanced perspective for making their own judgments about the specific questions addressed by this case and about T-Groups in general. In noting this, however, it is important to stress that it is impossible to present sufficient information for making an informed judgment about T-Groups in the brief space devoted to them here.)

To put my comments in perspective, it is important to note that I have been a T-Group facilitator since early 1960 and, based on that experience, I see T-Groups as having unusually high potential for helping people learn about themselves *when they are properly used.* Most recently, I have, for nearly ten years, been a facilitator for the American Management Association's (AMA) Executive Effectiveness Course, the first week of which uses a T-Group. It is one of the AMA's most popular courses. As part of that program, I have worked with more than thirty T-Groups along with six to eight other facilitators. In total, we have conducted more than 200 such groups in nearly ten years. Among the reasons organizations have been increasingly using the program as part of their approach to management develop-

---

*Basically, a T-Group is a group that helps its members learn from their own experience in the group. "T" is for "training" because the groups associated with the original T-Groups were intended to train people in communication and other skills. Although the purpose has shifted from training to providing a social setting within which people can learn, the original name has stuck.

ment, I think, is that, in addition to its popularity, they find it helpful for managers who must work together interdependently to learn a common language and common skills. That common learning multiplies the effects of the individual benefits; thus, the organizational benefits are substantially greater than the sum of the individual benefits.

My experience suggests that T-Groups have acquired a negative reputation for some people primarily because of occurrences early in the life of such groups. The first T-Groups were literally discovered by accident. We do not need to go into the details of the discovery, but its essential element was that spontaneous interaction within a small group can yield valuable learning by participants about themselves. A primary ingredient in producing that learning is *feedback* — namely, the information given to each person about how others in the group react to him or her during their unstructured, spontaneous interaction.

During the early T-Groups, everyone, including the "trainers," struggled with the problem of how to translate the unstructured experience of the T-Group into valuable learning for the participants. In the process, people made mistakes. Feedback was seen as a primary source of learning. Many people did have the feeling of being "torn apart," as suggested in the case, when they were subjected to feedback that was given *without regard for how it was expressed* and *without sensitivity to how it was received.* And in some cases, the results were unnecessarily hurtful and even harmful. In spite of that, most people were able to distill useful learning from the feedback in a way analogous to sorting grain from chaff. Most people were able to do that sorting with results they found extraordinarily valuable. And, in time, facilitators developed the knowledge and ability necessary to avoid mistakes and facilitate the process of giving and receiving feedback constructively and effectively. (Unfortunately, not everyone who purports to be a facilitator has the necessary knowledge and ability, which raises the issue of ethics related to assessing professional competence — but that is not the primary focus of this discussion.)

For those who have not experienced T-Groups, it will help

to understand that they are essentially groups in which a facilitator works with about ten people to help them learn about themselves by reflecting on their experience with one another in the group. The fact that the facilitator does not provide structure — in the form of lectures, skill practice exercises, or other activities in which participants are told what to do — is initially a source of frustration for some people. The ways they deal with that frustration and the ways they and others deal with the "leadership vacuum" created by the facilitator's not functioning as leader provide experience for the group and its members to reflect on as a starting point for learning about themselves. Before long the group's members have enough experience with one another that they can be encouraged to give feedback by describing how they perceive one another's behavior and how they react to such behavior. The person receiving feedback is encouraged to focus on understanding it and accepting it, even though he may not agree with it. He is also encouraged to view the feedback from other people as information about the perceptions of those other people and not as factual reports about him, and, at the same time, he is encouraged to recognize that if several people see the same behavior and react in similar ways, it is likely that other people in his work situation are seeing similar behavior and reacting in similar ways. *The responsibility for deciding the value of the feedback, if any, is explicitly left with him.*

The use of feedback involves some of the primary learning in the T-Group experience, including both feedback skills (giving and receiving) and specific content learning. Skill in *giving feedback effectively* includes such things as describing specific behavior (rather than using judgmental labels), suggesting alternative behavior, and focusing on things one likes (not just things one does not like). Feedback is given effectively if the recipient is able to understand and learn from it — or feels free to ignore it. Skill in *receiving feedback effectively* includes such things as asking for it, paraphrasing what others have said as a demonstration that the receiver does understand (even if she disagrees with or does not like what is being said), checking to see if others' perceptions and reactions to her behavior are similar or different, and responding to others' feedback in ways that encourage them to continue telling her the truth of their perceptions as they see her. It also involves the receiver's being able to tell the givers of feedback that she is having difficulty understanding them or that she may be getting more than she wants or is able to use at the moment, when that is the case. (A primary role of a facilitator is to ensure that recipients are able to do that and that the group respects their wishes. In early T-Groups that role was not always well understood.)

Specific content learning involves the specific feedback that people in the T-Group are given. For example, the recipients of the following feedback may be able to learn some things about their behavior and its effects. "I like your sense of humor, but there are times when it has a hostile edge. For example, when Fred said such and such, you said so and so. That sounded hostile to me and I didn't like it." "When Sally was talking about what she wanted us to do, you ignored what she was saying and took over the conversation. That bothered me, but, at the time, I was afraid to say anything." "I was very impressed with the way you asked Al how he felt about . . . He looked as if he wanted to talk, but it was your asking him that gave him the support he needed." "I like your ideas, but you seem to ramble and take so long expressing yourself that I begin to tune out and lose track of what you are saying. If you would be more concise, it would help me understand you better."

By using a T-Group to learn how to give and receive feedback constructively and effectively, participants increase competencies that are essential to their effectiveness as managers. By using a T-Group to learn about things they do that help and hinder their effectiveness with people in their T-Group, participants also learn things that will help them behave more effectively in their relations with people back home. Among other things, people frequently report that the most valuable transfers of learning have been to their family relations with wives, husbands, and children. In fact, a frequent response to feedback has been, "My wife has been telling me that for years." Over and above such specific skills and content learnings, those participants who benefit most from the T-Group experience also gain a heightened awareness of the process of the human relations in which they are involved on a moment-to-moment basis, an awareness that alerts them to their own and other people's feelings and reactions so they can act more effectively as a result.

With this as background, we can now turn to comments about the case.

Note: The commentaries on this case were originally presented at the annual meeting of the American Psychological Association, Los Angeles, August 1985. Commentators include the late Fred R. Berger, formerly a philosopher at the University of California, Davis; Rodney L. Lowman, a psychologist and director of the Career Development Laboratory, Houston, Texas; and Joan Sieber, a psychologist at California State University, Hayward.

Comments by Fred R. Berger

The handling of the situation in the T-Group case appears to be objectionable from a number of points of view: there is coercion, both formal and informal, that operates on Goldfarb; insufficient understanding is provided of the objectives and nature of the program and the sessions in order to guarantee truly informed consent to exposure to the situation; and those conducting the sessions appear to take too little responsibility in ensuring a fruitful outcome.

My chief objections, however, do not stem primarily from the manner of operating and organizing the program. I believe that for very deep moral reasons, the program itself is objectionable. The question is not one of whether it is successful; it should not have been undertaken even if its success could be guaranteed. I believe this to be a case of the corporation seeking control over employees in a way that involves deep moral objections. Corporate activities fall within the scrutiny of moral principle; there are limits to the activities that the corporation can legitimately undertake. I contend that as a matter of corporate responsibility, judged from the moral point of view, this sort of program ought not to be pursued at all.

In making an argument, I want to stress the notion of

being an autonomous person. A number of central moral themes converge in this concept. An *autonomous person* is someone who is self-determining, whose life mode, personal characteristics, and values reflect his or her own needs, choices, and judgments. Clearly, this is a matter of degree. We are necessarily social beings, and the very conditions of acquiring the capacities of choice and judgment are socially determined. But, to the extent someone *is* his or her "own person," whose actions spring from his or her character, to that extent we think the person an individual worthy of respect as such, rather than as a mere product stamped out to a given pattern by a machine, albeit a social mechanism. Autonomous persons have a dignity that is associated with their capacities for rational choice. This notion of being an autonomous person, then, brings together the important concepts of freedom and respect for persons as such. Freedom is involved because being free is part of what it is to be autonomous, and also because it is a necessary condition for determining our own lives, exercising our own judgment, and so on. Respect for persons as such is involved because only the autonomous person has a fully developed individual character and identity that has a worth independent of its social utility. The identity belongs to that person; it is not a mere social product.

From the perspective of autonomy, not all freedoms are on a par. For the corporation to set working hours, place of employment, and working conditions — all within limits, of course — is not to interfere significantly with being one's own person or determining what sort of person one is to be. Moreover, in an appropriately structured economy, employees may very well choose to accept certain restrictions on their freedoms in order to live the sorts of lives they desire. But, to the extent the corporation seeks to make employees over into certain sorts of persons, to that extent it does interfere with autonomy.

How does the T-Group training program stack up from this perspective? Note that its stated purpose is to "lead to greater self-awareness by providing participants with deeper insights into their implicit values concerning leadership and membership in an organization." But this is extraordinarily ambiguous in a number of ways. Is it intended to be for the employee's benefit? If so, then this somewhat coercive exposure of the individual's most private thoughts — his very persona — in a somewhat public setting, is objectionable as corporate paternalism. On the other hand, if it is intended to benefit the corporation — for example, to promote greater organizational efficiency or productivity — then it is a case of using the employee's very sense of self as a mere means to corporate ends. It is one thing to use employee skills, with the employee's fully knowing consent, and compensating the employee for such use. But to meddle with one's very identity because it could conceivably promote some vague corporate objective is odious.

To see this more clearly, one might consider a particular source of human commitment and values that is an important component of many persons' sense of themselves — religion. Would not one find it objectionable in the extreme if the corporation were to sponsor religious encounter sessions, where one's deepest religious convictions, beliefs, and values would be exposed, discussed, and, perhaps, criticized, because it could lead to deeper insights into employee values that relate to leadership and membership in an organization? If done for the employee's benefit, we would surely object that this is "not the corporation's business." And, if done for corporate objectives — greater efficiency or profit — we would object that these goals must give way to the more important values of religious integrity and independence. It seems to me that the T-Group case is simply the religion case extended to cover all aspects of individual personhood. As such, the program is morally pernicious.

Comments by Rodney L. Lowman

This case presents a number of ethical problems and dilemmas that commonly arise when methods developed for use in one setting are rather mechanistically applied in another — in this case an individual change program directed to organizational consultation. It actually matters little that the example, T-Groups, now is seldom used today as an organizational development tool. The principles and the problems would be the same had the case used a more current intervention such as survey feedback, quality circles, or an intervention directed to organizational culture.

In this particular case, Goldfarb was more or less pressured into participating in this experience. He was apprehensive and, left on his own, would probably not have chosen to participate voluntarily. The trainer, presumably a psychologist, owned primary responsibility for assuring that persons voluntarily chose to participate in this experience and that they were clearly advised in lay terms about what would take place in the sessions, including the psychological risks involved. In this regard, the trainer did not adequately execute professional responsibilities. Moreover, since the research literature has generally not supported the efficacy of sensitivity training as an organizational-level intervention, the trainer's competencies are further suspect.

The conduct of the T-Group itself must also be questioned. If Goldfarb was as psychologically withdrawn from the proceedings as the case depicts, the trainer had responsibility to help him and the group understand and confront this issue. Instead, at least as represented in the case, a caricature of confrontation occurred, with little evidence of meaningful learning having taken place either by Goldfarb or by the group. Group leaders in interventions must clearly be sensitive to more than the external words expressed by the participants; gestures, tone of voice, and an absence of psychological investment and authenticity should have been clues to the group leader that this participant was not having a positive growth experience.

On the other hand, Goldfarb must himself accept at least some responsibility for his own actions. He chose to participate in the experience (if only for reasons of perceived organizational pressure). He protected himself by pretending to participate in the experience while actually withdrawing psychologically. Even a thoroughly ethical and well-experienced psychologist cannot force help or learning upon an unwilling and/or disinterested participant.

The broader issue raised by this case is the extent to which implicit pressure to participate in psychological activities is appropriate, necessary, or even avoidable. While the psychologist must do as much as possible to avoid forcing organizational members to be part of psychological activities in which they voluntarily would choose not to participate, in reality there is never any way to know the extent to which participation in such circumstances is indeed voluntary. This places upon the psychological interventionist the grave responsibility not to undertake interventions of the sort described in this case unless (1) the system is healthy and supportive enough to withstand it and (2) there is clear and convincing evidence that the method will work in the manner prescribed. The interventionist must insist that the managers in an organization undertaking psychological activities that will involve "quasi coercion" understand the nature of the press to participate and offer an authentic and nonpunitive option not to participate. The psychologist must also work to ensure that there are no negative repercussions from a decision not to participate, so that great implicit pressure to attend will not arise. The psychologist has a special obligation to ensure that the system is indeed able to tolerate the intrusion (without requiring undue pressure) before proposing it.

Comments by Joan Sieber

Goldfarb's response is not unusual under the circumstances. This case illustrates the foolhardiness of coercing participation in "personal growth" meetings. The effect, if any, may have been to foster regression. Goldfarb probably would have done better to obey his first impulse—to stay home.

The corporation has an obligation to check out the credentials and reputation of the trainers they enlist, as well as to recruit participants in a way that is respectful of their autonomy. Similarly, the trainer has an obligation to ensure that participants are recruited in a noncoercive way.

This is a difficult case to discuss definitively. It is not clear that Goldfarb's perception of the T-Group and the context of recruitment is objective. It is conceivable that the experience was a rich and rewarding one for all of the other participants and that Goldfarb's resistance to openness will begin to break down later. However, it appears that the leader was highly superficial in his handling of Goldfarb's response.

The main ethical issues here are little different from those that govern research: Is the program valid? Are participants recruited respectfully? Are they told about the program in terms they can understand? Is the privacy of each individual respected and protected? Is there a debriefing where appropriate?

A less obvious ethical issue has to do with the naive paternalism of some professionals who seek to improve the mental health of others. Personal-growth groups provide a context in which some people open up and experience insight — or at least appear to do so. What many professionals fail to understand is that people who appear to need this experience are sometimes the ones who cannot handle it. If Goldfarb did not want to go, it was not a practical idea — let alone ethical practice — to railroad him into it.

Comments by William Gellermann

First, Dean, the HRD director, has a primary responsibility for assessing the competence of the program's sponsor and its facilitators. That is a matter of competence and ethics since, as the Statement (these references are to the Annotated Statement in Chapters Four and Five) indicates, the profession's ethics include a commitment to competence (Guideline II).

Second, assuming that Dean considers himself a member of the OD-HSD profession — that is, he takes a systems approach to his work, and meets the other conditions identified in the Annotated Statement in the notes following the Preamble — he values "freedom, responsibility, and self-control," "human potential and empowerment," and "respect, dignity, and integrity," among other things. These values would make him proceed very carefully when acting in ways that might be perceived as coercive by people like Goldfarb. Ideally, Goldfarb would have been given better information, a longer period of time to digest it, and a clear understanding that he was free to decide whether he was willing to participate. In other words, Dean and Ajax would have made the "opportunity" available in such a way that Goldfarb would truly feel free to say no.

However, it is also important to recognize that Goldfarb is a division sales manager and, therefore, is responsible for interacting with many people, including customers, a number of subordinate managers and the people who report to them, and his fellow managers. All these relations involve interdependence, and Dean and Ajax senior management are responsible for ensuring that Goldfarb relates to those people in ways that both respect and value them as human beings and, simultaneously, serve the purposes of the corporation. A T-Group experience can help Goldfarb increase his effectiveness in doing both those things *if he is willing to use the experience in that way.*

Although T-Group participation should be voluntary, organizations do "send" people in much the same way Goldfarb was sent. A competent facilitator can respect such people's freedom and dignity and see that their experience does them no harm (assuming they are not suffering significant emotional problems). Goldfarb, for example, seems to have endured his T-Group with neither pain nor harm. Often, after initial reluctance, such people learn to trust the group, the facilitator, and themselves enough to freely change their minds, become active participants, and derive great personal benefit.

This still leaves us with the difficult ethical question of whether a corporation, or an HRD director acting on its behalf, can require a manager to attend a T-Group–based management development program. The Annotated Statement offers some guidance. Guideline III–B–1 says to "inform people with whom we work about any activity or procedure in which we ask their participation" and item b adds that we should "inform them in a way that supports their free choice about their participation in activities initiated by us; also acknowledge that it may be appropriate for us to undertake activities initiated by recognized authorities in which participants do not have full freedom of choice." The notes under that guideline develop that idea further by saying: "For example, it may be appropriate to require managers with low interpersonal competence to participate in activities that will help them develop that competence. If they are unwilling, their freedom could still be respected by allowing them to choose a job that does not require such competence."

Clearly situations involving low interpersonal competence

present ethical dilemmas for OD-HSD professionals. On the one hand, such professionals value freedom and self-control and, on the other hand, they acknowledge the organization's responsibility for the well-being of all the people who work for it, including those who work for and with its managers. The organization does have a right to terminate people who are not competent to meet the requirements of their jobs, although OD-HSD's human values encourage looking for alternatives to termination. Preferably such people are helped to develop the necessary competence in ways that respect their freedom and integrity, but their freedom does not include the right to a job that requires competence they do not have and are unwilling to develop.

A case can be made that an OD-HSD professional, such as Dean, has moral justification for violating the moral rule "do not deprive of freedom" in a situation that requires the use of organizational power to protect other people from harm. However, we should note that the facts of Goldfarb's case do not clearly indicate that his situation requires such protection.

Finally, with regard to Teller, the T-Group facilitator, I would say that he has a primary responsibility for helping Goldfarb make a choice. Goldfarb's options include leaving the T-Group, even though the pressure he feels may make it seem as if he has no choice. Teller can help him acknowledge that, although he may choose not to risk losing his job by leaving the group, that *is* his choice. In view of the pressure, Goldfarb may decide to stay and see what happens. If he stays, Teller is responsible for encouraging him to take as much advantage of the opportunity as he is able based on his free choice, and, simultaneously, helping him and the group deal with any limits Goldfarb chooses to place on his participation. As I noted earlier, he may change his mind and become an active participant. In addition, I believe that Teller is responsible for encouraging the organizations that use his services to do so in a way that both informs prospective participants about the nature of those programs and makes it clear that the choice to participate is voluntary, although, when his services are offered through another organization, as in the case's Center for Holistic Development, it may be difficult to fulfill that responsibility. In any case, as

I've said, I think that facilitators can work effectively with groups in which some people have come reluctantly, but those facilitators have an ethical obligation to respect the freedom and integrity of such people.

Responsibility for What? And When?

1. Joe Brown, a professor in the management department at Metro State University, specializes in OD. He came to Metro State twelve years ago upon receiving his Ph.D. Brown teaches a heavy load of courses and does most of the student advising in the evening M.B.A. program. Nonetheless, he has succeeded, though not without difficulty at times, in establishing a productive record for himself in research. For the past seven years, Brown has worked intensively on a general theory of organizational change. He considers his theory, as developed in several recent publications, his most mature scholarly effort, and believes it has significant practical applications, which he strongly wants to explore. Unfortunately, despite repeated efforts, Brown has not succeeded in getting foundation support for a project in which he would carry out an actual OD intervention based upon his theory.

2. Brown receives a phone call one day in early March from the superintendent of a small suburban school district. The superintendent says that he "was really impressed" by a presentation Brown made at a weekend program for administrators last year, and thinks Brown could help his school district. According to the superintendent, inadequate communication between teachers and administrators has blocked effective problem solving both at individual schools and on a systemwide basis. A sense of inertia, he says, seems to pervade the district. Flattered and much pleased by the prospect of an opportunity to have his ideas put into practice, Brown makes an appointment to meet with the superintendent the next day.

3. At the meeting Brown lays out an approach he has developed for OD applications of his theory. Brown has no previous experience with school systems, but, according to his theory, the approach should work in virtually any organization.

It calls for distribution of survey questionnaires to all teachers in the district. When the questionnaires are completed, groups of teachers, headed by group leaders who the teachers select beforehand from among their ranks, analyze the survey data. Then they go to work in solving problems that the survey data analyses identify. The group leaders receive training prior to the distribution of the questionnaire in how to interpret survey data and guide small-group problem-solving efforts. To ensure communication between teacher groups and the school administration, the approach calls for the group leaders in a school to meet periodically with the principal. The approach also provides for a council consisting of administrators and faculty to confer on a regular basis. Brown describes his approach and its underlying theory with inspired eloquence and conviction. The superintendent responds enthusiastically.

4. Shortly after his first meeting with Brown, the superintendent arranges a meeting to include his "cabinet," which consists of two assistant superintendents. At the meeting Brown and the superintendent do almost all the talking. One assistant superintendent, however, raises a question about whether the climate in the district is right for Brown's approach. Before the meeting adjourns, the superintendent suggests that Brown and the cabinet do a little work to "sell the program."

5. For the next two months, Brown meets with many different groups. In a number of instances it is unclear to him why he is asked to confer with a particular group. Brown has assumed all along that the superintendent has authority to hire him as a consultant, but now he begins to have doubts, and asks for clarification about the matter. The superintendent assures Brown that he has the proper authority, but nonetheless wants "to touch all the bases." He asks Brown to attend one more meeting with a "representative group of faculty." At this meeting the faculty seem antagonistic to the superintendent. Several accuse him of initiating similar efforts in the past and not following through with enough support. One teacher asks whether the teacher groups will meet during released time. Afterward the superintendent says to Brown "It may take a while for the faculty to come around but I'm sure they will. The teachers,"

he says, "will go along." The next week Brown signs a contract with the school district for his services as a consultant.

6. Brown works out a schedule for implementing the program. He plans to distribute the questionnaire the first week of school. One week earlier the group leaders will begin a week of intensive training. A week before that, the principals will meet for a three-day session to introduce them to the program. Brown devotes the first part of the summer to preparing the survey questionnaire and the materials for training sessions. One day in mid July the superintendent calls and drops a bombshell. He tells Brown that ten days earlier he tendered his resignation from the school district. He also says that the school board has begun the search for a replacement and undoubtedly will find someone before school begins in the fall.

7. Two weeks before the start of the fall semester, the school board selects for the top job one of the two assistant superintendents — the one who doubted whether the district has the right climate for Brown's program. When Brown meets with him, the new superintendent asks him whether, in view of "organizational problems stemming from the transition from one administration to another," the length of the training session might be reduced. He proposes two days for the group leaders and one afternoon for the principals. Brown senses that he is not in a position to argue with the new superintendent. He tells himself that he will just have to do the best job he can.

8. Brown trains the group leaders intensively for two days. They readily absorb the necessary background for interpreting survey data, but at the end of the training period none of them has really picked up the group process skills. Several express anxiety about whether they will function effectively in their teaching groups. Five of the seven principals in the district attend the principals' introductory session. One is highly supportive, but the other four have grave reservations about the program. They appear to have no confidence in the ability of teacher groups to make constructive proposals about how to deal with problems in their schools. One principal seems hostile to Brown personally.

9. During the fall semester, the teachers complete the survey questionnaire and discuss the survey data in their groups.

All of the groups, however, experience difficulty in moving beyond the discussions to solve problems. Several groups stop
meeting altogether by the end of the fall term. Others continue
into the spring term and come up with a few suggestions about
relatively minor problems. These groups fizzle out, however,
at the end of the school year. Two group leaders complain to
Brown that their principals have never met with them. The program is discontinued the following academic year.

    10. In retrospect, Brown realizes that for many reasons
the school district was not a good place to implement an OD
program based upon his theory. A year later he writes up a case
study about his experience that is published in a leading journal. In the article, Brown identifies, with the aid of hindsight,
a number of factors that made the school district an inhospita-
ble environment for his intervention efforts.

Questions to Consider

1. What would you have done in Brown's position at each of
    the following points in the consultation/intervention process?
    - At the first meeting with the superintendent (end of
      paragraph 3)
    - After the first meeting with the cabinet (end of para-
      graph 4)
    - At the point of signing the contract with the superin-
      tendent (end of paragraph 5)
    - When the superintendent resigns (end of paragraph 6)
    - When Brown meets with the new superintendent (end
      of paragraph 7)
    - After the principals' introductory session (end of para-
      graph 8)
    - After the program is discontinued (end of paragraph 9)
2. Do you think it was morally incumbent upon Brown to ter-
    minate the consulting relationship at any point earlier than
    the discontinuation of the program? If so, when and why?

Note: The three commentaries on this case were originally
presented at the 12th annual Organizational Behavior Teaching Conference, Charlottesville, Va., June 1985. Kenneth D.

Alpern is a philosopher at DePaul University; Allan R. Cohen is professor of management at Babson College; and Peter B. Vaill is professor of human systems at George Washington University.

Comments by Kenneth D. Alpern

When to Terminate. We are asked to judge what Brown should have done at certain critical points in the case and whether he should have terminated his program earlier. To a large extent, these are questions to be answered with professional judgment and require detailed information, including not only what might be termed the "objective facts," but also the subtleties of tone and nuance. The proper question is this: At what point would sound professional judgment have determined that there were insufficient grounds to think that the program would provide the client (the superintendent) what it was represented as providing? If the client presses for continuation of the program against best professional judgment, it seems to me that one may stretch one's best professional judgment a bit—but only to a point. One has contracted to use one's expertise, not to pursue whatever unreachable end the client refuses to abandon.

It is clear that much has gone wrong at all stages of the case at hand. However, in reviewing any case, we need to remind ourselves that knowledge of the outcome (twenty-twenty hindsight) and the selectivity and emphasis unavoidable in presenting case studies create patterns of saliency that are much less evident in the thick of things.

Forcing the Program. I do think that one bit of conceptual clarification may help. The superintendent seemed to be railroading the program through. What precisely is the significance of this fact in terms of the propriety of Brown's choosing to press on with the program?

I do not think that the mere fact that the superintendent used his position to push along the program against objection and apathy is in itself a good reason to call into question the propriety of the program. Within reasonable limits, which seem here to be respected, the superintendent should be recognized as the person duly given authority to lead and make decisions for the school district. The main worry, as I see it, is not the fact that the superintendent is forcing the program on others, but rather, of what the resort to such force may be a symptom. The success of Brown's program depended on the interest and cooperation of the others involved: assistant superintendents, principals, and teachers. The fact that the superintendent resorted to force suggests that the needed cooperation might have been lacking. Again, some room must be allowed for the superintendent to exercise his leadership and "bring those others around," but to the extent that there is reason to think that cooperation will not be forthcoming, the propriety of continuing the program must be questioned.

Experimentation. Finally, a brief comment on the issue of experimentation. We may all agree that it would be valuable to know more about the conditions affecting the success or failure of such programs. And we may imagine that Brown's pushing on with his program could contribute to such knowledge. But we must recognize that these facts do not justify continuing with a doomed program, because (1) the client did not contract and pay for an experiment on conditions of success and failure and (2) such a study is not what the others involved have consented — however unenthusiastically — to participate in. There is no justification in this case to misrepresent the project to the participants. A project conducted in good faith that nonetheless fails may certainly be reported. Indeed, even where a project is purposely misrepresented, the negative findings, if valuable, should be reported; in such a case though, publishers and any academic institutions or funding agencies supporting the work should be informed of the fact of misrepresentation.

Comments by Allan R. Cohen

The case of Brown and his failed OD intervention demonstrates great incompetence by a consultant. Brown is so inept that I found the case painful to read. Like the proverbial child with a hammer, to whom everything looks like a nail, he is so desperate to try his theory that he pounds it at a situation requiring delicacy and caution. He lurches ahead despite many signals that he should back off and do some more learning before inflicting harm on his clients (and maybe himself). Perhaps Ph.D.'s should be forced to swear to the oath of "real" doctors, that the first principle for the doctor is at least to do no harm to patients!

Brown makes so many mistakes that it is probably sufficient to mention only a few:

1. He is so excited by the superintendent's call that he fails to ask about the nature of the "communication problem," who thinks there is a problem, what the causes might be, what has been done in the past on related issues, and what current relationships are among the various parties — including the superintendent, his staff, principals, teachers, and so on.
2. In spite of this woeful lack of fundamental knowledge about the situation, he proposes a "solution" that on the face of it does not even match the stated problem: teacher-led discussions of teacher survey data do not necessarily address "communication gaps" with principals.
3. When he encounters resistance and new data, he plunges ahead with no alteration in plans, except to reduce contact time with key players whose support is crucial.
4. He provides no support for the inappropriate process he has initiated, despite ample evidence that it is sorely needed.
5. He has no understanding of the school system as a political system, and blunders through the vested interests and rivalries.

The list could go on for quite some time; further elaboration would only add to my anguish. Not only does Brown miss the broad side of the barn, but he never notices that there is a barn in his path. Then, in a wonderful academic denouement, he writes an article on the school system's lack of readiness! Once again, he has missed by a mile. In my opinion, it is reasonable (maybe even obligatory) to try to capture knowledge from failure experiences, but blaming the dead patient for dying when struck by the surgeon's flailing hammer is hardly fair, and surely not very good science.

Is it unethical, however? I suppose that a surgeon who knowingly attempts a new operation without training and in a room without lights is pressing the boundaries of morality, although it is not hard to imagine situations, such as a battle zone, where such behavior would be heroic. Furthermore, no one springs full-blown into competence; it does take practice and a certain amount of risk to improve a professional's skills. Brown tries to learn from his experience, albeit ineptly, and he does not appear to misrepresent his lack of practical experience when he first meets with the superintendent. At the least we can demand full disclosure from any consultant proposing work, although when one is self-confident and a reasonably good improviser, it is tempting to omit information that is not directly inquired about by a prospective client.

In sum, I believe the case demonstrates just how readily poor or insufficient theory, experience, and consulting skill can lead to client failure; but in the OD world there is never sufficient supply of these precious commodities. Since I believe that consultant stretching is necessary and inevitable and that no one among us always anticipates all the complexities of client situations, I am reluctant to conclude that ineptness is unethical even when it is monumental. I confess, however, that behavior in this case makes me squirm with discomfort because it pushes against some nebulous boundary I realize I have. Nevertheless, it is competence that is needed, not greater ethical training or rules.

Ultimately, of course, this point of view requires that I spell out just what I believe competence in OD practice to be. As I've expressed in the above remarks, such competence includes:

1. Understanding of the power in organizations
2. Ability to diagnose stakeholders and help balance their interests

3. Knowledge of organizational structures and designs and their consequences
4. Understanding of the relationship between organizational processes and goals
5. Ability to educate clients about organizational option and consequences of alternative actions
6. Willingness to make difficult issues explicit and discussable, and to warn clients of impending diasters
7. Willingness to acknowledge personal limitations in terms of knowledge or skills
8. Avoidance of imposing theory on situations in which it does not fit
9. Understanding of the complexities of establishing who is the client
10. Willingness to alter course when mistakes have been made or disconfirming data are received
11. Care enough for clients' welfare that contracts having no chance of success are avoided and, when undertaken, are supplemented by personal time, if necessary

This is by no means a complete list, but it is one that any OD consultant should contemplate before leaping in to save the organizational world. Perhaps those of us who teach OD practitioners would be well advised to be certain that we appreciate the need for such competencies, and can impart them. Otherwise we must question the ethics of sending unprepared — and therefore dangerous — practitioners into a complex, needy world.

Comments by Peter B. Vaill

As with the case of Jones in "A Work System Design Contract," the ethics of Brown's position in the present case are intertwined with the quality of professional judgment he has exercised. He has tried to proceed with a design for a change process that is obviously dependent on the acceptance and support of participants in the face of consistent and insistent questioning of process by those very participants. Furthermore, he has made the assumption that because the superintendent is the *formal* leader of the system, his *informal* influence and prestige are strong enough to cope with doubts and fears felt by the teachers. It is a commonplace in the OD fields — or one would have thought so — never to assume that formal authority automatically includes informal influence and prestige. The fact that the superintendent wants the change only gets you in the door to begin talking with others, *and nothing more.*

Brown does not see that the installation of his elaborate framework for conducting a change process is itself a change process — one that is at least as complex and fragile as any changes that will flow from the use of his framework. That he does not recognize this is astonishing, and that he is later unaware of his increasingly questionable ethical position is of a piece with his basic misunderstanding of what he is doing as a change agent.

At some deep level, Brown is confused about means and ends. I draw this conclusion from his inability to pay attention to all the signals he gets — beginning with the initial phone call from the superintendent — that this system will not be an easy one in which to initiate change, especially change that is highly rational and theory-based, as is Brown's approach. It is an intensely political setting with many power centers and many separate, loosely coupled agendas being worked, which means that a great deal of action is being initiated at various points with little coordination and a high level of suspicion and negative fantasy. Apparently Brown is unaware that sound professional practice would suggest that one take such features seriously when considering what sort of change process to initiate.

For Brown, however, the question is not what sort of change process to initiate, for he has a favorite theory and is eager to install it somewhere. The end of installing his favorite theory drives out his sensitivity to the data from this system about what is needed. One suspects that he still does not see this in his case write-up. I feel fairly sure that Brown's write-up still makes the assumption that there are some systems somewhere that are perfect for applications of his theory. Brown does not understand that change is only a matter of minimal "front-end loading," and is much more a matter of working with energy of the form and kind that one finds already in the system.

Being confused about means and ends, Brown is therefore insensitive to ethical issues along the way. He implicitly accepts an ethic of power and authority: "What the superintendent wants and what I want conjoin, and since the superintendent can authorize me to proceed, I will align myself with him and go ahead." Having once made that ethical commitment, which of course he does not perceive as an ethical commitment, he is then unable to take seriously the alternative constructions of the situation and its needs as suggested by other parties in the situation. Their doubts and questions become tactical issues to be coped with rather than concerns grounded in other ethical priorities than those held by the superintendent. In short, having once aligned himself with the superintendent's ethics, he cannot take seriously the ethical norms and beliefs held by others in the situation. The problem is compounded by the fact that Brown is not even thinking in ethical terms. He does not see his alignment with the superintendent as a value judgment on his part. He does not see the questions and doubts held by others as ethical matters—that is, as others' ideas about how things should be and what should be done in the situation. Brown does not experience organizational change processes in ethical terms. He is doing social engineering and probably thinks it is science-based and, therefore, value-free.

In light of all this, any consideration of what Brown needs as a consultant and change agent ought to begin at a fairly basic level. He does not see organizational change as the interaction of ethical systems in terms of both what is desirable (ends) and what constitutes appropriate conduct (means). Of course, the reason he does not see organizational change in these terms is because it has rarely if ever been conceived of in these terms by the OD profession. It is certainly not taught in these terms. Matters of morals and ethics, if they are discussed at all, are discussed as limits and constraints to the change project—a fence of propriety surrounding action in the world, as it were, with the implication that as long as one stays inside the fence, one can pretty much do what one pleases. In the extreme case, the fence is defined only by official law.

This is a bankrupt view of morals and ethics, of course,

even though it is the dominant one in American society and in the OD profession in particular. What makes it bankrupt is its treatment of the human being—whether the one taking action or the one on whom it is taken—as primarily something other than a moral agent. In the business world, we would say that the manager is primarily a goal seeker and a problem solver. Secondarily, we may grant that such a manager must operate "within the bounds" of ethics, the law, and so on.

To suggest that people are something other than moral agents is the first mistake, and the rest of the tragedy in cases like Brown's follows inexorably. We are moral agents in the first instance. We experience ourselves as moral agents in that we do what we think we ought to do. We cannot prove that we ought to do what we do, yet we do what we think we ought to do. At bottom, our position rests on a belief in a moral order that grounds the action we are taking in the here and now.

We are moral agents also because we are experienced as such by others. Others note our actions and draw conclusions (make judgments) about whether we ought or ought not to be doing what we are doing. They act as moral agents in deciding whether we are exhibiting correct awareness of our responsibilities.

There is mutual perception of each other as moral agents, and yet when we assert that Brown is a moral agent in the first instance because he sees himself that way and because he is seen by others that way, we get an argument! No, we are told, Brown is a facilitator of change. Brown is a problem solver. Brown is an applied behavioral scientist. Brown is a . . . whatever. Anything but a moral agent.

Until we can reconceive such roles as Brown's, the superintendent's, and those of all the other case characters as roles played by moral agents, we will not know what we are talking about. Questions of ethics will be discussed as matters of limits and constraints and will constantly take a back seat to the instrumental concerns of those in the situation.

What this reconception of action roles into moral-ethical terms will involve, and what we will gain as we begin to make progress, are far too complex for this brief essay. But, surely, it is a process that must begin soon.

To Terminate or Continue?

Two OD consultants, Judy Chambers and Ryan Adams, are approached by Stan Winfield, the head of a public welfare agency, who is dissatisfied with his agency's performance. Winfield wants to explore ways to increase the work output of agency caseworkers while improving coordination between them and those responsible for evaluating their reports and deciding on eligibility for aid. The process is cumbersome and results in too many errors.

Chambers and Adams agree to investigate the problems Winfield describes and, on the basis of their findings, propose a plan of action. They examine existing procedures for preparing, filing, and evaluating case reports, and interview several caseworkers and case evaluators. All the caseworkers complain of being overworked and of having insufficient time to conduct thorough interviews. They blame this in large part on pressures from above to complete a certain number of case reports per week. The case evaluators express disappointment with inadequately detailed case reports, which complicate their task of judging eligibility. They also criticize the reports for the frequent appearance of evaluative comments from caseworkers, making it difficult for them to distinguish between the facts of the case and the caseworkers' perceptions and biases. The evaluators believe that the caseworkers have little understanding about how to prepare a useful case report.

After three months on the job, Chambers and Adams complete their diagnosis. They present their findings to Winfield and his top aides and propose a strategy designed to increase the efficiency of caseworkers, improve the quality of their reports, and reduce errors in determining eligibility. The intervention calls for a joint team of top agency officials, evaluators, and caseworkers to draw up a set of guidelines for conducting case interviews and writing reports. A draft of the guidelines will be circulated for comment among caseworkers before a final version is put into effect. In addition, Winfield will request additional funds to hire more caseworkers.

Winfield agrees to the proposal and requests that Chambers and Adams present their recommendations to a joint meeting of caseworkers and evaluators. The meeting produces general support for the proposal. Caseworkers are delighted with the prospects of having their ranks increased in order to lessen their individual work loads. They are equally pleased with the opportunity to provide input into the development of new interview and report guidelines. The case evaluators gladly accept responsibility for developing the new guidelines, which they believe will give more authority to their decisions regarding eligibility and enhance their influence within the agency. Top agency officials approve of the proposed guidelines, believing that they will help reduce errors and establish more objective standards for evaluating the performance of agency personnel. Moreover, the request for additional caseworkers presents little risk to them, yet promises substantial benefits if approved by the department. Chambers and Adams agree to return two months later to review progress.

When Chambers and Adams return, the process of drafting the guidelines is well under way, with a second draft in circulation. The request to hire several new caseworkers is somewhere in the departmental hierarchy, although a decision on the matter may take a few months. While top agency officials and most caseworkers and evaluators express satisfaction with the way the strategy is proceeding, others voice their disappointment to Chambers and Adams in private conversations. Some caseworkers and evaluators find the process too slow, a particular concern for caseworkers whose case loads remained heavy. Moreover, caseworkers feel betrayed by the guidelines development process, which they believe has not adequately taken into account their critique of the initial draft. Case evaluators are upset because they perceive top management taking over the drafting process even though the evaluators have the most appropriate experience and expertise for the task.

Chambers and Adams describe these concerns to Winfield in a private meeting. He expresses surprise at the accusation that top management is "taking over" the drafting process. Winfield assures them that this is not the case, although it is important to ensure that the final guidelines are consistent with

agency policy and the law, and that this is ultimately his responsibility within the agency. Winfield voices the opinion that the
drafting process is proceeding as quickly as can be expected,
although he, too, wishes that it could move more rapidly. But
the guidelines deal with sensitive matters that deserve everyone's careful attention. He deflects criticism by caseworkers that
their critique of the initial draft guidelines is not reflected in
the subsequent draft by observing that, although the drafting
process is an open one and all relevant parties are invited to
comment, some suggestions inevitably carry more weight than
others. Those critical of the process, Winfield notes, may simply be experiencing a natural disappointment in not having their
ideas accepted. After all, Winfield observes, the dissatisfaction
communicated to Chambers and Adams is expressed by relatively few persons. Most of those involved are prepared to continue with the intervention strategy.

Chambers and Adams are now faced with the decision
of how much more of a commitment they should make to the
ongoing process. Chambers has invested a considerable amount
of time in this project, which diverted her from taking on other
financially rewarding contracts. She is in favor of continuing
to observe, prompt, and exert influence on the process. She believes that since the intervention has not been fully implemented,
they have an obligation to continue to assist the parties toward
that end. She tells Adams that "many of those involved have
had their expectations raised by the strategy," and it is, in her
judgment, the consultants' "responsibility to see it through."
Adams, however, is not so sure. He is of the opinion that there
is little more they can or should do. The agency has requested
more caseworkers, but a final decision on funding is beyond the
consultants' control. The process of drafting new guidelines is
well under way, and any dispute over their content is a matter
to be resolved by those at the agency directly involved, not by
outside consultants untrained in the intricacies of public aid.
Moreover, he believes that to continue their consultation will
create false expectations about what changes they can actually
bring about, thereby creating a dependency on their expertise
that is not warranted.

Chambers counters that there is no reason to believe that the caseworkers or evaluators are sufficiently empowered to ensure that the agreed-upon intervention, when in place, will reflect their original expectations, and they are rightfully dependent on the consultants' assistance. To exit now would heighten their frustrations and perhaps cause the intervention to fail. But Adams is not persuaded by Chambers' position. "There are some things beyond our control," he argues. "We made a sound proposal that was accepted by all parties, and efforts to implement it are continuing." He points out that Winfield, the one with whom they made the original agreement to conduct the intervention, is satisfied with their work and prepared to have the agency carry it to its conclusion. Adams contends that "we can return if needed, but we should be helping them develop their own competence for handling similar problems in the future. We can't watch over them forever. There are other priorities and it's time to move on."

Questions to Consider

1. Placing yourself in the position of Chambers and Adams, what reasons would you give for either continuing or terminating the consulting relationship? What factors should OD consultants take into account when faced with the decision to continue or terminate a consulting arrangement?

2. For Chambers, terminating at this time risks frustrating some of the agency personnel and threatens to undermine the intervention strategy. For Adams, continuing risks creating false expectations about and greater dependency on the consultants and, therefore, is a more unacceptable prospect. He believes that the participants in the process must assume ultimate responsibility for making the strategy work. From an ethical perspective, how would you assess these two positions?

3. Any intervention is likely to raise expectations, some of which may not be fulfilled. What should OD consultants do, or not do, to avoid raising inflated expectations? How can those responsibilities be effectively discharged, either before or after the intervention?

Note: The commentaries by Jeanne Cherbeneau, Martin
Lonergan, Newton Margulies, Robert Tannenbaum, and Dorothy M. Tucker are based on presentations at the OD Network
Conference, San Francisco, October 1985. Cherbeneau is presi-
dent of Cherbeneau and Associates, Berkeley, California; Loner-
gan is a philosopher at the College of Professional Studies,
University of San Francisco; Margulies is professor of manage-
ment and former dean in the Graduate School of Management,
University of California, Irvine; Tannenbaum is professor emer-
itus of the development of human systems in the Anderson
Graduate School of Management, University of California, Los
Angeles; Tucker is a psychologist and external consultant.

Comments by Jeanne Cherbeneau

This case brings to the surface several issues of professional judgment and competence, as well as values and ethics.
Based on the information given, I would not want to conclude
that either Adams or Chambers is "rationalizing" a particular
position on the question of the timing and process of termination for primarily self-serving purposes, but this well may be
what they are doing. For example, the case does hint that Adams
may want to terminate because he has other pressing contracts.
It is possible that his eagerness to move on is influenced by the
apparent greater personal "payoff" of those "other priorities" and
may be biasing his assessment of the state of the contract. If
so, then acting on that desire to end the contract for purely self-
serving reasons would be professionally unethical. Implicit in
this is a possible conflict of interest between personal values associated with one's own survival/security/quality of life and
professional values associated with service/excellence/empower-
ment, among others. As in this case, the issue is often subtle
and it is understandable that a practitioner might want to rationalize away his professional responsibilities. Among other reasons, that is why Guideline I–E in "A Statement of Values . . . "
(April 1985) — namely, "Recognize my own personal needs and
desires and deal with them responsibly in the performance of
my professional roles" — is so important.

The case also hints that Chambers may be biased in favor of continuing because she "has invested a considerable amount of time in this project, which diverted her from taking on other financially rewarding contracts." That fact, however, could be an equally compelling reason for her to end the contract so that she might assume new, perhaps more lucrative, contracts. I would leave the issue of conscious or unconscious self-serving biases as an open question both consultants would be well advised to examine.

Additionally, in mentioning the considerable amount of time Chambers has invested, the implication is that it was more time than Adams committed. This could support an argument that she may have more or better information than Adams on which to base judgments about clients' needs and the appropriate timing of contract termination. On the other hand, it could be that she had become too close to and too invested in the client system, resulting in a diminished capacity to step back and be objective about what is "best" for the client. This possibility again calls for conscious self-examination, as reflected in Guidelines I–A, I–D, and I–E of the Statement regarding one's responsibility for self-knowledge and responsible practice, particularly with regard to termination issues.

My priority in examining this case is to identify the professional issues and questions involved and the options for addressing them. Those issues/questions address how to determine (1) realistic and mutual expectations, (2) mutual indicators of success, and (3) an appropriate termination process. All of these issues/questions, of course, are *front-end* contracting issues, defining realistic goals and objectives, problems, the task(s) at hand, client and consultant roles and philosophy, conditions for and indicators of success (primary and secondary) and process throughout, including the criteria for and process of termination. These agreements also should be reviewed with the client and all others involved periodically throughout the contract and modified as deemed mutually appropriate or necessary. Feedback should be sought throughout as well.

The concerns I have about the situation in this case are the following:

1. Neither the basis for termination nor a termination process appear to have been discussed at the front-end.
2. Indicators of success do not appear to have been agreed upon, or at least they were not clear enough to be indisputable when they were achieved. It is not clear at this point whether the agreed-upon goals have been achieved.
3. The consultants' philosophies and values regarding client empowerment—that is, dependency avoidance, ownership, and responsibility—do not appear to have been discussed at an early stage.
4. The client seems to have been left out of the discussion among the consultants regarding whether the intervention had reached a sufficient point of success and stability in achieving its goals or if Winfield and the others involved were sufficiently equipped to carry on effectively without further consultation. If not, what needed to be done to empower him and the others and to assure, to whatever degree possible, the achievement of the goals of the contract? Clearly, he and the others should have been involved in this discussion and included in the decision making with regard to determining (a) what still needed to be done, if anything, (b) the consultant roles and involvement, if any, and (c) when and how the consultants should have exited.

I would recommend that this whole discussion be opened up, first with Winfield and then with the caseworkers and evaluators. The process should include discussion about both current dissatisfaction with the process and results of the guidelines development (including the trust issues that have developed among the caseworkers, case evaluators, and management) and the importance and meaning of client empowerment, ownership, autonomy, responsibility, and trust. Problem solving and action planning need to take place, at which time the roles and need—or lack thereof—for the consultants should be addressed. The perspectives of management, the caseworkers, and case evaluators should be taken into account equally, and if it is anticipated or evident that any set of interests or group is going to be left "disempowered" by the consultants' departure, the expectations and concerns of that group need to be incorporated into any termination decision.

My judgment is that her contract is at the midpoint, not the end, and that the client system is not sufficiently empowered to indicate a reasonable level of assurance that it will carry on successfully. Adams himself acknowledges this when he says, "We should be helping them develop their own competence for handling similar problems in the future." If (1) the client system wants the consultants to continue, (2) all members of the system share the desire for empowerment and success of the overall effort, and (3) they can agree on and commit themselves to the necessary steps for success and empowerment and a basis for determining completion of the existing contract and the exit process of the consultants, then the consultants should stay and fulfill those agreements. Given these conditions, I believe it would become an ethical issue of premature termination—in fact, abandonment of the client—should the consultants decline to follow through with the contract.

Comments by Martin Lonergan

Many who read this case may be tempted to dismiss it as a case that involves no ethical issues. After all, the consultants, Chambers and Adams, have done a good job, and the welfare agency personnel accepted their proposal and are now doing their best to implement it. What else need be said? Why should not Chambers and Adams move on to something more interesting and perhaps more lucrative?

The merit of this case is that, in spite of its initial appearance, it is loaded with subtle ethical issues. Some citations from the Statement throw light on why this is true. The quotes are from Part II, Responsibilities to Clients and Significant Others.

Item A: Serve the . . . development of the client system and all its stakeholders.

Item B: Discuss candidly and fully goals, costs, risks, limitations, and anticipated outcomes of any program or other professional relationship under consideration.

Item H: Cease work with a client when it is clear that the
client is not benefiting or the contract has been
completed.

Item L-1:   Ensure a clear understanding of and mutual agreement on the services to be performed; do not shift
from that agreement without both a clearly defined
professional rationale for making the shift and the
informed consent of the clients/participants; withdraw from the agreement if circumstances beyond
my control prevent proper fulfillment.

These generalizations about how an OD consultant should behave in relationship to clients reflect an ethical perspective that
applies to the present case.

Kant's Categorical Imperative. The generalizations represent applications of ethical principles developed by Immanuel
Kant, one of the principal contributors to the development of
modern ethical theory. Kant's principles give us a way to argue
effectively for a resolution of ethical dilemmas. The principle
he left us is called the *categorical imperative.*

Why an imperative? Kant says that we need an imperative because we cannot rely on our feelings or our wants to determine what should be done. We need a command to follow,
no matter what our inclinations. That is the imperative. He contends, in other words, that no one can simply trust his judgment sufficiently to say, "I want to do this or that" and then be
sure that he is right in an ethical sense. If we were totally integrated and had what Kant calls a "good will," we would need
no such imperative. In Kant's (1949, p. 31) words: "A perfectly
good will would . . . be equally subject to objective laws ([namely],
laws of good), but could not be conceived as *obliged* thereby to
act lawfully . . . Therefore no imperatives hold for the Divine
will . . . *ought* is here out of place because the violation is already
of itself necessarily in unison with the law. Therefore imperatives are only formula to express the relation of objective laws
of all volition to the subjective imperfection of the will of this
or that rational being, for example, the human will."

Paton (1967, p. 135), in his famous commentary on the ethics of Kant, says in this connection, "No rational agent is entitled to make arbitrary exceptions to moral law in favor of himself . . . It cannot be determined merely by my desires."

Bierman (1980) of San Francisco State University explains: "Kant thinks of us as living in two worlds — the sensible, visible, palpable world and the intelligible, invisible, supersensible world. Humans, as residents of the intelligible world, look upon the sensible world, of which they are also residents, and find that the sensible world is not as good as it could be (p. 247). Because we are sensible and supersensible beings, we can have two kinds of feelings simultaneously (pathological and moral feelings). By "pathological" feeling Kant doesn't mean something diseased; he means the natural feeling aroused by the wants and desires of our sensible self. For example, suppose I am in desperate need of money. The thought of borrowing inclines me to promise to repay someone who can lend me money, even though I know I won't be able to do so . . . but at the same time I think about this policy, this maxim of "falsely" promising, and realize that the moral law bids me not to promise falsely" (p. 277).

The moral law Bierman refers to is the explicit formulation of the categorical imperative by Immanuel Kant: "Act only on that maxim whereby you can at the same time will that it should become a universal law" (Kant, 1949, p. 38). In this statement, *maxim* means the principle underlying one's choice in a particular situation. Kant says it is "the principle on which the subject *acts*" (p. 38, n. 7). When an OD consultant suggests this or that proposal for a particular situation, he is implicitly expressing a principle about what should be done. Kant's test of principles is utterly logical: if it is to be done this way now, it should be able to be done this way at all times under substantially similar conditions. If not, it is not ethical. If OD consultants examine their proposals from the ethical point of view, the test is very simple: Can this be a maxim for all times if the circumstances are substantially similar?

Kant does not speak here of specific details in an action plan. He is not looking at the details that must change with circumstances. He is looking at what is the same in all such cases.

Kant would hold that Chambers and Adams — and OD consultants generally — should ask themselves a question such as: When
you are experiencing unanticipated difficulties with a client,
should you terminate? The universalization principle would suggest a no answer because if all practitioners left under those conditions, no consultant could be trusted.

It is important to note that in the above application the
categorical imperative is not related to the specific issue of
whether the caseworkers should have a say in deciding about
the action plan. It is important to note this fact because there
is another formulation to the categorical imperative that would
touch on that issue. So far, the logic of Kant's approach to ethics
concerns itself with the universal issues, one of which would be,
in this instance, whether it is right to "quit when the going gets
tough."

Treating People as Ends, Never as Means Only. There is
another formulation of the categorical imperative that would
be more exactly applied to how one deals with the persons involved. It is as follows: "So act as to treat humanity, whether
in your own person or in that of any other, in every case as
an end withal, never as means only" (Kant, 1949, p. 46). "Means
only" refers to treating people as objects to be used. It is another
way of stating that some people manipulate others for their own
personal motives and that this manipulation is unethical if it
is done in a way that treats others as "means only."

Kant (1949, pp. 51–52) distinguishes between value and
dignity in clarifying this principle: "In the kingdom of ends
[where people are treated as ends in themselves], everything has
either value or dignity. Whatever has a value can be replaced
by something else which is *equivalent;* whatever, on the other
hand, is above all value, and therefore admits of no equivalent,
has a dignity. Whatever has reference to the general inclinations and wants of mankind has a *market value* . . . but that which
constitutes the condition under which alone anything can be an
end in itself, this has not merely a relative worth, that is, value,
but an intrinsic worth, that is, *dignity* . . . Thus morality, and
humanity as capable of it, is that which alone has dignity. Skill
and diligence in labor have a market value."

Paton (1967, p. 189) comments: "The fact that everything in the kingdom of ends has either a price or a dignity shows how concretely, indeed how prosaically, Kant is at times prepared to interpret his kingdom of ends . . . It is worth noting that throughout his discussion Kant is concerned with the value of human activities. As examples of market price he mentions skill and industry . . . It is only through morality that a rational being can be a law-making [maxim-generating] member of a kingdom of ends and consequently be an end in himself."

The distinction is subtle but important. We trade our skills. Chambers and Adams offer their skills to the company and, in turn, draw on the skills of the employees to make their proposal work. By staying with them and working out the proposal they maintain an exchange of values for what each can do for the other; the consultants can contribute their skills to drawing up a proposal for improved operations in the agency and the employees can contribute their skills to make the proposal work. The trouble here is that the consultants now want to leave and the issue is raised as to whether it would be right for them to do so at this time.

In the present case we see Chambers arguing against leaving the company because it would have an unfortunate effect on the people and would "heighten their frustrations." Adams, somewhat less noble, also wants to consider the people involved. However, his reasoning is different from that of Chambers. Adams feels that staying would be the less effective action because the members of the client system can just as well work out the situation themselves. As it is described, Adams's position suggests that perhaps he was in the operation only for his own benefit. If this is so — and such an assumption can be argued either way, since Adams may truly be concerned with the very autonomy that a view of people as ends in themselves would merit, rather than staying and telling them what to do — and he leaves while the job still needs his presence, such conduct would be unethical because he is treating others as mere means. Chambers sees this difficulty and argues the case for staying with the agency until the proposal has reached a more mature development. My own view would be similar to that of Chambers. It would seem that Adams does not sufficiently take into consideration the effect leaving would have on the workers who are, after all, some of the stakeholders in that decision. The Statement (1985) addresses this point: "Serve the . . . development of the client system and all its stakeholders" (Guideline II–A). This consideration of others is what the Kantian second principle means when it speaks about their "dignity."

Conclusions. Summing up, my position so far is that the consultants should not leave because (1) leaving would undermine trust; applying the universalization principle, if everyone left an intervention when it ceased to be of interest or because of other possible unforeseen difficulties, then who could be trusted to do the work of OD consultants? (2) leaving would reduce the people in the organization to mere means.

Objections could be made to these conclusions. For one thing, one could say that leaving might be the best thing under the circumstances. In instances where progress has slowed down so much that the consultants feel their work should be terminated, or where it seems that other more capable consultants should be brought into the case, one could indeed formulate a maxim that could be "made into a universal law" that in such circumstances leaving is the right thing to do, and then make arrangements to leave as soon as possible. Interestingly, the Statement states specifically: "Cease work with a client when it is clear that the client is not benefiting or the contract has been completed" (Guideline II–H). (The issue of contracts is discussed below.) A case could be made for the consultants leaving because the client is no longer benefiting from their work.

OD Contracting and Ethics. The issue of contracts is germane to the discussion at this point. It might be argued that there is no contract for the work or, at best, only a vague agreement "to investigate the problems Winfield describes and . . . propose a plan of action." Stated simply, how can one be expected to stay when there is no real agreement as to when this job will end?

The Statement says to "ensure mutual understanding and agreement by putting the contract in writing to the extent feasible" (Guideline II–L–2). Agreements are, after all, at the heart of all ethics.

Agreements do not have to be in writing. The Statement even recognizes (Guideline II–L–2–c) that sometimes it is not desirable. The present case is clearly one in which the lack of a written agreement makes the decision to leave a difficult one to justify.

One might, however, say that this contract issue really beclouds the ethical issue. The contract, it is here suggested, is a way to avoid relying upon feelings when one needs a rule to guide one through unexpected difficulties. To fail to put the agreement in writing is probably wrong. It is an ethical issue and one that the Statement addresses: "Ensure a clear understanding of and mutual agreement on the services to be performed" (Guideline II–L–1); "Ensure mutual understanding and agreement by putting the contract in writing to the extent feasible" (Guideline II–L–2).

In my judgment, then, the consultants must stay and see this proposal through. The success of the intervention with the welfare agency depends on it. Leaving under the circumstances described would not be in line with the Statement (as cited above; see Guideline II–H) and could not be a "universal law" because of the potential for failed trust. Leaving under the circumstances does not seem to contribute to the development of all the stakeholders (Guideline II–A) and seems to treat the workers of the agency as mere means.

Comments by Newton Margulies

The following are responses to questions posed at the end of the case.

1. Should the consultation continue? What factors should be considered in deciding? The decision to continue or to terminate the consulting arrangement must include (1) some sense of the client's preferences, particularly if the client is inclined to end the relationship, and (2) some discussion regarding the relative stage of the project's completion. If the project has met the original goals *jointly determined* by the client and the consultant at the project's initiation, then it is appropriate to consider terminating the client-consultant arrangement. If, on the other hand, both the client and the consultant agree that the project is not completed, it may be appropriate to review the original project goals and consulting arrangements, and consider a project redirection and, subsequently, a new consulting arrangement. All this, of course, is predicated on the fact that both the client and the consultant are satisfied with their working relationship—that is, they both believe that not only is there trust and support in their collaboration, but that, indeed, the consultants are providing competent expertise relevant to the project and its goals.

From the consultants' point of view, terminating the relationship might be founded on:

- A clear change in direction dictated by the client that the consultants do not believe is appropriate or is contrary to their particular orientation and values (note, for example, Winfield's conversation as described in the case)
- An evaluation by the client and consultants that the project has reached a point where the clients can legitimately carry on the project activities and the consultant's expertise is no longer necessary (Adams's position in the case seems to reflect some agreement that, given the client's perspective on the status of the project, the consultants are no longer needed but may be reengaged at some later point)

Terminating the relationship, then, may be based on a variety of factors, not the least of which is that the working relationship between the client and the consultant is not effective, cannot be improved, and is no longer workable. It may also be the judgment of both the client and the consultant that the project, though not yet completed, is well enough on the way to achieving the desired goals that it can be accomplished without further assistance from the consultant.

This case seems to require a judgment call. On the one hand, the process seems to be working adequately. The guidelines are in the process of being formulated, requisitions for additional personnel have been submitted, and things seem to be progressing as planned. On the other hand, there seems to be some dissatisfaction with the process (it is difficult to assess how much dissatisfaction) and it may be advantageous for the consultants to remain a bit longer to ensure that any major obstacles to fulfilling the project's objectives are not encountered.

To summarize, the decision to continue, as indicated above, should be based upon (1) the willingness of both the client and consultant to continue the project, (2) the degree to which the project has come to fruition and met the original goals jointly agreed upon, or (3) the desire of both the client and consultant to review the existing client-consultant relationship and modify their arrangement based on changes in the project.

2. How would you assess Chambers's and Adams's positions with regard to the decision to terminate or continue? The client may terminate the relationship with the consultant at any time. The decision whether to remain with this project is not totally theirs. The positions of the two consultants are classic positions related to each individual's personal sense of responsibility for the success of the project. The dependency issue that is implied in Adams's position is not one that suddenly emerges near the completion of a consulting project, but is, rather, an underlying characteristic of the basic client-consultant relationship that begins in the first stages of the contracting process. In this regard, responsibility for the project's success must be established in the initial steps of project development and relationship building with the client.

Adams may legitimately decide that if the client is willing and able to continue the project to completion without need for consultant intervention, it may be time to terminate the relationship. He assumes that major responsibility for project success must rest with the client. Chambers, on the other hand, seems concerned that some dissatisfactions may put the project in jeopardy and, therefore, its success depends on close consultant supervision. From a consultant's perspective, the question is, given the status of the project: Can I provide continuing assistance in the achievement of the project's goals, or can the client legitimately and capably bring the project to fruition? In responding to this question, I believe it is critical to ask whether there are personal reasons beyond the needs of the project for deciding whether to terminate or continue the arrangement. Decisions based on personal needs rather than project needs would be unethical, as per Guideline I–E of the Statement (1985).

3. What should OD-HSD consultants do to avoid inflating expectations? It is often difficult to present a realistic assessment of the potential success and benefits of a consulting project. Client needs are often immediate and fraught with pressures to resolve difficult organizational issues. Consultants, in addition to their own personal and professional objectives, are interested in successfully helping to solve managerial and organizational problems. In their desire to be careful, complete, and effective, they may often present a more detailed and longer-range perspective on the client's project. On the other hand, managers are often embedded in the needs for "quick-fix" solutions to sometimes difficult and pervasive issues.

OD consultants can avoid mixed expectations and sometimes inflated perceptions of what an OD project can produce by careful discussions in the beginning stages. The contracting process is often either overlooked or performed in a rather perfunctory manner that does not fully take advantage of the possibilities for joint clarification of objectives and expectations. Too, organizational problems may be symptomatic and rooted in the very culture of the organization, so that their solution can be neither short-term nor simple, but indeed must be understood as complex and quite fragile.

The most important activity for the consultant with regard to any OD project is a careful education of the client. It is particularly difficult when the client is anxious to proceed rapidly and experiencing the stress of immediate organizational problems. There is a need, therefore, to help the client understand what realistically can be done, the nature of the collaborative process, and the resources required in a successful project. This often requires strength of patience and persistence in spite of the client's desire to move quickly. A realistic sense of accomplishment, coupled with the promise of change and improvement, is the essence of good consultation and is the ethical response.

Adams seems rather quick to terminate the project, seemingly without detailed discussions with the client. On the other hand, Chambers is likewise quickly willing to remain, based on her "investment." The benefits of client-consultant discussions on the status of this project and on appropriate next steps might lead the client and consultants to a viable posture on this project.

Comments by Robert Tannenbaum

If I were in the position of Chambers and Adams, I would not want the decision to terminate or continue the consulting relationship to be a unilateral one. It should be made only after an open discussion with the client in which the pros and cons of the decision from all relevant perspectives are weighed. I might feel that the process we started was adequately embedded and that I or any other consultant was no longer centrally relevant to its continuation. I might feel that another or other colleague(s) could now be more relevant to the process than I. Perhaps I could sense that on personal grounds I have outworn my welcome. I might feel that my accepted task was unfinished. It is possible, at the given point in time, that my leaving would with high probability lead to a disintegration of what has already been accomplished. I might feel quite conflicted around the many pros and cons. I certainly would feel that the views of Winfield and other client system members—such as the joint team—were as relevant as mine to the decision. After a full discussion, we might all acquire new data or perspectives. In any event, the decision—ideally, both mine and the client's—to terminate or continue should be made only after full and open discussion. (See Guideline II–H of the Statement, 1985.)

Looking now more specifically at the conflicting positions of Chambers and Adams, they each have possible merit. To me, their positions are primarily based on assumptions about or predictions of the future — that is, that expectations of many of those involved in the project might be violated, that the consultants' services are still essential to the project, that their leaving now might cause the intervention to fail, that there is little more that they can and should do, that a continuation of their services would create a dependency on their expertise. The two consultants differ in how they predict the outcomes. I believe they should not primarily discuss their differences in the abstract, but should, as the discussions continue, anchor their predictions in as much here-and-now data as possible. They should then, at least, compare notes with Winfield and, even more desirable, with the existing joint team of top agency officials, evaluators, and caseworkers before making any decision to terminate or continue. (See Guideline II–B.)

Client Expectations and Dependency. Two of the issues involved in the Chambers-Adams discussion around termination or continuation merit special attention: client expectations and client dependency. Relative to expectations, the Statement (1985) suggests the following: "Discuss candidly and fully goals, costs, risks, limitations, and anticipated outcomes of any program or other professional relationship under consideration" (Guideline II–B). In my view, such candid and full discussion with everyone involved should take place not only early in a consultation but be reinforced as appropriate during the subsequent unfolding process. (Appropriateness depends upon a continuing discernment by the consultants of the development of unrealistic expectations on the part of the client system.) Rarely can the outcome of an intervention be predicted. There are typically too many unknowns, including the complexities of the personal, interpersonal, and contextual variables involved in the unfolding process. In the present case, the statement by Chambers that "many of those involved have had their expectations raised by the strategy" suggests that the two consultants never directly discussed expectations with the client system. Further, Chambers believes that a continuation of the consultation is *the* way to deal with expectations now held by system members, and Adams is concerned that to continue the consultation would create false expectations. It doesn't seem to occur to either of them to deal with this matter directly with system members.

Dependency can be both functional and dysfunctional. Consultants—teachers, parents, counselors, and so on—must be aware that in any developmental process there is typically an early period of dependency during which the knowledge and experience of the consultant are highly relevant to the client, and the support, understanding, and caring of the consultant facilitate the letting go of entrenched modes and the experimentation with and acceptance of new ones. Here, appropriate dependency can be highly functional. And yet it is essential that the consultant work in a way to reinforce the new learnings, to gradually and appropriately move away from the dependency, and ideally to reach a point where strong client independence in the new modes has been established such that the consultant's services are no longer required. In the present case, there is little evidence of anything that has been done by Chambers and Adams in the five months of the consultation explicitly to manage the dependency/independency flow within the client system. In fact, Adams states, "We should be helping [the clients] develop their own competence for handling similar problems in the future." Why this sudden awareness of an essential process after five months of work with the system? (See Guideline II–G.)

Consultant Competency. Some specific matters that occur during the consultation raise questions in my mind about the level of competency (see Guidelines I–B and I–C) and/or of self-knowledge (see Guideline I–D) of Chambers and Adams:

- There is no evidence that they, in arriving at their original diagnosis, attempted to probe more deeply behind the "facts and feelings" expressed by the interviewees, or that they in any way considered interpretations of the situation that might lead them beyond that which was explicitly stated by the interviewees.
- When Chambers and Adams returned after a two-month interval, they found most system members satisfied with the way the strategy was proceeding. But others "voiced their

disappointment in private conversation." Why had not this disappointment been previously expressed, why is it now expressed to the consultants in private, and is there any special and relevant meaning of the disappointment? Again, the consultants do not seem to ask themselves these questions. And they carry the disappointments to Winfield in private without creating a process for these feelings openly to become a part of the ongoing process.

- Winfield expresses surprise at what he hears in private. He refers to one of the concerns as an "accusation," he "deflects" some of the criticism by caseworkers, he assures the consultants that one of the expressed concerns was "not the case," and he concludes that those critical of the process "may simply be experiencing a natural disappointment in not having their ideas accepted." His response strongly suggests that he feels a need to defend himself and the ongoing process. There is no indication that the consultants attempt to understand Winfield better or help him understand the perceptions of the caseworkers and evaluators. It is also possible that Winfield's relationship to the process and to the individuals involved may be highly relevant to existing problems in the consultation, but Chambers and Adams do not seem even to have their interest or curiosity aroused. Further, the disappointments held by some participants and Winfield's defensiveness apparently do not enter as relevant considerations into the consultants' discussion of termination versus continuation.

- We are told that Chambers "has invested a considerable amount of time in this project, which diverted her from taking on other financially rewarding contracts." The ethical question should be raised as to whether this has influenced her desire to continue the consultation. If it has, then another ethical question should be raised as to whether she has any conscious awareness of her motivation in this instance. (See Guideline I–E.)

I raise the above issues relating to the level of competency and self-knowledge (both ethical issues) because in my judgment *the profession has thus far given inadequate attention to these important aspects of professionalism in matters of training for the profession, entry into the profession (including certification), and the monitoring of professional practice with reference to standards not yet established.* (*Editors' note:* Emphasis added to emphasize a point that is fundamental to the purpose of this book.)

Comments by Dorothy M. Tucker

"Cathy" is one of America's most read comic strips. She is consistently depicted as being in the middle. Whether the interaction is between the demands of her male friend, her mother, her father, her female friend, her boss, the store clerk, or others, Cathy cannot seem to decide to terminate or continue her interactions. She is caught between.

A colleague of mine commented recently that he thought "between" is where OD people periodically find themselves. His perceptions seemed accurate to me. Too often consultants do get in between in ways that may or may not be constructive for them as consultants or for the organizations in which they work. Chambers and Adams find themselves in between due to a combination of factors: expectations, powerlessness, and contracting.

Expectations. "To Terminate or Continue?" is an excellent case example for the discussion of violation of expectations coupled with overselling the illusion of OD as an intervention. In reviewing both consultants' interpretations of the situation, Chambers expresses guilt and stresses, in a semi-condescending fashion, that They need us, otherwise they cannot do it. Adams, on the other hand, says, We cannot make them dependent on us—the majority of the organization is satisfied; the boss is satisfied; let us get on with other commitments!

Clearly, Chambers and Adams are compromised by a design that did not generate the satisfaction expected by the participants. They oversold what data, information, and/or change they would utilize as interventions, which encouraged expectations that could not be met by the system. As a result, some of the participants experienced frustration.

The desire for a resolution is pursued by all sides, with Adams and Chambers caught in between. Both present convincing yet arguable positions. Technically, Adams is correct. The job has been completed according to the terms of the contract and all consultant obligations have been met. Chambers, however, suggests that consultants must adhere to more than just the specifics of an agreement; they must also feel and respond to the lack of closure. She argues that although the job may have been completed on paper, the paper contract becomes invalid if the expected outcomes are not satisfactory, a principle that is both ethically sound and central to effective consultation efforts. If consultants are not willing to take the time, energy, and expertise to follow through on their work to a productive, facilitative outcome, then they are subject to criticism for failing to meet their responsibilities to the clients. (See Guidelines II-A and II-M-1 of the Statement.) This appears to have happened with this agency, and it raises a number of questions about the ethical behavior of the consultants.

Powerlessness. Another variable exposed by this intervention was the inability of the caseworkers to influence change or exhibit power. The strategy identified by "the boss" in discussions with Chambers and Adams was to increase the efficiency level of caseworkers. The strategy from the outset did not address the real issue of powerlessness on the part of the caseworkers, the confrontations of the caseworkers with management and the case evaluators, or the process of decision making within the system.

In my opinion, the consultants erred in not providing a planning meeting for management and workers in the early phase of the project. The meeting would have been one vehicle for allowing both groups to reach an important understanding of the following questions:

1.   Who is in control?
2.   Who is directing the project?
3.   What are the ground rules?
4.   What are the long-term and short-term expectations, goals, strategies, and options?

5. What will the decision-making process be?
6. What will the implementation strategy be and how will it be measured and evaluated?
7. Who wants to participate?
8. What weight will be given to the views of those who participate in the decision-making process?

The generation of these data would have provided a valuable opportunity to discuss losses and gains and to collect a commitment for proceeding with the project that would probably have avoided the problem the consultants now face.

Contracting. Chambers and Adams investigated the problem and proposed a plan of action, which is all they really agreed to do. Agreeing to return later was not a part of the original contract/agreement. An awareness of this fact at this phase would have correctly directed them to negotiate a new contract, but they did not. Instead, they agreed to return, setting up expectations among workers that they would be there to look after them.

Adams expressed some concern for this issue when he concluded that the majority of the participants and the boss were satisfied, so it was time for the consultants to move on; to do otherwise risked making the client dependent on them. With this realization identified, the next valid step for the consultants would be to negotiate a new contract. This would also eliminate the distraction of Chambers's thoughts about "other financially rewarding contracts," or at least put it in perspective.

The question of unrealistic expectations, a major theme in this case, is very serious. It can be addressed with clients in many ways, one of which is used by a colleague of mine. He warns his client systems that if the outcome of the following story is going to occur, the project should not begin. This story is reported as taking place in the 1950s.

> There was a set of bones lying in a glass case at the Vatican. The sign underneath said, "These are the bones of St. Peter and they should be venerated." Pope Pius, who was the pope at the time,

decided that with all of the new carbon atomic dating systems, he would call in some scientists to validate the bones' authenticity. The scientists came, conducted tests, and concluded scientifically that these could not have been St. Peter's bones because they dated approximately 200 years from the time St. Peter lived. They gave their report to the pope, who declared that although these were not St. Peter's bones, they would continue to be venerated as if they were. So the sign continues to say that these are the bones of St. Peter.

This story raises the question, Why bother to do something if you are not going to change things based on what you find? In other words, if you intervene in an effort to make things right and you find that what you have is not what you want, you do something else. To act as if the findings validate the way things are is like continuing to venerate the bones of "St. Peter."

I suspect that some of that dynamic is working here. The critical mistake for Chambers and Adams was not having participants assist in setting the goals. The consultants were called in by Winfield, who defined the problem as work output in terms of numbers and procedures rather than interaction and trust. A session in which participants worked out a strategy of intervention would have helped eliminate feelings of exclusion.

In addition, the consultants failed to remember an old OD principle, which states that "consultants should start from where the organization is." This implies that consultants should begin by diagnosing the system. Systems, however, do not necessarily subscribe to this notion, nor do they like being "diagnosed." The term itself may even be experienced as offensive. Further, the system may not be ready for people who call themselves OD consultants. Chambers and Adams would probably have fared better had they taken the time to communicate more effectively, collect more data, build a sound strategy, understand how the client system members saw themselves and their situation, and, finally, understand the culture of the system. After all, OD cannot be forced on the organization or its people. It is the organization that has to define what is wrong and where it wants to go. The consultant is there only to guide the process. Consultants cannot ethically promise that they will bring about certain types of outcomes. Their role is to facilitate, work hard, and be sensitive and resourceful in responding to the situation as it unfolds.

Ethics Resources

▌▐▌

Because this book is intended, among other things, to function as an educational and reference tool, we have included two sets of resources for further use by interested readers. The first set is a select list of organizations specializing in education, research, or consultation in business or professional ethics. Readers should contact these organizations directly for description of their work and the services they provide. The second set of resources is a select list of journals and newsletters devoted to business and professional ethics issues. They range from those reporting predominantly on current scholarship to those offering information on current events and accessible resource materials. In either case, the wide range of periodicals listed should help to heighten the ethical consciousness of readers and inform their deliberations on ethical matters.

Organizations Specializing in Business
and Professional Ethics

Business Ethics Research Center
King's College
Strand
London, England WC2R 2LS

Canadian Society for the Study of Practical Ethics
c/o Department of Philosophy
York University
4700 Keele Street
North York, Ontario, Canada M3J 1P3

Center for Applied Ethics
Santa Clara University
Santa Clara, CA 95053 U.S.A.

Center for Business and Public Sector Ethics
6 Croftgate, Fulbrooke Road
Cambridge, England CB3 9EG

Center for Business Ethics
Bentley College
Waltham, MA 02154 U.S.A.

Center for Ethics and Social Policy
Graduate Theological Union
2465 LeConte Avenue
Berkeley, CA 94709 U.S.A.

Center for Ethics, Responsibilities and Values
The College of St. Catherine
2004 Randolph Avenue
St. Paul, MN 55105 U.S.A.

Center for Ethics Studies
Marquette University
Milwaukee, WI 53233 U.S.A.

Center for the Study of Ethics in the Professions
Illinois Institute of Technology
Chicago, IL 60616 U.S.A.

Ethics Resource Center
600 New Hampshire Avenue NW
Washington, DC 20037 U.S.A.

European Business Ethics Network
c/o European Foundation for Management Development
40 Rue Washington
B-1050 Brussels, Belgium

Hastings Center
255 Elm Road
Briarcliff Manor, NY 10510 U.S.A.

Institute for the Study of Applied and Professional Ethics
Dartmouth College
Hinman Box 6201
Hanover, NH 03755 U.S.A.

Institute of Business Ethics
12 Palace Steet
London, England SW1E 5JA

Josephson Institute for the Advancement of Ethics
310 Washington Street, Suite 104
Marina del Rey, CA 90292 U.S.A.

Olsson Center for Applied Ethics
Colgate Darden Graduate School of Business
    Administration
University of Virginia
P.O. Box 6550
Charlottesville, VA 22906 U.S.A.

Program in Ethics and the Professions
Harvard University
79 J.F.K. Street
Cambridge, MA 02138 U.S.A.

Social Values Research Centre
University of Hull
Hull, England HU6 7RX

Society for Business Ethics
c/o Department of Philosophy
Loyola University of Chicago
6525 North Sheridan Road
Chicago, IL 60626 U.S.A.

Trinity Center for Ethics and Corporate Policy
74 Trinity Place
New York, NY 10006 U.S.A.

Westminster Institute for Ethics and Human Values
361 Windermere Road
London, Ontario, Canada N6G 2K3

Periodicals

Business Ethics
1107 Hazeltine Blvd., Suite 530
Chaska, MN 55318 U.S.A.

Ethics Digest
Olsson Center for Applied Ethics
Colgate Darden Graduate School of Business
   Administration
University of Virginia
P.O. Box 6550
Charlottesville, VA 22906 U.S.A.

Ethics: Easier Said Than Done and *Ethics in Action*
Josephson Institute for the Advancement of Ethics
310 Washington Street, Suite 104
Marina del Rey, CA 90292 U.S.A.

Ethics Resource Center Report
Ethics Resource Center
600 New Hampshire Avenue, NW
Washington, DC 20037 U.S.A.

Ethikos
799 Broadway, Suite 541
New York, NY 10211 U.S.A.

European Business Ethics Newsletter
European Business Ethics Network
c/o European Foundation for Management Development
40 Rue Washington
B-1050 Brussels, Belgium

Hastings Center Report
Hastings Center
255 Elm Road
Briarcliff Manor, NY 10510 U.S.A.

International Journal of Value-Based Management
Hagan School of Business
Iona College
New Rochelle, NY 10801 U.S.A.

Issues in Ethics
Center for Applied Ethics
Santa Clara University
Santa Clara, CA 95053 U.S.A.

Journal of Business Ethics
Kluwer Academic Publishers
Spuiboulevard 50, P.O. Box 17
3300 AA Dordrecht
The Netherlands

Perspectives on the Professions
Center for the Study of Ethics in the Professions
Illinois Institute of Technology
Chicago, IL 60616 U.S.A.

Professional Ethics Report
American Association for the Advancement of Science
1333 H Street, NW
Washington, DC 20005 U.S.A.

How the Statement
Was Developed

▮▮▮▮▮▮▮▮▮▮▮▮▮▮▮▮▮▮▮▮▮▮▮▮▮▮▮▮▮▮▮▮

The process leading to the development of the Statement pre-sented in Chapters Four and Five and Appendix B (currently in its twenty-second version) began in 1981. That process has been endorsed by the leadership groups of most of the leading OD-oriented professional organizations, associations, and networks in the United States. These include the Association for Creative Change (ACC), the OD Division of the American Society of Training and Development (ASTD), Certified Consultants International (CCI), NTL Institute, the OD Institute, the OD Network, and the Human Systems Development Consortium (HSDC). It was also endorsed unanimously by the participants in the 1984 OD World Congress at Southhampton, England, and in the International OD Association's business meeting during its 1989 annual conference at Irsee, Bavaria (West Germany). And nearly three hundred people at the 1989 annual conference of the U.S. OD Network in San Diego also endorsed the process.

Up to this point, it is the *process* of developing a Statement that has been endorsed by those groups and not the Statement's *content*. We have intentionally not sought endorsement of the Statement's content since, in spite of substantial support, responses still indicate opportunities for improvement. In mid 1989, for example, many of the newsletters of the United States Regional OD Networks circulated a one-page Summary Statement, along with a survey questionnaire. Responses (n = 230) indicated that: 215 consider OD a profession; 211 consider themselves members of the OD profession; 225 agree that, among other things, being a profession requires clear ethics; 191 could accept the Summary Statement as it was but 57 had suggestions for improvement, and another 26 could accept it if certain changes were made. Those results suggest that a one-page summary is too short to describe our ethical position adequately, so a longer, but still concise, Statement has been developed (see Appendix B).

To date, more than five hundred people from more than twenty countries have participated in the process. The countries from which contributions were received include Belgium, Canada, Finland, France, Great Britain, Hungary, India, Israel, Japan, Mexico, the Netherlands, Norway, the Philippines, Poland, Saudi Arabia, Singapore, South Africa, Spain, the United States, West Germany, and Yugoslavia.

The process has involved drafting a version, sending it out with a request for comments and suggestions, redrafting based on the responses, sending it out again, and so on. We expect this process to continue with increasing participation by people throughout the profession until we can truly say we have achieved substantial consensus — and even then we expect to keep the process open.

Among other sources, the Statement is based on statements by and contributions from many professional associations, including: the Association for Creative Change; the Academy of Management; the American Psychological Association; the American Society for Personnel Administration; Certified Consultants International; the Dutch Association of Organizational Experts en Advisors; the European Institute for Transnational Studies in Group and Organizational Development; Gesellschaft für Organisationentwicklung; the Gestalt Institute of Cleveland; the Human Systems Development Consortium; the International Consultants Foundation; the International Human Resources Development Corporation; the International Organization Development Association; the International Registry of Organization Development Professionals; the National Association of Social Workers; NTL Institute; the OD Division of the American Society for Training and Development; the OD Institute; the OD Networks of both the United Kingdom and the United States; Organization Renewal, Inc.; the Société Internationale pour le Développement des Organisations (SIDO); Society for Applied Anthropology; and study groups from Reseau OD Canada and SANNO Institute of Business Administration (Japan).

The Statement's development was supported, in part, by a project grant from the National Science Foundation (NSF) (Grant Nos. RII-8409933 and RII-8696147). Among other things, it has enabled us to develop this Statement, conduct panels on values and ethics in OD at annual meetings of six of the major OD-oriented professional associations, develop a set of cases for ethical analysis (see Chapters Six through Eleven and Appendix D), publish an extensive annotated bibliography on OD-HSD values and ethics (Frankel, 1987), and initiate a Clearinghouse on Information about OD-HSD Values and Ethics as a means of further institutionalizing coordination by our profession with regard to its values and ethics. (Note: The project funded by the grant has been a cooperative effort by the Human Systems Development Consortium, the American Association for the Advancement of Science (AAAS) [through its Scientific Freedom and Responsibility Programs], and the Center for the Study of Ethics in the Professions at the Illinois Institute of Technology (IIT). We owe NSF, AAAS, and IIT a debt of gratitude.)

References

Ackoff, R. *Management in Small Doses.* New York: Wiley, 1986.

Adler, M. *We Hold These Truths: Understanding the Ideas and Ideals of the Constitution.* New York: Macmillan, 1987.

Adler, M. *Reforming Education: The Opening of the American Mind.* New York: MacMillan, 1988.

Argyris, C. *Intervention Theory and Method: A Behavioral Science View.* Reading, Mass.: Addison-Wesley, 1970.

Aristotle. *Nichomachean Ethics,* Books I and II. In R. McKeon (ed.), *The Basic Works of Aristotle.* New York: Random House, 1941.

Bayles, M. D. *Professional Ethics.* (2nd ed.) Belmont, Calif.: Wadsworth, 1989.

Beer, M., and Walton, E. "Organizational Change and Development." In M. Rosenzweig and L. Porter (eds.), *Annual Review of Psychology.* Palo Alto, Calif.: Annual Reviews, 1987.

Benne, K. "Some Ethical Problems in Group and Organizational Consultation." *Journal of Social Issues,* 1959, *15,* 60–67.

Bennis, W. "A New Role for the Behavioral Sciences: Effecting Organizational Change." *Administrative Science Quarterly,* 1963, *8,* 125–165.

507

Bierman, A. K. *Life and Morals: An Introduction to Ethics.* New York: Harcourt Brace Jovanovich, 1980.

Blanchard, K. "Situational Leadership Revisited." In A. Ritvo and A. G. Sargent (eds.), *The NTL Manager's Handbook.* Arlington, Va.: NTL Institute, 1983.

Boulding, K. *The World as a Total System.* Newbury Park, Calif.: Sage, 1985.

Branden, N. "Building Self-Esteem." (Audiocassette.) Washington, D.C.: American Psychological Association, 1985.

Brown, M. "Care and Justice." *Organizational Ethics Newsletter,* 1987, *4* (9), 3–5.

Brown, M. "Ethics in Organizations." *Issues in Ethics,* 1988–1989, *2* (1), 1.

Camenisch, P. F. *Grounding Professional Ethics in a Pluralistic Society.* New York: Haven, 1983.

Chase, T. "Monthly Quote." *New York Organization Development Network Newsletter,* Oct. 1989, p. 8.

Consultation Skills Laboratory. *Life: Strengths and Weaknesses.* Bethel, Maine: NTL Institute, 1984.

Cummings, T., and Molloy, E. *Improving Productivity and the Quality of Working Life.* New York: Praeger, 1977.

Davis, M. "Conflict of Interest." *Journal of Business and Professional Ethics,* 1982, *1* (4), 17–27.

Dewey, J. *Art as Experience.* New York: Putnam, Capricorn Books, 1958.

Diagonali, J. "December NYODN Meeting." *New York Organization Development Network Newsletter,* Feb. 1984, pp. 2–4.

Dworkin, R. *Law's Empire.* Cambridge, Mass.: Harvard University Press, 1986.

Eisen, S., Steele, H., and Cherbeneau, J. "An Environmental Scan for the OD Profession: A Continuing Delphi Conference: 1988 Update." *OD Practitioner,* 1988, *20* (4), 8–10.

Ellington, J. W., Jr. *Grounding for the Metaphysics of Morals.* Indianapolis, Ind.: Hackett, 1981.

Elliston, F., and others. *Whistleblowing: Managing Dissent in the Workplace.* New York: Praeger, 1985.

Emerson, R. W. "Monthly Quote." *New York Organization Development Network Newsletter,* Feb. 1988, p. 8.

Fishbein, M., and Ajzen, I. *Belief, Atttitude, Intention and Behavior: An Introduction to Theory and Research.* Reading, Mass.: Addison-Wesley, 1975.

Frankel, M. S. "Ethical Considerations for Personnel Administrators and Human Resource Managers." Paper presented at national conference of the American Society of Personnel Administrators, Chicago, 1984.

Frankel, M. S., *Values and Ethics in Organization and Human Systems Development: An Annotated Bibliography.* Washington, D.C.: American Association for the Advancement of Science, 1987.

Frankel, M. S. "Professional Codes: Why, How, and with What Impact?" *Journal of Business Ethics,* 1989, *8,* 109–115.

Freire, P. *Pedagogy of the Oppressed.* New York: Herder and Herder, 1970.

French, W. L., and Bell, C. H., Jr. *Organization Development: Behavioral Science Interventions for Organization Improvement.* Englewood Cliffs, N.J.: Prentice-Hall, 1973.

Friedlander, F., and Brown, L. D. "Organization Development." In M. Rosenzweig and L. Porter (eds.), *Annual Review of Psychology.* Palo Alto, Calif.: Annual Reviews, 1974.

Frizell, N., and Gellermann, W. "Integrating the Business and Human Dimensions of Management and Organization Development." In S. Mailick, S. Hoberman, and S. Wall (eds.), *The Practice of Management.* New York: Praeger, 1988.

Fullan, M., Miles, M., and Taylor, G. "Organization Development in the Schools: The State of the Art." *Review of Educational Research,* 1980, pp. 121–183.

Fuller, L. L. *The Morality of Law.* New Haven, Conn.: Yale University Press, 1964.

Gellermann, W. "A Statement of Values and Ethics for Organization Development Professionals." New York: W. Gellermann, Feb. 1984a. (Photocopy.)

Gellermann, W. "Issues in Developing a Statement of Values and Ethics for Organization Development Professionals." *Organization Development Journal,* 1984b, *2* (1), 39–47.

Gellermann, W. "A Statement of Values and Ethics for Professionals in Organization and Human System Development." New York: W. Gellermann, Apr. 1985a. (Photocopy.)

Gellermann, W. "Values and Ethical Issues for Human Systems Development Practitioners." In R. Tannenbaum, N. Margulies, F. Massarik, and Associates, *Human Systems Development: New Perspectives on People and Organizations.* San Francisco: Jossey-Bass, 1985b.

Gellermann, W. "The Core of Professional Identity: Common Purpose, Values, and Ethics." *OD Practitioner,* 1990, *22* (3), 1–3.

Gert, B. *The Moral Rules.* New York: Harper & Row, 1970.

Gert, B. *Morality: A New Justification of the Moral Rules.* (Paperback ed.) New York: Oxford University Press, 1989.

Goldman, A. H. "Professional Values and the Problem of Regulation." *Business and Professional Ethics Journal,* n.d., *5* (2), 47–59.

Golembiewski, R. T., Billingsley, K., and Yeager, S. "Measuring Change and Persistence in Human Affairs: Types of Change Generated by OD Designs." *Journal of Applied Behavioral Science,* 1976, *12,* 133–157.

Goodstein, L., and Hunt, J. "Commentary: Do American Theories Apply Abroad?" *Organizational Dynamics,* 1981, *10* (1), 49–62.

Harman, W., and Rheingold, H. *Higher Creativity: Liberating the Unconscious for Breakthrough Insights.* Los Angeles: Tarcher, 1984.

Hart, H.L.A. *The Concept of Law.* Oxford: Oxford University Press, 1961.

Hillard, A. "Free Your Mind, Back to the Source: African Origins." *Behavioral Criteria in the Study of Racism.* Vol. 1. Washington, D.C.: Office of Naval Research, 1978.

Hinckley, S., Jr. "Challenges Facing the Profession of Human Systems Development." Paper presented at Certified Consultants International conference, New York, Oct. 1986.

Hofstede, G. "Motivation, Leadership and Organization: Do American Theories Apply Abroad?" *Organizational Dynamics,* 1980, *9* (1), 42–68.

Hofstede, G. "Do American Theories Apply Abroad: A Reply to Goodstein and Hunt." *Organizational Dynamics,* 1981, *10* (1), 63–68.

"In the News." *Professional Ethics Report,* 1988, *1* (3), 1.

Isenberg, D. J. "How Senior Managers Think." *Harvard Business Review*, 1984, *4* (6), 80–90.

Jennings, B., Callahan, D., and Wolf, S. M. "The Professions: Public Interest and Common Good." *Hastings Center Report* (Special Supplement), 1987, *17* (1), 3–10.

Kant, I. *Fundamental Principles of the Metaphysics of Morals*. New York: Library of Liberal Arts, 1949.

Kaufman, W. (ed.). *Basic Writings of Nietzsche*. New York: Random House, 1966. (See especially "The Genealogy of Morals.")

Kegan, D. "Organization Development as OD Network Members See It." *Group and Organization Studies*, 1982, *7* (1), 5–9.

Kiefer, C., and Stroh, P. "A New Paradigm for Organization Development." *Training and Development Journal*, 1983, *37* (4), 26–35.

Klein, J. "The Race Mess: A City on the Verge of a Nervous Breakdown." *New York*, 1990, *23* (1), 32–37.

Kushner, H. *When All You Ever Wanted Isn't Enough: The Search for a Life That Matters*. New York: Pocket Books, 1986.

Ladd, J. "Philosophical Remarks on Professional Responsibility in Organizations." In A. Flores (ed.), *Designing for Safety*. Troy, N.Y.: Albert Flores, 1982.

Lande, N., and Slade, A. *Stages: Understanding How You Make Your Moral Decisions*. New York: Harper & Row, 1979.

Lebacqz, K. *Professional Ethics: Power and Paradox*. Nashville, Tenn.: Abingdon Press, 1985.

Lowman, R. (ed.). *Casebook on Ethics and Standards for the Practice of Psychology in Organizations*. College Park, Md.: Society for Industrial and Organization Psychology, 1985.

MacIntyre, A. *After Virtue*. Notre Dame, Ind.: Notre Dame University Press, 1981.

McLagan, P. A. *Models for Excellence: The Conclusions and Recommendations of the ASTD Training and Development Competency Study*. Alexandria, Va.: American Society for Training and Development, 1983.

McLagan, P. A. *Models for HRD Practice*. Alexandria, Va.: American Society for Training and Development, 1989.

Maslow, A. "A Theory of Human Motivation." *Psychological Review*, 1943, *50*, 370–396.

Mason, R. *Participatory and Workplace Democracy.* Carbondale, Ill.: Southern Illinois University, 1982.

Merton, R. K. "Functions of the Professional Association." In A. Rosenblatt and T. F. Gieryn (eds.), *Robert K. Merton: Social Research and the Practicing Professions.* Cambridge, Mass.: ABT Books, 1982.

Morton, R. "'Straight from the Shoulder'—Leveling with Others on the Job." *Personnel,* Nov.-Dec. 1966, pp. 65-70.

Nicholas, J. "The Comparative Impact of Organization Development Interventions on Hard Criteria Measures." *Academy of Management Review,* 1982, *7,* 531-542.

Ouchi, W. G. *Theory Z.* Reading, Mass.: Addison-Wesley, 1981.

Owen, H. *Spirit: Transformation and Development in Organizations.* Potomac, Md.: Abbott, 1987.

Paton, H. J. *The Categorical Imperative.* New York: Harper & Row, 1967.

Pedrazzini, L., and Gable, C. "Art as a Tool for Self-Integration in the Workplace." Paper presented at the Organizational Development Network national conference, San Diego, Calif.: Nov. 1989.

Peters, M. B., Gellermann, W., and Herald-Marlowe, K. "A Model of the Organization Development Profession." Paper presented at Certified Consultants International conference, New York, Oct. 1986.

Plato. *Republic.* (G.M.A. Grube, trans.) Indianapolis, Ind.: Hackett, 1974.

Porras, J., and Berg, P. "Evaluation Methodology in Organization Development: An Analysis and Critique." *Journal of Applied Behavioral Science,* 1978, *14,* 151-173.

Reidenbach, R. E., and Robin, D. "A Conceptual Model of Corporate Moral Development." Paper presented at 1989 conference of the Society for Business Ethics, Washington, D.C., Aug. 1989.

Rush, H. *Organization Development: A Reconnaissance.* New York: The Conference Board, 1973.

Shea, G. *Practical Ethics, AMA Management Briefing.* New York: American Management Association, 1988.

Shepard, H. "Rules of Thumbs for Change Agents." Paper presented at Consultation Skills Laboratory, NTL Institute, Carmel, Calif., 1973.

Shepard, H. "The Irony of a Mature Helping Profession." *CCI News,* Summer 1983, pp. 6–7.

Sher, G. (ed.). *Utilitarianism.* Indianapolis, Ind.: Hackett, 1979.

Simmons, J., and Mares, W. *Working Together.* New York: Knopf, 1983.

Tannenbaum, R., and Davis, S. "Values, Man, and Organization." In W. Eddy and others (eds.), *Behavioral Science and the Manager's Role.* Washington, D.C.: NTL Institute for Applied Behavioral Science, 1969.

Tannenbaum, R., Margulies, N., Massarik, F., and Associates. *Human Systems Development: New Perspectives on People and Organizations.* San Francisco: Jossey-Bass, 1985.

Terborg, J., Howard, G., and Maxwell, S. "Evaluating Planned Organizational Change: A Method for Assessing Alpha, Beta, and Gamma Change." *Academy of Management Review,* 1980, *5,* 109–121.

Tuohy, C. J., and Wolfson, A. D. "The Political Economy of Professionalism: A Perspective." In Consumer Research Council, *Four Aspects of Professionalism.* Ottawa, Ontario: Consumer Research Council, 1977.

Wachtel, P. *The Poverty of Affluence.* Philadelphia: New Society, 1989.

Walton, R. E. "Ethical Issues in the Practice of Organization Development." In G. Bermant, H. C. Kelman, and D. P. Warwick (eds.), *The Ethics of Social Intervention.* Washington, D.C.: Hemisphere, 1978.

Walton, R. E., and Warwick, D. "The Ethics of Organization Development." *Journal of Applied Behavioral Science,* 1973, *9,* 681–698.

Warwick, D. "Types of Harm in Social Research." In T. L. Beauchamp and R. Faden (eds.), *Ethical Issues in Social Science Research.* Baltimore, Md.: Johns Hopkins University Press, 1982.

Welsing, F. "Black Value Systems and Strategies." In J. Chun (ed.), *The Survival of Black Children and Youth.* Washington, D.C.: Nuclassics and Science, 1974.

White, L., and Wooten, K. *Professional Ethics and Practice in Organizational Development: A Systematic Analysis of Issues, Alternatives, and Approaches.* New York: Praeger, 1986.

Wilbur, K. *Eye to Eye: The Quest for the New Paradigm.* Garden City, New York: Anchor Books, 1983.

Williams, B. *Ethics and the Limits of Philosophy.* Cambridge, Mass.: Harvard University Press, 1985.

Williams, P. (ed.). *The International Bill of Human Rights.* Glen Ellen, Calif.: Entwhistle Books, 1981.

Wolfson, A. D., Trebilcock, M. J., and Tuohy, C. J. "Regulating the Professions: A Theoretical Framework." In S. Rottenberg (ed.), *Occupational Licensure and Regulation.* Washington, D.C.: American Enterprise Institute, 1980.

Wooten, K., and White, L. "Ethical Problems in the Practice of Organization Development." *Training and Development Journal,* 1983, *37* (4), 16–23.

Wright, B. *The Psychopathic Racial Personality.* Chicago: Institute of Positive Education, 1975.

Index

∎∎∎∎∎∎∎∎∎∎∎

515